500 Common Chinese Idioms

500 Common Chinese Idioms is the ideal tool for all intermediate to advanced learners of Chinese. Based on large corpuses of authentic language data, it presents the 500 most commonly used Chinese idioms or **chéngyǔ**, along with a variety of synonyms, antonyms and the most common structures, enabling the reader to make educated guesses about the meanings of hundreds of unfamiliar idioms.

Key features include:

- the idiom in both simplified and traditional characters
- a literal English translation and English equivalents
- two suitable example sentences, plus explanations and usage notes
- a pinyin index and stroke order index.

This practical dictionary is suitable both for class use and independent study and will be of interest to students and teachers of Chinese alike.

Liwei Jiao is Lecturer in Chinese at the University of Pennsylvania. His publications include *The Routledge Advanced Chinese Multimedia Course: Crossing Cultural Boundaries* (co-authored with Kun-shan Carolyn Lee, Hsin-Hsin Liang and Julian Wheatley, Routledge 2009).

Cornelius C. Kubler is Stanfield Professor of Asian Studies at Williams College. He has authored or co-authored nine books and over 50 articles on Chinese language pedagogy and linguistics.

Weiguo Zhang is Emeritus Professor of Chinese Linguistics at Renmin University of China. He is currently Visiting Professor and Co-director of the Confucius Institute for Ireland at University College Dublin. He has published several books on computer language.

500 Common Chinese Idioms

An annotated frequency dictionary

Liwei Jiao, Cornelius C. Kubler and Weiguo Zhang

Routledge
Taylor & Francis Group

LONDON AND NEW YORK

First published 2011
by Routledge
2 Park Square, Milton Park, Abingdon, Oxon OX14 4RN

Simultaneously published in the USA and Canada
by Routledge
270 Madison Ave, New York, NY 10016

Routledge is an imprint of the Taylor & Francis Group, an informa business

Typeset in GraphSwift Light
by Graphicraft Limited, Hong Kong
Printed and bound in Great Britain
by MPG Books Group, UK

British Library Cataloguing in Publication Data
A catalogue record for this book is available from the British Library

Library of Congress Cataloging in Publication Data
Jiao, Liwei.
500 common Chinese idioms / Liwei Jiao, Cornelius C. Kubler,
Weiguo Zhang. — 1st ed.
    p. cm.
    Chinese language—Idioms—Dictionaries—English.   2. Chinese language—
    Terms and phrases.   I. Kubler, Cornelius C.   II. Zhang, Weiguo.
    III. Title.   IV. Title: Five hundred common Chinese idioms.
    PL1273.J53 2010
    495.1′313—dc22

                                                            2010019805

ISBN 13: 978-0-415-59893-4 (hbk)
ISBN 13: 978-0-415-77682-0 (pbk)
ISBN 13: 978-0-203-83914-0 (ebk)

Contents

Introduction   vi
Chinese idioms and why they are important   vi
Special characteristics of this dictionary   vii
How the entries of this dictionary were determined   viii
How this dictionary is organized   ix
How to use this dictionary   x
Background of the compilation of this dictionary and acknowledgments   xi

List of entries   xii

500 common Chinese idioms   1

Appendix one: common structural patterns of Chinese idioms   298

Appendix two: Pinyin index of 500 common Chinese idioms   301

Appendix three: stroke index of 500 common Chinese idioms   307

Introduction

500 Common Chinese Idioms: An Annotated Frequency Dictionary is a dictionary of common Chinese idioms that is based on frequency statistics. Designed for native English-speaking learners of Chinese at the intermediate level or above, it is designed so that it can both serve as a reference work and also function as a supplementary textbook for either class instruction or independent learning. In addition, the dictionary can be used as a resource by teachers of Chinese as a second/foreign language for developing pedagogical materials or assessment tools.

Chinese idioms and why they are important

There exist in both spoken and written Chinese a great number of idioms called 成语 (成語 chéngyǔ), literally 'set language' or 'set expressions,' which we here translate into English as 'idiom.' These may be general in nature or they may allude to famous events or stories from Chinese history, or they may be direct quotations from famous works of Chinese literature. The great majority of Chinese idioms is composed of four characters, which usually – though not always – can be parsed in groups of two. Chinese idioms are usually composed in Classical Chinese and thus typically have a different grammatical structure from that of Modern Chinese. In their speech and writing, Chinese people make frequent use of idioms, since these often sum up succinctly a meaning which it would otherwise take many words to express.

Contextually appropriate use of idioms tends to impress hearers as to the educational level and eloquence of the speaker. Since idioms are frequently used in formal speech and higher-level written materials, such as newspaper editorials and commentaries, they serve as a useful medium for helping learners move up on the proficiency ladder. Familiarity with idioms can also be helpful for the non-native in gaining credibility in Chinese society. Indeed, almost nothing impresses a Chinese person more than an aptly used idiom coming from the mouth of a foreigner.

There is a great number of idioms in Chinese, with certain dictionaries of idioms including well over 20,000 entries. All Chinese people know idioms, even though the total number known by any one individual will depend on her or his education, linguistic talent, general intelligence, etc. Idioms are such an important part of Chinese popular culture that there even exists a game called 成语接龙 (成語接龍 chéngyǔ jiēlóng) that involves someone calling out an idiom, with someone else then being supposed to think of another idiom to link up with the first one, so that the last character of the first idiom is the same as the first character of the second idiom, and so forth. According to the Chinese search engine Baidu, the longest idiom chain ever created was all of 1,788 idioms long!

For the learner of Chinese as a second/foreign language, idioms are not so easy to understand, since the functional meaning of idioms is often different from the surface meaning and may, to quote an English idiom, be 'greater than the sum of its parts.' This is because Chinese idioms frequently involve literary allusions, extended meanings, and metaphors. For example, take the idiom 雪中送炭 (雪中送炭 xuě zhōng sòng tàn). This could be translated literally as 'in the snow to deliver charcoal'; however, the actual meaning usually has nothing at all to do with 'snow' or 'charcoal,' but rather involves the rendering of aid to someone at a time of need.

Similarly, it is not so easy to use idioms. For example, consider the idiom 衣食住行 (衣食住行 yī shí zhù xíng). The literal meaning of this idiom is 'food, clothing, shelter, and transportation,' that is, 'the basic necessities of life.' This would seem to be not that difficult to understand. However, in speech or in written compositions, students will frequently produce a sentence such as *每个人都有衣食住行, with the intended meaning: 'Everyone possesses the basic necessities of life'; yet this idiom cannot be used in such a way. The basic problem here is that students understand only the general meaning of the idiom but are not clear about how to use it appropriately in their own speech or writing. And precisely because idioms are difficult to use appropriately, students tend to avoid them in their Chinese.

Idioms have a long history in Chinese, with some having existed for well over 2,000 years. Indeed, the grammatical structure of most Chinese idioms is that of Classical Chinese. There are three common origins of idioms: ancient fables and historical tales; Buddhist and Confucian classics as well as other works of ancient Chinese literature; and habitual collocations of terms that gradually came to be stable and used in a certain way, even though their exact origin is not known today.

To use a Chinese idiom, we could say there are in the Chinese language as many idioms 'as there are hairs on an ox' (多如牛毛 duō rú niú máo 'many as ox hairs'). So, how many idioms should a foreign learner of Chinese learn? We have found that, based on our own statistical surveys, whether one employs a larger corpus consisting of several tens of millions of characters (which would include 6,000–7,000 idioms) or a smaller corpus consisting of several hundred thousand to a few million characters, 500 idioms will in either case cover about 40 percent to 50 percent of the total of the frequency of occurrence of all idioms. This is the reason why it was decided to include 500 entries in this dictionary.

Special characteristics of this dictionary

There are many dictionaries of Chinese idioms on the market in China, with the largest containing over 20,000 entries. However, none of these dictionaries is particularly suitable for the use of non-native Chinese language learners. This is primarily for the following reasons:

First, the choice of idioms to be included is often not practical or otherwise appropriate for non-native learners of Chinese. For example, in not a few monolingual dictionaries of Chinese idioms, the first entry is 阿鼻地狱 (阿鼻地獄 Ābí Dìyù) 'Avici Hell (in Buddhism)' – not exactly a particularly useful idiom for the average non-native learner and, indeed, one that even many Chinese readers would not readily understand. Second, most dictionaries of idioms in China lack English translations, and the Chinese used for explanation and exemplification is typically too difficult for someone whose native language is not Chinese; in fact, the language of the explanations is in many cases even harder than the idiom being explained! Third, there may not even be Pinyin romanization provided. Also, in many monolingual Chinese dictionaries of idioms there are no example sentences, or else the example sentences are too difficult, deriving from famous works of classical literature such as *Dream of the Red Chamber*. Perhaps such examples are appropriate for native Chinese users, but certainly they are not very helpful for non-native users. Also, usage explanations, if present at all, may be quite vague and without information on common collocations. Finally, the great majority of dictionaries of idioms are arranged according to Pinyin romanization, stroke order, or meaning categories. Though arranging entries based on Pinyin or stroke order may be convenient for looking up idioms, such an arrangement is definitely not the most conducive for learning.

The idioms included in this dictionary were chosen and arranged based on their frequency and practicality for non-native learners. Moreover, all the example sentences have been written in clear, everyday Modern Chinese and provide an invaluable context for the idiom being exemplified. Indeed, most of the example sentences were written only after examining 200 or more instances of actual use in the linguistic corpuses on which the dictionary was based. Also included are synonyms, antonyms, sociolinguistic information, and fairly detailed descriptions of usage that provide information on grammatical functions and, when applicable, common collocations.

How the entries of this dictionary were determined

In determining the 500 entries to be included here and their order in the dictionary, we considered the following six corpuses:

Name of corpus	1. *People's Daily* newspaper, all issues from 1996–2000	2. Professor Weiguo Zhang's personal corpus	3. Balanced Corpus from Academia Sinica, Taiwan	4. Spoken Beijing Dialect Corpus by Hu Mingyang and Zhang Weiguo	5. 2009 PRC elementary/ secondary school language textbooks (24 volumes)	6. Peking University Center for Chinese Linguistics (CCL) corpus
Number of characters	45 million	9.5 million	8 million	1 million	1–2 million	307 million
Type of material	primarily news; general	primarily literature	general	speech	general	general

Regarding corpus 3, while we did consult the frequency list for that corpus, it should be noted that the list includes only those idioms that occur ten or more times in the corpus. As for corpus 6, though it was not possible for us to search all of the idioms in that corpus, we did consult that corpus in deciding the order for the entries included in our dictionary.

The procedure for determining the entries was as follows: First, an exhaustive search was conducted of all the idioms in corpuses 1 and 2 above, with the goal of compiling for each of these corpuses a list of the 800 highest-frequency idioms. It turned out that the two lists of 800 idioms had 305 idioms in common; therefore, it was decided that these 305 idioms should form the basis for this dictionary.

Next to be selected were a group of 75 idioms that were relatively high in frequency in corpuses 3, 4, and 5, but which happened not to be included among the 305 idioms described in the preceding paragraph. Adding them to the 305 idioms just mentioned, a list of of 380 entries was obtained. Finally, after tabulating all the idioms in the first five corpuses, an additional 120 high-frequency idioms that did not appear on the list of 380 entries were selected. In this way, the grand total of 500 entries was arrived at. The frequency of occurrence of the 500 entries in all the different corpuses was then added together, and it was thus that the overall frequency number of each entry was obtained.

It should be pointed out that, among the 500 idioms, there are 50 that derive from fables or tales from Chinese history. After we obtained the overall frequencies of occurrence for each of the 500 idioms, we took the 50 idioms that derive from fables or Chinese history and arranged them according to frequency, and then ordered them so that one would occur as every tenth idiom, from idiom number 10 through idiom number 500. With this one exception, the 500 entries were arranged strictly according to frequency of occurrence.

The reason why we decided the order of fables and historical idioms separately from the other entries is that, if we had proceeded purely by frequency, then most of these idioms would not have been included in the dictionary; and yet these idioms are often even more concise and embody even more Chinese culture than 'ordinary' idioms. It is for these reasons that we gave what one might call 'special handling' to these idioms that derive from fables and tales from ancient Chinese culture, which we recommend to learners for their learning and use, when appropriate.

How this dictionary is organized

Each entry in this dictionary consists of the following:

1. *Number of the idiom.* On the first line of each entry is the number of the idiom in this dictionary.
2. *Idiom in simplified characters.* Next on the first line is the idiom printed in simplified characters [indicated by thick brackets].
3. *Idiom in traditional characters.* Also on the first line is the idiom printed in traditional characters (indicated by thin parentheses).
4. *Idiom in Pinyin romanization.* The last item on the first line of each entry is the idiom written in Pinyin romanization.
5. *English translation of idiom.* Starting on the second line of each entry is the English translation and/or explanation of the idiom. When possible, the individual characters that make up the idiom are also translated. These are often

followed by a literal translation of the whole idiom and one or more freer translations of the idiom.

6. *Example sentences.* Next, two example sentences are provided for each idiom to illustrate how the idiom is used. We urge users of this dictionary to study the examples carefully and to pay special attention to the linguistic context in which the entries occur. Each example sentence is given first in simplified Chinese characters and then in Pinyin romanization, followed by an English translation. In translating the examples, we have in most cases not attempted to find an equivalent English idiom, which could be confusing for learners, since they might not understand which part of the Chinese corresponds to which part of the English. Instead, we have usually translated into ordinary prose. To help learners understand the structure of the Chinese original, the English translations tend to follow the structure of the Chinese quite closely; as a result, some of the English in the translations is rather stilted. Our concern was that, had we translated into smoother English, many learners might have been puzzled how we got from the Chinese to the English. As concerns the examples, we should state here that the example sentences are merely linguistic examples, not in any way being indicative of the authors' personal beliefs or advocations.

7. *Usage.* For most of the entries, comments on usage are provided. Here, we try to indicate the main grammatical functions of the idiom; for example, whether it occurs as subject, predicate, complement, attributive, or adverbial. Comments on common collocations, that is, other words together with which the entry frequently occurs, are sometimes included. These comments are based on approximately 200 examples in the corpuses and the authors' own judgment.

8. *Allusion.* If applicable, information is included on literary or historical allusions related to the idiom. In these cases, we often provide a somewhat simplified version, in English translation, of the Chinese story of how the idiom came into common use.

9. *Note.* Many entries include a note on the sociolinguistic function of the idiom, for example, whether its use is complimentary or derogatory. Information may also be included here on the origin of the idiom, or on whether it is used primarily in speaking or writing, etc.

10. *Near synonyms.* So as to help more advanced students expand their vocabulary, we list near synonyms of the main entry when they exist. These are presented in simplified characters [in brackets], in Pinyin and traditional characters (in parentheses), and in English translation 'in single quotation marks.'

11. *Antonyms.* Common antonyms of the main entry are also provided. As with the near synonyms, these are presented in simplified characters [in brackets], Pinyin and traditional characters (in parentheses), and in English 'in single quotation marks.'

How to use this dictionary

This dictionary can be used as a reference to look up idioms that you have read or heard. If you know the pronunciation of the idiom, you may look it up in the

Pinyin index at the end of the volume (Appendix Two), which is arranged in alphabetical order. On the other hand, if you do not know the pronunciation of at least the first syllable of the idiom, then you may look up the idiom by the stroke order of the first character in the stroke order index at the end of the volume (Appendix Three).

Though every entry in this dictionary is independent and complete and the dictionary can serve for general reference purposes just like any other reference work, it is our hope that, since the dictionary is arranged in order of frequency, readers will – if at all possible – study this dictionary in the order of the entries, from beginning to end. In this way, by the time they have finished working their way through the dictionary, readers will have in the most efficient way possible raised their overall proficiency level in understanding and using Chinese idioms. In an organized Chinese language class, the instructor could assign one to five idioms to be studied for each class session. In the case of independent learners, they could take up one to five idioms per day, depending on the amount of time they have available.

Background of the compilation of this dictionary and acknowledgments

In 2007, Liwei Jiao devised a plan for writing a dictionary of idioms and invited Cornelius C. Kubler and Weiguo Zhang to join him in the project. Weiguo Zhang subsequently undertook a statistical frequency survey of idioms in linguistic corpuses 1, 2, and 4, as described above. He suggested taking the 305 idioms that overlapped on the first 800 entries of corpuses 1 and 2 as the basis for the dictionary. Liwei Jiao was responsible for the remainder of the statistical work and determined the 500 entries to be included in the dictionary as well as their order. He then proceeded to draft in Chinese the explanations of the idioms, example sentences, and usage notes, and compiled the lists of near synonyms and antonyms. Later, Liwei Jiao also added the traditional characters and initial versions of the Pinyin romanization, as well as writing the Chinese version of Appendix One. Kubler translated all of the Chinese in this book into English, edited the Pinyin romanization, and provided input regarding the explanations, example sentences, and this Introduction.

The three authors wish to express here their appreciation to the following for their assistance in the compilation of this dictionary: Professor Shuiguang Deng of the Department of Computer Science of Zhejiang University, P.R.C.; Ms. Lijun Wu, also of the P.R.C.; Mr. William Xuefeng Wang of Canada; and Ms. Margaret Howard, Ms. Sarah Basham, and Ms. Barbara Wei, all of the U.S. Finally, the authors would be remiss not to also thank our families for their crucial support, without which this dictionary would surely never have seen the light of day.

List of entries

1	实事求是	40	纸上谈兵	79	截然不同	118	任重道远
2	艰苦奋斗	41	名副其实	80	愚公移山	119	无家可归
3	千方百计	42	日新月异	81	所作所为	120	入木三分
4	全心全意	43	得天独厚	82	后顾之忧	121	意味深长
5	无论如何	44	情不自禁	83	德才兼备	122	继往开来
6	前所未有	45	不以为然	84	相辅相成	123	耳目一新
7	坚定不移	46	络绎不绝	85	讨价还价	124	循序渐进
8	引人注目	47	不约而同	86	同心同德	125	挺身而出
9	因地制宜	48	千千万万	87	理直气壮	126	滔滔不绝
10	自相矛盾	49	齐心协力	88	身体力行	127	天翻地覆
11	成千上万	50	卧薪尝胆	89	义不容辞	128	不言而喻
12	卓有成效	51	大街小巷	90	画龙点睛	129	再接再厉
13	当务之急	52	不由自主	91	琳琅满目	130	杞人忧天
14	独立自主	53	应运而生	92	耐人寻味	131	风云变幻
15	脱颖而出	54	形形色色	93	繁荣昌盛	132	淋漓尽致
16	无可奈何	55	名列前茅	94	难能可贵	133	忧心忡忡
17	莫名其妙	56	家喻户晓	95	一模一样	134	直截了当
18	自力更生	57	兴高采烈	96	突飞猛进	135	眼花缭乱
19	一如既往	58	排忧解难	97	刮目相看	136	不屈不挠
20	扑朔迷离	59	自强不息	98	风风雨雨	137	语重心长
21	不可思议	60	走马观花	99	旗帜鲜明	138	栩栩如生
22	坚持不懈	61	长治久安	100	破釜沉舟	139	呕心沥血
23	供不应求	62	安居乐业	101	独一无二	140	毛遂自荐
24	行之有效	63	惊心动魄	102	兢兢业业	141	方兴未艾
25	众所周知	64	脚踏实地	103	不折不扣	142	聚精会神
26	全力以赴	65	徇私舞弊	104	五花八门	143	比比皆是
27	理所当然	66	不知所措	105	求同存异	144	高瞻远瞩
28	四面八方	67	来之不易	106	无能为力	145	无动于衷
29	兴致勃勃	68	发扬光大	107	一无所知	146	迫在眉睫
30	一鸣惊人	69	顾全大局	108	一席之地	147	触目惊心
31	想方设法	70	八仙过海	109	轻而易举	148	无济于事
32	千家万户	71	自然而然	110	亡羊补牢	149	应有尽有
33	举足轻重	72	以身作则	111	默默无闻	150	南辕北辙
34	见义勇为	73	层出不穷	112	迫不及待	151	有朝一日
35	举世瞩目	74	轰轰烈烈	113	有声有色	152	大有可为
36	小心翼翼	75	息息相关	114	一心一意	153	史无前例
37	源远流长	76	一丝不苟	115	突如其来	154	随心所欲
38	弄虚作假	77	微不足道	116	异军突起	155	丰功伟绩
39	自言自语	78	刻不容缓	117	喜闻乐见	156	不动声色

157	取而代之	204	顺理成章	251	不择手段	298	生气勃勃
158	根深蒂固	205	大刀阔斧	252	津津有味	299	天经地义
159	久而久之	206	不遗余力	253	深入浅出	300	狐假虎威
160	四面楚歌	207	字里行间	254	相提并论	301	了如指掌
161	急功近利	208	不解之缘	255	深恶痛绝	302	别有用心
162	始终不渝	209	一无所有	256	不可多得	303	五光十色
163	一目了然	210	守株待兔	257	沸沸扬扬	304	不合时宜
164	量力而行	211	百花齐放	258	雪上加霜	305	富丽堂皇
165	浩浩荡荡	212	力不从心	259	风尘仆仆	306	马不停蹄
166	雨后春笋	213	异口同声	260	朝三暮四	307	开门见山
167	一举一动	214	背道而驰	261	心平气和	308	别具一格
168	有目共睹	215	势在必行	262	德高望重	309	一针见血
169	欣欣向荣	216	当之无愧	263	燃眉之急	310	草木皆兵
170	三顾茅庐	217	咄咄逼人	264	不厌其烦	311	专心致志
171	五彩缤纷	218	四通八达	265	别出心裁	312	堂堂正正
172	一本正经	219	可歌可泣	266	不见经传	313	泣不成声
173	恍然大悟	220	惊弓之鸟	267	蔚然成风	314	无与伦比
174	视而不见	221	真心实意	268	大惊小怪	315	素不相识
175	有条不紊	222	恰到好处	269	千辛万苦	316	堂而皇之
176	别开生面	223	津津乐道	270	东施效颦	317	训练有素
177	锲而不舍	224	取长补短	271	因势利导	318	刻骨铭心
178	全神贯注	225	喜出望外	272	千里迢迢	319	不屑一顾
179	万无一失	226	本来面目	273	格格不入	320	对牛弹琴
180	按图索骥	227	脍炙人口	274	如火如荼	321	助人为乐
181	诸如此类	228	自由自在	275	肃然起敬	322	衣食住行
182	精益求精	229	气喘吁吁	276	扬长避短	323	不胜枚举
183	一帆风顺	230	画蛇添足	277	蒸蒸日上	324	赞不绝口
184	审时度势	231	座无虚席	278	胸有成竹	325	大名鼎鼎
185	谈何容易	232	夜以继日	279	肆无忌惮	326	如数家珍
186	大势所趋	233	持之以恒	280	囫囵吞枣	327	跃跃欲试
187	潜移默化	234	针锋相对	281	异乎寻常	328	古色古香
188	掉以轻心	235	相得益彰	282	赏心悦目	329	推波助澜
189	此起彼伏	236	念念不忘	283	古往今来	330	班门弄斧
190	名落孙山	237	深思熟虑	284	大有作为	331	光明磊落
191	引人入胜	238	独树一帜	285	集思广益	332	川流不息
192	不堪设想	239	惊天动地	286	一应俱全	333	迎刃而解
193	义无反顾	240	东窗事发	287	不得而知	334	对症下药
194	焕然一新	241	铺天盖地	288	提心吊胆	335	热火朝天
195	一视同仁	242	大张旗鼓	289	货真价实	336	不足为奇
196	五颜六色	243	彬彬有礼	290	鸡犬升天	337	脱胎换骨
197	束手无策	244	熙熙攘攘	291	奋不顾身	338	扬眉吐气
198	十字路口	245	无影无踪	292	精打细算	339	荡然无存
199	与日俱增	246	至高无上	293	目不转睛	340	叶公好龙
200	拔苗助长	247	司空见惯	294	车水马龙	341	一脉相承
201	博大精深	248	接二连三	295	一望无际	342	置之不理
202	喜气洋洋	249	斩钉截铁	296	一成不变	343	身先士卒
203	不可或缺	250	滥竽充数	297	脱口而出	344	精神抖擞

345	侃侃而谈	385	同甘共苦	425	同日而语	464	立竿见影
346	诚心诚意	386	明目张胆	426	曾几何时	465	冲锋陷阵
347	千军万马	387	耳闻目睹	427	高高在上	466	水到渠成
348	绞尽脑汁	388	啼笑皆非	428	一往情深	467	危言耸听
349	垂头丧气	389	死灰复燃	429	痛心疾首	468	何去何从
350	掩耳盗铃	390	塞翁失马	430	鹬蚌相争，	469	有求必应
351	日复一日	391	口口声声		渔翁得利	470	杯弓蛇影
352	奄奄一息	392	水落石出	431	无时无刻	471	风平浪静
353	千载难逢	393	我行我素	432	欢天喜地	472	逍遥法外
354	未雨绸缪	394	望而却步	433	殚精竭虑	473	灯红酒绿
355	居高临下	395	有血有肉	434	通情达理	474	顶天立地
356	心安理得	396	天涯海角	435	从天而降	475	有鉴于此
357	一意孤行	397	轻描淡写	436	井井有条	476	义愤填膺
358	三令五申	398	哭笑不得	437	苦口婆心	477	不可告人
359	依依不舍	399	自告奋勇	438	人山人海	478	指手画脚
360	乐不思蜀	400	指鹿为马	439	运筹帷幄	479	简明扼要
361	叹为观止	401	设身处地	440	才高八斗	480	螳螂捕蝉，
362	大有人在	402	天方夜谭	441	沾沾自喜		黄雀在后
363	雪中送炭	403	雅俗共赏	442	皆大欢喜	481	一举两得
364	一筹莫展	404	无所适从	443	大千世界	482	置之度外
365	水泄不通	405	不容置疑	444	举一反三	483	永垂不朽
366	相依为命	406	流连忘返	445	不了了之	484	美中不足
367	街头巷尾	407	翻来覆去	446	得不偿失	485	人声鼎沸
368	无微不至	408	无中生有	447	偷工减料	486	天真烂漫
369	不假思索	409	庞然大物	448	高屋建瓴	487	就事论事
370	江郎才尽	410	黔驴技穷	449	恋恋不舍	488	大手大脚
371	不相上下	411	三三两两	450	围魏救赵	489	漫山遍野
372	居安思危	412	发号施令	451	花团锦簇	490	刻舟求剑
373	近在咫尺	413	心旷神怡	452	悲欢离合	491	生龙活虎
374	卷土重来	414	雷厉风行	453	今非昔比	492	不甘示弱
375	冰天雪地	415	朝夕相处	454	一事无成	493	循循善诱
376	有的放矢	416	踌躇满志	455	不伦不类	494	万家灯火
377	一尘不染	417	金碧辉煌	456	家常便饭	495	执迷不悟
378	事半功倍	418	同舟共济	457	平心而论	496	千疮百孔
379	不同凡响	419	志同道合	458	变本加厉	497	悬崖勒马
380	井底之蛙	420	唇亡齿寒	459	名正言顺	498	半斤八两
381	大同小异	421	柳暗花明	460	望梅止渴	499	共襄盛举
382	谈笑风生	422	袖手旁观	461	意气风发	500	五十步笑百步
383	不亦乐乎	423	豁然开朗	462	双管齐下		
384	承前启后	424	诗情画意	463	含辛茹苦		

500 common
Chinese idioms

1. 【实事求是】(實事求是) shí shì qiú shì

实 means 'actual,' 事 means 'situation,' 求 means 'seek,' and 是 means 'original way.' The meaning of this idiom is 'to handle matters according to their actual situation.' This idiom is conventionally translated as 'seek truth from facts.'

Example 1: 我们应该坚持**实事求是**的原则，把理论和实践结合起来。

Wǒmen yīnggāi jiānchí shíshì-qiúshì de yuánzé, bǎ lǐlùn hé shíjiàn jiéhé qǐlai.

'We should insist on the principle of seeking truth from facts, and integrate theory and practice.'

Example 2: 大家要**实事求是**地评价毛泽东的历史地位，不能因为有了文化大革命就全盘否定他以前的贡献。

Dàjiā yào shíshì-qiúshì de píngjià Máo Zédōng de lìshǐ dìwèi, bù néng yīnwèi yǒule Wénhuà Dà Gémìng jiù quán pán fǒudìng tā yǐqián de gòngxiàn.

'Everyone should evaluate Mao Zedong's position in history by seeking truth from facts; one can't totally repudiate his earlier contributions because of the Cultural Revolution.'

Usage: Functions mainly as attributive and predicate; can also serve as adverbial.

Note: Because 实事求是 is part of the contents of Mao Zedong thought, these four characters can be seen on the buildings of many Chinese organizations. The photograph below was taken at the entrance to Renmin University in Beijing. The four characters in the photograph are 实事求是, with 實 being the traditional form of the simplified character 实.

courtesy of Du Jian

Antonym: [弄虚作假] (nòng xū zuò jiǎ 弄虚作假) 'use trickery or deception to create a false appearance.'

2. 【艰苦奋斗】(艱苦奮鬥) jiān kǔ fèn dòu

艰苦 means 'difficult' and 奋斗 means 'struggle.' The meaning of the whole idiom is 'difficult struggle, arduous struggle.'

Example 1: 即使在今天，我们也不应该丢掉**艰苦奋斗**的精神。

Jíshǐ zài jīntiān, wǒmen yě bù yīnggāi diūdiào jiānkǔ-fèndòu de jīngshen.

'Even today, we should not lose our spirit of hardworking struggle.'

Example 2: 经济困难时期，全国人民都**艰苦奋斗**，最后终于渡过难关。

Jīngjì kùnnán shíqī, quánguó rénmín dōu jiānkǔ-fèndòu, zuìhòu zhōngyú dùguò nánguān.

'In difficult economic times, all the people of the country struggled arduously; in the end, they finally got through the difficult period.'

Usage: Functions mainly as attributive or predicate. As attributive, usually followed by nouns such as 精神 (jīngshen) 'spirit,' 作风 (zuòfeng 作風) 'way of working,' and 传统 (chuántǒng 傳統) 'tradition.'

Note: Complimentary in meaning.

Near Synonyms: [克勤克俭] (kè qín kè jiǎn 克勤克儉) 'hardworking and thrifty,' [奋发图强] (fèn fā tú qiáng 奮發圖強) 'work hard for the strength and prosperity of the country.'

Antonyms: [花天酒地] (huā tiān jiǔ dì 花天酒地) 'flowers in the sky and wine on the ground – lead a frivolous life,' [铺张浪费] (pū zhāng làng fèi 鋪張浪費) 'extravagant and wasteful,' [骄奢淫逸] (jiāo shē yín yì 驕奢淫逸) 'indulge oneself in a proud and extravagant lifestyle.'

3. 【千方百计】(千方百計) qiān fāng bǎi jì

The literal meaning is 'by every possible means,' with a freer translation being 'by hook or by crook.'

Example 1: 由于农民的收入跟城市居民的收入差距比较大，所以政府**千方百计**地增加农民的收入。

Yóuyú nóngmín de shōurù gēn chéngshì jūmín de shōurù chājù bǐjiào dà, suǒyǐ zhèngfǔ qiānfāng-bǎijì de zēngjiā nóngmín de shōurù.

'Due to the relatively large gap between the salaries of rural residents and those in the city, the government increased rural residents' salaries by every possible means.'

Example 2: 这家工厂**千方百计**地降低产品的成本。

Zhè jiā gōngchǎng qiānfāng-bǎijì de jiàngdī chǎnpǐn de chéngběn.

'This factory decreased the production costs of its products by every possible means.'

Usage: Functions mainly as adverbial modifier.

Near Synonyms: [想方设法] (xiǎng fāng shè fǎ 想方設法) 'try every possible means,' 绞尽脑汁 (jiǎo jìn nǎo zhī 絞盡腦汁) 'rack one's brains,' [费尽心机] (fèi jìn xīn jī 費盡心機) 'think of every possible means.'

Antonyms: [无计可施] (wú jì kě shī 無計可施) 'have no plan to carry out – at one's wit's end,' [束手无策] (shù shǒu wú cè 束手無策) 'tied hands without plan – at a complete loss about what to do.'

4. 【全心全意】(全心全意) quán xīn quán yì

The literal meaning is 'complete heart complete intention,' with a freer translation being 'with all one's heart and all one's soul, wholeheartedly.'

Example 1: 公务员应该**全心全意**地为人民服务。

Gōngwùyuán yīnggāi quánxīn-quányì de wèi rénmín fúwù.

'Civil servants should serve the people with all their heart and all their soul.'

Example 2: 她一边哭一边说，"我这样**全心全意**地对你，你为什么对我有二心？"

Tā yì biān kū yì biān shuō, "Wǒ zhèyàng quánxīn-quányì de duì nǐ, nǐ wèishénme duì wǒ yǒu èrxīn?"

'She cried as she said, "I treat you like this with all my heart and all my soul; why are you disloyal to me?"'

Usage: Functions mainly as adverbial, often followed by 为人民服务 (wèi rénmín fúwù 為人民服務) 'to serve (for) the people.'

Note: Somewhat complimentary in meaning.

Near Synonym: [一心一意] (yì xīn yí yì 一心一意) 'with one heart and one mind, wholeheartedly.'

Antonyms: [三心二意] (sān xīn èr yì 三心二意) 'of two minds, half-hearted,' [朝三暮四] (zhāo sān mù sì 朝三暮四) 'fickle and inconstant.'

5. 【无论如何】(無論如何) wú lùn rú hé

无论 means 'no matter' and 如何 means 'how?' The meaning of the whole idiom is 'no matter how, no matter what, in any event, in any case.'

Example 1: 你们**无论如何**都要在三天内把这件事情做完。

Nǐmen wúlùn-rúhé dōu yào zài sān tiān nèi bǎ zhè jiàn shìqing zuòwán.

'No matter what, you should complete this matter within three days.'

Example 2: 我看她非常面熟，但是**无论如何**都想不起她的名字来。

Wǒ kàn tā fēicháng miànshú, dànshì wúlùn-rúhé dōu xiǎngbuqǐ tā de míngzi lái.

'When I look at her, she's very familiar, but no matter what I can't think of her name.'

Usage: Functions as adverbial.

Near Synonym: [在所不惜] (zài suǒ bù xī 在所不惜) 'will not grudge, will spare no effort, will not hesitate to.'

6. 【前所未有】(前所未有) qián suǒ wèi yǒu

未 means 'did not, not yet.' The meaning of the whole idiom is 'never happened before in the past, unprecedented.'

Example 1: 她遇到了**前所未有**的挑战。

Tā yùdàole qiánsuǒwèiyǒu de tiǎozhàn.

'She encountered unprecedented challenges.'

Example 2: 这次行动规模之大、速度之快，在历史上是**前所未有**的。

Zhè cì xíngdòng guīmó zhī dà, sùdù zhī kuài, zài lìshǐ shàng shì qiánsuǒwèiyǒu de.

'The scale and speed of the operation this time were unprecedented in history.'

Usage: Functions mainly as attributive; can also serve as predicate.

Near Synonyms: [史无前例] (shǐ wú qián lì 史無前例) 'in history there is no precedent, unprecedented,' [前无古人] (qián wú gǔ rén 前無古人) 'no ancients who can compare – peerless, unprecedented.'

Antonym: [司空见惯] (sī kōng jiàn guàn 司空見慣) 'get used to seeing something and no longer find it strange.'

7. 【坚定不移】(堅定不移) jiān dìng bù yí

坚定 means 'firm, steadfast' and 移 means 'move, change.' A literal translation of the whole idiom is 'firm and unchanging.' Freer translations include 'firm and unswerving, steadfast and unchanging, resolute.'

Example 1: 在一场政治危机中，他**坚定不移**地站在总统一边。

Zài yì cháng zhèngzhì wēijī zhōng, tā jiāndìng-bùyí de zhàn zài zǒngtǒng yì biān.

'In a political crisis, he steadfastly stood on the side of the president.'

Example 2: 中国将**坚定不移**地推进改革开放。

Zhōngguó jiāng jiāndìng-bùyí de tuījìn gǎigé kāifàng.

'China will steadfastly advance the policy of reform and opening up.'

Usage: Functions mainly as adverbial.

Note: Complimentary in meaning.

Near Synonyms: [始終不渝] (shǐ zhōng bù yú 始終不渝) 'from beginning to end not changing – steady, steadfast,' [矢志不渝] (shǐ zhì bù yú 矢志不渝) 'arrow(-like) determination not to change – determined not to change.'

Antonyms: [举棋不定] (jǔ qí bú dìng 舉棋不定) 'hold a chess piece without deciding – indecisive,' [见异思迁] (jiàn yì sī qiān 見異思遷) 'see something different and want to change – fickle, capricious.'

8. 【引人注目】 (引人注目) yǐn rén zhù mù

引 means 'attract' and 注目 means 'fix one's eyes on, gaze at.' A literal translation would be 'attract other people's attention.' Freer translations include 'draw attention, noticeable, conspicuous.'

Example 1: 在一场**引人注目**的比赛中，他的运气及发挥都很好，因此轻松战胜对手。

Zài yì chǎng yǐnrén-zhùmù de bǐsài zhōng, tā de yùnqì jí fāhuī dōu hěnhǎo, yīncǐ qīngsōng zhànshèng duìshǒu.

'In an attention-grabbing competition, his luck and his performance were both very good, therefore he defeated his opponents without effort.'

Example 2: 台湾电子行业的迅速发展格外**引人注目**。

Táiwān diànzǐ hángyè de xùnsù fāzhǎn géwài yǐnrén-zhùmù.

'The rapid development of Taiwan's electronics industry especially attracts people's attention.'

Usage: Functions mainly as predicate and attributive.

Antonyms: [隐姓埋名] (yǐn xìng mái míng 隱姓埋名) 'conceal one's identity,' [无人问津] (wú ré wèn jīn 無人問津) 'no one asks about the ford – no one shows any interest.'

9. 【因地制宜】 (因地制宜) yīn dì zhì yí

因 here means 'according to,' 地 means 'locality,' 制 means 'formulate,' and 宜 means 'appropriate measures.' A literal translation of the whole idiom is 'according to the locality formulate appropriate measures,' with a freer translation being 'adapt to local conditions.'

Example 1: 那座城市有几座历史名胜古迹，因此该城市**因地制宜**地大力发展旅游业。

Nà zuò chéngshì yǒu jǐ zuò lìshǐ míngshèng-gǔjì, yīncǐ gāi chéngshì yīndì-zhìyí de dàlì fāzhǎn lǚyóuyè.

'That city has several famous historical sites; therefore, the aforementioned city is vigorously developing tourism, adopting appropriate measures according to concrete local conditions.'

Example 2: 国家在推行一些地方政策的时候要**因地制宜**，不能搞一刀切。

Guójiā zài tuīxíng yìxiē dìfāng zhèngcè de shíhou yào yīndì-zhìyí, bù néng gǎo yì dāo qiē.

'When the country implements local policies, it should enact appropriate policies based on local conditions; it must not adopt a cookie-cutter approach.'

Usage: Functions mainly as predicate and adverbial.

Near Synonyms: [对症下药] (duì zhèng xià yào 對癥下藥) 'suit the medicine to the illness,' [因势利导] (yīn shì lì dǎo 因勢利導) 'guided by the circumstances.'

Antonym: [一成不变] (yì chéng bú biàn 一成不變) 'fixed and unalterable.'

10. 【自相矛盾】(自相矛盾) zì xiāng máo dùn

自 means 'self,' 相 means 'mutually,' 矛 means 'spear,' and 盾 means 'shield.' The connotation is 'self-contradictory.'

Example 1: 那个政治家显然在撒谎，上个月说的话跟这个月说的话**自相矛盾**。

Nàge zhèngzhìjiā xiǎnrán zài sāhuǎng, shàng ge yuè shuōde huà gēn zhège yuè shuō de huà zìxiāng-máodùn.

'That politician is obviously lying; what he said last month and what he said this month are self-contradictory.'

Example 2: 他的文章的逻辑不太清楚，有**自相矛盾**的地方。

Tā de wénzhāng de luójí bú tài qīngchu, yǒu zìxiāng-máodùn de dìfang.

'The logic of his essay is not very clear; there are places that are self-contradictory.'

Usage: Functions mainly as predicate or attributive.

Allusion: There was a man who was selling a spear and a shield at the same time. He boasted about his shield, saying, "My shield is the strongest in the world! There is nothing that can penetrate it." He also said, "My spear is the sharpest in the world! There is nothing it can't penetrate." Consequently someone asked him, "If you use your spear to stab your shield, what will happen?" The man could not answer. (from *Han Feizi*)

Antonyms: [自圆其说] (zì yuán qí shūo 自圓其説) 'make one's argument consistent and not self-contradictory,' [无懈可击] (wú xiè kě jī 無懈可擊) 'with no chink in one's armour, leave no room for criticism.'

11. 【成千上万】(成千上萬) chéng qiān shàng wàn

成 here means 'becoming' and 上 mean 'surpassing.' The meaning of the whole idiom is 'tens of thousands of.'

Example 1: 为了找到一个好位置来看他们喜爱的歌星，**成千上万**的歌迷一下子挤进了体育场。

Wèile zhǎodào yí ge hǎo wèizhì lái kàn tāmen xǐ'ài de gēxīng, chéngqiān-shàngwàn de gēmí yíxiàzi jǐ jìnle tǐyùchǎng.

'In order to find a good spot to see their beloved singing star, tens of thousands of fans all at once pushed their way into the stadium.'

Example 2: 这部新的法律影响到**成千上万**人的利益，所以引起了大家热烈的讨论。

Zhè bù xīn de fǎlǜ yǐngxiǎng dào chéngqiān-shàngwàn rén de lìyì, suǒyǐ yǐnqǐle dàjiā rèliè de tǎolùn.

'This new law affected the interests of tens of thousands of people, so it touched off passionate discussions by everyone.'

Usage: Functions mainly as attributive and predicate.

Near Synonym: [不计其数] (bú jì qí shù 不計其數) 'not calculate its number – too numerous to count.'

Antonym: [寥寥无几] (liáo liáo wú jǐ 寥寥無幾) 'very few.'

12. 【卓有成效】(卓有成效) zhuó yǒu chéng xiào

卓 means 'outstanding, excellent' and 成效 means 'effect, result.' A literal translation of the whole idiom is 'outstanding and having effect,' with freer translations including 'with outstanding results, highly effective.'

Example 1: 近年来，双方在文化领域内进行了**卓有成效**的合作。

Jìn nián lái, shuāngfāng zài wénhuà lǐngyù nèi jìnxíngle zhuóyǒuchéngxiào de hézuò.

'In recent years, both sides have carried out extremely effective cooperation in cultural spheres.'

Example 2: 政府的新经济政策**卓有成效**，受到人民的高度赞扬。

Zhèngfǔ de xīn jīngjì zhèngcè zhuóyǒuchéngxiào, shòudào rénmín de gāodù zànyáng.

'The government's new economic policy is highly effective; it has received a high degree of approval from the people.'

Usage: Functions mainly as attributive. Often preceded by the verbs 进行 (jinxing 進行) 'carry out' and 开展 (kāizhǎn 開展) 'develop'; often followed by the noun 合作 (hézuò 合作) 'cooperation.' Can also serve as predicate and adverbial.

Note: Complimentary in meaning.

Near Synonym: [行之有效] (xíng zhī yǒu xiào 行之有效) 'implement with efficiency, efficient.'

Antonyms: [无济于事] (wú jì yú shì 無濟於事) 'not help matters, of no avail, to no effect,' [劳而无功] (láo ér wú gōng 勞而無功) 'endeavor but have no success – work with no gain.'

13. 【当务之急】(當務之急) dāng wù zhī jí

当 means 'should,' 务 means 'pursue,' and 急 means 'an urgent matter.' The literal meaning is 'an urgent matter that should be pursued.' The whole idiom means 'a matter of great urgency.'

Example 1: 如何保持经济持续发展，是我们的**当务之急**。

Rúhé bǎochí jīngjì chíxù fāzhǎn, shì wǒmen de dāngwù-zhījí.

'How to maintain continued economic development is a matter of great urgency for us.'

Example 2: 二十世纪五六十年代，迅速推广普通话是语言文字工作者的**当务之急**。

Èrshí shìjì wǔ-liùshí niándài, xùnsù tuīguǎng pǔtōnghuà shì yǔyán wénzì gōngzuòzhě de dāngwù-zhījí.

'In the 1950s and 60s, the rapid spread of Putonghua was a matter of great urgency for language and writing specialists.'

Usage: Nominal element, functions mainly as object and subject.

Near Synonyms: [燃眉之急] (rán méi zhī jí 燃眉之急) 'the urgency of fire singeing the eyebrows – a matter of great urgency,' [迫在眉睫] (pò zài méi jié 迫在眉睫) 'pressing on the eyebrows and eyelashes – very urgent,' [刻不容缓] (kè bù róng huǎn 刻不容緩) 'allow no delay, extremely urgent.'

Antonyms: [一拖再拖] (yì tuō zài tuō 一拖再拖) 'drag on or delay without end,' [遥遥无期] (yáo yáo wú qī 遙遙無期) 'not in the foreseeable future.'

14. 【独立自主】(獨立自主) dú lì zì zhǔ

独立 means 'independent' and 自主 means 'be one's own master.' The whole idiom can be translated as 'independent and being one's own master' or 'independent and possessing the right of self-determination.'

Example 1: 中国一贯奉行**独立自主**的和平外交政策。

Zhōngguó yíguàn fèngxíng dúlì-zìzhǔ de hépíng wàijiāo zhèngcè.

'China has all along pursued an independent and peaceful diplomatic policy.'

Example 2: 那位亿万富翁的儿子不想借助他父亲的影响，而愿意**独立自主**地开创他自己的事业。

Nà wèi yìwànfùwēng de érzǐ bù xiǎng jièzhù tā fùqīn de yǐngxiǎng, ér yuànyì dúlì-zìzhǔ de kāichuàng tā zìjǐ de shìyè.

'That billionaire's son does not want to make use of his father's influence, but wants to independently establish his own career.'

Usage: Functions mainly as object or adverbial.

Note: Complimentary in meaning. 独立自主 is a foreign policy of China; therefore, this idiom often appears in diplomatic contexts.

Near Synonyms: [自力更生] (zì lì gēng shēng 自力更生) 'one's own strength changes one's life – rely on one's own efforts,' [自食其力] (zì shí qí lì 自食其力) 'oneself eat one's own strength – support oneself by one's own labor.'

Antonyms: [仰人鼻息] (yǎng rén bí xī 仰人鼻息) 'rely on other people's noses for breath – slavishly dependent,' [寄人篱下] (jì rén lí xià 寄人籬下) 'live as a dependent or parasite in another's home – rely or depend on others.'

15. 【脱颖而出】(脱穎而出) tuō yǐng ér chū

脱 means 'break free from, escape from' and 颖 means 'an awn of wheat' (i.e., the bristle-like fiber in the wheat). This refers to the fibers that often stick through a sack of wheat. By metaphor, this has come to mean 'talent being fully exposed, talent revealing itself.'

Example 1: 尽管很多人批评高考，但是高考的确能使很多优秀的人才**脱颖而出**。

Jǐnguǎn hěn duō rén pīpíng gāokǎo, dànshì gāokǎo díquè néng shǐ hěn duō yōuxiù de réncái tuōyǐng-érchū.

'Even though many people criticize the Chinese college entrance examination, it really can make many outstanding people of talent be revealed.'

Example 2: 第一次世界大战以后，梵高的作品**脱颖而出**，受到人们的重视。

Dìyī cì shìjiè dàzhàn yǐhòu, Fàn Gāo de zuòpǐn tuōyǐng-érchū, shòudào rénmen de zhòngshì.

'After World War I, Van Gogh's works became fully revealed, and were greatly valued by people.'

Usage: Functions as predicate.

Note: Complimentary in meaning.

Near Synonym: [崭露头角] (zhǎn lù tóu jiǎo 嶄露頭角) 'distinguish oneself.'

Antonym: [韬光养晦] (tāo guāng yǎng huì 韜光養晦) 'conceal one's abilities and bide one's time.'

16. 【无可奈何】(無可奈何) *wú kě nài hé*

The literal meaning is 'helpless; have no alternative; there's no way out.'

Example 1: 他**无可奈何**地说："对不起，这件事我帮不了你。"

Tā wúkěnàihé de shuō: "Duìbuqǐ, zhè jiàn shì wǒ bāng bùliǎo nǐ."

'Having no alternative, he said: "I'm sorry, I can't help you with this."'

Example 2: 辛普森案判决以后，虽然不少人都感到不满，但是**无可奈何**。

Xīnpǔsēn àn pànjué yǐhòu, suīrán bù shǎo rén dōu gǎndào bùmǎn, dànshì wúkěnàihé.

'After the verdict of the Simpson case, although a good number of people felt unsatisfied, there was nothing they could do about it.'

Usage: Functions mainly as predicate or adverbial modifier.

Near Synonyms: [爱莫能助] (ài mò néng zhù 愛莫能助) 'want to help but not be in a position to do so,' [无计可施] (wú jì kě shī 無計可施) 'at one's wit's end.'

Antonym: [花样百出] (huā yàng bǎi chū 花樣百出) 'one pattern or scheme after another.'

17. 【莫名其妙】(莫名其妙) *mò míng qí miào*

The literal meaning is 'no one can explain it; unable to make head or tail of something; be baffled.'

Example 1: 他一会儿说这样做，一会儿说那样做，大家都感到**莫名其妙**。

Tā yíhuìr shuō zhèyàng zuò, yíhuìr shuō nàyàng zuò, dàjiā dōu gǎndào mòmíng-qímiào.

'One moment he said to do it this way. The next moment he said to do it that way. Everyone felt baffled.'

Example 2: 我的手机**莫名其妙**地不见了。

Wǒ de shǒujī mòmíng-qímiào de bú jiàn le.

'My cell phone inexplicably disappeared.'

Usage: Functions mainly as predicate, complement, or adverbial modifier; can also serve as attribute. Common combinations include 让人～ (ràng rén ～ 讓人～), 感到～ (gǎndào～), and ～的话 / 病 (～ de huà/bìng 的話 / 病).

Note: There is an alternative form 莫明其妙 (mò míng qí miào).

Near Synonym: [匪夷所思] (fěi yí suǒ sī 匪夷所思) 'who would have thought it, unthinkable.'

Antonym: [洞若观火] (dòng ruò guān huǒ 洞若觀火) 'see something as clearly as a blazing fire.'

18. 【自力更生】(自力更生) zì lì gēng shēng

自力 means 'rely on one's own efforts' and 更生 means 'revive, rejuvenate.' The meaning of the whole idiom is 'one's own strength changes one's life – rely on one's own efforts.'

Example 1: 二十世纪六十年代，中国在失去苏联援助的情况下，**自力更生**，艰苦奋斗，在尖端科技方面并没有落后太多。

Èrshí shìjì liùshí niándài, Zhōngguó zài shīqù Sūlián yuánzhù de qíngkuàng xià, zìlì-gēngshēng, jiānkǔ-fèndòu, zài jiānduān kējì fāngmiàn bìng méiyǒu luòhòu tài duō.

'In the 1960s, China – in the situation of having lost the Soviet Union's assistance – relied on its own efforts in its development and struggled arduously, not falling behind too much in the advanced sciences.'

Example 2: 灾区人民**自力更生**，很快完成了家园的重建工作。

Zāiqū rénmín zìlì-gēngshēng, hěn kuài wánchéngle jiāyuán de chóngjiàn gōngzuò.

'The people of the disaster area relied on their own efforts; they quickly finished the work of reconstructing their homeland.'

Usage: Functions mainly as predicate and adverbial.

Note: Complimentary in meaning. Used mainly in slogans, often together with other idioms such as 艰苦奋斗 (jiān kǔ fèn dòu 艱苦奮鬥) 'arduous struggle,' 艰苦创业 (jiān kǔ chuàng yè 艱苦創業) 'experience great difficulty in starting an undertaking,' or 奋发图强 (fèn fā tú qiáng 奮發圖強) 'work hard for the strength and prosperity of the country.'

Near Synonyms: [自强不息] (zì qiáng bù xī 自強不息) 'strive constantly for self-improvement,' [自食其力] (zì shí qí lì 自食其力) 'oneself eat one's own strength – support oneself by one's own labor.'

Antonyms: [仰人鼻息] (yǎng rén bí xī 仰人鼻息) 'rely on other people's noses for breath – slavishly dependent,' [寄人篱下] (jì rén lí xià 寄人籬下) 'live as a dependent or parasite in another's home – rely or depend on others.'

19. 【一如既往】(一如既往) yì rú jì wǎng

既往 means 'formerly, in the past.' The meaning of the whole idiom is 'exactly the same as in the past, as before.'

Example 1: 中国将一**如既往**地加强同非洲国家的友好关系。

Zhōngguó jiāng yìrújìwǎng de jiāqiáng tóng Fēizhōu guójiā de yǒuhǎo guānxi.

'China will, exactly as in the past, strengthen friendly relations with African nations.'

Example 2: 今天，那位老教授**一如既往**地提前十分钟来到了教室。

Jīntiān, nà wèi lǎo jiàoshòu yìrújìwǎng de tíqián shí fēn zhōng láidàole jiàoshì.

'Today that old professor, exactly as in the past, came to the classroom ten minutes ahead of time.'

Usage: Functions as adverbial, often preceded by 将 (jiāng 將) 'will.'

Near Synonyms: [一成不变] (yì chéng bú biàn 一成不變) 'fixed and unalterable,' [始终如一] (shǐ zhōng rú yī 始終如一) 'beginning and end like one – consistent, constant.'

Antonyms: [一反常态] (yì fǎn cháng tài 一反常態) 'depart from one's normal behavior,' [朝三暮四] (zhāo sān mù sì 朝三暮四) 'fickle and inconstant.'

20. 【扑朔迷离】(撲朔迷離) pū shuò mí lí

扑朔 means 'move all over the place' and 迷离 means 'dim, blurred.' The original meaning of this idiom had to do with the difficulty of distinguishing between male and female rabbits (see note below). The extended meaning is 'things are intricate and complicated and difficult to distinguish clearly.' A freer translation is 'confusing, hard to distinguish, all mixed up.'

Example 1: 中国古典长篇小说的线索往往比较多，因此故事情节**扑朔迷离**。

Zhōngguó gǔdiǎn chángpiān xiǎoshuō de xiànsuǒ wǎngwǎng bǐjiào duō, yīncǐ gùshi qíngjié pūshuò-mílí.

'There are often rather many threads in Classical Chinese novels; because of this, the plot of the story is confusing.'

Example 2: 这次多方谈判，由于每一方都尽力维护自己的利益，所以谈判的前景**扑朔迷离**。

Zhè cì duōfāng tánpàn, yóuyú měi yì fāng dōu jìnlì wéihù zìjǐ de lìyì, suǒyǐ tánpàn de qiánjǐng pūshuò-mílí.

'In the current multiparty negotiations, because each side is trying its best to protect its own interests, the prospects for the negotiations are murky.'

Usage: About half the time functions as predicate, often occurring at the end of a sentence. Can also serve as attributive.

Allusion: A Northern Dynasties folk song, *Mulan Ci*, sang the praises of the young woman Mulan, who joined the military on behalf of her father. Mulan had been in the military for twelve years and involved in many military exploits when she was finally recognized by her comrades as being a woman. Her explanation then was this: "The male rabbit's foot moves all over, the female rabbit's eyes are dim. When both rabbits are running on the ground, how can one distinguish whether they are male or female?" The meaning of this is that when rabbits are grabbed by their ears so they can't move, the male rabbit's feet will keep moving wildly, while the female rabbit's eyes will half close, which makes it easy to distinguish males from females. But when two rabbits – one male, one female – are moving next to each other, how can one easily distinguish male from female? The story of Mulan spread far and wide in China; in 1998 in the U.S., the Disney film studios produced the animated film *Mulan*, which was based on this story.

Antonym: [一清二楚] (yī qīng èr chǔ 一清二楚) 'completely clear.'

21. 【不可思议】(不可思議) bù kě sī yì

The whole idiom means 'unthinkable, inconceivable, unimaginable.'

Example 1: 她一百米跑了九秒七零，简直太**不可思议**了！

Tā yìbǎimǐ pǎole jiǔ miǎo qīlíng, jiǎnzhí tài bùkě-sīyì le!

'She ran 100 meters in 9.7 seconds, which is simply inconceivable!'

Example 2: 他的性格有一点儿奇怪，有时候会做出一些**不可思议**的事情。

Tā de xìnggé yǒu yìdiǎnr qíguài, yǒu shíhou huì zuò chū yìxiē bùkě-sīyì de shìqing.

'His temperament is a little strange; sometimes he does unthinkable things.'

Usage: Functions mainly as predicate and attributive.

Near Synonym: [匪夷所思] (fěi yí suǒ sī 匪夷所思) 'who would have thought it, unthinkable.'

22. 【坚持不懈】(堅持不懈) jiān chí bú xiè

坚持 means 'persist' and 懈 means 'relax, let up.' A literal translation of this idiom is 'persist and not relax.' Freer translations are 'persist, persevering, unremitting.'

Example 1: 不管社会怎么变化，都应该**坚持不懈**地抓好青少年的思想教育工作。

Bùguǎn shèhuì zěnme biànhuà, dōu yīnggāi jiānchí-búxiè de zhuā hǎo qīngshàonián de sīxiǎng jiàoyù gōngzuò.

'No matter how society changes, we should persevere without letting up in getting a good grip on the work of the youth's ideological education.'

Example 2: 经过**坚持不懈**的努力，艾滋病蔓延的势头终于被遏制了。

Jīngguò jiānchí-búxiè de nǔlì, àizībìng mànyán de shìtóu zhōngyú bèi èzhì le.

'Through persistent efforts, the momentum of the spread of AIDS has finally been contained.'

Usage: Functions mainly as adverbial; can also serve as attributive.

Note: Complimentary in meaning.

Near Synonyms: [持之以恒] (chí zhī yǐ héng 持之以恆) 'persevere,' [锲而不舍] (qiè ér bù shě 鍥而不捨) 'work with perseverence.'

Antonyms: [浅尝辄止] (qiǎn cháng zhé zhǐ 淺嘗輒止) 'shallowly taste then stop – stop after gaining a little knowledge of something,' [半途而废] (bàn tú ér fèi 半途而廢) 'give up halfway.'

23. 【供不应求】(供不應求) gōng bù yìng qiú

供 means 'supply,' 应 means 'respond to,' and 求 means 'demand.' A literal translation of the whole idiom is 'supply does not respond to demand,' with freer translations being 'supply does not meet demand' and 'in short supply.'

Example 1: 在美国，医护人员**供不应求**。

Zài Měiguó, yīhù rényuán gōngbùyìngqiú.

'In the U.S., medical personnel are in short supply.'

Example 2: 据说那种中药能够治疗艾滋病，于是大家纷纷抢购，那种中药一夜之间出现了**供不应求**的情况。

Jùshuō nà zhǒng zhōngyào nénggòu zhìliáo àizībìng, yúshì dàjiā fēnfēn qiǎnggòu, nà zhǒng zhōngyào yí yè zhījiān chūxiànle gōngbùyìngqiú de qíngkuàng.

'It's said that kind of Chinese medicine can cure AIDS, so everyone one after another rushed off to purchase it; regarding that kind of Chinese medicine, overnight there emerged a situation of supply not meeting demand.'

Usage: Functions mainly as predicate and attributive. As attributive, usually followed by 局面 (júmiàn) 'situation,' 情况 (qíngkuàng 情況) 'circumstances,' or 现象 (xiànxiàng 現象) 'phenomenon.'

Near Synonym: [僧多粥少] (sēng duō zhōu shǎo 僧多粥少) 'monks many but gruel little – not enough to go around.'

Antonym: [供过于求] (gōng guò yú qiú 供過於求) 'supply exceeds demand.'

24. 【行之有效】(行之有效) xíng zhī yǒu xiào

行 means 'put into practice,' 之 means 'it,' and 效 means 'effect, efficiency.' A literal translation of the whole idiom is 'put it into practice having effect or efficiency.' Freer translations include 'implement with efficiency' and 'efficient.'

Example 1: 这是一套**行之有效**的实验方法，很多大实验室都使用过，从来没有出现过错误。

Zhè shì yí tào xíngzhī-yǒuxiào de shíyàn fāngfǎ, hěn duō dà shíyànshì dōu shǐyòngguo, cónglái méiyǒu chūxiànguo cuòwù.

'This is a very effective method of experimentation; many large laboratories have used it; mistakes have never occurred.'

Example 2: 专家呼吁，有关部门应该采取**行之有效**的政策来切实保护农民工的权利。

Zhuānjiā hūyù, yǒuguān bùmén yīnggāi cǎiqǔ xíngzhī-yǒuxiào de zhèngcè lái qièshí bǎohù nóngmíngōng de quánlì.

'Experts have appealed that the relevant departments should adopt effective policies to protect, in a practical manner, the rights of migrant workers.'

Usage: Functions mainly as attributive; often followed by nouns such as 办法 (bànfǎ 辦法) 'method,' 方法 (fāngfǎ) 'method,' 做法 (zuòfǎ) 'method of doing,' 措施 (cuòshī) 'measure,' and 政策 (zhèngcè) 'policy.'

Note: Complimentary in meaning.

Near Synonyms: [卓有成效] (zhuó yǒu chéng xiào 卓有成效) 'with outstanding results, highly effective,' [屡试不爽] (lǚ shì bù shuǎng 屢試不爽) 'repeated tests never deviate – effective every time.'

Antonyms: [劳而无功] (láo ér wú gōng 勞而無功) 'endeavor but have no success – work with no gain.'

25. 【众所周知】 (眾所周知) zhòng suǒ zhōu zhī

The literal meaning is 'as is known to all; it is well-known that; it is common knowledge that. . . .'

Example 1: **众所周知**，中国人是很讲究饭桌上的客套的。

Zhòngsuǒzhōuzhī, Zhōngguórén shì hěn jiǎngjiu fànzhuō shàng de kètào de.

'As everyone knows, Chinese people are very particular about etiquette at the dinner table.'

Example 2: 孩子学习外语比成年人学得快，这是**众所周知**的道理。

Háizi xuéxí wàiyǔ bǐ chéngniánrén xué de kuài, zhè shì zhòngsuǒzhōuzhī de dàolǐ.

'Children learn foreign languages faster than adults – this is a truth that is known to all.'

Usage: In general used at the beginning of sentences or as an attribute.

Note: This is written-style usage.

Near Synonym: [家喻户晓] (jiā yù hù xiǎo 家喻戶曉) 'known to every family, widely known.'

Antonym: [默默无闻] (mò mò wú wén 默默無聞) 'unknown to the public.'

26. 【全力以赴】 (全力以赴) quán lì yǐ fù

赴 means 'go.' A literal translation is 'with all one's strength go to some place,' with a freer translation being 'put all one's energy into something, spare no effort.'

Example 1: 面对困难，大家**全力以赴**，终于克服了困难。

Miànduì kùnnán, dàjiā **quánlì-yǐfù**, zhōngyú kèfúle kùnnán.

'In facing the difficulties, everyone spared no effort, so that in the end they overcame the difficulties.'

Example 2: 中国正在**全力以赴**地进行经济建设，因此一个稳定的国际环境非常重要。

Zhōngguó zhèngzài **quánlì-yǐfù** de jìnxíng jīngjì jiànshè, yīncǐ yíge wěndìng de guójì huánjìng fēicháng zhòngyào.

'China is putting all her energy into undertaking economic construction; therefore, a stable international environment is very important.'

Usage: Functions as adverbial and predicate.

Note: Somewhat complimentary in meaning.

Near Synonym: [竭尽全力] (jié jìn quán lì 竭盡全力) 'do one's utmost.'

27. 【理所当然】(理所當然) lǐ suǒ dāng rán

理 means '(according to) reason' and 当然 means 'should be like this.' The meaning of the whole idiom is 'of course, naturally, needless to say, it is only right and proper that. . . .'

Example 1: 有钱的人拿出一部分钱来回馈社会，帮助穷人，这是**理所当然**的。

Yǒuqián de rén náchū yíbùfen qián lái huíkuì shèhuì, bāngzhù qióngrén, zhè shì **lǐsuǒ-dāngrán** de.

'That rich people should take out part of their money to give back to society and help poor people is only right and proper.'

Example 2: 二十一世纪是生物医学的世纪，所以国家在生物医学方面加大投资是**理所当然**的事情。

Èrshíyī shìjì shì shēngwù yīxué de shìjì, suǒyǐ guójiā zài shēngwù yīxué fāngmiàn jiādà tóuzī shì **lǐsuǒ-dāngrán** de shìqing.

'The 21st century is the century of biomedicine, so for a country to increase its investment in the area of biomedicine is completely natural.'

Usage: Functions mainly as predicate, adverbial, and attributive.

Near Synonyms: [天经地义] (tiān jīng dì yì 天經地義) 'unalterable principle, entirely justified,' [名正言顺] (míng zhèng yán shùn 名正言順) 'perfectly justifiable.'

28. 【四面八方】(四面八方) sì miàn bā fāng

面 here means 'side' and 方 means 'direction.' The literal meaning of this idiom is 'the four sides and the eight directions,' with a freer translation being 'all directions, all around, far and wide.'

Example 1: 每年的三月，中国的人大代表都会由**四面八方**进入北京，举行一年一次的全国人民代表大会。

Měi nián de sānyuè, Zhōngguó de Réndà Dàibiǎo dōu huì yóu sìmiàn-bāfāng jìnrù Běijīng, jǔxíng yì nián yí cì de Quánguó Rénmín Dàibiǎo Dàhuì.

'In March of every year, representatives from China's National People's Congress enter Beijing from far and wide to hold the annual National People's Congress.'

Example 2: 杭州是中国的旅游胜地，常年吸引**四面八方**的游客前去旅游。

Hángzhōu shì Zhōngguó de lǚyóu shèngdì, chángnián xīyǐn sìmiàn-bāfāng de yóukè qiánqù lǚyóu.

'Hangzhou is a famous tourist spot in China; year in and year out it attracts tourists from all over to go there to tour.'

Usage: Functions mainly as object and attributive.

Near Synonym: [五湖四海] (wǔ hú sì hǎi 五湖四海) 'from the five lakes to the four seas – throughout the land.'

29. 【兴致勃勃】(興致勃勃) xìng zhì bó bó

兴致 means 'interest' and 勃勃 means 'full of life, exuberant.' The meaning of the whole idiom is 'full of interest and enthusiasm.'

Example 1: 总理**兴致勃勃**地参观了当地的一所小学并且与小学教师进行了亲切的交谈。

Zǒnglǐ xìngzhì-bóbó de cānguānle dāngdì de yì suǒ xiǎoxué bìngqiě yǔ xiǎoxué jiàoshī jìnxíngle qīnqiè de jiāotán.

'Full of enthusiasm, the prime minister visited a local elementary school and engaged in a cordial conversation with the teachers.'

Example 2: 新闻发布会后，总统**兴致勃勃**地邀请客人到他的乡下别墅继续会谈。

Xīnwén fābùhuì hòu, zǒngtǒng xìngzhì-bóbó de yāoqǐng kèrén dào tā de xiāngxià biéshù jìxù huìtán.

'After the news briefing, the prime minister, full of enthusiasm, invited the guests to his country villa to continue the talks.'

Usage: Functions as adverbial, often followed by verbs such as 参观 (cānguān 參觀) 'visit,' 参加 (cānjiā 參加) 'participate in,' 游览 (yóulǎn 遊覽) 'sight-see,' and 访问 (fǎngwèn 訪問) 'visit.'

Note: Complimentary in meaning.

Near Synonym: [兴趣盎然] (xìng qù àng rán 興趣盎然) 'with great interest.'

Antonyms: [无精打采] (wú jīng dǎ cǎi 無精打采) 'listless, in low spirits,' [垂头丧气] (chuí tóu sàng qì 垂頭喪氣) 'hang one's head in dejection.'

30. 【一鸣惊人】(一鳴驚人) yì míng jīng rén

鸣 means 'cry (of birds)' and 惊 means 'surprise.' A literal translation of the whole idiom is 'one cry surprises others,' with freer translations being 'amaze the world with a single brilliant feat, achieve overnight success.'

Example 1: 她在这次奥运会上**一鸣惊人**，打破了保持了三十年的世界纪录。

Tā zài zhè cì Àoyùnhuì shàng yìmíng-jīngrén, dǎpòle bǎochí le sānshí nián de shìjiè jìlù.

'She amazed the world in this Olympic Games; she broke a world record that had held for thirty years.'

Example 2: 我在咖啡店看见了前几天**一鸣惊人**的女歌手。

Wǒ zài kāfēidiàn kànjiànle qián jǐ tiān yìmíng-jīngrén de nǚ gēshǒu.

'In a coffee shop I saw the female singer who had shocked the world a few days ago.'

Usage: Functions mainly as predicate; can also serve as attributive and adverbial. Often preceded by 不鸣则已 (bù míng zé yǐ 不鳴則已).

Allusion: In the middle of the 4th century, B.C.E., there was a king in the country of Qi who loved metaphorical language but who frequently indulged himself in pleasure. His country declined and it seemed as though it might soon be conquered by other countries, yet no one dared to try to stop him. One day, a man by the name of Chunyu Kun said to the king: "In our country, there is a big bird which stays in your courtyard, but for three years it has neither flown nor cried. What kind of bird is it?" The king answered, "Once it flies, it will fly high into the sky; once it cries, it will surprise the whole world." Subsequently, the king began governing his country strictly by law, and ended up making his country the strongest among many. (from "Huaji Liezhuan" in *Records of the Grand Historian*)

Near Synonyms: [一举成名] (yì jǔ chéng míng 一舉成名) 'one action become famous – achieve instant fame,' [一步登天] (yí bù dēng tiān 一步登天) 'one step ascend the sky – attain the highest level in one step' (derogatory in meaning).

Antonym: [臭名远扬] (chòu míng yuǎn yáng 臭名遠揚) 'bad reputation widely spread – notorious.'

31. 【想方设法】(想方設法) xiǎng fāng shè fǎ

方 means 'method,' 设 means 'presume, suppose,' and 法 means 'way.' A literal translation is 'think of methods and presume ways,' with a freer translation being 'think of all kinds of ways, try every possible means.'

Example 1: 现在很多国家都**想方设法**吸引外国的优秀人才前来工作。

Xiànzài hěn duō guójiā dōu xiǎngfāng-shèfǎ xīyǐn wàiguó de yōuxiù réncái qiánlái gōngzuò.

'Now many countries try every possible means to attract foreigners of talent to come to their countries to work.'

Example 2: 遇到困难的时候他总是自己**想方设法**去解决。

Yùdào kùnnán de shíhou tā zǒngshì zìjǐ xiǎngfāng-shèfǎ qù jiějué.

'When encountering difficulties, he always tries every possible way to resolve them by himself.'

Usage: Functions mainly as predicate; followed by a verbal element.

Near Synonym: [千方百计] (qiān fāng bǎi jì 千方百計) 'by every possible means.'

Antonym: [无计可施] (wú jì kě shī 無計可施) 'at one's wit's end.'

32. 【千家万户】(千家萬戶) qiān jiā wàn hù

千 means 'thousand,' 家 means 'home,' 万 means 'ten thousand,' and 户 means 'household.' The literal translation of this idiom is 'thousand families ten thousand households,' with freer translations being 'innumerable households, every family.'

Example 1: 即使在农村，计算机也早已走进**千家万户**，不再是高档的商品了。

Jíshǐ zài nóngcūn, jìsuànjī yě zǎoyǐ zǒujìn qiānjiā-wànhù, búzài shì gāodàng de shāngpǐn le.

'Even in the countryside, computers also early on already entered innumerable households, no longer being upmarket merchandise.'

Example 2: 春节的时候，**千家万户**喜气洋洋，全都笼罩在节日的喜庆气氛中。

Chūnjié de shíhou, qiānjiā-wànhù xǐqì-yángyáng, quándōu lǒngzhào zài jiérì de xǐqìng qìfēn zhōng.

'At the time of the Chinese New Year, multitudes of families are bursting with happiness; they are all enveloped in the celebratory atmosphere of the holiday.'

Usage: Nominal element, functions mainly as object or subject.

Near Synonym: [家家户户] (jiā jiā hù hù 家家戶戶) 'family family household household – every home and household.'

Antonyms: [独门独户] (dú mén dú hù 獨門獨戶) 'single door single household – self-contained house not shared with others, home with private entrance,' [孤家寡人] (gū jiā guǎ rén 孤家寡人) 'originally meant "I" as spoken by the emperor, nowadays means "an isolated man, a loner."' (used mostly in speech)

33. 【举足轻重】(舉足輕重) jǔ zú qīng zhòng

举 means 'raise,' 足 means 'foot,' 轻 means 'light,' and 重 means 'heavy.' A literal translation of the whole idiom is 'raise one's feet and influence lightness and heaviness,' with freer translations being 'play a decisive role, be pivotal in importance.'

Example 1: 中国的家电产品在世界市场上占有**举足轻重**的地位。

Zhōngguó de jiādiàn chǎnpǐn zài shìjiè shìchǎng shàng zhànyǒu jǔzú-qīngzhòng de dìwèi.

'Chinese household electrical appliances occupy a pivotal position in the world market.'

Example 2: 法国在欧洲的政治事务中有着**举足轻重**的影响。

Fǎguó zài Ōuzhōu de zhèngzhì shìwù zhōng yǒuzhe jǔzú-qīngzhòng de yǐngxiǎng.

'France has a pivotal influence in Europe's political affairs.'

Usage: Functions mainly as attributive, often followed by words such as 地位 (dìwèi) 'position,' 作用 (zuòyòng) 'function,' 影响 (yǐngxiǎng) 'influence,' 人物 (rénwù) 'person,' and 角色 (jiǎosè) 'role.'

Near Synonyms: [至关重大] (zhì guān zhòng dà 至關重大) 'extremely important.'

Antonyms: [无足轻重] (wú zú qīng zhòng 無足輕重) 'of no importance,' [无关大局] (wú guān dà jú 無關大局) 'have no bearing on the general situation – unimportant.'

34. 【见义勇为】 (見義勇為) jiàn yì yǒng wéi

义 means 'righteousness,' 勇 means 'courage,' and 为 means 'do, make.' The meaning of the whole idiom is 'see what is right and have the courage to do it.'

Example 1: 现在社会上特别缺乏**见义勇为**的行为和观念了。

Xiànzài shèhuì shàng tèbié quēfá jiànyì-yǒngwéi de xíngwéi hé guānniàn le.

'Nowadays in society we especially lack the kind of behavior and concept where you see what is right and have the courage to do it.'

Example 2: 大会表彰了二十位**见义勇为**的英雄人物。

Dàhuì biǎozhāngle èrshí wèi jiànyì-yǒngwéi de yīngxióng rénwù.

'At the mass meeting, they publicly commended twenty heroes who saw what was right and had the courage to do it.'

Usage: Functions mainly as attributive.

Note: Complimentary in meaning.

Near Synonyms: [当仁不让] (dāng rén bú ràng 當仁不讓) 'not shirk one's duty.'

Antonyms: [见利忘义] (jiàn lì wàng yì 見利忘義) 'when you see profit forget what is right,' [袖手旁观] (xiù shǒu páng guān 袖手旁觀) 'stand idly by.'

35. 【举世瞩目】 (舉世矚目) jǔ shì zhǔ mù

举 here means 'whole,' 世 means 'world,' 瞩 means 'gaze at,' and 目 means 'eyes.' A literal translation of the whole idiom is 'the whole world gazes at with the eyes,' with freer translations including 'the entire world focuses its attention on' and 'attract world-wide attention.'

Example 1: 中国在改革开放以后的三十年中，取得了**举世瞩目**的成就。

Zhōngguó zài gǎigé kāifàng yǐhòu de sānshí nián zhōng, qǔdéle jǔshì-zhǔmù de chéngjiù.

'In the thirty years after carrying out reforms and opening up to the outside world, China obtained achievements that have attracted world-wide attention.'

Example 2: 最高法院会不会判总统有罪，这成了**举世瞩目**的焦点。

Zuì Gāo Fǎyuàn huì bú huì pàn zǒngtǒng yǒu zuì, zhè chéngle jǔshì-zhǔmù de jiāodiǎn.

'Whether or not the Supreme Court will judge the president guilty has become the focus of world-wide attention.'

Usage: Functions mainly as attributive, usually followed by 成就 (chéngjiù) 'accomplishment' or 成绩 (chéngjì 成績) 'achievement.'

Near Synonyms: [举世闻名] (jǔ shì wén míng 舉世聞名) 'world famous.'

Antonyms: [默默无闻] (mò mò wú wén 默默無聞) 'unknown to the public.'

36. 【小心翼翼】 (小心翼翼) xiǎo xīn yì yì

翼翼 means 'cautious.' A literal translation of this idiom is 'careful and cautious.' It is often used adverbially in the sense 'cautiously, carefully.'

Example 1: 考古工作者**小心翼翼**地检查考古现场的每一件东西。

Kǎogǔ gōngzuòzhě xiǎoxīn-yìyì de jiǎnchá kǎogǔ xiànchǎng de měi yí jiàn dōngxi.

'Archeological workers very carefully and cautiously inspect every item from the archeological site.'

Example 2: 他的生活过于谨慎，凡事都**小心翼翼**，生怕惹别人不高兴。

Tā de shēnghuó guòyú jǐnshèn, fán shì dōu xiǎoxīn-yìyì, shēngpà rě biérén bù gāoxìng.

'His life is overcautious; regarding every matter, he is careful and cautious, deathly afraid that he will cause others to be upset.'

Usage: Functions mainly as adverbial; can also serve as predicate.

Near Synonym: [谨小慎微] (jǐn xiǎo shèn wēi 謹小慎微) 'cautious even in very small things.'

Antonym: [粗心大意] (cū xīn dà yì 粗心大意) 'careless, negligent.'

37. 【源远流长】(源遠流長) yuán yuǎn liú cháng

源 means 'source,' 远 means 'distant,' 流 means 'the length the water flows,' and 长 means 'long.' A literal translation is 'the source (of a stream) is distant and (the water) flows a long distance.' Freer translations include 'age-old, long-standing, well-established.'

Example 1: 两国人民的友谊**源远流长**。

Liǎng guó rénmín de yǒuyì **yuányuǎn-liúcháng**.

'The friendship between the peoples of the two countries is long-standing and well-established.'

Example 2: 中国有着**源远流长**的茶文化。

Zhōngguó yǒuzhe **yuányuǎn-liúcháng** de chá wénhuà.

'China has an age-old tea culture.'

Usage: Functions mainly as predicate; can also serve as attributive.

Note: Complimentary in meaning.

Antonyms: [无源之水] (wú yuán zhī shuǐ 無源之水) 'no source water – without a source,' [无本之木] (wú běn zhī mù 無本之木) 'tree without roots – have no foundation,' [空穴来风] (kōng xué lái fēng 空穴來風) 'empty hole makes wind come in – leave oneself open to rumors.'

38. 【弄虚作假】(弄虚作假) nòng xū zuò jiǎ

弄 here means 'use,' 虚 means 'empty,' 作 means 'fabricate,' and 假 means 'false.' A literal translation of the whole idiom is 'use emptiness to create a false appearance,' with a freer translation being 'use trickery or deception to create a false appearance.'

Example 1: 那家大公司在对外公布业绩报告的时候**弄虚作假**，欺骗投资者。

Nà jiā dà gōngsī zài duì wài gōngbù yèjì bàogào de shíhou **nòngxū-zuòjiǎ**, qīpiàn tóuzīzhě.

'When that large company announced its business report to the outside, it used trickery to create a false appearance, deceiving the investors.'

Example 2: 应该严厉批评**弄虚作假**的行为和风气。

Yīnggāi yánlì pīpíng **nòngxū-zuòjiǎ** de xíngwéi hé fēngqì.

'One should severely criticize behavior or an atmosphere where deception is used to create a false appearance.'

Usage: Functions mainly as predicate and adverbial.

Note: Derogatory in meaning.

Near Synonyms: [招摇撞骗] (zhāo yáo zhuàng piàn 招搖撞騙) 'swindle and bluff,' [歪门邪道] (wāi mén xié dào 歪門邪道) 'crooked doors evil paths – dishonest ways.'

Antonym: [实事求是] (shí shì qiú shì 實事求是) 'seek truth from facts.'

39. 【自言自语】(自言自語) zì yán zì yǔ

A literal translation of the whole idiom is 'self talk self say,' with freer translations being 'talk to oneself, think out loud.'

Example 1: 她**自言自语**地说："真奇怪，明明刚才还在这里，怎么一会儿就不见了呢？"

Tā zìyán-zìyǔ de shuō: "Zhēn qíguài, míngmíng gāngcái hái zài zhèlǐ, zěnme yíhuìr jiù bú jiàn le ne?"

'She said to herself: "That's really strange; it clearly was here just a minute ago, how could it disappear so quickly?"'

Example 2: 他跟别人说话的时候不看对方的眼睛，声音又小，别人觉得他好像**自言自语**。

Tā gēn biérén shuōhuà de shíhou bú kàn duìfāng de yǎnjing, shēngyīn yòu xiǎo, biérén juéde tā hǎoxiàng zìyán-zìyǔ.

'When he talks with others, he doesn't look into their eyes, and his voice is low; other people think it's as if he's talking to himself.'

Usage: Functions mainly as adverbial and predicate.

Near Synonym: [喃喃自语] (nán nán zì yǔ 喃喃自語) 'mutter to oneself.'

40. 【纸上谈兵】(紙上談兵) zhǐ shàng tán bīng

兵 here means 'military force.' A literal translation of this idiom is 'on paper speak of warfare.' The extended meaning is 'engage in empty talk that does nothing to solve problems.' One freer translation is 'be an armchair strategist.'

Example 1: 她的计划不过是**纸上谈兵**，没有什么实际价值。

Tā de jìhuà búguò shì zhǐshàng-tánbīng, méiyǒu shénme shíjì jiàzhí.

'Her plan is only empty talk; it has no real value.'

Example 2: 他是一个只会**纸上谈兵**的家伙，并没解决过实际问题。

Tā shì yí ge zhǐ huì zhǐshàng-tánbīng de jiāhuo, bìng méi jiějuéguo shíjì wèntí.

'He's a fellow who can only engage in armchair strategies; he has never solved any real problems.'

Usage: Functions mainly as predicate; can also serve as attributive.

Allusion: During the Warring States Period (475–221 B.C.E.), the countries of Qin and Zhao were confronting each other. The Zhao general employed defensive tactics, so there was nothing the Qin army could do. Later, Zhao fell victim to Qin's stratagem of sowing discord and a man by the name of Zhao Kuo was chosen to substitute for the original general. Now, Zhao Kuo was someone who had thoroughly studied books on military strategy; in discussing military theory, he even surpassed his father, a famous general. But despite this, the father predicted that the country of Zhao would some day be destroyed at the hands of his own son. And sure enough, after Zhao Kuo became general, he fell for one of the Qin army's stratagems with the result that not only did he die, but more than 400,000 Zhao soldiers were buried alive by the Qin forces. Known in history as the Battle of Changping (260 B.C.E.), this major historical event influenced the course of Chinese history since thirty-two years later, Qin destroyed Zhao and, seven years after that, Qin united all of China. And the key factor in determining the success or failure of the Battle of Changping had been General Zhao Kuo, a man who could only "speak of warfare on paper." (from *Records of the Grand Historian*)

Note: Derogatory in meaning.

Near Synonyms: [华而不实] (huá ér bù shí 華而不實) 'flowers but no fruit – flashy but lacking substance,' [夸夸其谈] (kuā kuā qí tán 誇誇其談) 'full of boasts and exaggerations.'

Antonym: [真才实学] (zhēn cái shí xué 真才實學) 'genuine talent, real ability.'

41. 【名副其实】(名副其實) míng fù qí shí

副 means 'correspond to,' 其 means 'its,' and 实 means 'reality, truth.' The literal meaning is 'the name corresponds to its reality,' with a freer translation being 'worthy of the name or reputation.'

Example 1: 虽然在《美国新闻与世界报道》上没有排名第一，但是大家都认为哈佛大学才是**名副其实**的世界上最好的大学。

Suīrán zài *Měiguó Xīnwén yǔ Shìjiè Bàodào* shàng méi yǒu páimíng dìyī, dànshì dàjiā dōu rènwéi Hāfó Dàxué cái shì míngfù-qíshí de shìjiè shàng zuì hǎo de dàxué.

'Even though it wasn't ranked as number one in *U.S. News and World Report*, everyone believes that Harvard University is worthy of the reputation of being the best university in the world.'

Example 2: 到了中国，你就会深刻体会到中国是**名副其实**的自行车王国。

Dàole Zhōngguó, nǐ jiù huì shēnkè tǐhuìdào Zhōngguó shì míngfù-qíshí de zìxíngchē wángguó.

'When you arrive in China, you will have the profound realization that China is worthy of the name "kingdom of bicycles."'

Usage: Functions mainly as attributive; can also serve as predicate.

Note: Sometimes written as 名符其实 (míng fú qí shí), with the same meaning, but note the different character and different tone for the second syllable.

Near Synonym: [表里如一] (biǎo lǐ rú yī 表裏如一) 'outside and inside are as one – one's deeds correspond with one's thoughts.'

Antonym: [名不副实] (míng bú fù shí 名不副實) 'unworthy of the name.'

42. 【日新月异】(日新月異) rì xīn yuè yì

异 means 'different.' The literal translation of this idiom is 'day new month different,' with a freer translation being 'change rapidly with each new day.'

Example 1: 当代科学技术的发展**日新月异**，人们的生活越来越舒适。

Dāngdài kēxué jìshù de fāzhǎn rìxīn-yuèyì, rénmen de shēnghuó yuè lái yuè shūshì.

'Modern science and technology have been developing rapidly with each new day, and people's lives have been getting more and more comfortable.'

Example 2: 改革开放后的几十年内，北京、上海等大城市发生了**日新月异**的变化。

Gǎigé kāifàng hòu de jǐ shí nián nèi, Běijīng, Shànghǎi děng dà chéngshì fāshēngle rìxīn-yuèyì de biànhuà.

'In the decades since the reforms and opening up to the outside world, with the passing of each new day there have taken place rapid changes in the big cities such as Beijing and Shanghai.'

Usage: Functions mainly as predicate; can also serve as attributive.

Note: Complimentary in meaning.

Near Synonym: [一日千里] (yí rì qiān lǐ 一日千里) 'one day a thousand miles – at a tremendous pace.'

Antonym: [一成不变] (yì chéng bú biàn 一成不變) 'fixed and unalterable.'

43. 【得天独厚】(得天獨厚) dé tiān dú hòu

得 means 'obtain,' 天 means 'nature,' 独 means 'by oneself,' and 厚 means 'favorable.' A literal translation of the whole idiom is 'by oneself obtain favorable natural conditions,' with freer translations being 'enjoy exceptional advantages' and 'in a favorable position.'

Example 1: 欧洲人学语言有**得天独厚**的优势。

Ōuzhōu rén xué yǔyán yǒu détiān-dúhòu de yōushì.

'Europeans enjoy exceptional advantages in learning languages.'

Example 2: 深圳靠近香港，因此发展经济有**得天独厚**的条件。

Shēnzhèn kàojìn Xiānggǎng, yīncǐ fāzhǎn jīngjì yǒu détiān-dúhòu de tiáojiàn.

'Shenzhen is close to Hong Kong; therefore, with regard to developing the economy, it has extremely favorable conditions.'

Usage: Functions mainly as attributive, often followed by 优势 (yōushì 優勢) 'advantage' or 条件 (tiáojiàn 條件) 'condition.'

Near Synonym: [天时地利] (tiān shí dì lì 天時地利) 'opportune time, advantageous terrain – advantageous situation.'

Antonym: [先天不足] (xiān tiān bù zú 先天不足) 'congenitally deficient.'

44. 【情不自禁】(情不自禁) qíng bú zì jìn

情 means 'emotions' and 禁 means 'control, restrain.' A literal translation is 'emotions not by oneself restrain.' The meaning of the whole idiom is 'unable to restrain one's emotions, excited, cannot help.'

Example 1: 看完这部电影，她**情不自禁**地大声说，"太好了！太好了！"

Kànwán zhè bù diànyǐng, tā qíngbúzìjìn de dàshēng shuō, "Tài hǎole! Tài hǎole!"

'When she had seen the movie, she said, unable to restrain her emotions, "It's fantastic, it's fantastic!"'

Example 2: 听到那首熟悉的音乐，他**情不自禁**地跳起舞来了。

Tīngdào nà shǒu shúxī de yīnyuè, tā qíngbúzìjìn de tiàoqǐ wǔ láile.

'When he heard that familiar piece of music, he began dancing, unable to restrain his emotions.'

Usage: Functions as adverbial.

Near Synonym: [不由自主] (bù yóu zì zhǔ 不由自主) 'involuntarily, spontaneously.'

45. 【不以为然】(不以爲然) bù yǐ wéi rán

然 means 'like that.' 不以为然 means 不以之为然 'not take it to be like that.' A freer translation would be 'think otherwise, take exception to, disapprove.'

Example 1: 当别人对她的成绩感到很惊奇的时候，她却**不以为然**地说，"没什么了不起的。"

Dāng biérén duì tā de chéngjì gǎndào hěn jīngqí de shíhou, tā què bùyǐwéirán de shuō, "Méi shénme liǎobùqǐ de."

'When others felt amazement at her grades, she took exception by saying, "It's nothing remarkable."'

Example 2: 不少年轻人对老年人的看法很**不以为然**，认为他们的看法通通陈旧了。

Bùshǎo niánqīngrén duì lǎoniánrén de kànfǎ hěn bùyǐwéirán, rènwéi tāmen de kànfǎ tōngtōng chénjiù le.

'The view that many young people have of older people is very disapproving, believing that their views are all outdated.'

Usage: Functions mainly as predicate and adverbial.

Near Synonym: [嗤之以鼻] (chī zhī yǐ bí 嗤之以鼻) 'snort at contemptuously with one's nose.'

Antonyms: [言听计从] (yán tīng jì cóng 言聽計從) 'listen to someone's words and follow someone's plan – follow someone's advice,' [五体投地] (wǔ tǐ tóu dì 五體投地) 'the five parts of the body thrown upon the floor – prostrate oneself before someone in utmost admiration.'

46. 【络绎不绝】 (絡繹不絕) luò yì bù jué

络绎 means 'continuous, endless' and 绝 means 'break off, cut off.' The literal meaning is 'endless and not cutting off,' with a freer translation being 'continuous flow, unending stream.'

Example 1: 他是名医，所以找他看病的人**络绎不绝**。

Tā shì míngyī, suǒyǐ zhǎo tā kànbìng de rén luòyì-bùjué.

'He's a famous doctor, so there is an unending stream of people who seek him out for medical treatment.'

Example 2: 每天，到天安门广场瞻仰毛泽东遗体的人**络绎不绝**。

Měi tiān, dào Tiānānmén Guǎngchǎng zhānyǎng Máo Zédōng yítǐ de rén luòyì-bùjué.

'Every day there is a continuous stream of people who go to Tiananmen Square to pay their respects to the remains of Mao Zedong.'

Usage: Functions mainly as predicate; can also serve as adverbial and attributive. Generally used to describe people.

Near Synonyms: [川流不息] (chuān liú bù xī 川流不息) 'continuous flow without stopping (of people or traffic),' [连绵不断] (lián mián bú duàn 連綿不斷) 'continuously without being cut off.'

Antonym: [寥寥无几] (liáo liáo wú jǐ 寥寥無幾) 'very few.'

47. 【不约而同】 (不約而同) bù yuē ér tóng

约 means 'agree' and 同 means 'same.' The meaning of the whole idiom is 'have the same view or take the same action as someone else but without prior consultation with them.'

Example 1: 当老师问是谁打碎了玻璃的时候，两个学生**不约而同**地说"是他"。

Dāng lǎoshī wèn shì shéi dǎsuìle bōli de shíhou, liǎng ge xuésheng bùyuē'értóng de shuō 'shì tā.'

'When the teacher asked who had broken the glass, two students spoke up simultaneously: "It was him!"'

Example 2: 提到北京，大家会**不约而同**地想到故宫和天安门。

Tídào Běijīng, dàjiā huì bùyuē'értóng de xiǎngdào Gùgōng hé Tiān'ānmén.

'When you mention Beijing, everyone automatically thinks of the Forbidden Palace and Tiananmen.'

Usage: Functions adverbially.

Near Synonym: [不谋而合] (bù móu ér hé 不謀而合) 'agree without prior consultation.'

Antonyms: [见仁见智] (jiàn rén jiàn zhì 見仁見智) 'different people have different views,' [众说纷纭] (zhòng shuō fēn yún 衆説紛紜) 'opinions vary greatly.'

48. 【千千万万】(千千萬萬) qiān qiān wàn wàn

The literal meaning is 'thousand thousand ten thousand ten thousand,' with a freer translation being 'tens of thousands, numerous, a great number of.'

Example 1: 医学上的这项重大发现挽救了**千千万万**患者的生命。

Yīxué shàng de zhè xiàng zhòngdà fāxiàn wǎnjiùle qiānqiān-wànwàn huànzhě de shēngmìng.

'This major medical discovery saved the lives of thousands upon thousands of sufferers.'

Example 2: 他的演讲打动了**千千万万**的听众的心。

Tā de yǎnjiǎng dǎdòngle qiānqiān-wànwàn de tīngzhòng de xīn.

'His lecture touched the hearts of tens of thousands of people in the audience.'

Usage: Functions as attributive, usually describes people.

Note: Distinguish from 千万千万 (qiān wàn qiān wàn) 'absolutely, no matter what happens' (followed by a negative).

Near Synonym: [成千上万] (chéng qiān shàng wàn 成千上萬) 'tens of thousands of.'

49. 【齐心协力】(齊心協力) qí xīn xié lì

齐 means 'together,' 心 means 'heart, mind,' and 协力 means 'join forces, combine efforts.' A literal translation of the whole idiom is 'put together minds combine forces.' This refers to minds thinking together, and strength and forces working together. A freer translation is 'make a united effort, work as one.'

Example 1: 他们三个人**齐心协力**，顺利地完成了那项工作。

Tāmen sān ge rén qíxīn-xiélì, shùnlì de wánchéngle nà xiàng gōngzuò.

'The three of them put forth a united effort, and smoothly completed that piece of work.'

Example 2: 国际社会应该**齐心协力**，共同打击恐怖主义。

Guójì shèhuì yīnggāi qíxīn-xiélì, gòngtóng dǎjī kǒngbù zhǔyì.

'Global society should make a united effort, and jointly combat terrorism.'

Usage: Functions mainly as predicate.

Note: Complimentary in meaning.

Near Synonyms: [同心同德] (tóng xīn tóng dé 同心同德) 'of one heart and mind,' [万众一心] (wàn zhòng yì xīn 萬眾一心) 'ten thousand crowd one heart – united with one heart.'

Antonym: [貌合神离] (mào hé shén lí 貌合神離) 'appearance united spirits apart – seemingly agreed but actually at variance, in name or appearance only.'

50. 【卧薪尝胆】(臥薪嘗膽) wò xīn cháng dǎn

卧 means 'lie down,' 薪 means 'firewood,' 尝 means 'taste, lick,' and 胆 means 'gall bladder.' A literal translation of this idiom is 'sleep on firewood and taste gall bladder.' This is a metaphor for 'undergo hardships to achieve one's purpose' or 'steel oneself for revenge.'

Example 1: 中国女排经过十多年的**卧薪尝胆**，终于又回到世界顶尖水平。

Zhōngguó nǚpái jīngguò shí duō nián de wòxīn-chángdǎn, zhōngyú yòu huídào shìjiè dǐngjiān shuǐpíng.

'Chinese women's volleyball, after steeling itself for revenge for more than ten years, finally again returned to the world's top level.'

Example 2: 他被赶下台之后，**卧薪尝胆**，八年以后重新当选总统。

Tā bèi gǎnxià tái zhīhòu, wòxīn-chángdǎn, bā nián yǐhòu chóngxīn dāngxuǎn zǒngtǒng.

'After being driven out of office, he underwent great hardships, steeling himself for revenge, and eight years later was once again elected president.'

Usage: Functions mainly as attributive; sometimes also occurs independently.

Allusion: In 494 B.C.E., during the Spring and Autumn Period, the king of the state of Yue, Gou Jian, was defeated by the state of Wu, so Gou Jian was constantly thinking of revenge. When he slept, he didn't sleep on a bed but instead slept on pieces of firewood; and in front of his seat he hung a gall bladder, so every day before he sat down to rest and before he lay down to sleep, he had to look at that gall bladder; and before he ate or drank anything, he had to lick the gall bladder. At the same time, he intensified the training of his troops. After many years, in 482 B.C.E., Gou Jian finally defeated the state of Wu, and in 473 B.C.E. he destroyed the state of Wu. (from "Yue Wang Gou Jian Shijia" in *Records of the Grand Historian*)

Note: Complimentary in meaning.

Near Synonyms: [发奋图强] (fā fèn tú qiáng 發奮圖強) 'exert oneself and strive to be strong,' [痛定思痛] (tòng dìng sī tòng 痛定思痛) 'learn from a painful experience,' [忍辱负重] (rěn rǔ fù zhòng 忍辱負重) 'endure humiliation to perform one's duty.'

Antonym: [乐不思蜀] (lè bù sī Shǔ 樂不思蜀) 'so happy one doesn't think of the ancient state of Shu – so happy as to forget home and duty.'

51. 【大街小巷】 (大街小巷) dà jiē xiǎo xiàng

街 means 'street' and 巷 means 'lane,' with the pattern 大 . . . 小 . . . here meaning 'all.' The meaning of the whole idiom is 'all the streets and lanes.'

Example 1: 春节的时候，北京的**大街小巷**都挂满了红色的灯笼。

Chūnjié de shíhou, Běijīng de dàjiē-xiǎoxiàng dōu guà mǎnle hóngsè de dēnglóng.

'At the time of the Chinese New Year, red lanterns hang in all of Beijing's streets and lanes.'

Example 2: 小贩们沿着**大街小巷**叫卖他们的东西。

Xiǎofànmen yánzhe dàjiē-xiǎoxiàng jiàomài tāmen de dōngxi.

'Peddlers were hawking their wares along all the streets and lanes.'

Usage: Functions mainly as noun, either in subject or object position.

Near Synonym: [街头巷尾] (jiē tóu xiàng wěi 街頭巷尾) 'streets and lanes.'

52. 【不由自主】 (不由自主) bù yóu zì zhǔ

由 means 'from' or 'by,' 自 means 'oneself,' and 主 means 'be master of.' The literal meaning of the whole idiom is 'not be master over oneself.' A freer translation would be 'not be able to restrain oneself, feel an irresistible urge; involuntarily, spontaneously.'

Example 1: 那个男人坐得离她很近，于是她**不由自主**地往旁边挪了一下。

Nàge nánrén zuò de lí tā hěn jìn, yúshì tā bùyóuzìzhǔ de wǎng pángbiān nuóle yíxià.

'That man was sitting quite close to her, and so without being aware of it, she automatically moved a bit to the side.'

Example 2: 地震了，人们**不由自主**地从房间里往外跑。

Dìzhènle, rénmen bùyóuzìzhǔ de cóng fángjiān lǐ wǎng wài pǎo.

'When the earthquake occurred, people spontaneously ran from inside their rooms to the outside.'

Usage: Mainly used as adverbial.

Near Synonyms: [身不由己] (shēn bù yóu jǐ 身不由己) 'having no control over one's body or actions,' [鬼使神差] (guǐ shǐ shén chāi 鬼使神差) 'directed by spirits and gods.'

53. 【应运而生】(應運而生) yìng yùn ér shēng

应 means 'respond to,' 运 here means 'fate' or 'opportune moment,' and 生 means 'arise.' The whole idiom means 'arise in response to the needs of the times.'

Example 1: 因为人们的实际购买力下降，各种形式的 "一元店" **应运而生**。

Yīnwèi rénmen de shíjì gòumǎilì xiàjiàng, gèzhǒng xíngshì de "yīyuándiàn" yìngyùn-érshēng.

'Because people's real purchasing power has declined, various forms of "one dollar stores" have arisen in response to the needs of the times.'

Example 2: 美式快餐在中国获得巨大成功，于是中国的快餐店也**应运而生**。

Měishì kuàicān zài Zhōngguó huòdé jùdà chénggōng, yúshì Zhōngguó de kuàicāndiàn yě yìngyùn-érshēng.

'U.S.-style fast food achieved great success in China, and so Chinese fast food establishments also arose in response to the needs of the times.'

Usage: Functions as predicate.

Antonym: [听天由命] (tīng tiān yóu mìng 聽天由命) 'abide by the will of heaven, accept one's fate.'

54. 【形形色色】(形形色色) xíng xíng sè sè

形 means 'outward appearance' and 色 means 'color.' The meaning of the whole idiom is 'of all different outward appearances and colors, of all kinds.'

Example 1: 在火车站里，你会遇到**形形色色**的人，有急着乘车的旅客，也有各种各样的骗子和小偷儿。

Zài huǒchēzhàn lǐ, nǐ huì yùdào xíngxíng-sèsè de rén, yǒu jízhe chéngchē de lǚkè, yě yǒu gèzhǒng-gèyàng de piànzi hé xiǎotōur.

'In a train station, you will meet all kinds of people; there are travelers anxious to get on their trains, and there are also all kinds of swindlers and thieves.'

Example 2: 最近社会上出现了**形形色色**的投资公司，基本上都是骗钱的。

Zuìjìn shèhuì shàng chūxiànle xíngxíng-sèsè de tóuzī gōngsī, jīběnshàng dōu shì piàn qián de.

'Recently in society there has appeared every kind of investment company; basically they're all out to cheat you of your money.'

Usage: Functions mainly as attributive.

Note: Derogatory in meaning.

Near Synonyms: [五花八门] (wǔ huā bā mén 五花八門) 'various, of all kinds,' [鱼龙混杂] (yú lóng hùn zá 魚龍混雜) 'fish and dragons mixed together – good and bad people or things mixed up.'

Antonyms: [千篇一律] (qiān piān yí lǜ 千篇一律) 'a thousand essays uniform – follow the same pattern, stereotyped,' [如出一辙] (rú chū yì zhé 如出一轍) 'as if emerging from the same track – one and the same, cut from the same cloth.'

55. 【名列前茅】(名列前茅) míng liè qián máo

名 means 'name,' 列 means 'ranked at,' and 前茅 means 'front ranks.' A literal translation of this idiom is 'one's name is ranked at the top of the list.' This refers to coming out in front or on top in an examination or a competition. A freer English translation is 'rank among the very top, be at the top of the list.'

Example 1: 他的学习成绩一向很优秀，每次考试都**名列前茅**。

Tā de xuéxí chéngjì yíxiàng hěn yōuxiù, měi cì kǎoshì dōu míngliè-qiánmáo.

'His achievements in his studies have always been superior; every time he tests he comes out on top.'

Example 2: 这个品牌的啤酒的销量在国际市场**名列前茅**。

Zhège pǐnpái de píjiǔ de xiāoliàng zài guójì shìchǎng míngliè-qiánmáo.

'Sales volume for this brand of beer is at the top of the list in international markets.'

Usage: Functions mainly as predicate.

Note: Complimentary in meaning.

Near Synonyms: [首屈一指] (shǒu qū yì zhǐ 首屈一指) 'second to none,' [榜上有名] (bǎng shàng yǒu míng 榜上有名) 'on name list there is the name – have one's name on a list of successful candidates.'

Antonym: [名落孙山] (míng luò Sūn Shān 名落孫山) 'one's name falls behind Sun Shan – fail to pass an examination, fail to be a successful candidate.'

56. 【家喻户晓】(家喻戶曉) jiā yù hù xiǎo

喻 means 'understand,' 户 means 'household,' and 晓 means 'know.' A literal translation of the whole idiom is '(every) family understands and (every) household knows,' with freer translations being 'known to every family,' 'widely known' and 'a household word.'

Example 1: 在美国，Oprah Winfrey 是一位**家喻户晓**的人物。

Zài Měiguó, Oprah Winfrey shì yí wèi jiāyù-hùxiǎo de rénwù.

'In the U.S., Oprah Winfrey is a person who has become a household word.'

Example 2: 她的歌声美妙动人，一夜之间成了**家喻户晓**的明星。

Tā de gēshēng měimiào dòngrén, yí yè zhījiān chéngle jiāyù-hùxiǎo de míngxīng.

'Her singing voice is splendid and touching; she has overnight become a widely known star.'

Usage: Functions mainly as attributive and predicate.

Near Synonyms: [众所周知] (zhòng suǒ zhōu zhī 眾所周知) 'as is known to all,' [妇孺皆知] (fù rú jiē zhī 婦孺皆知) 'women and children all know.'

Antonyms: [默默无闻] (mò mò wú wén 默默無聞) 'unknown to the public,' [寂寂无名] (jì jì wú míng 寂寂無名) 'quiet and nameless.'

57. 【兴高采烈】(興高采烈) xìng gāo cǎi liè

兴 means 'interest, enthusiasm,' 采 means 'energy, spirit,' and 烈 means 'strong.' A literal translation of this idiom is 'interest high energy strong,' with a freer translation being 'in high spirits, jubilant, elated.'

Example 1: 在回家的路上，球迷们依然**兴高采烈**地谈论着刚才的那场比赛。

Zài huíjiā de lùshang, qiúmímen yīrán xìnggāo-cǎiliè de tánlùnzhe gāngcái de nà chǎng bǐsài.

'On their way home, the sports fans were still elatedly discussing that game just now.'

Example 2: 他今天的情绪特别好，像过年一样**兴高采烈**。

Tā jīntiān de qíngxù tèbié hǎo, xiàng guònián yíyàng xìnggāo-cǎiliè.

'His mood today is especially good, as jubilant as at Chinese New Year.'

Usage: Functions mainly as adverbial.

Note: Complimentary in meaning.

Near Synonym: [欢天喜地] (huān tiān xǐ dì 歡天喜地) 'overjoyed.'

Antonym: [无精打采] (wú jīng dǎ cǎi 無精打采) 'listless, in low spirits.'

58. 【排忧解难】(排憂解難) pái yōu jiě nàn

排 means 'remove,' 忧 means 'worry,' 解 means 'relieve,' and 难 means 'difficulty.' A literal translation of the whole idiom is 'remove worries relieve difficulties.' A freer translation is 'help other people overcome their difficulties.'

Example 1: 我们要多为残疾人**排忧解难**。

Wǒmen yào duō wèi cánjírén páiyōu-jiěnàn.

'We should do more to alleviate concerns and relieve difficulties for handicapped people.'

Example 2: 那位市长在竞选的时候提出要为市民们**排忧解难**，解决他们生活上的实际困难。

Nà wèi shìzhǎng zài jìngxuǎn de shíhou tíchū yào wèi shìmínmen páiyōu-jiěnàn, jiějué tāmen shēnghuó shàng de shíjì kùnnán.

'That mayor at the time of the election proposed that he would on behalf of the city's residents alleviate their concerns and relieve their worries, and solve the real difficulties in their lives.'

Usage: Functions as predicate, often preceded by the structure 为 (wèi 為) + person 'for (someone).'

Near Synonym: [助人为乐] (zhù rén wéi lè 助人為樂) 'enjoy helping others.'

Antonym: [无事生非] (wú shì shēng fēi 無事生非) 'when there are no problematic matters give birth to trouble – create problems when none exist.'

59. 【自强不息】(自強不息) zì qiáng bù xī

自 means 'self,' 强 means 'strengthen,' and 息 means 'stop.' A literal translation of the whole idiom is 'strengthen oneself not stop,' with freer translations being 'strive constantly for self-improvement.'

Example 1: 他热情地鼓励大家越是在不利的情况下，越要发扬**自强不息**的民族精神。

Tā rèqíng de gǔlì dàjiā yuè shì zài búlì de qíngkuàng xià, yuè yào fāyáng zìqiáng-bùxī de mínzú jīngshen.

'He enthusiastically encouraged everyone: the less beneficial the circumstances, the more one should promote a national spirit of constantly striving for self-improvement.'

Example 2: 他们**自强不息**、顽强拼搏的精神值得我们学习。

Tāmen zìqiáng-bùxī, wánqiáng pīnbó de jīngshen zhíde wǒmen xuéxí.

'Their spirit of constantly striving for self-improvement and tenaciously struggling is worthy of our learning from.'

Usage: Functions mainly as attributive, usually followed by 精神 (jīngshen) 'spirit.'

Note: Complimentary in meaning. The motto of Tsinghua University in China – 自强不息，厚德载物 (zì qiáng bù xī, hòu dé zài wù 自强不息，厚德載物) – contains this idiom.

Near Synonyms: [自力更生] (zì lì gēng shēng 自力更生) 'one's own strength changes one's life – rely on one's own efforts,' [发奋图强] (fā fèn tú qiáng 發奮圖強) 'exert oneself and strive to be strong,' [卧薪尝胆] (wò xīn cháng dǎn 臥薪嘗膽) 'steel oneself for revenge.'

Antonym: [自暴自弃] (zì bào zì qì 自暴自棄) 'give up on oneself, despair.'

60. 【走马观花】(走馬觀花) zǒu mǎ guān huā

走马 means 'ride a galloping horse' and 观 means 'look at.' A literal translation of the whole idiom is 'look at flowers while riding on a galloping horse.' This is a metaphor for 'observe in a hurried and rough manner' or 'give a cursory look and gain a shallow understanding of something.'

Example 1: 他在纽约只玩儿了一天，只能算是**走马观花**，了解不深入。

Tā zài Niǔyuē zhǐ wánrle yì tiān, zhǐ néng suàn shì zǒumǎ-guānhuā, liǎojiě bù shēnrù.

'He visited New York for only one day, which can only be considered a superficial visit; he does not have a deep understanding.'

Example 2: 我**走马观花**地参观了附近的几家公司。

Wǒ zǒumǎ-guānhuā de cānguānle fùjìn de jǐ jiā gōngsī.

'I quickly and cursorily visited several nearby companies.'

Usage: Functions mainly as adverbial and predicate, often followed by verbs such as 参观 (cānguān 參觀) 'visit,' 逛 (guàng) 'stroll through,' or 浏览 (liúlǎn 瀏覽) 'glance, browse.'

Allusion: This idiom originates from a popular legend about two families. The first family had a handsome son who was, however, crippled; the second family had a beautiful daughter who had, however, a flat nose. Someone wanted to serve as matchmaker for the two of them, so he told the young man not to dismount from the horse he was riding when he went to the "get-acquainted" meeting with the young woman; and he told the young woman to hide her nose with a flower. The two of them did this and, after meeting hurriedly, were satisfied. As a result, they didn't discover each other's shortcomings until the day of their marriage, by which time it was already too late.

Note: Neutral or slightly derogatory in meaning.

Near Synonyms: [蜻蜓点水] (qīng tíng diǎn shuǐ 蜻蜓點水) 'dragonfly skims surface of water – just scratch the surface of something without going into it deeply,' [浮光掠影] (fú guāng lüè yǐng 浮光掠影) 'floating light passing shadows – skimming over the surface, cursory.'

Antonyms: [入木三分] (rù mù sān fēn 入木三分) 'enter wood 3/10 of an inch (in calligraphy) – forceful, bold, sharp,' [下马看花] (xià mǎ kàn huā 下馬看花) 'get off horse and look at flowers – conduct in-depth on-the-spot investigations.'

61. 【长治久安】(長治久安) cháng zhì jiǔ ān

长 means 'long,' 治 means 'order,' 久 means 'long in time,' and 安 means 'peace.' The literal meaning of the whole idiom is 'long order long peace,' with a freer translation being 'long-term peace, long-lasting peace and good government.'

Example 1: 这是关系国家发展和**长治久安**的重大问题。

Zhè shì guānxì guójiā fāzhǎn hé chángzhì-jiǔ'ān de zhòngdà wèntí.

'This is a major issue that has a bearing on the country's development and long-term peace and order.'

Example 2: 只有彻底根除黑势力，社会才能**长治久安**。

Zhǐyǒu chèdǐ gēnchú hēishìlì, shèhuì cáinéng chángzhì-jiǔ'ān.

'Only if we thoroughly eliminate unlawful influence can society have long-term peace and order.'

Usage: Functions mainly as predicate.

Note: Complimentary in meaning.

Near Synonym: [天下太平] (tiān xià tài píng 天下太平) 'all under heaven is peaceful – all is at peace.'

Antonyms: [动荡不安] (dòng dàng bù ān 動蕩不安) 'move wave not peaceful – be in turmoil,' [兵荒马乱] (bīng huāng mǎ luàn 兵荒馬亂) 'soldiers in disorder horses confused – the chaos and tumult of war.'

62. 【安居乐业】(安居樂業) ān jū lè yè

安 means 'peaceful,' 居 means 'live, reside,' 乐 means 'happy,' and 业 means 'business, occupation.' A literal translation is 'live peacefully and be content with one's occupation.' Freer translations include 'live and work in peace and happiness, lead a peaceful and happy life.'

Example 1: 那个城市经济发达，社会治安良好，人们**安居乐业**。

Nàge chéngshì jīngjì fādá, shèhuì zhì'ān liánghǎo, rénmen ānjū-lèyè.

'That city's economy is developed, and public security is good; its people live peacefully and work happily.'

Example 2: 南极洲常年严寒，但是企鹅却能在那里**安居乐业**。

Nánjízhōu chángnián yánhán, dànshì qǐ'é què néng zài nàlǐ ānjū-lèyè.

'Antarctica is bitterly cold throughout the year, but penguins can live there peacefully and happily.'

Usage: Functions mainly as predicate.

Note: Complimentary in meaning.

Near Synonyms: [丰衣足食] (fēng yī zú shí 豐衣足食) 'abundant clothing sufficient food – be well-clothed and well-fed,' [国泰民安] (guó tài mín ān 國泰民安) 'country prosperous people peace – the country is prosperous and the people content.'

Antonyms: [背井离乡] (bèi jǐng lí xiāng 背井離鄉) 'turn one's back on one's wells and leave one's native place – be forced to leave one's hometown,' [流离失所] (liú lí shī suǒ 流離失所) 'wander about and lose one's place – destitute and homeless,' [民不聊生] (mín bù liáo shēng 民不聊生) 'people cannot support their lives – be destitute and have nothing on which to depend for survival.'

63. 【惊心动魄】(驚心動魄) jīng xīn dòng pò

惊心 means 'startle the heart' and 动魄 means 'move the soul.' The meaning of the whole idiom is 'soul-stirring.'

Example 1: 电影《泰坦尼克》场面宏大，看得观众**惊心动魄**。

Diànyǐng *Tàitǎnníkè* chǎngmiàn hóngdà, kàn de guānzhòng jīngxīn-dòngpò.

'The movie *Titanic* has many grand scenes, for an audience to see it is a soul-stirring experience.'

Example 2: 经过一场**惊心动魄**的较量，狮子最终战胜了老虎。

Jīngguò yì cháng jīngxīn-dòngpò de jiàoliàng, shīzi zuìzhōng zhànshèngle lǎohǔ.

'After a soul-stirring contest, the lion eventually defeated the tiger.'

Usage: Functions mainly as attributive and predicate.

Near Synonyms: [心惊肉跳] (xīn jīng ròu tiào 心驚肉跳) 'fearful and apprehensive,' [魂飞魄散] (hún fēi pò sàn 魂飛魄散) 'the soul flies and the spirit scatters – scared out of one's wits.'

Antonyms: [心如止水] (xīn rú zhǐ shuǐ 心如止水) 'heart like stopped waters – have no emotions,' [泰然自若] (tài rán zì ruò 泰然自若) 'composed, unperturbed.'

64. 【脚踏实地】(腳踏實地) jiǎo tà shí dì

脚 means 'foot,' 踏 means 'step on,' and 实 means 'real, true, solid.' The literal meaning is 'plant one's feet on solid ground,' with a freer translation being 'conscientious and dependable, with honesty and dedication.'

Example 1: 所有的人都应该**脚踏实地**地做好自己的本职工作。

Suǒyǒu de rén dōu yīnggāi jiǎotà-shídì de zuòhǎo zìjǐ de běnzhí gōngzuò.

'Everyone should with honesty and dedication do a good job performing their own work.'

Example 2: 她为人很谦虚，**脚踏实地**，从来不炫耀自己。

Tā wéirén hěn qiānxū, jiǎotà-shídì, cónglái bú xuànyào zìjǐ.

'As a person, she's modest; she's conscientious and dependable, and she never shows off.'

Usage: Functions mainly as adverbial and predicate.

Note: Complimentary in meaning.

Near Synonym: [踏踏实实] (tā tā shí shí 踏踏實實) 'steady, solid, reliable' (limited mostly to spoken Chinese).

Antonym: [好高骛远] (hào gāo wù yuǎn 好高鶩遠) 'reach for something beyond one's grasp.'

65. 【徇私舞弊】(徇私舞弊) xùn sī wǔ bì

徇 means 'submit to,' 私 means 'personal gains,' and 舞弊 means 'fraudulent or corrupt practices.' The meaning of the whole idiom is 'play favoritism and commit irregularities, do wrong to serve one's relatives or friends.'

Example 1: 他发生了**徇私舞弊**的丑闻，因此，寻求连任几乎不可能。

Tā fāshēngle xùnsī-wǔbì de chǒuwén, yīncǐ, xúnqiú liánrèn jīhū bù kěnéng.

'He was involved in a scandal that involved playing favoritism and committing irregularities; therefore, it is almost impossible for him to seek to serve another term in office.'

Example 2: 在没有法律监督的国家里，官员们常常**徇私舞弊**。

Zài méiyǒu fǎlǜ jiāndū de guójiā lǐ, guānyuánmen chángcháng xùnsī-wǔbì.

In countries where there is no legal supervision, government officials often play favoritism and commit irregularities.

Usage: Functions mainly as predicate and attributive.

Note: Derogatory in meaning.

Near Synonyms: [以权谋私] (yǐ quán móu sī 以權謀私) 'abuse one's power to seek personal gain,' [徇私枉法] (xùn sī wǎng fǎ 徇私枉法) 'bend the law to suit one's selfish ends.'

Antonyms: [大公无私] (dà gōng wú sī 大公無私) 'great impartiality and unselfishness, perfectly impartial,' [公事公办] (gōng shì gōng bàn 公事公辦) 'do official business according to official principles,' [廉洁奉公] (lián jié fèng gōng 廉潔奉公) 'have integrity and work in the interests of the public.'

66. 【不知所措】(不知所措) bù zhī suǒ cuò

措 means 'handle.' The meaning of the whole idiom is 'not know what to do.'

Example 1: 他站在那里**不知所措**，非常尴尬。

Tā zhàn zài nàli bùzhī-suǒcuò, fēicháng gān'gà.

'He stood there not knowing what to do, it being extremely awkward.'

Example 2: 这个消息对她来说太突然了，她**不知所措**地说，"这是真的吗？"

Zhège xiāoxi duì tā lái shuō tài tūrán le, tā bùzhī-suǒcuò de shuō: 'Zhè shì zhēnde ma?'

'This news was too sudden for her; bewildered, she said, "Is this true?"'

Usage: Functions mainly as predicate and adverbial.

Near Synonyms: [惊慌失措] (jīng huāng shī cuò 驚慌失措) 'so frightened and confused one doesn't know what to do – panic-stricken,' [手足无措] (shǒu zú wú cuò 手足無措) 'have no idea what to do with one's hands and feet – at a loss as to what to do, bewildered.'

Antonyms: [从容不迫] (cóng róng bú pò 從容不迫) 'calm and unhurried,' [应付自如] (yìng fù zì rú 應付自如) 'able to deal with a situation effortlessly.'

67. 【来之不易】(來之不易) lái zhī bú yì

来 means 'cause to come,' 之 means 'it,' and 易 means 'easy.' A literal translation of the whole idiom is 'causing it to come is not easy.' Freer translations include 'not easily obtained, hard-won, hard-earned.'

Example 1: 父母教育孩子珍惜**来之不易**的家庭条件。

Fùmǔ jiàoyù háizi zhēnxī láizhī-búyì de jiātíng tiáojiàn.

'In educating their children, the parents cherish the family conditions, which were not easily obtained.'

Example 2: 这样的成果确实**来之不易**。

Zhèyàng de chéngguǒ quèshí láizhī-búyì.

'This kind of result is indeed hard-won.'

Usage: Functions mainly as attributive and predicate.

Antonym: [轻而易举] (qīng ér yì jǔ 輕而易舉) 'light and easy to lift – easy.'

68. 【发扬光大】(發揚光大) fā yáng guāng dà

发扬 means 'promote' and 光大 means '(make) brilliant.' The whole idiom can be translated as 'promote, develop, enhance, carry forward.'

Example 1: 我们应该把前人艰苦奋斗的精神不断**发扬光大**。

Wǒmen yīnggāi bǎ qiánrén jiānkǔ-fèndòu de jīngshen búduàn fāyáng-guāngdà.

'We should continuously promote and enhance the spirit of arduous struggle of the people who came before.'

Example 2: 这些都是我们宝贵的精神财富，我们不但不应该抛弃它们，反而应该使它们**发扬光大**。

Zhèxiē dōu shì wǒmen bǎoguì de jīngshen cáifù, wǒmen búdàn bù yīnggāi pāoqì tāmen, fǎn'ér yīnggāi shǐ tāmen fāyáng-guāngdà.

'All these are our precious spiritual riches; not only should we not abandon them, but we should cause them to be promoted and developed.'

Usage: Functions mainly as predicate of a 把 (bǎ) sentence structure. The usual structure is 把 (bǎ) ／ 将 (jiāng 將) ／ 使 (shǐ) etc. + something + 发扬光大.

Antonyms: [斩草除根] (zhǎn cǎo chú gēn 斬草除根) 'cut grass dig up roots – root out and destroy,' [斩尽杀绝] (zhǎn jìn shā jué 斬盡殺絕) 'behead exhaust kill deplete – exterminate.'

69. 【顾全大局】(顧全大局) gù quán dà jú

顾 means 'look at, take into account.' The meaning of the whole idiom is 'take the entire situation into account, consider the overall situation.'

Example 1: 她做事坚持原则，**顾全大局**，不计较个人得失。

Tā zuòshì jiānchí yuánzé, gùquán-dàjú, bú jìjiào gèrén déshī.

'In her work she sticks to principles and considers the overall situation, disregarding personal gains or losses.'

Example 2: 为了**顾全大局**，他解雇了自己的办公室主任。

Wèile gùquán-dàjú, tā jiěgùle zìjǐ de bàngōngshì zhǔrèn.

'Taking the overall situation into account, he laid off his own office manager.'

Usage: Functions mainly as predicate; can also serve as attributive.

Antonym: [因小失大] (yīn xiǎo shī dà 因小失大) 'for a small gain lose a lot.'

70. 【八仙过海】(八仙過海) bā xiān guò hǎi

八仙 refers to the Eight Immortals (in Taoism) and 过海 means 'cross the (East China) sea.' A literal translation is 'the Eight Immortals cross the East China Sea.' The extended meaning is 'use one's own particular talents to solve problems' or 'use one's own individual resources to achieve great goals.'

Example 1: 自从旅游业放开之后，旅行社之间竞争激烈，**八仙过海**，各显神通，想尽办法吸引游客。

Zìcóng lǚyóuyè fàngkāi zhīhòu, lǚxíngshè zhījiān jìngzhēng jīliè, bāxiān-guòhǎi, gè xiǎn shén tōng, xiǎngjìn bànfǎ xīyǐn yóukè.

'Ever since the loosening up of the travel industry, travel agencies have been competing intensely with each other; when the Eight Immortals crossed the sea, each of them showed her or his own remarkable power; (similarly, the various travel agencies) are doing everything in their power to attract tourists.'

Example 2: 今天的晚会没有固定的节目，请大家**八仙过海**，各显其能，把你们的本事都使出来。

Jīntiān de wǎnhuì méiyǒu gùdìng de jiémù, qǐng dàjiā bāxiān-guòhǎi, gè xiǎn qí néng, bǎ nǐmen de běnshi dōu shǐchūlái.

'This evening's party has no set program; as when the Eight Immortals were crossing the sea, each of you please show your own abilities and put forth your own talents.'

Usage: Usually followed by 各显其能 (gè xiǎn qí néng 各顯其能) or 各显神通 (gè xiǎn shén tōng 各显神通), both of which mean 'each shows her or his own remarkable ability.' Together with one of these phrases, this idiom functions as an independent predicate.

Allusion: This idiom originates from a popular legend about the Eight Immortals in Taoism, who defended people against injustices and helped the weak. One day the Eight Immortals were going to cross the East China Sea. One of them suggested to the others that each should throw some item on the sea surface and then avail themselves of that item to cross the sea, without using a boat. And so all of them, one after another, threw various treasures into the water, including an iron walking stick, a calabash, a palm-leaf fan, a paper donkey, and so forth. One after another, each of them displayed his or her own special skills.

Note: Complimentary in meaning.

Antonym: [黔驴技穷] (Qián lú jì qióng 黔驢技窮) 'the Guizhou donkey's skills have been exhausted – exhaust one's bag of clumsy tricks' (derogatory).

71. 【自然而然】(自然而然) zì rán ér rán

自然 means 'naturally.' The meaning of the whole idiom is 'naturally, of itself.'

Example 1: 经济高度发展了，民主**自然而然**地成了大家讨论的话题。

Jīngjì gāodù fāzhǎnle, mínzhǔ zìrán-érrán de chéngle dàjiā tǎolùn de huàtí.

'The economy has developed to a high degree; democracy has naturally become a topic of conversation discussed by everyone.'

Example 2: 人的生、老、病、死都是**自然而然**的事，你抗拒不了的。

Rén de shēng, lǎo, bìng, sǐ dōu shì zìrán-érrán de shì, nǐ kàngjùbùliǎo de.

'Human beings' birth, aging, illness, and death all are natural things, you can't defy them.'

Usage: Functions mainly as adverbial and attributive.

Near Synonym: [水到渠成] (shuǐ dào qú chéng 水到渠成) 'water arrives and channel is formed – when conditions are ripe success is achieved; achieved naturally and without effort.'

Antonyms: [矫揉造作] (jiǎo róu zào zuò 矯揉造作) 'affected' (pejorative), [事在人为] (shì zài rén wéi 事在人為) 'everything depends on human effort.'

72. 【以身作则】 (以身作則) yǐ shēn zuò zé

身 means 'oneself' and 则 means 'rule, model.' A literal translation is 'take oneself as the model,' with a freer translation being 'set an example for others, practice what one preaches.'

Example 1: 周恩来总理严以律己、**以身作则**，为别人树立了榜样。

Zhōu Ēnlái zǒnglǐ yányǐlǜjǐ, yǐshēn-zuòzé, wèi biérén shùlìle bǎngyàng.

'Premier Zhou Enlai was strict on himself and set himself as an example, establishing a model for others.'

Example 2: 如果领导干部不能**以身作则**，下面的工作人员就可想而知了。

Rúguǒ lǐngdǎo gànbù bù néng yǐshēn-zuòzé, xiàmiàn de gōngzuò rényuán jiù kěxiǎng'érzhī le.

'If the leading cadres cannot practice what they preach, then you can imagine how it will be with the workers below.'

Usage: Functions mainly as predicate.

Note: Complimentary in meaning.

Near Synonyms: [言传身教] (yán chuán shēn jiào 言傳身教) 'teach by personal example,' [身体力行] (shēn tǐ lì xíng 身體力行) 'personally set an example.'

Antonyms: [上行下效] (shàng xíng xià xiào 上行下效) 'the actions of superiors are imitated by subordinates,' [以身试法] (yǐ shēn shì fǎ 以身試法) 'defy the law.'

73. 【层出不穷】 (層出不窮) céng chū bù qióng

层 means 'layer' and 穷 means 'exhaust.' The meaning of the whole idiom is 'pile up or emerge one after another without stopping.'

Example 1: 在现代社会里，新事物、新产品**层出不穷**。

Zài xiàndài shèhuì lǐ, xīn shìwù, xīn chǎnpǐn céngchū-bùqióng.

'In modern society, new things and new products pile up one after another.'

Example 2: 改革开放以后，中国出现了英语热，各种英语培训班**层出不穷**。

Gǎigé kāifàng yǐhòu, Zhōngguó chūxiànle yīngyǔ rè, gèzhǒng yīngyǔ péixùnbān céngchū-bùqióng.

'After the reforms and opening up of the late 1970s, there appeared in China a phenomenon of English being "hot," with all kinds of English training classes emerging one after another.'

Usage: Functions mainly as predicate.

Near Synonyms: [屡见不鲜] (lǚ jiàn bù xiān屡見不鮮) 'often seen and nothing remarkable,' [比比皆是] (bǐ bǐ jiē shì 比比皆是) 'can be found everywhere.'

Antonym: [寥寥无几] (liáo liáo wú jǐ 寥寥無幾) 'very few.'

74. 【轰轰烈烈】(轟轟烈烈) hōng hōng liè liè

轰轰 describes loud noise while 烈烈 refers to blazing fire. The meaning of the whole idiom is 'grand and gigantic, bold and dynamic.'

Example 1: 一个人一辈子不干一番**轰轰烈烈**的大事，是不是白活了？

Yí ge rén yíbèizi bú gàn yì fān hōnghōng-lièliè de dàshì, shìbúshì báihuó le?

'If someone during their whole life long never does something grand and bold and dynamic, is it the case that they have lived in vain?'

Example 2: 她一回国就参加了**轰轰烈烈**的革命运动。

Tā yì huíguó jiù cānjiāle hōnghōng-lièliè de gémìng yùndòng.

'As soon as she returned to her native country, she took part in the great revolutionary movement.'

Usage: Functions mainly as attributive and predicate.

Note: Complimentary in meaning.

Near Synonym: [惊世骇俗] (jīng shì hài sú 驚世駭俗) 'astound the world, earth-shaking.'

Antonym: [无声无息] (wú shēng wú xī 無聲無息) 'no sound no breath – silent.'

75. 【息息相关】(息息相關) xī xī xiāng guān

息 means 'breath,' 相 means 'mutually,' and 关 means 'related.' A literal translation of the whole idiom is 'mutually related as one breath is to another,' with freer translations being 'interrelated, closely linked.'

Example 1: 美国高科技的进步与她吸引人才的政策**息息相关**。

Měiguó gāo kējì de jìnbù yǔ tā xīyǐn réncái de zhèngcè xīxī-xiāngguān.

'The U.S.'s progress in high-tech is very closely related to her policy of attracting people of talent.'

Example 2: 政府应该花大力气解决与老百姓生活**息息相关**的问题。

Zhèngfǔ yīnggāi huā dà lìqi jiějué yǔ lǎobǎixìng shēnghuó xīxī-xiāngguān de wèntí.

'Government should expend a great deal of effort to solve those problems that are closely linked to the lives of ordinary citizens.'

Usage: Functions mainly as predicate and attributive, often preceded by coverbs such as 与 (yǔ 與), 跟 (gēn), and 和 (hé).

Near Synonyms: [休戚相关] (xiū qī xiāng guān 休戚相關) 'share joys and sorrows,' [息息相通] (xī xī xiāng tōng 息息相通) 'interrelated.'

Antonyms: [水火不容] (shuǐ huǒ bù róng 水火不容) 'as incompatible as water and fire,' [风马牛不相及] (fēng mǎ niú bù xiāng jí 風馬牛不相及) 'have nothing to do with one another.'

76. 【一丝不苟】(一絲不苟) yì sī bù gǒu

一丝 means 'even a little, at all' and 苟 means 'careless.' The meaning of the whole idiom is 'not the least bit negligent, scrupulous about every detail, conscientious and meticulous, perfectionist.'

Example 1: 她是公众人物，每天的衣着打扮都很注意，**一丝不苟**。

Tā shì gōngzhòng rénwù, měi tiān de yīzhuó dǎbàn dōu hěn zhùyì, yìsī-bùgǒu.

'She is a public figure; she pays great attention to her daily attire and make-up, being scrupulous about every detail.'

Example 2: 科学研究需要**一丝不苟**的态度和作风。

Kēxué yánjiū xūyào yìsī-bùgǒu de tàidu hé zuòfeng.

'Scientific research requires a perfectionist attitude and work style.'

Usage: Functions mainly as attributive, adverbial, and predicate.

Note: Complimentary in meaning.

Near Synonyms: [兢兢业业] (jīng jīng yè yè 兢兢業業) 'cautious and attentive,' [小心翼翼] (xiǎo xīn yì yì 小心翼翼) 'cautiously.'

Antonyms: [马马虎虎] (mǎ mǎ hū hū 馬馬虎虎) 'casual, careless,' [粗枝大叶] (cū zhī dà yè 粗枝大葉) 'careless, crude, sloppy.'

77. 【微不足道】(微不足道) wēi bù zú dào

微 means 'small,' 足 means 'worth,' and 道 means 'say, mention.' The meaning of the whole idiom is 'too trifling to deserve mention, insignificant.'

Example 1: 这点儿小事**微不足道**，你不必那么客气。

Zhè diǎr xiǎo shì wēibùzúdào, nǐ búbì nàme kèqi.

'Something as small as this is just not worth mentioning; you needn't be so polite.'

Example 2: 那家**微不足道**的小公司，十年以后成了同行业的巨头。

Nà jiā wēibùzúdào de xiǎo gōngsī, shí nián yǐhòu chéngle tónghángyè de jùtóu.

'That insignificant little company in ten years became a giant in the profession.'

Usage: Functions mainly as predicate and attributive.

Near Synonym: [不足挂齿] (bù zú guà chǐ 不足掛齒) 'not worth hanging on the teeth – not worth mentioning.'

Antonym: [举足轻重] (jǔ zú qīng zhòng 舉足輕重) 'play a decisive role.'

78. 【刻不容缓】(刻不容緩) kè bù róng huǎn

刻 means 'short period of time,' 容 means 'allow,' and 缓 means 'delay.' A literal translation of the whole idiom is 'short time not allow delay,' with a freer translation being 'it is not allowed to delay for even a short period of time.' The meaning of the whole idiom is 'allow no delay, extremely urgent.'

Example 1: 打击黑社会的行动**刻不容缓**。

Dǎjī hēi shèhuì de xíngdòng kèbùrónghuǎn.

'Operations to crack down on organized crime allow for no delay.'

Example 2: 解决失业人口的生计问题，是本届政府**刻不容缓**的任务。

Jiějué shīyè rénkǒu de shēngjì wèntí, shì běnjiè zhèngfǔ kèbùrónghuǎn de rènwù.

'Solving livelihood issues of the unemployed population is an urgent responsibility of this administration.'

Usage: Functions mainly as predicate; can also serve as attributive.

Near Synonyms: [分秒必争] (fēn miǎo bì zhēng 分秒必争) 'every minute or second counts,' [迫不及待] (pò bù jí dài 迫不及待) 'too impatient to wait,' [迫在眉睫] (pò zài méi jié 迫在眉睫) 'very urgent.'

Antonym: [一拖再拖] (yì tuō zài tuō 一拖再拖) 'drag on or delay without end.'

79. 【截然不同】(截然不同) jié rán bù tóng

截然 means 'completely.' The meaning of the whole idiom is 'completely different.'

Example 1: 两个人从小一起长大，后来在同一所大学上学，可是毕业后的命运却**截然不同**。

Liǎng ge rén cóng xiǎo yìqǐ zhǎngdà, hòulái zài tóng yì suǒ dàxué shàngxué, kěshì bìyè hòu de mìngyùn què jiérán-bù tóng.

'The two of them grew up together from the time they were children, and later they attended the same university, but their fate after graduation was completely different.'

Example 2: 对于同一个问题，由于大家的立场不一样，所以产生了两种**截然不同**的观点。

Duìyú tóng yí ge wèntí, yóuyú dàjiā de lìchǎng bù yíyàng, suǒyǐ chǎnshēngle liǎng zhǒng jiérán-bùtóng de guāndiǎn.

'Because everyone's standpoint was different, there arose two completely different views about the same issue.'

Usage: Functions mainly as predicate and attributive.

Near Synonym: [天壤之别] (tiān rǎng zhī bié 天壤之別) 'as different as heaven and earth.'

Antonyms: [一模一样] (yì mú yí yàng 一模一樣) 'exactly alike,' [半斤八两] (bàn jīn bā liǎng 半斤八兩) 'six of one and half a dozen of the other.'

80. 【愚公移山】(愚公移山) yú gōng yí shān

愚 means 'foolish,' 公 means 'old man,' and 移 means 'move.' A literal translation of this idiom is 'the foolish old man moved the mountain.' This is a metaphor for 'have inexhaustible willpower and an unyielding spirit.' Possible English translations include 'where there's a will there's a way' or 'with sufficient effort anything can be achieved.'

Example 1: 我们要发扬**愚公移山**的精神，把家乡建设好。

Wǒmen yào fāyáng yúgōng-yíshān de jīngshen, bǎ jiāxiāng jiànshèhǎo.

'We should develop and promote the spirit of "the old man who moved a mountain," doing a good job of reconstructing our hometown.'

Example 2: 他们继承了老一辈**愚公移山**的精神，踏踏实实地做出了许多贡献。

Tāmen jìchéngle lǎo yíbèi yúgōng-yíshān de jīngshen, tātā-shíshí de zuòchūle xǔduō gòngxiàn.

'They inherited the older generation's spirit of "the old man who moved a mountain," steadily making many contributions.'

Usage: Functions mainly as attributive, often followed by 精神 (jīngshen) 'spirit.'

Allusion: There was an old man by the name of Yu Gong who was around ninety years of age. Directly across from the front door of his home were two mountains, making it hard for him to go out. So he called together everyone in his family for a meeting to discuss moving the mountains. One after another, they all agreed to this. But Yu Gong's wife brought up a problem: where should they move the earth and stones from the mountains? Yu Gong replied that they should be transported to the distant sea, so he himself led three younger people and they began to transport the earth and stones to the sea. Now, it was very far from Yu Gong's home to the sea, so each year they were able to transport earth and stones only one time. There was another old man who made fun of Yu Gong: "You're not very smart. You're over ninety, you don't even have the strength to pull out the grass on the mountain; how are you going to handle all that earth and all those stones?" Yu Gong heaved a sigh and said: "My goodness, you're just too stubborn in your thinking, you're even worse than widows or children. Just think, after I die there will still be my sons, and after my sons there will be my grandsons; going on like that, there will be generation after generation of my descendants. But these mountains are not going to become any higher, so why worry about not being able to move them?" Even the gods in the heavens were moved by Yu Gong's spirit, and so in the space of one night, the gods moved the two mountains. And from this time on, there were no longer any large mountains obstructing the way in front of Yu Gong's home. (from "Tang Wen" in *Liezi*)

Note: Complimentary in meaning. This idiom, which was already common, came into even wider use after Mao Zedong used it in a 1945 essay of the same name.

Near Synonyms: [锲而不舍] (qiè ér bù shě 鍥而不捨) or [持之以恒] (chí zhī yǐ héng 持之以恆) 'work with perseverance, persevere.'

Antonyms: [浅尝辄止] (qiǎn cháng zhé zhǐ 淺嘗輒止) 'shallowly taste then stop – stop after gaining a little knowledge of something,' [拈轻怕重] (niān qīng pà zhòng 拈輕怕重) 'prefer the light to the heavy.'

81. 【所作所为】(所作所為) suǒ zuò suǒ wéi

为 means 'do.' The literal meaning of this idiom is 'what one does,' with a freer translation being 'everything one does, all of a person's actions.'

Example 1: 父母的**所作所为**会对孩子的行为产生直接的影响。

Fùmǔ de suǒzuò-suǒwéi huì duì háizi de xíngwéi chǎnshēng zhíjiē de yǐngxiǎng.

'Everything that parents do will have a direct influence on children's behavior.'

Example 2: 我对自己的**所作所为**毫不后悔。

Wǒ duì zìjǐ de suǒzuò-suǒwéi háo bú hòuhuǐ.

'I don't in the slightest regret my own actions.'

Usage: Functions mainly as object.

Near Synonym: [一举一动] (yì jǔ yí dòng 一舉一動) 'every action and every movement.'

82. 【后顾之忧】(後顧之憂) hòu gù zhī yōu

后 means 'in the back,' 顾 means 'look back,' and 忧 means 'worry.' A literal translation of the whole idiom is 'the worries of looking back,' with a freer translation being 'things to worry about back home or in the rear.'

Example 1: 公司为所有员工买了养老保险，解决了员工们的**后顾之忧**。

Gōngsī wèi suǒyǒu yuángōng mǎile yǎnglǎo bǎoxiǎn, jiějuéle yuángōngmen de hòugù-zhīyōu.

'The company bought retirement insurance for all the employees; it solved the employees' domestic worries.'

Example 2: 在一场有关黑社会的审判中，有关部门表示，绝对保证证人的安全，这样就解除了证人的**后顾之忧**。

Zài yì cháng yǒuguān hēi shèhuì de shěnpàn zhōng, yǒuguān bùmén biǎoshì, juéduì bǎozhèng zhèngrén de ānquán, zhèyàng jiù jiěchúle zhèngrén de hòugù-zhīyōu.

'In a trial concerning organized crime, the departments concerned indicated that they would absolutely guarantee the safety of witnesses; in this way they relieved the domestic worries of the witnesses.'

Usage: Functions mainly as object, often preceded by the verbs 解除 (jiěchú) 'eliminate' or 解决 (jiějué 解决) 'solve.'

Near Synonym: [投鼠忌器] (tóu shǔ jì qì 投鼠忌器) 'when throwing it at a rat have fears about the dish (breaking) – cautious about harming evildoers lest the innocent be hurt.'

Antonym: [高枕无忧] (gāo zhěn wú yōu 高枕無憂) 'high pillow no worries – rest easy.'

83. 【德才兼备】(德才兼備) dé cái jiān bèi

德 means 'moral character,' 才 means 'ability, talent,' 兼 means 'simultaneously,' and 备 means 'equipped with.' A literal translation of the entire idiom is 'simultaneously be equipped with moral character and talent.' A freer translation is 'possess both moral integrity and professional competence.'

Example 1: 他是一个**德才兼备**的青年，很有发展前途。

Tā shì yí ge décái-jiānbèi de qīngnián, hěn yǒu fāzhǎn qiántú.

'He is a youth of good character and great ability; he has great prospects for development.'

Example 2: 提拔干部的时候得坚持**德才兼备**的原则。

Tíbá gànbù de shíhou děi jiānchí décái-jiānbèi de yuánzé.

'When promoting cadres, one must insist on the principle of their possessing both moral integrity and professional competence.'

Usage: Functions mainly as object.

Note: Complimentary in meaning.

Near Synonym: [品学兼优] (pǐn xué jiān yōu 品學兼優) 'excellent in character and learning.'

Antonym: [寡廉鲜耻] (guǎ lián xiǎn chǐ 寡廉鮮恥) 'few honesty little shame – have no sense of shame.'

84. 【相辅相成】(相輔相成) xiāng fǔ xiāng chéng

相 means 'mutually,' 辅 means 'help,' and 成 means 'facilitate, bring about.' A literal translation of the whole idiom is 'help each other and facilitate each other,' with a freer translation being 'complement each other.'

Example 1: 保护环境和发展经济是**相辅相成**的。

Bǎohù huánjìng hé fāzhǎn jīngjì shì xiāngfǔ-xiāngchéng de.

'Protecting the environment and developing the economy complement each other.'

Example 2: 这种药能止咳，那种药能化痰，二者**相辅相成**。

Zhè zhǒng yào néng zhǐké, nà zhǒng yào néng huàtán, èrzhě xiāngfǔ-xiāngchéng.

'This kind of medicine can stop coughing, and that kind of medicine can dissolve mucus; the two of them complement each other.'

Usage: Often functions as predicate, in the construction ... 是相辅相成的 (shì xiāngfǔ-xiāngchéng de).

Near Synonyms: [不可或缺] (bù kě huò quē 不可或缺) 'indispensable,' [相得益彰] (xiāng dé yì zhāng 相得益彰) 'each improves by association with the other.'

Antonyms: [势不两立] (shì bù liǎng lì 勢不兩立) 'irreconcilable, incompatible,' [两败俱伤] (liǎng bài jù shāng 兩敗俱傷) 'both sides lose and are equally wounded.'

85. 【讨价还价】(討價還價) tǎo jià huán jià

讨价 means 'ask a price' and 还价 means 'make a counter-offer.' The meaning of the whole idiom is 'bargain back and forth, negotiate back and forth.'

Example 1: 经过一番**讨价还价**，买卖双方最终达成了协议。

Jīngguò yì fān tǎojià-huánjià, mǎimài shuāngfāng zuìzhōng dáchéngle xiéyì.

'After a series of negotiations, the buyer and seller in the end reached an agreement.'

Example 2: **讨价还价**之后，他辞去了行政职务，但是继任者给他增加了薪水。

Tǎojià-huánjià zhīhòu, tā cíqùle xíngzhèng zhíwù, dànshì jìrènzhě gěi tā zēngjiāle xīnshuǐ.

'After negotiations, he resigned his administrative post, but his successor increased his salary.'

Usage: Functions mainly as predicate and object.

Note: Slightly derogatory in meaning.

Near Synonym: [斤斤计较] (jīn jīn jì jiào 斤斤計較) 'haggle over every catty – calculating.'

86. 【同心同德】 (同心同德) tóng xīn tóng dé

同 means 'same,' 心 means 'mind,' and 德 here means 'belief.' A literal translation of this idiom is 'same mind same beliefs.' Freer translations include 'of one heart and mind, united in thought and belief.'

Example 1: 他号召全国人民**同心同德**，为民族的伟大复兴而努力奋斗。

Tā hàozhào quánguó rénmín tóngxīn-tóngdé, wèi mínzú de wěidà fùxīng ér nǔlì fèndòu.

'He appealed to the people of the whole country to be of one heart and mind, and to work hard and struggle for the great rejuvenation of the nation.'

Example 2: 他们解决好内部矛盾以后，**同心同德**工作起来。

Tāmen jiějué hǎo nèibù máodùn yǐhòu, tóngxīn-tóngdé gōngzuò qǐlai.

'After they had solved the internal conflict, they began to work with united hearts and minds.'

Usage: Functions mainly as predicate and adverbial.

Note: Complimentary in meaning.

Near Synonyms: [志同道合] (zhì tóng dào hé 志同道合) 'have the same aspirations, have common goals,' [齐心协力] (qí xīn xié lì 齊心協力) 'work as one.'

Antonym: [同床异梦] (tóng chuáng yì mèng 同床異夢) 'same bed different dreams – work together but for different ends.'

87. 【理直气壮】 (理直氣壯) lǐ zhí qì zhuàng

理 means 'reason,' 直 means 'correct,' 气 means 'spirit,' and 壮 means 'strong.' The meaning of the whole idiom is 'bold through being in the right, with righteous self-assurance.'

Example 1: 他在法庭上**理直气壮**地说："我是清白的，我没有犯罪。"

Tā zài fǎtíng shàng lǐzhí-qìzhuàng de shuō: "Wǒ shì qīngbái de, wǒ méiyǒu fànzuì."

'In court he said with righteous self-assurance: "I'm unstained, I didn't commit a crime."'

Example 2: 她**理直气壮**地回答："绝对不可能。"

Tā lǐzhí-qìzhuàng de huídá: 'Juéduì bù kěnéng.'

'She answered righteously and boldly: "That is absolutely impossible."'

Usage: Functions mainly as attributive.

Near Synonym: [义正词严] (yì zhèng cí yán 義正詞嚴) 'speak righteously and sternly.'

Antonyms: [理屈词穷] (lǐ qū cí qióng 理屈詞窮) 'in the wrong and out of arguments,' [强词夺理] (qiǎng cí duó lǐ 強詞奪理) 'use far-fetched arguments.'

88. 【身体力行】(身體力行) shēn tǐ lì xíng

身 means 'oneself,' 体 means 'learn from experience,' 力 means 'strive hard to do something,' and 行 means 'put into practice.' The literal meaning is 'What oneself has learned from experience one should try hard to put into practice,' with a freer translation being 'practice what you preach, personally set an example.'

Example 1: 他不光努力宣传这种健康的生活方式，而且**身体力行**，为其他人做了一个榜样。

Tā bù guāng nǔlì xuānchuán zhè zhǒng jiànkāng de shēnghuó fāngshì, érqiě shēntǐ-lìxíng, wèi qítā rén zuòle yí ge bǎngyàng.

'He not only works hard in publicizing this kind of healthy lifestyle, but also practices what he preaches, serving as an example to others.'

Example 2: 各级领导干部都应该**身体力行**，发扬自强不息的精神。

Gè jí lǐngdǎo gànbù dōu yīnggāi shēntǐ-lìxíng, fāyáng zìqiáng-bùxī de jīngshen.

'Leading cadres at all levels should all serve as an example to others, developing and promoting a spirit of striving constantly for self-improvement.'

Usage: Functions mainly as predicate.

Antonym: [光说不做] (guāng shuō bú zuò 光說不做) 'only talk not do – all talk and no action' (used mostly in speech).

89. 【义不容辞】(義不容辭) yì bù róng cí

义 means 'duty, obligation,' 容 means 'allow,' and 辞 means 'decline, refuse.' A literal translation of this idiom is 'duty does not allow one to decline,' with a freer translation being 'duty-bound not to refuse.'

Example 1: 为人民服务是各级领导干部**义不容辞**的责任。

Wèi rénmín fúwù shì gè jí lǐngdǎo gànbù yìbùróngcí de zérèn.

'To serve the people is the responsibility of leading cadres at all levels, which they are duty-bound not to decline.'

Example 2: 救助病人是医生**义不容辞**的责任。

Jiùzhù bìngrén shì yīshēng yìbùróngcí de zérèn.

'Helping patients is a doctor's responsibility, which he or she is duty-bound not to shirk.'

Usage: Functions mainly as attributive, usually followed by 责任 (zérèn 責任) 'responsibility.' Can also serve as predicate.

Note: Complimentary in meaning.

Near Synonyms: [天经地义] (tiān jīng dì yì 天經地義) 'unalterable principle, entirely justified,' [义无反顾] (yì wú fǎn gù 義無反顧) 'duty-bound not to turn back,' [理所当然] (lǐ suǒ dāng rán 理所當然) 'of course, naturally.'

Antonym: [推三阻四] (tuī sān zǔ sì 推三阻四) 'decline with all sorts of excuses.'

90. 【画龙点睛】(畫龍點睛) huà lóng diǎn jīng

画 means 'draw,' 龙 means 'dragon,' 点 means 'dot, adorn,' and 睛 means 'eye.' A literal translation of the whole idiom is 'draw a dragon and add on the eyes.' This is a metaphor for 'add the perfect finishing touch' or 'say or write something crucially important that completes a matter.'

Example 1: 文章最后的一段虽然不长，但是起到了**画龙点睛**的作用。

Wénzhāng zuìhòu de yí duàn suīrán bù cháng, dànshì qǐdàole huàlóng-diǎnjīng de zuòyòng.

'Though the last section of the essay is not long, it had the effect of adding the perfect finishing touch.'

Example 2: 有人说，克林顿总统的朝鲜之旅，是到那时候为止他的政治生命的**画龙点睛**之笔。

Yǒu rén shuō, Kèlíndùn zǒngtǒng de Cháoxiǎn zhī lǚ, shì dào nà shíhou wéi zhǐ tā de zhèngzhì shēngmìng de huàlóng-diǎnjīng zhī bǐ.

'Some people say that President Clinton's trip to Korea was the perfect finishing touch for his political life up until that time.'

Usage: Functions mainly as attributive.

Allusion: The famous Southern Dynasties painter Zhang Sengyao drew four dragons on the wall of a temple in Nanjing, but he didn't add eyes to any of them. When people asked him why, he would always say that if he added eyes, the dragons would fly away. People didn't believe him, feeling this was absurd, so he added eyes to one of the dragons. After a while, there was thunder, and lightning struck the wall; then one of the dragons, riding the clouds, flew up into the heavens. But those dragons to which eyes hadn't been added were still on the wall. (from the section on Zhang Sengyao in *Famous Paintings from Successive Dynasties* by Zhang Yanyuan, Tang Dynasty)

Note: Complimentary in meaning.

Near Synonyms: [锦上添花] (jǐn shàng tiān huā 錦上添花) 'on brocade add flowers – improve to perfection,' [点石成金] (diǎn shí chéng jīn 點石成金) 'touch stone and it becomes gold – turn one's worthless words into gold.'

Antonyms: [画蛇添足] (huà shé tiān zú 畫蛇添足) 'draw snake add feet – add something superfluous,' [弄巧成拙] (nòng qiǎo chéng zhuō 弄巧成拙) 'too clever for one's own good.'

91. 【琳琅满目】(琳瑯滿目) lín láng mǎn mù

琳琅 means 'beautiful jade' and functions as a metaphor for precious things. 满目 means 'fill the eyes – seen everywhere.' The meaning of the whole idiom is 'a dazzling collection of beautiful and precious things.'

Example 1: 购物中心里**琳琅满目**，世界各国的奢侈品都有。

Gòuwù zhōngxīn lǐ línláng-mǎnmù, shìjiè gè guó de shēchǐpǐn dōu yǒu.

'In the shopping mall there was a dazzling collection of beautiful and precious things, luxury goods from countries all over the world being present.'

Example 2: 小商品批发市场里商品**琳琅满目**，要什么有什么。

Xiǎoshāngpǐn pīfā shìchǎng lǐ shāngpǐn línláng-mǎnmù, yào shénme yǒu shénme.

'The goods in the small commodities wholesale market were like a dazzling collection of beautiful and precious things, whatever you might want was there.'

Usage: Functions mainly as predicate; can also serve as attributive.

Note: Somewhat complimentary in meaning.

Near Synonym: [金碧辉煌] (jīn bì huī huáng 金碧辉煌) 'resplendent in bright colors.'

Antonyms: [光怪陆离] (guāng guài lù lí 光怪陸離) 'grotesque and gaudy,' [满目疮痍] (mǎn mù chuāng yí 滿目瘡痍) 'everywhere the eyes look there is devastation.'

92. 【耐人寻味】(耐人尋味) nài rén xún wèi

耐 means 'endure, withstand,' 寻 means 'seek,' and 味 means 'flavor,' with 寻味 meaning 'ponder, think over.' The literal meaning is 'can withstand people's pondering something.' A freer translation is 'giving food for thought, thought-provoking.'

Example 1: 这个故事意义深刻，**耐人寻味**。

Zhège gùshi yìyì shēnkè, nàirén-xúnwèi.

'This story has a profound significance and is food for thought.'

Example 2: 他说了一段**耐人寻味**的话："两只小老鼠掉进一桶奶油里，第一只很快放弃了希望，便淹死了；第二只则没有放弃，它如此努力挣扎，最后竟然把奶油搅成了黄油，然后爬了出来。"

Tā shuōle yí duàn nàirén-xúnwèi de huà: "Liǎng zhī xiǎo lǎoshǔ diàojìn yì tǒng nǎiyóu lǐ, dìyī zhī hěn kuài fàngqìle xīwàng, biàn yānsǐle; dì'èr zhī zé méiyǒu fàngqì, tā rúcǐ nǔlì zhēngzhá, zuìhòu jìngrán bǎ nǎiyóu jiǎochéngle huángyóu, ránhòu pále chūlái."

'He said the thought-provoking words: "Two little mice fell in a bucket of cream. The first mouse quickly gave up and drowned. The second mouse, wouldn't quit.

He struggled so hard that eventually he churned that cream into butter and crawled out."' (from the film *Catch Me If You Can*)

Usage: Functions mainly as predicate and attributive.

Near Synonym: [回味无穷] (huí wèi wú qióng 回味無窮) 'recollect or remember without end.'

Antonyms: [索然无味] (suǒ rán wú wèi 索然無味) 'dull and without flavor – insipid,' [枯燥无味] (kū zào wú wèi 枯燥無味) 'dry and without flavor – dull.'

93. 【繁荣昌盛】 (繁榮昌盛) fán róng chāng shèng

繁荣 means 'prosperous' and 昌盛 means 'thriving,' so the whole idiom can be translated as 'prosperous and thriving.' This typically refers to an industry, society, or nation.

Example 1: 衷心祝愿伟大祖国**繁荣昌盛**。

Zhōngxīn zhùyuàn wěidà zǔguó fánróng-chāngshèng.

'From the bottom of my heart, I wish that my great motherland may prosper and thrive.'

Example 2: 服务业又复活了，社会呈现出**繁荣昌盛**的景象。

Fúwùyè yòu fùhuó le, shèhuì chéngxiàn chū fánróng-chāngshèng de jǐngxiàng.

'The service industry has come back to life, and society presents an appearance of flourishing prosperity.'

Usage: Functions mainly as predicate and attributive.

Note: Complimentary in meaning.

Near Synonyms: [欣欣向荣] (xīn xīn xiàng róng 欣欣向榮) 'thriving, flourishing,' [蒸蒸日上] (zhēng zhēng rì shàng 蒸蒸日上) 'progress day by day.'

Antonyms: [满目疮痍] (mǎn mù chuāng yí 滿目瘡痍) 'everywhere the eyes look there is devastation,' [江河日下] (jiāng hé rì xià 江河日下) 'rivers and streams daily decline – deteriorate day by day, go from bad to worse,' [国破家亡] (guó pò jiā wáng 國破家亡) 'state broken family dead – the country is defeated and the family is ruined.'

94. 【难能可贵】 (難能可貴) nán néng kě guì

难能 here means 'hard to do' and 可贵 means 'valuable, praiseworthy.' A literal translation of the whole idiom is 'hard to do and (therefore) praiseworthy.' Freer translations of the idiom include 'praiseworthy, commendable.'

Example 1: 他虽然年轻，但是做事很稳重，这是**难能可贵**的。

Tā suīrán niánqīng, dànshì zuòshì hěn wěnzhòng, zhè shì nánnéng-kěguì de.

'Though he's young, he does things very steadily; this is very praiseworthy.'

Example 2: 这家公司不但在经济危机中生存了下来，更加**难能可贵**的是，他们把成功的经验无偿地介绍给其他竞争对手。

Zhè jiā gōngsī búdàn zài jīngjì wēijī zhōng shēngcúnle xiàlái, gèngjiā nánnéng-kěguì de shì, tāmen bǎ chénggōng de jīngyàn wúcháng de jièshào gěi qítā jìngzhēng duìshǒu.

'This company has not only survived during the economic crisis, what is even more commendable is that they took their successful experience and, without compensation, introduced it to other competitors.'

Usage: Functions mainly as predicate or as a nominal phrase added on at the end of one sentence that serves as the subject of a second sentence.

Note: Complimentary in meaning.

Near Synonym: [来之不易] (lái zhī bú yì 來之不易) 'not easily obtained, hard-won.'

Antonym: [不足为奇] (bù zú wéi qí 不足為奇) 'not at all surprising.'

95. 【一模一样】(一模一樣) yì mú yí yàng

模 means 'model' and 样 means 'pattern.' A literal translation is 'one model one pattern.' The meaning of the whole idiom is 'identical, completely the same, exactly alike.'

Example 1: 这对双胞胎长得一**模**一**样**，连他们的父母有时候都分不开。

Zhè duì shuāngbāotāi zhǎngde yìmú-yíyàng, lián tāmen de fūmǔ yǒu shíhou dōu fēnbukāi.

'This pair of twins looks exactly the same; even their parents sometimes can't tell them apart.'

Example 2: 两篇文章除了作者的名字不同以外，其余的一**模**一**样**，肯定有人抄袭。

Liǎng piān wénzhāng chúle zuòzhě de míngzi bù tóng yǐwài, qíyú de yìmú-yíyàng, kěndìng yǒu rén chāoxí.

'As for these two essays, except for the author's name being different, everything else is identical; somebody is certainly plagiarizing.'

Usage: Functions mainly as predicate; can also serve as attributive.

Near Synonyms: [如出一辙] (rú chū yì zhé 如出一轍) 'as if emerging from the same track – one and the same, cut from the same cloth,' [毫发不爽] (háo fà bù shuǎng 毫髮不爽) 'not the least bit off.'

Antonyms: [截然不同] (jié rán bù tóng 截然不同) 'completely different,' [天壤之别] (tiān rǎng zhī bié 天壤之別) 'as different as heaven and earth.'

96. 【突飞猛进】(突飛猛進) tū fēi měng jìn

突 means 'suddenly, quickly,' 飞 means 'fly, leap,' 猛 means 'vigorously,' and 进 means 'progress forward, advance.' A literal translation of the whole idiom is 'quickly leap vigorously advance,' with freer translations including 'advance rapidly, progress by leaps and bounds, make great strides.'

Example 1: 计算机出现后，科学技术**突飞猛进**，取得了惊人的成就。

Jìsuànjī chūxiàn hòu, kēxué jìshù tūfēi-měngjìn, qǔdéle jīngrén de chéngjiù.

'After computers emerged, scientific technology advanced in leaps and bounds, obtaining astonishing achievements.'

Example 2: 去年，该国的出口**突飞猛进**，比前年增长了五倍。

Qùnián, gāi guó de chūkǒu tūfēi-měngjìn, bǐ qiánnián zēngzhǎngle wǔ bèi.

'Last year, that country's exports made great strides, increasing five times compared with the year before last.'

Usage: Functions mainly as predicate, can also function as attributive and adverbial.

Note: Complimentary in meaning.

Near Synonyms: [日新月异] (rì xīn yuè yì 日新月異) 'change rapidly with each new day,' [一日千里] (yí rì qiān lǐ 一日千里) 'one day a thousand miles – at a tremendous pace.'

Antonyms: [江河日下] (jiāng hé rì xià 江河日下) 'rivers and streams daily decline – deteriorate day by day, go from bad to worse,' [停滞不前] (tíng zhì bù qián 停滯不前) 'stop and stagnate and not advance – come to a standstill, get bogged down.'

97. 【刮目相看】(刮目相看) guā mù xiāng kàn

刮目 means 'rub one's eyes.' The meaning of the whole idiom is 'have great respect for, hold someone in high esteem.'

Example 1: 这座城市最近三十年的发展令世界**刮目相看**。

Zhè zuò chéngshì zuìjìn sānshí nián de fāzhǎn lìng shìjiè guāmù-xiāngkàn.

'This city's development in the last thirty years has earned the respect of the whole world.'

Example 2: 他在很短的时间内就做成了几件大事，让人们**刮目相看**。

Tā zài hěn duǎn de shíjiān nèi jiù zuòchéngle jǐ jiàn dà shì, ràng rénmen guāmù-xiāngkàn.

'Within a short time he completed several major projects, making people hold him in high esteem.'

Usage: Functions as predicate, mainly in the pattern 令 (lìng) / 让 (ràng 讓) / 使 (shǐ) 'make' + 人 (rén) 'people' / 世界 (shìjiè) 'world' + 刮目相看.

Note: Complimentary in meaning.

Near Synonyms: [另眼看待] (lìng yǎn kàn dài 另眼看待) 'look at from a new point of view,' [拭目以待] (shì mù yǐ dài 拭目以待) 'wait for eagerly.'

98. 【风风雨雨】(風風雨雨) fēng fēng yǔ yǔ

A literal translation of the whole idiom is 'wind wind rain rain.' This is often used metaphorically to mean 'repeated difficulties, frequent hardships.'

Example 1: 最近几年她可不容易，经历了多少**风风雨雨**。

Zuìjìn jǐ nián tā kě bù róngyì, jīnglì le duōshǎo fēngfēng-yǔyǔ.

'The last few years she really hasn't had it easy; she has undergone so many repeated difficulties.'

Example 2: 二十年的**风风雨雨**把他磨练得无比坚强。

Èrshí nián de fēngfēng-yǔyǔ bǎ tā móliàn de wúbǐ jiānqiáng.

'Twenty years of frequent hardships have disciplined him so that he is incomparably strong.'

Usage: Nominal element, functions mainly as object. Often preceded or followed by words expressing length of time.

Near Synonyms: [风霜雨雪] (fēng shuāng yǔ xuě 風霜雨雪) 'many hardships,' [栉风沐雨] (zhì fēng mù yǔ 櫛風沐雨) 'exposed to the elements,' [饱经风霜] (bǎo jīng fēng shuāng 飽經風霜) 'have experienced hardships to the full,' [曲曲折折] (qū qū zhé zhé 曲曲折折) 'tortuous, full of complications.'

Antonym: [养尊处优] (yǎng zūn chǔ yōu 養尊處優) 'have a respected position and live in affluence.'

99. 【旗帜鲜明】(旗幟鮮明) qí zhì xiān míng

旗帜 means 'banner' or 'flag' and 鲜明 means 'bright' or 'distinct.' A literal translation of the entire idiom is 'banners are bright and distinct.' This originally referred to the brilliant colors of an army's banners. Freer translations include 'have a clear standpoint, take a clear position, take a clear political stand.'

Example 1: 我们要**旗帜鲜明**地反对民族分裂主义。

Wǒmen yào qízhì-xiānmíng de fǎnduì mínzú fēnliè zhǔyì.

'We must have a clear position opposing national secessionism.'

Example 2: 在原则性问题上必须**旗帜鲜明**。

Zài yuánzéxìng wèntí shàng bìxū qízhì-xiānmíng.

'One must take a clear stand on questions of principle.'

Usage: Functions mainly as adverbial, can also function as predicate.

Near Synonym: [爱憎分明] (ài zèng fēn míng 愛憎分明) 'love hate demarcate clearly – clearly distinguish between what one hates and what one loves.'

Antonym: [模棱两可] (mó léng liǎng kě 模棱兩可) 'ambiguous.'

100. 【破釜沉舟】(破釜沉舟) pò fǔ chén zhōu

破 means 'break,' 釜 means 'kettle, pot,' 沉 means 'sink,' and 舟 means 'boat.' The literal meaning is 'break the kettles and sink the boats.' The connotation is 'burn one's bridges, cut off all means of retreat.'

Example 1: 现在我们不能再犹豫了，必须**破釜沉舟**，这样还有一点儿希望。

Xiànzài wǒmen bù néng zài yóuyù le, bìxū pòfǔ-chénzhōu, zhèyàng hái yǒu yìdiǎnr xīwàng.

'Now we can hesitate no longer; we must cut off all means of retreat; this way, there is still a little hope.'

Example 2: 这种**破釜沉舟**的做法虽然勇敢，但是考虑得不够全面。

Zhè zhǒng pòfǔ-chénzhōu de zuòfǎ suīrán yǒnggǎn, dànshì kǎolǜ de bú gòu quánmiàn.

'Although this method of cutting off all means of retreat is brave, it does not take enough into consideration.'

Usage: Functions mainly as predicate or attributive.

Allusion: In 207 B.C.E., the state of Chu was fighting against the Qin empire. Xiang Yu (232–202 B.C.E.) was then a lieutenant general of Chu. Since the general fought reluctantly, Xiang Yu killed him. After crossing a river, Xiang Yu ordered all the soldiers to sink their boats, smash their cooking pots, set fire to their huts, and each take only three days' worth of food. Sure enough, the soldiers fought heroically and defeated the enemy. (from "Xiang Yu Ben Ji" in *Records of the Grand Historian*)

Near Synonyms: [孤注一掷] (gū zhù yí zhì 孤注一擲) 'bet all or stake everything on a single throw – put all one's eggs into one basket,' [背水一战] (bèi shuǐ yí zhàn 背水一戰) 'fight with one's back to the river – fight to win or die, a win-or-die battle.'

Antonyms: [瞻前顾后] (zhān qián gù hòu 瞻前顧後) 'look in front and turn around to look behind – look ahead into the future and back into the past, consider cautiously and carefully,' [优柔寡断] (yōu róu guǎ duàn 優柔寡斷) 'irresolute and hesitant, indecisive.'

101. 【独一无二】(獨一無二) dú yī wú èr

独 means 'only.' A literal translation of the whole idiom is 'only one without a second one,' with freer translations being 'unique, unparalleled.'

Example 1: 据说，每个人的视网膜都是**独一无二**的，可以作为鉴别不同的人的最可靠的依据。

Jùshuō, měi ge rén de shìwǎngmó dōu shì dúyī-wú'èr de, kěyǐ zuòwéi jiànbié bùtóng de rén de zuì kěkào de yījù.

'It's said that every person's retina is unique; it can serve as the most accurate basis for discriminating among different people.'

Example 2: 耶路撒冷对于宗教研究有着**独一无**二的研究价值。

Yēlùsālěng duìyú zōngjiào yánjiū yǒuzhe dúyī-wú'èr de yánjiū jiàzhí.

'Jerusalem has unique research value for religious research.'

Usage: Functions as attributive and predicate.

Near Synonyms: [举世无双] (jǔ shì wú shuāng 舉世無雙) 'matchless, unrivaled,' [绝无仅有] (jué wú jǐn yǒu 絕無僅有) 'unique, one of a kind.'

Antonyms: [不足为奇] (bù zú wéi qí 不足為奇) 'not at all surprising,' [无独有偶] (wú dú yǒu ǒu 無獨有偶) 'not singly but in pairs,' [司空见惯] (sī kōng jiàn guàn 司空見慣) 'get used to seeing something and no longer find it strange,' [屡见不鲜] (lǚ jiàn bù xiān 屢見不鮮) 'often seen and nothing remarkable.'

102. 【兢兢业业】 (兢兢業業) jīng jīng yè yè

兢兢 means 'cautious' and 业业 means 'anxious.' A literal translation of the whole idiom is 'cautious and anxious.' Note that this idiom often conveys the additional sense of 'conscientious.' Freer translations include 'cautious and attentive' and 'careful and conscientious.'

Example 1: 他做任何事情都**兢兢业业**，让别人很放心。

Tā zuò rènhé shìqing dōu jīngjīng-yèyè, ràng biérén hěn fàngxīn.

'Whatever he does, he is careful and conscientious, letting others feel reassured.'

Example 2: 王老师教了几十年，**兢兢业业**地培养了一批又一批学生。

Wáng lǎoshī jiāole jǐ shí nián, jīngjīng-yèyè de péiyǎngle yì pī yòu yì pī xuésheng.

'Professor Wang has taught for several decades, carefully and conscientiously training one group of students after another.'

Usage: Functions mainly as predicate and adverbial.

Note: Complimentary in meaning.

Near Synonyms: [一丝不苟] (yì sī bù gǒu 一絲不苟) 'not the least bit negligent,' [脚踏实地] (jiǎo tà shí dì 腳踏實地) 'foot steps on solid ground – conscientious and dependable.'

Antonym: [敷衍了事] (fū yǎn liǎo shì 敷衍了事) 'do a perfunctory job.'

103. 【不折不扣】(不折不扣) bù zhé bú kòu

折 means 'discount' and 扣 'deduct.' The meaning of the whole idiom is 'to the letter, in every sense of the term, dyed-in-the-wool.'

Example 1: 她是个**不折不扣**的共产主义者。

Tā shì ge bùzhé-búkòu de gòngchǎnzhǔyìzhě.

'She is a dyed-in-the-wool Communist.'

Example 2: 地方政府应该**不折不扣**地执行中央的政策。

Dìfāng zhèngfǔ yīnggāi bùzhé-búkòu de zhíxíng zhōngyāng de zhèngcè.

'The local government should carry out the policies of the central government to the letter.'

Usage: Functions mainly as adverbial.

Near Synonyms: [地地道道] (dì dì dào dào 地地道道) 'genuine,' [彻头彻尾] (chè tóu chè wěi 徹頭徹尾) 'from head to foot.'

Antonyms: [添油加醋] (tiān yóu jiā cù 添油加醋) 'add oil add vinegar – add inflammatory details, embellish,' [画蛇添足] (huà shé tiān zú 畫蛇添足) 'draw snake add feet – add something superfluous.'

104. 【五花八门】(五花八門) wǔ huā bā mén

五花 or 'five flowers' refers to the Five Row battle formation and 八门 or 'eight gates' refers to the Eight Trigram battle formation in ancient Chinese military strategy. Both of these strategies involved many different kinds of tactics. Nowadays, this idiom means 'various, of all kinds, miscellaneous.'

Example 1: 这个商店出售**五花八门**的帽子。

Zhège shāngdiàn chūshòu wǔhuā-bāmén de màozi.

'This store sells hats of all kinds.'

Example 2: 她说尽管哲学上的流派**五花八门**，但是基本上可以归为两类，唯物主义和唯心主义。

Tā shuō jǐnguǎn zhéxué shàng de liúpài wǔhuā-bāmén, dànshì jīběn shàng kěyǐ guīwéi liǎng lèi, wéiwù zhǔyì hé wéixīn zhǔyì.

'She said that although there are various schools of philosophy, basically they can be categorized into two types, materialism and idealism.'

Usage: Functions as attributive and predicate.

Note: Slightly complimentary in meaning.

Near Synonyms: [形形色色] (xíng xíng sè sè 形形色色) 'of all hues, of all kinds,' [光怪陆离] (guāng guài lù lí 光怪陸離) 'grotesque and gaudy.'

Antonym: [一成不变] (yì chéng bú biàn 一成不變) 'fixed and unalterable.'

105. 【求同存异】(求同存異) qiú tóng cún yì

求 means 'seek,' 同 means 'similarity,' 存 means 'preserve,' and 异 means 'difference.' A literal translation of the whole idiom is 'seek sameness maintain difference.' A freer translation is 'seek common ground while maintaining differences.'

Example 1: 在这个问题上，虽然我们之间有一些分歧，但是也有不少共识，我们不妨**求同存异**，在此基础上寻求进一步的合作。

Zài zhège wèntí shàng, suīrán wǒmen zhījiān yǒu yìxiē fēnqí, dànshì yě yǒu bùshǎo gòngshí, wǒmen bùfáng qiútóng-cúnyì, zài cǐ jīchǔ shàng xúnqiú jìnyíbù de hézuò.

'Concerning this question, though there are a few differences between us, there are also quite a few points of consensus; we might as well maintain our differences while seeking common ground, and on this foundation seek further cooperation.'

Example 2: 我们本着**求同存异**的原则，希望与贵方发展友好关系。

Wǒmen běnzhe qiútóng-cúnyì de yuánzé, xīwàng yǔ guì fāng fāzhǎn yǒuhǎo guānxi.

'On the basis of the principle of maintaining our differences while seeking common ground, we hope to develop friendly relations with you.'

Usage: Functions mainly as predicate, can also function as attributive.

Near Synonyms: [百花齐放] (bǎi huā qí fàng 百花齊放) 'hundred flowers together open – different points of view exist simultaneously,' [取长补短] (qǔ cháng bǔ duǎn 取長補短) 'draw on the strong points of others to make up for one's own deficiencies,' [兼容并包] (jiān róng bìng bāo 兼容併包) 'simultaneously accommodate equally contain – indiscriminately all-inclusive.'

Antonyms: [求全责备] (qiú quán zé bèi 求全責備) 'seek perfection and find fault with everyone and everything,' [唯我独尊] (wéi wǒ dú zūn 唯我獨尊) 'only I alone respect – self-important, conceited.'

106. 【无能为力】(無能為力) wú néng wéi lì

无能 means 'have no ability to, be powerless to' and 为力 means 'exert oneself, make an effort.' A literal translation of the whole idiom is 'have no ability to make an effort,' with a freer translation being 'powerless, helpless.'

Example 1: 这件事情太大，即使总理也**无能为力**。

Zhè jiàn shìqing tài dà, jíshǐ zǒnglǐ yě wúnéng-wéilì.

'This matter is too big; even if it were the premier, he also would be powerless.'

Example 2: 医生耸了耸肩，表示**无能为力**了。

Yīshēng sǒngle sǒng jiān, biǎoshì **wúnéng-wéilì** le.

'The doctor shrugged her shoulders, indicating there was nothing she could do.'

Usage: Functions mainly as predicate.

Near Synonyms: [力不从心] (lì bù cóng xīn 力不從心) 'lack the ability to do what one would like to do,' [爱莫能助] (ài mò néng zhù 愛莫能助) 'want to help but not be in a position to do so.'

Antonyms: [得心应手] (dé xīn yìng shǒu 得心應手) 'do or handle expertly,' [举手之劳] (jǔ shǒu zhī láo 舉手之勞) 'the work involved in raising one's hand – slight effort, easy.'

107. 【一无所知】(一無所知) yì wú suǒ zhī

The meaning of this idiom is 'know absolutely nothing about something.'

Example 1: 不少人对于世界历史一**无所知**。

Bù shǎo rén duìyú shìjiè lìshǐ yìwúsuǒzhī.

'Not a few people know absolutely nothing about world history.'

Example 2: 那位国会议员说，他对儿子的违法行为一**无所知**。

Nà wèi guóhuì yìyuán shuō, tā duì érzi de wéifǎ xíngwéi yìwúsuǒzhī.

'That member of the National Assembly said he knew absolutely nothing about the illegal activities of his son.'

Usage: Functions mainly as predicate; usually preceded by 对 (duì 對).

Near Synonyms: [一窍不通] (yí qiào bù tōng 一竅不通) 'one gate not opened – know nothing about something,' [知之甚少] (zhī zhī shèn shǎo 知之甚少) 'know very little.'

Antonyms: [了如指掌] (liǎo rú zhǐ zhǎng 瞭如指掌) 'understand as well as one's own fingers and palms – completely clear,' [博古通今] (bó gǔ tōng jīn 博古通今) 'know much about both ancient and modern learning,' [学贯东西] (xué guàn dōng xī 學貫東西) 'thoroughly conversant with both Asian and Western knowledge.'

108. 【一席之地】(一席之地) yì xí zhī dì

席 means 'mat.' A literal translation of the whole idiom is 'the place for one mat.' By metaphor, this has come to mean 'a deserved place' or 'a proper place.'

Example 1: 席勒在德国文学史上占有一**席之地**。

Xílè zài Déguó wénxuéshǐ shàng zhànyǒu yìxí-zhīdì.

'Schiller has a deserved place in German literary history.'

Example 2: 张艺谋的电影为中国电影在世界舞台赢得**一席之地**。

Zhāng Yìmóu de diànyǐng wèi Zhōngguó diànyǐng zài shìjiè wǔtái yíngdé yìxí-zhīdì.

'Zhang Yimou's films have earned a deserved place for Chinese films on the world stage.'

Usage: Functions mainly as object, often preceded by verbs such as 占有 (zhànyǒu 佔有) 'possess,' 占据 (zhànjù 佔據) 'occupy,' or 赢得 (yíngdé 贏得) 'win.'

Near Synonym: [立锥之地] (lì zhuī zhī dì 立錐之地) '(enough) land to set up an awl – a scrap of land.'

Antonyms: [无边无际] (wú biān wú jì 無邊無際) 'without sides without borders – limitless,' [泰山北斗] (Tài Shān Běidǒu 泰山北斗) 'Mount Tai and the North Star – an eminent authority (in a learned field).'

109. 【轻而易举】(輕而易舉) qīng ér yì jǔ

轻 means 'light, not heavy,' 易 means 'easy,' and 举 means 'lift, raise.' The literal meaning is 'light and easy to lift,' with a freer translation being 'easy, easy as pie, without much effort.'

Example 1: 这件事看似简单，但是绝非一件**轻而易举**的事。

Zhè jiàn shì kànsì jiǎndān, dànshì juéfēi yíjiàn qīng'éryìjǔ de shì.

'This matter looks simple, but it's absolutely not a very easy thing.'

Example 2: 那支足球队太强大，因此**轻而易举**地战胜了对手。

Nà zhī zúqiúduì tài qiángdà, yīncǐ qīng'éryìjǔ de zhànshèngle duìshǒu.

'That soccer team is too powerful, so they easily defeated their opponents.'

Usage: Functions mainly as attributive; can also serve as adverbial and predicate.

Near Synonym: [易如反掌] (yì rú fǎn zhǎng 易如反掌) 'as easy as turning one's palms over – very easy.'

Antonym: [难于上青天] (nán yú shàng qīng tiān 難於上青天) 'harder than ascending into the blue sky.'

110. 【亡羊补牢】(亡羊補牢) wáng yáng bǔ láo

亡 means 'lose,' 补 means 'mend, repair,' and 牢 means 'sheep pen.' A literal translation of the idiom is 'mend the sheep pen when one loses sheep.' This is a metaphor for it never being too late to figure out a way to solve a problem that has arisen. English translations include 'it's never too late' and 'better late than never.'

Example 1: 虽然她在预赛中失利，但是**亡羊补牢**，决赛中取得了优异的成绩。

Suīrán tā zài yùsài zhōng shīlì, dànshì wángyáng-bǔláo, juésài zhōng qǔdéle yōuyì de chéngjì.

'Even though she suffered a setback in the preliminary competition, it's never too late to fix a problem; so she obtained outstanding results in the finals.'

Example 2: 你不要过分责备自己，**亡羊补牢**，还不算晚，以后多注意就是了。

Nǐ búyào guòfèn zébèi zìjǐ, wángyáng-bǔláo, hái bú suàn wǎn, yǐhòu duō zhùyì jiù shìle.

'Don't reproach yourself excessively; it's never too late to solve a problem; just pay more attention in the future.'

Usage: Usually used independently, often followed by expressions such as 犹未晚 也 (yóu wèi wǎn yě 猶未晚也) or 为时未晚 (wéi shí wèi wǎn 為時未晚), both of which mean 'not yet late.'

Allusion: In ancient times there was a herdsman who kept many sheep in his household. One night, his sheep pen broke and a sheep was carried off by a wolf. The next day a neighbor came to comfort him and urged him to repair the sheep pen. But he said: "Since the sheep has already been carried off, what use is repairing the sheep pen? That sheep is not coming back." The neighbor said earnestly: "Haven't you heard the old saying 'To not send hunting dogs outside until you see rabbits is not considered too late; and to not repair a sheep pen until you lose a sheep is not considered tardy'? If you don't repair the sheep pen, you will suffer even greater losses." The herdsman didn't believe him; and so the next morning, three of his sheep were carried off by the wolf. (from "Stratagems of Chu," No. 4, in *Stratagems of the Warring States*)

Near Synonym: [知错就改] (zhī cuò jiù gǎi 知錯就改) 'as soon as you realize a mistake, correct it.'

Antonym: [屡教不改] (lǚ jiào bù gǎi 屢教不改) 'repeatedly teach someone but they don't change their ways.'

111. 【默默无闻】(默默無聞) mò mò wú wén

默默 means 'silently' and 闻 means 'hear of.' A literal translation of the whole idiom is 'silently and without anyone hearing of someone or something.' Freer translations include 'unknown to the public, anonymous.'

Example 1: 她以前是个**默默无闻**的歌手，但是上了春节晚会以后，一夜成名。

Tā yǐqián shì ge mòmò-wúwén de gēshǒu, dànshì shàngle chūnjié wǎnhuì yǐhòu, yí yè chéngmíng.

'She formerly was an unknown singer, but after she was on the Chinese New Year's evening program, she became famous overnight.'

Example 2: 老李在这个工作岗位上**默默无闻**地工作了三十年了。

Lǎo Lǐ zài zhège gōngzuò gǎngwèi shàng mòmò-wúwén de gōngzuòle sānshí nián le.

'Old Li has been working in this position quietly and unknown to the public for thirty years.'

Usage: Functions mainly as attributive, adverbial, and predicate.

Near Synonym: [无声无息] (wú shēng wú xī 無聲無息) 'no sound no breath – silent.'

Antonyms: [众所周知] (zhòng suǒ zhōu zhī 眾所周知) 'as is known to all,' [家喻户晓] (jiā yù hù xiǎo 家喻戶曉) 'known to every family, widely known,' [鼎鼎大名] (dǐng dǐng dà míng 鼎鼎大名) 'very famous, renowned,' [赫赫有名] (hè hè yǒu míng 赫赫有名) 'celebrated and famous, illustrious.'

112. 【迫不及待】(迫不及待) pò bù jí dài

迫 means 'urgent, pressing,' 不及 means 'not be up to,' and 待 means 'wait.' The meaning of the whole idiom is 'too impatient to wait, be itching to do something, unable to hold oneself back.'

Example 1: 还没等客人把话说完，孩子就**迫不及待**地打开了客人送的礼物。

Hái méi děng kèrén bǎ huà shuōwán, háizi jiù pòbùjídài de dǎkāile kèrén sòng de lǐwù.

'Without waiting for the guests to finish talking, the children – who were too impatient to wait – opened the presents that the guests had given them.'

Example 2: 收到大学的录取通知书后，她**迫不及待**地把这个好消息告诉了所有的好朋友。

Shōudào dàxué de lùqǔ tōngzhīshū hòu, tā pòbùjídài de bǎ zhège hǎo xiāoxi gàosule suǒyǒu de hǎo péngyou.

'When she received the college's letter of admission, she couldn't wait to tell all her best friends this good news.'

Usage: Functions mainly as adverbial.

113. 【有声有色】(有聲有色) yǒu shēng yǒu sè

声 means 'sound' and 色 means 'color.' A literal translation of this idiom is 'have sound have color.' A freer translation is 'full of sound and color, vivid.'

Example 1: 他做了学生会主席以后，把学生会的活动搞得**有声有色**的。

Tā zuòle xuéshenghuì zhǔxí yǐhòu, bǎ xuéshenghuì de huódòng gǎode yǒushēng-yǒusè de.

'When he became chair of the student association, he did much to liven up the association's activities.'

Example 2: "读书月" 活动开展得**有声有色**。

"Dúshū Yuè" huódòng kāizhǎnde yǒushēng-yǒusè.

'"Reading Month" activities were launched full of sound and color.'

Usage: Functions mainly as verb complement, usually occurring after verbs such as 搞 (gǎo) 'do,' 办 (bàn 辦) 'handle,' 开展 (kāizhǎn 開展) 'develop,' and 进行 (jìnxíng 進行) 'conduct.'

Note: Complimentary in meaning.

Near Synonyms: [绘声绘色] (huì shēng huì sè 繪聲繪色) 'vivid, life-like,' [像模像样] (xiàng mó xiàng yàng 像模像樣) 'presentable, respectable' (used in spoken Chinese).

Antonym: [无声无息] (wú shēng wú xī 無聲無息) 'no sound no breath – silent.'

114. 【一心一意】(一心一意) yì xīn yí yì

A literal translation of this idiom is 'with one heart and one mind.' Freer translations include 'wholeheartedly, very attentively, with complete concentration.'

Example 1: 中国的政策是不在国际上出头，**一心一意**搞经济建设。

Zhōngguó de zhèngcè shì bú zài guójì shàng chūtóu, yìxīn-yíyì gǎo jīngjì jiànshè.

'Chinese policy is not to raise its head internationally, concentrating wholeheartedly on engaging in economic construction.'

Example 2: 他不一**心一意**地工作，在工作的时间炒股，因此被解雇了。

Tā bú yìxīn-yíyì de gōngzuò, zài gōngzuò de shíjiān chǎogǔ, yīncǐ bèi jiěgùle.

'He doesn't work with complete concentration; during working hours he traded stocks, therefore he was let go.'

Usage: Functions as adverbial.

Note: Complimentary in meaning.

Near Synonyms: [专心致志] (zhuān xīn zhì zhì 專心致志) 'with single-minded devotion,' [全心全意] (quán xīn quán yì 全心全意) 'with all one's heart and all one's soul,' [心无旁骛] (xīn wú páng wù 心無旁騖) 'single-minded.'

Antonyms: [三心二意] (sān xīn èr yì 三心二意) 'of two minds, half-hearted,' [心猿意马] (xīn yuán yì mǎ 心猿意馬) 'heart (agile as an) ape and thoughts (swift as a) horse – fanciful and fickle, capricious,' [朝三暮四] (zhāo sān mù sì 朝三暮四) 'fickle and inconstant.'

115. 【突如其来】(突如其來) tū rú qí lái

突 means 'sudden.' The meaning of the whole idiom is 'something that has come suddenly.'

Example 1: 大家都被这**突如其来**的消息吓呆了。

Dàjiā dōu bèi zhè tūrúqílái de xiāoxi xiàdāile.

'Everyone was scared out of their wits by this sudden news.'

Example 2: 一场**突如其来**的大地震夺走了几万个人的生命。

Yì cháng tūrúqílái de dà dìzhèn duózǒule jǐ wàn ge rén de shēngmìng.

'A sudden major earthquake took away the lives of tens of thousands of people.'

Usage: Functions mainly as attributive.

Near Synonym: [从天而降] (cóng tiān ér jiàng 從天而降) 'fall from the sky.'

Antonym: [意料之中] (yì liào zhī zhōng 意料之中) 'as might be expected.'

116. 【异军突起】(異軍突起) yì jūn tū qǐ

异 means 'another,' 军 means 'army,' 突 means 'suddenly,' and 起 means 'arise, emerge.' A literal translation of the whole idiom is 'another army suddenly emerges.' This is a metaphor meaning 'sudden appearance of a new force or new trend.'

Example 1: 去年以来，中国女子网球选手**异军突起**，在世界大赛上屡次获得好成绩。

Qùnián yǐlái, Zhōngguó nǚzǐ wǎngqiú xuǎnshǒu yìjūn-tūqǐ, zài shìjiè dàsài shàng lǚcì huòdé hǎo chéngjì.

'Since last year, the Chinese women's tennis players have turned a new leaf; at major international competitions, they have repeatedly obtained good results.'

Example 2: 那座城市的博彩业**异军突起**，占全市税收的百分之五十以上。

Nà zuò chéngshì de bócǎiyè yìjūn-tūqǐ, zhàn quán shì shuìshōu de bǎifēnzhī wǔshí yǐshàng.

'That city's gambling industry has started a new trend; it constitutes over fifty percent of the tax revenues for the whole city.'

Usage: Functions mainly as predicate; can also serve as attributive.

Near Synonym: [别开生面] (bié kāi shēng miàn 別開生面) 'start something new.'

Antonym: [万马齐喑] (wàn mǎ qí yīn 萬馬齊喑) 'ten thousand horses together mute – with nobody expressing an opinion.'

117. 【喜闻乐见】(喜聞樂見) xǐ wén lè jiàn

喜 means 'like,' 闻 means 'hear,' 乐 means 'glad,' and 见 means 'see.' A literal translation of the whole idiom is 'like to hear and glad to see.' A freer translation is 'love to see and hear.'

Example 1: 相声是人们**喜闻乐见**的艺术形式.

Xiàngshēng shì rénmen xǐwén-lèjiàn de yìshù xíngshì.

'Comic dialogues are an art form that people love to see and hear.'

Example 2: 近年来，她创作了大量的老百姓**喜闻乐见**的作品。

Jìn nián lái, tā chuàngzuòle dàliàng de lǎobǎixìng xǐwén-lèjiàn de zuòpǐn.

'During recent years, she created many works that the common people love to see and hear.'

Usage: Functions mainly as attributive.

Note: Complimentary in meaning.

Near Synonyms: [脍炙人口] (kuài zhì rén kǒu 膾炙人口) 'on everyone's lips,' [下里巴人] (xià lǐ bā rén 下里巴人) 'popular literature and art.'

Antonym: [阳春白雪] (yáng chūn bái xuě 陽春白雪) 'highbrow culture.'

118. 【任重道远】(任重道遠) rèn zhòng dào yuǎn

任 means 'burden' and 道 means 'road.' A literal translation of the whole idiom is 'the burden is heavy and the road is far,' with a freer translation being 'have heavy responsibilities that take a long time to fulfill.'

Example 1: 对全世界来说，消除贫苦**任重道远**。

Duì quán shìjiè lái shuō, xiāochú pínkǔ rènzhòng-dàoyuǎn.

'For the whole world, eliminating poverty is a heavy responsibility that will take a long time to fulfill.'

Example 2: 中国男足成为世界强队这一目标**任重道远**。

Zhōngguó nánzú chéngwéi shìjiè qiáng duì zhè yī mùbiāo rènzhòng-dàoyuǎn.

'This goal of China's male soccer team to become a strong team in the world is a heavy responsibility that will take many years of hard work to achieve.'

Usage: Functions mainly as predicate.

Antonym: [无所事事] (wú suǒ shì shì 無所事事) 'have nothing to do.'

119. 【无家可归】(無家可歸) wú jiā kě guī

归 means 'go back.' A literal translation is 'have no home that you can return to,' with a freer translation being 'homeless.'

Example 1: 台风过后，十万人**无家可归**。

Táifēng guò hòu, shíwàn rén wújiā-kěguī.

'After the typhoon had passed, 100,000 people were homeless.'

Example 2: 这个机构专门收养那些**无家可归**的小动物。

Zhège jīgòu zhuānmén shōuyǎng nàxiē wújiā-kěguī de xiǎo dòngwù.

'This organization specializes in adopting homeless small animals.'

Usage: Functions as predicate and attributive. Note also the expression 无家可归者 (wú jiā kě guī zhě 無家可歸者) 'homeless person.'

Near Synonym: [流离失所] (liú lí shī suǒ 流離失所) 'wander about and lose one's place – be destitute and homeless.'

Antonym: [四海为家] (sì hǎi wéi jiā 四海為家) 'the four seas are one's home – the whole world is one family, be able to move anywhere and feel at home.'

120. 【入木三分】(入木三分) rù mù sān fēn

A literal translation of the whole idiom is 'enter wood 3/10 of an inch (in calligraphy) – forceful, bold, sharp.' Originally, this referred to great strength in writing Chinese calligraphy, but later it came to be used as a metaphor for 'deep, astute, keen, or sharp.'

Example 1: 她对这部电影的评论**入木三分**，非常深刻。

Tā duì zhè bù diànyǐng de pínglùn rùmù-sānfēn, fēicháng shēnkè.

'Her review of this film is quite astute and extremely deep.'

Example 2: 他看人真是**入木三分**，一下子就看到别人的本质。

Tā kàn rén zhēn shì rùmù-sānfēn, yíxiàzi jiù kàndào biérén de běnzhì.

'He really is very astute in his observations of people, immediately seeing the basic character of others.'

Usage: Functions mainly as predicate and attributive.

Allusion: Wang Xizhi (303–361 C.E.) of the Jin Dyansty was the most famous calligrapher in Chinese history. He was not only naturally talented and smart but also very assiduous in his practice. He practiced writing characters at the bank of a pond, and every time when he finished writing, he would wash his brush and inkstone in the pond. As time went on, all the water in the pond turned black. Once, the emperor wanted to go to the outskirts of the city to offer sacrifices to the gods and told Wang Xizhi to write prayers on a wooden board with his brush. The emperor then had workers engrave the brush characters. But when the workers engraved the characters, they discovered that Wang Xizhi had so much power in his brush strokes that his calligraphy actually penetrated three-tenths of an inch into the wood.

Note: Complimentary in meaning.

Near Synonym: [一针见血] (yì zhēn jiàn xuě 一針見血) 'one prick of the needle and see blood – hit the nail on the head.'

Antonyms: [不得要领] (bù dé yào lǐng 不得要領) 'not obtain the essence – miss the point,' [略见一斑] (lüè jiàn yì bān 略見一斑) 'get just a glimpse of.'

121. 【意味深长】 (意味深長) yì wèi shēn cháng

意味 means 'meaning, significance' and 深长 means 'profound.' The meaning of the whole idiom is 'have profound significance.'

Example 1: 他**意味深长**地说，"是时候了。"

Tā yìwèi-shēncháng de shuō, "Shì shíhou le."

'With profound significance, he said, "It's time."'

Example 2: 邓小平的话总是很简单，但是却**意味深长**，比方说那个有名的"猫和老鼠"的评论。

Dèng Xiǎopíng de huà zǒngshì hěn jiǎndān, dànshì què yìwèi-shēncháng, bǐfāng shuō nàge yǒumíng de "māo hé lǎoshǔ" de pínglùn.

'Deng Xiaoping's words were always very simple, but they had a profound significance, for example, that famous comment about "the cat and the mouse."'

Usage: Functions mainly as adverbial, predicate, and attributive; often used in connection with verbs meaning 'say.'

Note: Complimentary in meaning.

Near Synonyms: [语重心长] (yǔ zhòng xīn cháng 語重心長) 'sincere, heartfelt,' [余音袅袅] (yú yīn niǎo niǎo 餘音裊裊) 'lingering sound.'

Antonyms: [戛然而止] (jiá rán ér zhǐ 戛然而止) 'stop suddenly,' [索然无味] (suǒ rán wú wèi 索然無味) 'dull and without flavor – insipid.'

122. 【继往开来】 (繼往開來) jì wǎng kāi lái

继 means 'succeed, continue,' 往 means 'the past,' 开 means 'open up, initiate,' and 来 means 'the future.' A literal translation of the whole idiom is 'succeed the past and initiate the future,' with freer translations being 'carry on the glorious traditions of the past and open up the way to the future.'

Example 1: 这是一次承前启后、**继往开来**的重要会议。

zhè shì yí cì chéngqián-qǐhòu, jìwǎng-kāilái de zhòngyào huìyì.

'This is an important conference that continues the past and develops the future, that carries on the fine traditions of the past and opens up the way to the future.'

Example 2: 新领导呼吁大家**继往开来**、再创辉煌。

Xīn lǐngdǎo hūyù dàjiā jìwǎng-kāilái, zài chuàng huīhuáng.

'The new leader appealed to everyone to carry on the traditions of the past and open up the way to the future, and recreate glory.'

Usage: Functions mainly as attributive and predicate.

Note: Complimentary in meaning.

Near Synonyms: [承前启后] (chéng qián qǐ hòu 承前啟後) 'continue the past and develop the future,' [承上启下] (chéng shàng qǐ xià 承上啟下) 'link the preceding with the following.'

Antonyms: [空前绝后] (kōng qián jué hòu 空前絕後) 'never before or since,' [青黄不接] (qīng huáng bù jiē 青黃不接) 'old crop and new crop don't connect – temporary shortage.'

123. 【耳目一新】(耳目一新) ěr mù yì xīn

耳 means 'ear' and 目 means 'eye.' The literal meaning of this idiom is 'ear eye entirely new.' Freer translations include 'brand-new sounds and sights, find everything fresh and new, the whole atmosphere has changed for the better, a whole new look, refreshing.'

Example 1: 他既熟悉中国的情况，又了解美国的情况，所以他的建议令人**耳目一新**。

Tā jì shúxī Zhōngguó de qíngkuàng, yòu liǎojiě Měiguó de qíngkuàng, suǒyǐ tā de jiànyì lìng rén ěrmù-yìxīn.

'He is both familiar with China's situation and also understands the U.S.'s situation, so his proposals make people feel they are very novel and refreshing.'

Example 2: 这种新产品的材料和样式都很特别，给人一种**耳目一新**的感觉。

Zhè zhǒng xīn chǎnpǐn de cáiliào hé yàngshì dōu hěn tèbié, gěi rén yì zhǒng ěrmù-yìxīn de gǎnjué.

'The materials and style of this kind of new product are both very special; they give people a kind of new and refreshing feeling.'

Usage: Functions mainly as predicate or attributive. As predicate, usually used after 让 (ràng 讓) / 令 (lìng) / 使人 (shǐrén) 'make people (feel) . . . .' As attributive, usually used in the phrases 给人～的感觉 (gěi rén ～ de gǎnjué 給人～的感覺) and 给人～之感 (gěi rén ～ zhī gǎn 給人～之感) 'give people a . . . feeling.'

Note: Has a positive connotation.

Near Synonym: [焕然一新] (huàn rán yì xīn 煥然一新) 'look brand-new, change beyond recognition.'

Antonyms: [一成不变] (yì chéng bú biàn 一成不變) 'fixed and unalterable,' [依然如故] (yī rán rú gù 依然如故) 'still the same as before.'

124. 【循序渐进】(循序漸進) xún xù jiàn jìn

循 means 'follow,' 序 means 'order,' 渐 means 'gradually,' and 进 means 'move forward.' A literal translation of the whole idiom is 'according to the order gradually move forward,' with a freer translation being 'follow in order and proceed step by step.'

Example 1: 做事不能太着急，要**循序渐进**，一步一个脚印。

Zuòshì bù néng tài zháojí, yào xúnxù-jiànjìn, yí bù yí ge jiǎoyìn.

'In one's work one must not be too anxious; one should follow the established order and proceed step by step, one step and one footprint at a time.'

Example 2: 国家已经制定政策，要**循序渐进**地发展农村的基础教育。

Guójiā yǐjīng zhìdìng zhèngcè, yào xúnxù-jiànjìn de fāzhǎn nóngcūn de jīchǔ jiàoyù.

'The nation has already formulated the policy; we should proceed step by step in developing basic education in the countryside.'

Usage: Functions mainly as adverbial and attributive.

Note: Complimentary in meaning.

Near Synonym: [按部就班] (àn bù jiù bān 按部就班) 'do things in an orderly fashion.'

Antonyms: [一蹴而就] (yí cù ér jiù 一蹴而就) 'accomplish in one move,' [过犹不及] (guò yóu bù jí 過猶不及) 'going too far is as bad as not going far enough.'

125. 【挺身而出】(挺身而出) tǐng shēn ér chū

挺 means 'straighten' and 身 means 'body.' The literal meaning of this idiom is 'straighten one's body and come out.' A freer translation is 'step forward courageously, come out boldly.'

Example 1: 出现不公正的事情的时候，老李总是**挺身而出**，说公道话。

Chūxiàn bù gōngzhèng de shìqing de shíhou, Lǎo Lǐ zǒngshì tǐngshēn-érchū, shuō gōngdào huà.

'When unjust things happen, Old Li always steps forward courageously and speaks fairly.'

Example 2: 面对凶恶的犯罪分子，警察**挺身而出**，保护了受害者。

Miànduì xiōng'è de fànzuì fènzǐ, jǐngchá tǐngshēn-érchū, bǎohùle shòuhàizhě.

'Facing vicious criminals, the policemen stepped forward bravely and protected the victim.'

Usage: Functions as predicate.

Note: Complimentary in meaning.

Near Synonym: [奋不顾身] (fèn bú gù shēn 奮不顧身) 'act boldly without regard for one's own life.'

Antonym: [畏缩不前] (wèi suō bù qián 畏縮不前) 'afraid to advance.'

126. 【滔滔不绝】(滔滔不絕) tāo tāo bù jué

滔滔 describes the continuous flow of water and 绝 means 'cut off.' The meaning of the whole idiom is 'talking on and on without stopping, incessant.'

Example 1: 他**滔滔不绝**地讲了两个小时，没有一句重复的话。

Tā tāotāo-bùjué de jiǎngle liǎng ge xiǎoshí, méiyǒu yí jù chóngfù de huà.

'He talked incessantly for two hours, without a single repeated phrase.'

Example 2: 说起年轻时候的事情来，她**滔滔不绝**。

Shuōqǐ niánqīng shíhou de shìqing lái, tā tāotāo-bùjué.

'When she starts talking about things from when she was young, she just keeps on talking without stopping.'

Usage: Functions mainly as adverbial and predicate.

Near Synonyms: [口若悬河] (kǒu ruò xuán hé 口若懸河) 'mouth like a fast-flowing river – eloquent,' [源源不断] (yuán yuán bú duàn 源源不斷) 'in an endless stream,' [侃侃而谈] (kǎn kǎn ér tán 侃侃而談) 'speak with confidence and conviction.'

Antonyms: [张口结舌] (zhāng kǒu jié shé 張口結舌) 'open mouth tie tongue – at a loss for words,' [哑口无言] (yǎ kǒu wú yán 啞口無言) 'dumb and without words – speechless.'

127. 【天翻地覆】(天翻地覆) tiān fān dì fù

翻 means 'turn over' and 覆 means 'overturn.' A literal translation is 'heavens overturn earth overturns.' A freer translation is 'earth-shaking, causing cataclysmic changes.'

Example 1: 改革开放以后，中国发生了**天翻地覆**的变化。

Gǎigé kāifàng yǐhòu, Zhōngguó fāshēngle tiānfān-dìfù de biànhuà.

'After the reforms and opening to the outside world, in China there occurred earth-shaking changes.'

Example 2: 夫妻吵架，把整个大家庭闹得**天翻地覆**。

Fūqī chǎojià, bǎ zhěng ge dà jiātíng nàode tiānfān-dìfù.

'The husband and wife quarreled, causing a huge ruckus for the whole big family.'

Usage: Functions mainly as complement, attributive, and predicate.

Antonym: [一成不变] (yì chéng bú biàn 一成不變) 'fixed and unalterable.'

128. 【不言而喻】(不言而喻) bù yán ér yù

言 means 'speak' and 喻 means 'understand.' The whole idiom means 'it goes without saying, be obvious.'

Example 1: 在总统选举中，他出了丑闻，结果**不言而喻**。

Zài zǒngtǒng xuǎnjǔ zhōng, tā chūle chǒuwén, jiéguǒ bùyán-éryù.

'In the presidential election, a scandal arose about him, with the obvious result.'

Example 2: 中国有七亿多农民，所以农业问题在中国的经济中**不言而喻**。

Zhōngguó yǒu qī yì duō nóngmín, suǒyǐ nóngyè wèntí zài Zhōngguó de jīngjì zhōng bùyán-éryù.

'China has over 700 million peasants, so in China's economy, agricultural issues are obvious in their importance.'

Usage: Functions as predicate.

Near Synonym: [显而易见] (xiǎn ér yì jiàn 顯而易見) 'obviously, clearly.'

Antonym: [模棱两可] (mó léng liǎng kě 模棱兩可) 'ambiguous.'

129. 【再接再厉】(再接再厲) zài jiē zài lì

再 means 'again,' 接 here means 'join (battle),' and 厉 here means 'sharpen.' A literal translation of the whole idiom is 'again join (battle) again sharpen (one's weapon).' This originally referred to the habit some roosters had of sharpening their beaks prior to fighting. Freer translations of the idiom include 'redouble one's efforts' and 'make sustained and persistent efforts.'

Example 1: 你们已经取得了很大的成绩，希望你们**再接再厉**，取得更大的成绩。

Nǐmen yǐjīng qǔdéle hěn dà de chéngjì, xīwàng nǐmen zàijiē-zàilì, qǔdé gèng dà de chéngjì.

'You have already attained great achievements; I hope you redouble your efforts and attain even greater achievements.'

Example 2: 她输了前两盘，但是赢了第三盘，后来**再接再厉**，赢了最后两盘，最终以3:2取得了胜利。

Tā shūle qián liǎng pán, dànshì yíngle dìsān pán, hòulái zàijiē-zàilì, yíngle zuìhòu liǎng pán, zuìzhōng yǐ sān bǐ èr qǔdéle shènglì.

'She lost the first two games, but won the third game; later she redoubled her efforts and won the last two games, in the end attaining victory with a score of 3 to 2.'

Usage: Functions as predicate.

Note: Complimentary in meaning.

Near Synonyms: [不屈不挠] (bù qū bù náo 不屈不撓) 'refuse to submit,' [屡败屡战] (lǚ bài lǚ zhàn 屢敗屢戰) 'repeatedly be defeated repeatedly fight – fight on despite repeated setbacks.'

Antonym: [得过且过] (dé guò qiě guò 得過且過) 'drift or muddle along.'

130. 【杞人忧天】(杞人憂天) Qǐ rén yōu tiān

杞 is the name of a country in ancient China and 忧 means 'worry about.' A literal translation of the whole idiom is '(like) the person from Qi who worried about the sky (falling down).' This is a metaphor for 'groundless fears' or 'alarmism.'

Example 1: 把心放到肚子里去吧，不会有事的。你这是**杞人忧天**。

Bǎ xīn fàngdào dùzi lǐ qù ba, bú huì yǒu shì de. Nǐ zhè shì Qǐrén-yōutiān.

'Put your heart at ease, nothing will happen. You're being like the man of Qi who was worried about the sky falling in.'

Example 2: 教练们的担心并非**杞人忧天**，世界排名第一的选手有过被排名一百以外的选手打败的例子。

Jiàoliànmen de dānxīn bìngfēi Qǐrén-yōutiān, shìjiè páimíng dìyī de xuǎnshǒu yǒuguo bèi páimíng yìbǎi yǐwài de xuǎnshǒu dǎbài de lìzi.

'The coaches' worries were not totally groundless; there were examples of athletes ranked number one in the world who had been defeated by athletes who didn't rank in the top 100.'

Usage: Functions mainly as predicate, often preceded by 是 (shì) 'be a situation of' or 并非 (bìngfēi 並非) 'by no means be a situation of.'

Allusion: In the country of Qi there was a man who worried all day long that the sky would collapse and the earth would sink, and that he would then have no place to stay. For this reason, he couldn't eat all day or sleep well all night. The man had a friend who was worried about him, who explained: "The sky is a mass of air and air is everywhere. All of your breaths and actions take place in air; and you're worried that the sky will fall in?" The man responded: "If the sky is a mass of air, then wouldn't the sun, moon, and stars in the sky fall down?" His friend replied: "Those are merely things in the air that emit light; even if they fell, they wouldn't hurt anyone." Then the man asked: "What should we do if the earth sinks?" His friend answered: "The earth is merely clumps of earth that have been piled up. They have filled up all places everywhere, there being no place that does not have clumps of earth. You walk on the earth every day; why do you worry that the earth will sink?" After he had heard his friend's words, the man felt reassured and became happier. And his friend was happy, too. (from "Tian Rui" in *Liezi*)

Note: Derogatory in meaning.

Near Synonym: [庸人自扰] (yōng rén zì rǎo 庸人自擾) 'mediocre people bring troubles upon themselves.'

Antonyms: [无忧无虑] (wú yōu wú lǜ 無憂無慮) 'have no worries or anxieties at all,' [怡然自得] (yí rán zì dé 怡然自得) 'content and pleased with oneself.'

131. 【风云变幻】(風雲變幻) fēng yún biàn huàn

风 means 'wind,' 云 means 'cloud,' and 变幻 means 'change often and unpredictably.' A literal translation of this idiom is 'wind and clouds change often,' with freer translations including 'constantly changing, changeable.'

Example 1: 国际局势**风云变幻**，我们得做好充分准备。

Guójì júshì fēngyún-biànhuàn, wǒmen děi zuò hǎo chōngfèn zhǔnbèi.

'The international situation is constantly changing; we must make full preparations.'

Example 2: 在**风云变幻**的股票市场，任何疏忽都会造成巨大的损失。

Zài fēngyún-biànhuàn de gǔpiào shìchǎng, rènhé shūhū dōu huì zàochéng jùdà de sǔnshī.

'In the constantly shifting stock market, any negligence will cause giant losses.'

Usage: Functions mainly as attributive and predicate.

Near Synonyms: [捉摸不定] (zhuō mō bú dìng 捉摸不定) 'difficult to ascertain, hard to fathom,' [波谲云诡] (bō jué yún guǐ 波譎雲詭) 'wave cheats cloud deceives – change constantly.'

Antonym: [一成不变] (yì chéng bú biàn 一成不變) 'fixed and unalterable.'

132. 【淋漓尽致】(淋漓盡致) lín lí jìn zhì

The literal meaning of this idiom is 'soak thoroughly until dripping wet,' but it is usually used in the sense of 'thoroughly.'

Example 1: 比赛中，她把自己的特长发挥得**淋漓尽致**，最终取得了比赛的胜利。

Bǐsài zhōng, tā bǎ zìjǐ de tècháng fāhuī de línlí-jìnzhì, zuìzhōng qǔdéle bǐsài de shènglì.

'During the competition, she brought her special skills into thorough play, ultimately winning the competition.'

Example 2: 这部小说**淋漓尽致**地反映了十九世纪英国煤矿工人的生活。

Zhè bù xiǎoshuō línlí-jìnzhì de fǎnyìngle shíjiǔ shìjì Yīngguó méikuàng gōngrén de shēnghuó.

'This novel thoroughly reflects the life of 19th century English coal miners.'

Usage: Functions mainly as complement and attributive; can also serve as attributive.

Near Synonym: [酣畅淋漓] (hān chàng lín lí 酣暢淋漓) 'to one's heart's content.'

133. 【忧心忡忡】(憂心忡忡) yōu xīn chōng chōng

忧心 means 'worry' and 忡忡 means 'sad and worried.' The meaning of the whole idiom is 'sad and worried.'

Example 1: 父母们对电视上的涉及暴力和性内容的节目**忧心忡忡**，生怕孩子受到不良习气的影响。

Fùmǔmen duì diànshì shàng de shèjí bàolì hé xìng nèiróng de jiémù yōuxīn-chōngchōng, shēngpà háizi shòudào bù liáng xíqì de yǐngxiǎng.

'The parents were very worried about the programs on television that involved violence and sexual content, very much afraid that their child would be influenced by the bad habits.'

Example 2: 总理**忧心忡忡**地说，"没想到情况这么严重。"

Zǒnglǐ yōuxīn-chōngchōng de shuō: "Méi xiǎngdào qíngkuàng zhème yánzhòng."

'The premier said, sad and worried, "I wouldn't have thought the situation would be so serious."'

Usage: Functions mainly as predicate, adverbial, and attributive.

Near Synonyms: [心事重重] (xīn shì chóng chóng 心事重重) 'in one's heart have layer upon layer of worries,' [惴惴不安] (zhuì zhuì bù ān 惴惴不安) 'fearful and uneasy.'

Antonyms: [满面春风] (mǎn miàn chūn fēng 滿面春風) 'whole face spring breeze – radiant with happiness,' [喜上眉梢] (xǐ shàng méi shāo 喜上眉梢) 'radiant with joy.'

134. 【直截了当】(直截了當) zhí jié liǎo dàng

直截 means 'direct' and 了当 means 'straightforward.' The meaning of the whole idiom is 'direct, straightforward.'

Example 1: 你有什么话就**直截了当**地说吧，别绕弯子。

Nǐ yǒu shénme huà jiù zhíjié-liǎodàng de shuō ba, bié rào wānzi.

'If you have anything to say, say it directly, don't beat around the bush.'

Example 2: 记者**直截了当**地问，"你跟她到底什么关系？"

Jìzhě zhíjié-liǎodàng de wèn: "Nǐ gēn tā dàodǐ shénme guānxi?"

'The reporter asked directly, "What's your relationship to her?"'

Usage: Functions mainly as adverbial.

Note: Complimentary in meaning; used to describe speech or actions. Also written as 直接了当 (zhí jiē liǎo dàng 直接了當), with the second syllable in tone one.

Near Synonyms: [开门见山] (kāi mén jiàn shān 開門見山) 'open the door and see the mountain – come straight to the point,' [单刀直入] (dān dāo zhí rù 單刀直入) 'single sword enters straight – come straight to the point.'

Antonym: [转弯抹角] (zhuǎn wān mò jiǎo 轉彎抹角) 'a tortuous route, beat around the bush.'

135. 【眼花缭乱】(眼花繚亂) yǎn huā liáo luàn

眼花 means 'blurry vision' and 缭乱 means 'confused, chaotic.' The meaning of the whole idiom can be either 'confused, dazzled' or 'confusing, dazzling.'

Example 1: 中国武打片里**眼花缭乱**的动作让外国人看了大吃一惊。

Zhōngguó wǔdǎpiān lǐ **yǎnhuā-liáoluàn** de dòngzuò ràng wàiguó rén kànle dà chī yì jīng.

'The dazzling movements in Chinese acrobatic fighting films astonish foreigners when they have seen them.'

Example 2: 十多个人竞争民主党总统候选人，每个人都有一套自己的政治主张，这可能让部分选民**眼花缭乱**。

Shí duō ge rén jìngzhēng Mínzhǔdǎng zǒngtǒng hòuxuǎnrén, měi ge rén dōu yǒu yí tào zìjǐ de zhèngzhì zhǔzhāng, zhè kěnéng ràng bùfen xuǎnmín **yǎnhuā-liáoluàn**.

'More than a dozen people competing for Democratic presidential nominee, each with his or her own political views – this may confuse a portion of the voters.'

Usage: Functions as predicate in the structure 令 (lìng) / 让 (ràng 讓) 'make' + 人 (rén) 'people' + 眼花缭乱.

Near Synonyms: [目不暇接] (mù bù xiá jiē 目不暇接) 'so much that the eyes cannot take it all in,' [头昏眼花] (tóu hūn yǎn huā 頭昏眼花) 'head unconscious eyes blurred – dizzy,' [五花八门] (wǔ huā bā mén 五花八門) 'various, of all kinds.'

Antonym: [心如止水] (xīn rú zhǐ shuǐ 心如止水) 'heart like stopped waters – have no emotions.'

136. 【不屈不挠】(不屈不撓) bù qū bù náo

屈 means 'submit' and 挠 means 'bent, crooked.' The whole idiom means 'refuse to submit, stick to one's guns.'

Example 1: 在困难面前，他**不屈不挠**，努力奋斗，最后胜利了。

Zài kùnnán miànqián, tā **bùqū-bùnáo**, nǔlì fèndòu, zuìhòu shènglì le.

'In the face of difficulty he refused to submit, struggling hard and succeeding in the end.'

Example 2: 中国人民经过**不屈不挠**的斗争，最终赢得了独立。

Zhōngguó rénmín jīngguò bùqū-bùnáo de dòuzhēng, zuìzhōng yíngdéle dúlì.

'After an unyielding struggle, the Chinese people ultimately won independence.'

Usage: Functions mainly as attributive and predicate. As attributive, some kind of 'struggle' is often mentioned after it.

Note: Complimentary in meaning.

Near Synonym: [百折不挠] (bǎi zhé bù náo 百折不撓) 'undaunted despite many setbacks.'

Antonyms: [卑躬屈膝] (bēi gōng qū xī 卑躬屈膝) 'bow low and humiliate oneself, submissive or deferential,' [奴颜婢膝] (nú yán bì xī 奴顏婢膝) 'servility, subservience.'

137. 【语重心长】(語重心長) yǔ zhòng xīn cháng

语 here means 'manner of speaking,' 重 means 'serious,' 心 means 'intention,' and 长 here means 'profound.' A literal translation of the whole idiom is 'with a serious manner of speaking and profound intention,' with freer translations being 'sincere' and 'heartfelt.'

Example 1: 母亲**语重心长**地对女儿说："孩子，找对象绝对不能找三心二意的。"

Mǔqīn yǔzhòng-xīncháng de duì nǚ'ér shuō: "Háizi, zhǎo duìxiàng juéduì bù néng zhǎo sānxīn-èryì de."

'The mother said in a heartfelt manner to her daughter: "Child, when you look for someone to marry, you absolutely must not look for someone who is of two minds."'

Example 2: 看着灾民，总理**语重心长**地说："你们受苦了，有什么困难就跟政府说。"

Kànzhe zāimín, zǒnglǐ yǔzhòng-xīncháng de shuō: "Nǐmen shòukǔ le, yǒu shénme kùnnán jiù gēn zhèngfǔ shuō."

'Seeing the disaster victims, the premier said in a very heartfelt way: "You all have suffered hardship; tell the government about whatever hardships you have."'

Usage: Functions mainly as adverbial, usually followed by the verb 说 (shuō 說) 'say.'

Note: Complimentary in meaning.

Near Synonyms: [推心置腹] (tuī xīn zhì fù 推心置腹) 'treat someone honestly and sincerely,' [情真意切] (qíng zhēn yì qiē 情真意切) 'with genuine feelings and warm intentions.'

Antonyms: [轻描淡写] (qīng miáo dàn xiě 輕描淡寫) 'treat a matter lightly and superficially,' [不痛不痒] (bú tòng bù yǎng 不痛不癢) 'not hurt not itch – scratching the surface, superficial.'

138. 【栩栩如生】(栩栩如生) xǔ xǔ rú shēng

栩栩 means 'lively, vivid, lifelike' and 如生 means 'like life.' The meaning of the whole idiom is 'lifelike.'

Example 1: 杜莎夫人蜡像馆里的蜡像个个**栩栩如生**。

Dùshā fūrén làxiàngguǎn lǐ de làxiàng gègè xǔxǔ-rúshēng.

'Every one of the wax figures in Madame Tussaud's wax museum is very lifelike.'

Example 2: 那幅画上的马**栩栩如生**，就像真的马在奔跑。

Nà fú huà shàng de mǎ xǔxǔ-rúshēng, jiù xiàng zhēn de mǎ zài bēnpǎo.

'The horses in that painting are very lifelike, just like real horses that are running.'

Usage: Functions mainly as predicate and attributive; can also serve as adverbial.

Note: Complimentary in meaning.

Near Synonyms: [惟妙惟肖] (wéi miào wéi xiào 惟妙惟肖) and [活灵活现] (huó líng huó xiàn 活靈活現) 'lifelike.'

Antonyms: [奄奄一息] (yǎn yǎn yì xī 奄奄一息) 'breathe feebly, dying,' [死气沉沉] (sǐ qì chén chén 死氣沉沉) 'lifeless.'

139. 【呕心沥血】(嘔心瀝血) ǒu xīn lì xuè

呕 means 'vomit,' 沥 means 'drip, trickle,' and 血 means 'blood.' A literal translation of the whole idiom is 'vomit one's heart and let drip out one's blood,' with a freer translation being 'work one's heart out.'

Example 1: 父母为了儿女长大以后能够过上幸福的生活，可以说是**呕心沥血**。

Fùmǔ wèile érnǚ zhǎngdà yǐhòu nénggòu guòshàng xìngfú de shēnghuó, kěyǐ shuō shì ǒuxīn-lìxuè.

'So that their children after they grow up can lead a happy life, one could say that parents work their hearts out.'

Example 2: 他几十年来**呕心沥血**地改造沙漠，挽救了几万亩良田。

Tā jǐ shí nián lái ǒuxīn-lìxuè de gǎizào shāmò, wǎnjiùle jǐ wàn mǔ liángtián.

'The last few decades he has been working his heart out to transform the desert, saving tens of thousands of acres of fertile farmland.'

Usage: Functions mainly as predicate; can also serve as adverbial and attributive.

Note: Complimentary in meaning.

Near Synonyms: [殚精竭虑] (dān jīng jié lǜ 殫精竭慮) 'rack one's brains,' [鞠躬尽瘁] (jū gōng jìn cuì 鞠躬盡瘁) 'do one's utmost to the point of exhaustion,' [煞费苦心] (shà fèi kǔ xīn 煞費苦心) 'take great pains.'

Antonyms: [无所用心] (wú suǒ yòng xīn 無所用心) 'not give serious thought to something,' [敷衍塞责] (fū yǎn sè zé 敷衍塞責) 'do a perfunctory job.'

140. 【毛遂自荐】 (毛遂自薦) Máo Suì zì jiàn

毛遂 is the name of a person and 荐 means 'recommend.' A literal translation is 'Mao Sui recommended himself,' with a freer translation of the whole idiom being 'volunteer.'

Example 1: 电影剧组还缺一位演男二号的人，她**毛遂自荐**，化妆后演了那个角色。

Diànyǐng jùzǔ hái quē yí wèi yǎn nán èrhào de rén, tā Máo Suì-zìjiàn, huàzhuāng hòu yǎnle nàge juésè.

'In the film crew they are still lacking someone to play the role of male number two; she volunteered and, after putting on make-up, played that role.'

Example 2: 他用**毛遂自荐**的方式给附近各个公司的人事部门经理打电话，希望能够找到一份工作。

Tā yòng Máo Suì-zìjiàn de fāngshì gěi fùjìn gègè gōngsī de rénshì bùmén jīnglǐ dǎ diànhuà, xīwàng nénggòu zhǎodào yí fèn gōngzuò.

'He used the way of Mao Sui when he recommended himself, calling the managers of the personnel departments of all the companies in the vicinity, in hopes of being able to find a job.'

Usage: Functions mainly as predicate.

Allusion: Mao Sui (approx. 285–228 B.C.E.) was a retainer of Lord Pingyuan, prince of Zhao during the Warring States Period. Lord Pingyuan had over 3,000 retainers, of which Mao Sui was one of the lowest-ranking. In 259 B.C.E., the army of the state of Qin surrounded the capital of Zhao, and Lord Pingyuan was about to go to the state of Chu in the south to seek relief. He was planning to take along twenty retainers. When he had chosen nineteen of them, Mao Sui demanded to be included. Lord Pingyuan said to Mao Sui: "You've been in my household for three years but I've never heard anyone talk about you, so you must not have any special abilities." Mao Sui replied: "That's because you've never made use of my talents before; otherwise, my talents would have been obvious long ago." So Lord Pingyuan took Mao Sui along to the state of Chu. When they arrived in Chu, Lord Pingyuan and the king of Chu talked for half a day without any result, so Mao Sui – risking his life – explained clearly to the king of Chu the benefits for the state of Chu in cooperating with the state of Zhao; in the end, he convinced the king of Chu. The state of Chu then sent its army to rescue the state of Zhao. When all this was over, Lord Pingyuan evaluated Mao Sui as follows: "With his persuasive speaking skills, this gentleman is stronger than a million troops. In the future, I shall never again dare to evaluate someone without taking the task very seriously." And so he promoted Mao Sui to be a very high-ranking retainer. (from "Pingyuan Jun Yuqing Liezhuan" in *Records of the Grand Historian*)

Note: Complimentary in meaning.

Near Synonym: [自告奋勇] (zì gào fèn yǒng 自告奮勇) 'volunteer.'

Antonyms: [韬光养晦] (tāo guāng yǎng huì 韜光養晦) 'conceal one's abilities and bide one's time,' [自惭形秽] (zì cán xíng huì 自慚形穢) 'feel inferior, feel unworthy.'

141. 【方兴未艾】(方興未艾) fāng xīng wèi ài

方 here means 'just now,' 兴 means 'rise,' 未 means 'not yet,' and 艾 means 'stop.' A literal translation of the whole idiom is 'just now rising and not yet stopped,' with freer translations being 'on the rise, on the upswing.'

Example 1: 在中国 "英语热" **方兴未艾**。

Zài Zhōngguó "Yīngyǔ rè" fāngxīng-wèi'ài.

'In China, the "English craze" is still on the upswing.'

Example 2: 据说这家电信巨头要在**方兴未艾**的生物医学领域投入大笔资金。

Jùshuō zhè jiā diànxìn jùtóu yào zài fāngxīng-wèi'ài de shēngwù yīxué lǐngyù tóurù dà bǐ zījīn.

'It is said that this telecommunications magnate wants to invest a huge sum of capital in the rapidly rising realm of biomedicine.'

Usage: Functions mainly as predicate and attributive.

Near Synonym: [崭露头角] (zhǎn lù tóu jiǎo 嶄露頭角) 'distinguish oneself.'

Antonyms: [穷途末路] (qióng tú mò lù 窮途末路) 'dead end, impasse,' [日暮途穷] (rì mù tú qióng 日暮途窮) 'in the evening when one's road is exhausted – toward the end of one's days.'

142. 【聚精会神】(聚精會神) jù jīng huì shén

聚 means 'collect,' 会 means 'concentrate,' and the noun object 精神 (which is here split into 精 and 神) means 'energy.' The meaning of the whole idiom is 'with total concentration.'

Example 1: 上课的时候，学生们**聚精会神**地听老师讲课。

Shàngkè de shíhou, xuéshengmen jùjīng-huìshén de tīng lǎoshī jiǎngkè.

'In class, the students listened to the teacher lecture with total concentration.'

Example 2: 中国需要一个和平稳定的周边环境，以便**聚精会神**地搞国内建设。

Zhōngguó xūyào yí ge hépíng wěndìng de zhōubiān huánjìng, yǐbiàn jùjīng-huìshén de gǎo guónèi jiànshè.

'China needs a peaceful and stable peripheral environment, so that it can with total concentration engage in domestic construction.'

Usage: Functions mainly as adverbial; can also serve as predicate.

Near Synonyms: [专心致志] (zhuān xīn zhì zhì 專心致志) 'with single-minded devotion,' [全神贯注] (quán shén guan zhù 全神貫注) 'give one's undivided attention to.'

Antonyms: [心不在焉] (xīn bú zài yān 心不在焉) 'heart is not there – absent-minded, distracted,' [神不守舍] (shén bù shǒu shè 神不守舍) 'not thinking straight,' [心猿意马] (xīn yuán yì mǎ 心猿意馬) 'heart (agile as an) ape and thoughts (swift as a) horse – fanciful and fickle, capricious.'

143. 【比比皆是】(比比皆是) bǐ bǐ jiē shì

比比 means 'everywhere' and 皆 means 'all.' A literal translation of the whole idiom is 'everywhere in all cases it is,' with freer translations being 'can be found everywhere, great in number, in abundance.'

Example 1: 这是一个富人区，豪华轿车**比比皆是**。

Zhè shì yíge fùrén qū, háohuá jiàochē bǐbǐ-jiēshì.

'This is a district of rich people; luxury automobiles can be found everywhere.'

Example 2: 在欧洲，会说五种以上语言的人**比比皆是**。

Zài Ōuzhōu, huì shuō wǔ zhǒng yǐshàng yǔyán de rén bǐbǐ-jiēshì.

'In Europe, people who can speak five or more languages can be found everywhere.'

Usage: Functions as predicate.

Near Synonym: [俯拾皆是] (fǔ shí jiē shì 俯拾皆是) 'so many you can bend down and pick them up easily.'

Antonyms: [寥寥无几] (liáo liáo wú jǐ 寥寥無幾) 'very few,' [屈指可数] (qū zhǐ kě shǔ 屈指可數) 'can be counted on the fingers, very few.'

144. 【高瞻远瞩】(高瞻遠矚) gāo zhān yuǎn zhǔ

瞻 means 'gaze' and 矚 here means 'look at with attention.' A literal translation of the whole idiom is 'look out from on high and see far,' with freer translations including 'far sighted' and 'take a long-range or long-term approach to something.'

Example 1: 她**高瞻远瞩**，在能源危机到来以前很多年，就提出了要发展新能源的主张。

Tā gāozhān-yuǎnzhǔ, zài néngyuán wēijī dào lái yǐqián hěn duō nián, jiù tíchūle yào fāzhǎn xīn néngyuán de zhǔzhāng.

'She is very far sighted, having many years before the coming of the energy crisis already put forward the suggestion to develop new sources of energy.'

Example 2: 邓小平**高瞻远瞩**，用"一国两制"的办法成功地解决了香港和澳门问题。

Dèng Xiǎopíng gāozhān-yuǎnzhǔ, yòng "Yì Guó Liǎng Zhì" de bànfǎ chénggōng de jiějuéle Xiānggǎng hé Àomén wèntí.

'Deng Xiaoping was very far sighted, using the means of "One Country, Two Systems" to successfully solve the problem of Hong Kong and Macao.'

Usage: Functions mainly as predicate; can also serve as attributive and adverbial.

Note: Complimentary in meaning.

Near Synonym: [深谋远虑] (shēn móu yuǎn lǜ 深謀遠慮) 'circumspect and far sighted.'

Antonym: [鼠目寸光] (shǔ mù cùn guāng 鼠目寸光) 'rat eyes see (only) an inch of light – short sighted.'

145. 【无动于衷】(無動於衷) wú dòng yú zhōng

动 means 'move' and 衷 means 'heart.' A literal translation is 'there is no moving in the heart,' with freer translations of the whole idiom being 'unmoved, unconcerned.'

Example 1: 因为经历得多了，好像对这种事就**无动于衷**了。

Yīnwèi jīnglìde duōle, hǎoxiàng duì zhè zhǒng shì jiù wúdòng-yúzhōng le.

'Because she has experienced so much, it seems she is unmoved by this kind of thing.'

Example 2: 他**无动于衷**地说："不是我无情，而是没有办法。"

Tā wúdòng-yúzhōng de shuō: "Bú shì wǒ wúqíng, ér shì méiyǒu bànfǎ."

'Quite unmoved, he said: "It's not that I have no feelings, but that there is nothing that can be done."'

Usage: Functions mainly as predicate, often preceded by 对 (duì 對) 'by, about.'

Near Synonyms: [不动声色] (bú dòng shēng sè 不動聲色) 'not change one's voice or composure – calm and collected,' [漠不关心] (mò bù guān xīn 漠不關心) 'indifferent' (pejorative), [麻木不仁] (má mù bù rén 麻木不仁) 'numb, apathetic' (pejorative).

Antonym: [感人肺腑] (gǎn rén fèi fǔ 感人肺腑) 'deeply moving' (complimentary).

146. 【迫在眉睫】(迫在眉睫) pò zài méi jié

迫 here means 'urgent, pressing,' with 眉 meaning 'eyebrow' and 睫 meaning 'eyelash.' A literal translation of the whole idiom is 'pressing on the eyebrows and eyelashes.' Freer translations include 'very urgent' and 'imminent.'

Example 1: 社会养老保障制度的改革已经**迫在眉睫**。

Shèhuì yǎnglǎo bǎozhàng zhìdù de gǎigé yǐjīng pòzài-méijié.

'Reforms in Social Security Retirement System (lit. "social retirement protection system") are already imminent.'

Example 2: 对于这个公司来说，从银行得到贷款是**迫在眉睫**的问题。

Duìyú zhège gōngsī lái shuō, cóng yínháng dédào dàikuǎn shì pòzài-méijié de wèntí.

'For this company, to obtain a loan from a bank is an urgent problem.'

Usage: Functions mainly as predicate; can also serve as attributive.

Near Synonyms: [燃眉之急] (rán méi zhī jí 燃眉之急) 'the urgency of fire singeing the eyebrows – a matter of great urgency,' [火烧眉毛] (huǒ shāo méi máo 火燒眉毛) 'fire burns eyebrows – extremely urgent matter' (spoken Chinese).

Antonyms: [远在天边] (yuǎn zài tiān biān 遠在天邊) 'as remote as the ends of the earth,' [慢条斯理] (màn tiáo sī lǐ 慢條斯理) 'leisurely.'

147. 【触目惊心】(觸目驚心) chù mù jīng xīn

触目 means 'strike the eye, see' and 惊心 means 'alarmed in one's heart.' The meaning of the whole idiom is 'frightening, shocking.'

Example 1: 看到这些**触目惊心**的照片，没有人不会流泪。

Kàndào zhèxiē chùmù-jīngxīn de zhàopiàn, méiyǒu rén búhuì liúlèi.

'If they saw these shocking photographs, there is no one who would not shed tears.'

Example 2: 这种悲惨的情景让人**触目惊心**。

Zhè zhǒng bēicǎn de qíngjǐng ràng rén chùmù-jīngxīn.

'A tragic scene like this makes one feel shocked.'

Usage: Functions mainly as predicate and attributive. In general used for negative things.

Near Synonym: [心惊胆战] (xīn jīng dǎn zhàn 心驚膽戰) (also written as [心惊胆颤] (xīn jīng dǎn chàn 心驚膽顫)) 'terror-stricken.'

Antonym: [司空见惯] (sī kōng jiàn guan 司空見慣) 'get used to seeing something and no longer find it strange.'

148. 【无济于事】(無濟於事) wú jì yú shì

济 means 'help.' A literal translation of this idiom is 'has no help to matters.' A freer translation is 'to not help matters, of no avail, to no effect.'

Example 1: 父母一再劝说孩子，但是已经**无济于事**，孩子还是决定退学。

Fùmǔ yízài quànshuō háizi, dànshì yǐjīng wújì-yúshì, háizi háishì juédìng tuìxué.

'The parents repeatedly exhorted their child, but it was already of no avail; the child still decided to drop out of school.'

Example 2: 病人疼得厉害，这时候用普通的药物已经**无济于事**了，只能用那种进口的特效药。

Bìngrén téngde lìhai, zhè shíhou yòng pǔtōng de yàowù yǐjīng wújì-yúshì le, zhǐ néng yòng nà zhǒng jìnkǒu de tèxiàoyào.

'The patient was in great pain; at this time to use ordinary medicine no longer helped matters; they could only use that kind of imported, specially potent medicine.'

Usage: Functions as predicate.

Near Synonym: [于事无补] (yú shì wú bǔ 於事無補) 'of no help to matters.'

Antonym: [行之有效] (xíng zhī yǒu xiào 行之有效) 'implement with efficiency, efficient.'

149. 【应有尽有】(應有盡有) yīng yǒu jìn yǒu

尽 means 'all.' A literal translation of this idiom is 'have everything that should be had,' with a freer translation being 'lack nothing, complete.'

Example 1: 中国的大商场里一般都有一层美食城，里面各地风味小吃**应有尽有**。

Zhōngguó de dà shāngchǎng lǐ yìbān dōu yǒu yì céng měishíchéng, lǐmiàn gè dì fēngwèi xiǎochī yīngyǒu-jìnyǒu.

'In the larger department stores in China there is usually a "fine foods city," in which local delicacies from everywhere are to be had, with nothing lacking.'

Example 2: 最新的手机，集中了许多产品的功能，例如电话、电子邮件、网络、录音机、照相机、全球卫星定位系统等等，可以说是**应有尽有**。

Zuì xīn de shǒujī, jízhōngle xǔduō chǎnpǐn de gōngnéng, lìrú diànhuà, diànzǐ yóujiàn, wǎngluò, lùyīnjī, zhàoxiàngjī, quánqiú wèixīng dìngwèi xìtǒng děngděng, kěyǐ shuō shì yīngyǒu-jìnyǒu.

'The newest cell phones have concentrated in one place the functions of several products, such as telephone, e-mail, Internet, tape recorder, camera, GPS, etc.; it can be said they have everything that's required.'

Usage: Functions as predicate. Used at the end of a sentence.

Note: Complimentary in meaning.

Near Synonyms: [一应俱全] (yì yīng jù quán 一應俱全) 'complete with everything,' [包罗万象] (bāo luó wàn xiàng 包羅萬象) 'covering ten thousand phenomena – all-inclusive, comprehensive,' [面面俱到] (miàn miàn jù dào 面面俱到) 'complete and thorough.'

Antonym: [一无所有] (yì wú suǒ yǒu 一無所有) 'have absolutely nothing, destitute.'

150. 【南辕北辙】(南轅北轍) nán yuán běi zhé

辕 means 'shaft (of a vehicle)' and 辙 means 'rut, groove, track (left by a wheel in the ground).' A literal translation is 'south shaft north rut,' which could be translated more freely as 'go south by driving north.' By metaphor this means 'head in the wrong direction,' 'one's goal and one's actions are exactly opposite,' or 'defeat one's purpose.'

Example 1: 要想改变贫困人口的生活状况，得给他们足够的教育和就业机会，一味地给他们钱会产生相反的结果的，会**南辕北辙**的。

Yào xiǎng gǎibiàn pínkùn rénkǒu de shēnghuó zhuàngkuàng, děi gěi tāmen zúgòu de jiàoyù hé jiùyè jīhuì, yíwèi de gěi tāmen qián huì chǎnshēng xiāngfǎn de jiéguǒ de, huì nányuán-běizhé de.

'If one wants to change the living conditions of the impoverished population, one must give them sufficient educational and employment opportunities, always to give them money will produce the opposite result, it will defeat one's purpose.'

Example 2: 他们的做法和目的正好**南辕北辙**。

Tāmen de zuòfǎ hé mùdì zhènghǎo nányuán-běizhé.

'Their practices and their goals are exactly opposite.'

Usage: Functions mainly as predicate.

Allusion: In ancient times, there was a man who wanted to travel to a country in the south, but in a rush to find a vehicle he could take, he ended up traveling to the north instead. A good-hearted person told him he had gone in the wrong direction and that he should go south, but he said it didn't matter, that he had a good horse that ran very quickly. The good-hearted person said that if the man kept going, he would be further and further from his goal, but the man again said it didn't matter, that he had brought along a lot of money. The good-hearted person then said that though the man might have a lot of money, he was wasting it. But the man again said it didn't matter, that his servant was very good at driving vehicles. In the end, the good-hearted person said: "You have a good horse, a lot of money, and a servant who is good at driving vehicles; but all this will only make you be further and further from your goal. You won't get to where you want to go at all!" (from "Stratagems of Wei," No. 4, in *Stratagems of the Warring States*)

Note: Derogatory in meaning.

Near Synonyms: [背道而驰] (bèi dào ér chí 背道而馳) 'run counter to, diametrically opposed,' [事与愿违] (shì yǔ yuàn wéi 事與違) 'things do not turn out the way one wishes.'

151. 【有朝一日】(有朝一日) yǒu zhāo yí rì

朝 means 'morning, day.' The meaning of the whole idiom is 'some day in the future.'

Example 1: 他每个星期都买一次彩票，希望**有朝一日**能够中大奖。

Tā měi ge xīngqī dōu mǎi yí cì cǎipiào, xīwàng yǒuzhāo-yírì nénggòu zhòng dà jiǎng.

'He buys a lottery ticket every week, hoping that one day in the future he can win a major prize.'

Example 2: 如果**有朝一日**中国成为超级大国，那么汉语会不会变得跟英语一样重要？

Rúguǒ yǒuzhāo-yírì Zhōngguó chéngwéi chāojí dà guó, nàme Hànyǔ huì bú huì biànde gēn Yīngyǔ yíyàng zhòngyào?

'If some day in the future China becomes a superpower, then will the Chinese language become as important as English?'

Usage: Functions as adverbial; often preceded by verbs such as 希望 (xīwàng) 'hope,' 期待 (qīdài) 'await,' and 梦想 (mèngxiǎng 夢想) 'dream,' or by conjunctions such as 如果 (rúguǒ) and 倘若 (tǎngruò), both of which mean 'if.'

Near Synonym: [总有一天] (zǒng yǒu yì tiān 總有一天) 'eventually there will be a day, the day will come' (spoken Chinese).

Antonym: [遥遥无期] (yáo yáo wú qī 遙遙無期) 'not in the foreseeable future.'

152. 【大有可为】（大有可為）dà yǒu kě wéi

大 here means 'greatly, very much,' 可 means 'can,' and 为 means 'do.' A literal translation of the whole idiom is 'greatly have things one can do.' Freer translations of the idiom include 'very promising, have bright prospects, have great potential.'

Example 1: 未来几十年中，新能源行业**大有可为**。

Wèilái jǐ shí nián zhōng, xīn néngyuán hángyè dàyǒu-kěwéi.

'In the next few decades, businesses dealing with new sources of energy will have bright prospects.'

Example 2: 政府鼓励青年到中西部去找工作，说中西部开发**大有可为**。

Zhèngfǔ gǔlì qīngnián dào zhōngxībù qù zhǎo gōngzuò, shuō zhōngxībù kāifā dàyǒu-kěwéi.

'The government encourages young people to go to the Midwest to look for work, saying that the development of the Midwest has great potential.'

Usage: Functions mainly as predicate.

Near Synonyms: [前途无量] (qián tú wú liàng 前途無量) 'future without limit – have boundless prospects,' [前程似锦] (qián chéng sì jǐn 前程似錦) 'road ahead resembles brocade – have splendid prospects.'

Antonym: [不可救药] (bù kě jiù yào 不可救藥) 'cannot be saved with medicine – incurable, hopeless situation.'

153. 【史无前例】(史無前例) shǐ wú qián lì

史 means 'history' and 前例 means 'precedent.' A literal translation of this idiom is 'in history there is no precedent.' A common translation is 'unprecedented.'

Example 1: 在这次足球世界杯比赛中，他平均每场踢进两个球，这是**史无前例**的。

Zài zhè cì zúqiú shìjièbēi bǐsài zhōng, tā píngjūn měi chǎng tījìn liǎng ge qiú, zhè shì shǐwúqiánlì de.

'In this soccer world cup competition, he on average in each game has been kicking in two balls, which is unprecedented.'

Example 2: 在那次**史无前例**的唐山大地震中，死亡的人数多达二十四万人，超过了受伤的人数。

Zài nà cì shǐwúqiánlì de Tángshān dà dìzhèn zhōng, sǐwáng de rénshù duōdá èrshisì wàn rén, chāoguòle shòushāng de rénshù.

'In the unprecedented great earthquake of Tangshan that time, the number of those who died was as many as 240,000, which surpassed the number injured.'

Usage: Functions mainly as predicate and attributive. As predicate, it is preceded by 是 (shì) 'be' and followed by 的 (de).

Near Synonyms: [前所未有] (qián suǒ wèi yǒu 前所未有) 'never happened before in the past, unprecedented,' [绝无仅有] (jué wú jǐn yǒu 絕無僅有) 'unique, one of a kind,' [空前绝后] (kōng qián jué hòu 空前絕後) 'never before or since.'

Antonym: [比比皆是] (bǐ bǐ jiē shì 比比皆是) 'can be found everywhere.'

154. 【随心所欲】(隨心所欲) suí xīn suǒ yù

随 means 'follow' and 欲 means 'want, desire.' The literal meaning is 'follow what the heart desires.' This idiom is often translated as 'do exactly as one pleases, at will, anything goes.'

Example 1: 她是个大画家，画什么像什么，已经达到**随心所欲**的地步了。

Tā shì ge dà huàjiā, huà shénme xiàng shénme, yǐjīng dádào suíxīn-suǒyù de dìbù le.

'She is a great painter, and whatever she paints looks real; she has already reached the point where she can do anything she wants.'

Example 2: 他是个亿万富翁，可以**随心所欲**地买他喜欢的东西。

Tā shì ge yìwàn fùwēng, kěyǐ suíxīn-suǒyù de mǎi tā xǐhuan de dōngxi.

'He's a billionaire, so he can buy the things he likes at will.'

Usage: Functions mainly as adverbial; can also serve as predicate and attributive.

Near Synonyms: [为所欲为] (wéi suǒ yù wéi 為所欲為) 'do what one pleases,' [无所顾忌] (wú suǒ gù jì 無所顧忌) 'have no scruples or misgivings' (pejorative in meaning).

Antonyms: [谨小慎微] (jǐn xiǎo shèn wēi 謹小慎微) 'cautious even in very small things,' [缩手缩脚] (suō shǒu suō jiǎo 縮手縮腳) 'draw in one's hands and feet – overcautious.'

155. 【丰功伟绩】 (豐功偉績) fēng gōng wěi jì

丰 means 'abundant,' 功 means 'accomplishment,' 伟 means 'great,' and 绩 means 'achievement.' A literal translation of the whole idiom is 'abundant accomplishment great achievement,' with freer translations being 'great achievement, magnificent accomplishment.'

Example 1: 这本画册形象地记录了他的**丰功伟绩**。

Zhè běn huàcè xíngxiàng de jìlùle tā de fēnggōng-wěijì.

'This album vividly recorded his grand achievements.'

Example 2: 她为世界和平建立的**丰功伟绩**永远留在人们心里。

Tā wèi shìjiè hépíng jiànlì de fēnggōng-wěijì yǒngyuǎn liú zài rénmen xīnlǐ.

'The grand contributions she made for world peace will forever remain in people's hearts.'

Usage: Nominal element, can function as subject and object.

Note: Complimentary in meaning.

Near Synonym: [汗马功劳] (hàn mǎ gōng láo 汗馬功勞) 'sweating horse meritorious service – a great deed in battle.'

Antonyms: [罪大恶极] (zuì dà è jí 罪大惡極) 'guilt great evil extreme – commit a horrible crime,' [恶贯满盈] (è guàn mǎn yíng 惡貫滿盈) 'full of evil – have committed countless crimes.'

156. 【不动声色】 (不動聲色) bú dòng shēng sè

声 means 'voice' and 色 here means 'facial complexion.' A literal translation of this idiom is 'not change one's voice or complexion.' More freely, the idiom means 'calm and collected, maintain one's composure.'

Example 1: 在演讲的过程中他得到消息，他家里出了大事，但是他却**不动声色**，按计划做完了演讲。

Zài yǎnjiǎng de guòchéng zhōng tā dédào xiāoxi, tā jiālǐ chūle dàshì, dànshì tā què búdòng-shēngsè, àn jìhuà zuòwánle yǎnjiǎng.

'During the course of his speech, he received the news that something big had happened at his home, but he maintained his composure and finished the speech according to plan.'

Example 2: 外面有一点动静，于是几名特工**不动声色**地贴近了总统，以防出事。

Wàimiàn yǒu yìdiǎn dòngjìng, yúshì jǐ míng tègōng búdòng-shēngsè de tiējìnle zǒngtǒng, yǐfáng chūshì.

'There was the sound of something moving outside, so several Secret Service agents, calm and collected, drew closer to the president, so as to prevent something from happening.'

Usage: Functions mainly as adverbial, can also serve as predicate or attributive.

Near Synonyms: [镇定自若] (zhèn dìng zì ruò 鎮定自若) 'perfectly calm and collected, in possession of oneself,' [稳如泰山] (wěn rú Tài shān 穩如泰山) 'as stable as Mount Tai – standing firmly in place,' [无动于衷] (wú dòng yú zhōng 無動於衷) 'unmoved, unconcerned' (derogatory).

Antonyms: [大惊失色] (dà jīng shī sè 大驚失色) 'turn pale with fright,' [惊慌失措] (jīng huāng shī cuò 驚慌失措) 'so frightened and confused one doesn't know what to do – panic-stricken,' [手足无措] (shǒu zú wú cuò 手足無措) 'have no idea what to do with one's hands and feet – at a loss as to what to do, bewildered,' [不知所措] (bù zhī suǒ cuò 不知所措) 'not know what to do.'

157. 【取而代之】(取而代之) qǔ ér dài zhī

取 means 'take,' 代 means 'replace,' and 之 means 'it.' A literal translation of the whole idiom is 'take and replace it,' with freer translations being 'replace (someone or something), take over, supersede.'

Example 1: 北京老城的小胡同渐渐消失了，**取而代之**的是宽阔、平坦的大马路。

Běijīng lǎo chéng de xiǎo hútòng jiànjiàn xiāoshīle, qǔ'érdàizhī de shì kuānkuò, píngtǎn de dà mǎlù.

'The *hutong* (small alleys) of the old city of Beijing are gradually disappearing; what is replacing them are broad and level avenues.'

Example 2: 石油资源总有一天会用尽的，我们将用什么新能源**取而代之**？

Shíyóu zīyuán zǒng yǒu yì tiān huì yòngjìn de, wǒmen jiāng yòng shénme xīn néngyuán qǔ'érdàizhī?

'Petroleum resources will some day be exhausted; what new energy source shall we use to replace them?'

Usage: Functions mainly as subject followed by 的 (de); can also serve as predicate.

Near Synonym: [推陈出新] (tuī chén chū xīn 推陳出新) 'make new things on the basis of the old.'

Antonyms: [一如既往] (yì rú jì wǎng 一如既往) 'exactly the same as in the past,' [李代桃僵] (lǐ dài táo jiāng 李代桃僵) 'substitute one thing for another, sacrifice oneself for someone else' (allusion to a story about a plum tree that sacrificed itself for a peach tree when the latter was bitten by a worm).

158. 【根深蒂固】(根深蒂固) gēn shēn dì gù

根 means 'root,' 深 means 'deep,' 蒂 means 'stem,' and 固 means 'firm, solid.' A literal translation of the whole idiom is 'roots deep stem firm,' with freer translations being 'deep-rooted, rock solid, ingrained.'

Example 1: 农民的一些思想**根深蒂固**，即使生活条件改善了，那些思想还是不容易改变。

Nóngmín de yìxiē sīxiǎng gēnshēn-dìgù, jíshǐ shēnghuó tiáojiàn gǎishàn le, nàxiē sīxiǎng háishì bù róngyì gǎibiàn.

'Some of the thinking of the peasants is deep-rooted; even if living conditions have improved, that thinking is still not easy to change.'

Example 2: 新来的官员不敢轻易触犯在当地**根深蒂固**的大家族的利益。

Xīn lái de guānyuán bù gǎn qīngyì chùfàn zài dāngdì gēnshēn-dìgù de dà jiāzú de lìyì.

'The newly arrived official does not dare rashly to offend the interests of the entrenched big clans of the area.'

Usage: Functions mainly as predicate and attributive.

Near Synonyms: [积重难返] (jī zhòng nán fǎn 積重難返) 'old habits die hard' (derogatory), [盘根错节] (pán gēn cuò jié 盤根錯節) 'twisted roots and gnarled branches – complicated, deep-rooted.'

Antonym: [立足未稳] (lì zú wèi wěn 立足未穩) 'one's footing is not yet steady.'

159. 【久而久之】(久而久之) jiǔ ér jiǔ zhī

The meaning of this idiom is 'in the course of time, gradually.'

Example 1: 她每天坚持学习十个新生词，**久而久之**，英语水平有了明显的提高。

Tā měi tiān jiānchí xuéxí shí ge xīn shēngcí, jiǔ'érjiǔzhī, Yīngyǔ shuǐpíng yǒule míngxiǎn de tígāo.

'She persisted in learning ten new vocabulary words every day; in time, her English level experienced a clear improvement.'

Example 2: 两个人本来矛盾不深，但是由于缺乏沟通，**久而久之**，矛盾竟然不可调和了。

Liǎng ge rén běnlái máodùn bù shēn, dànshì yóuyú quēfá gōutōng, jiǔ'érjiǔzhī, máodùn jìngrán bùkě tiáohé le.

'Originally the conflict between them was not deep, but due to a lack of communication, over the course of time, their conflict actually became irreconcilable.'

Usage: Functions mainly as time adverbial, used by itself in isolation from other sentence elements.

Near Synonym: [日久天长] (rì jiǔ tiān cháng 日久天長) 'in the course of time.'

Antonym: [一朝一夕] (yì zhāo yì xī 一朝一夕) 'in a single day.'

160. 【四面楚歌】(四面楚歌) sì miàn Chǔ gē

楚 was the name of a state in ancient China. A literal translation of this idiom is 'four sides Chu songs,' with a freer translation being 'everywhere there were the sounds of soldiers from the state of Chu who were singing.' This is a metaphor for being in a situation where one is attacked by enemies everywhere and one is isolated and cut off from help. English translations include 'find oneself besieged on all sides,' 'deserted by one's allies,' and 'in dire straits.'

Example 1: 很多部长都反对总统，最后连副总统也反对了，总统处于**四面楚歌**之中。

Hěn duō bùzhǎng dōu fǎnduì zǒngtǒng, zuìhòu lián fùzǒngtǒng yě fǎnduìle, zǒngtǒng chǔyú sìmiàn-Chǔgē zhīzhōng.

'Many ministers opposed the president; in the end even the vice president opposed him; the president found himself besieged on all sides.'

Example 2: 银行不给贷款，商品卖不出去，这家公司陷于**四面楚歌**的境地。

Yínháng bù gěi dàikuǎn, shāngpǐn màibuchūqù, zhè jiā gōngsī xiànyú simian-Chǔgē de jìngdì.

'When the banks did not make loans, the goods could not be sold, and this company fell into dire straits.'

Usage: Functions mainly as attributive; can also serve as predicate.

Allusion: Xiang Yu (232–202 B.C.E.), who is known as "The Conqueror of Western Chu," can be considered the most famous military commander in Chinese history. During his ill-fated war with Liu Bang (the first emperor of the future Western Han Dynasty), Xiang Yu's troops were besieged by layer upon layer of enemy troops. Because Xiang Yu and the troops under his command were all extremely valiant, it was very difficult for Liu Bang's troops to destroy Xiang Yu's troops. A general under Liu Bang by the name of Han Xin then came up with a plan: he had the soldiers all sing songs from Chu, since Xiang Yu and the troops under him were mostly from Chu. At that time, because they had been fighting year in year out, Xiang Yu's soldiers were all quite homesick; when they heard the songs of their native places, everybody's confidence wavered. When Xiang Yu heard the Chu songs everywhere at night, he was shocked, thinking that Liu Bang must have occupied even his native place of Chu. Later, when Xiang Yu was defeated in battle, he committed suicide because he felt that he didn't have the "face" to look at the villagers in Chu. (from "Xiang Yu Ben Ji" in *Records of the Grand Historian*)

Note: Derogatory in meaning.

Near Synonyms: [十面埋伏] (shí miàn mái fú 十面埋伏) 'ambushed on ten sides,' [腹背受敌] (fù bèi shòu dí 腹背受敵) 'attacked front and rear,' [山穷水尽] (shān qióng shuǐ jìn 山窮水盡) 'mountains and rivers exhausted – at the end of one's rope.'

Antonyms: [夹道欢迎] (jiá dào huān yíng 夾道歡迎) 'line the streets to welcome,' [众望所归] (zhòng wàng suǒ guī 眾望所歸) 'where the multitude's hopes converge – the center of popular hope and confidence.'

161. 【急功近利】(急功近利) jí gōng jìn lì

急 means 'impatient,' 功 means 'success,' and 利 means 'benefit.' A literal translation of the whole idiom is 'impatient to achieve success and benefit,' with a freer translation being 'eager for quick success and immediate gain.'

Example 1: 教育的目的是培养人才，而人才的成长需要时间，所以教育不能**急功近利**。

Jiàoyù de mùdì shì péiyǎng réncái, ér réncái de chéngzhǎng xūyào shíjiān, suǒyǐ jiàoyù bù néng jígōng-jìnlì.

'The purpose of education is to cultivate human talent, and the growth of human talent takes time; so education must not be eager for quick success and immediate gain.'

Example 2: 股票刚涨了百分之五他就急于把股票卖出去，显示了他**急功近利**的心理。

Gǔpiào gāng zhǎngle bǎifēnzhīwǔ tā jiù jíyú bǎ gǔpiào màichūqù, xiǎnshìle tā jígōng-jìnlì de xīnlǐ.

'Stocks have just risen five percent and he is already anxious to sell the stocks, which has demonstrated his mindset of being eager for quick success and immediate gain.'

Usage: Functions mainly as attributive and adverbial; can also serve as predicate.

Note: Derogatory in meaning.

Near Synonyms: [急于求成] (jí yú qiú chéng 急於求成) 'impatient for success,' [鼠目寸光] (shǔ mù cùn guāng 鼠目寸光) 'rat eyes see (only) an inch of light – short sighted.'

Antonyms: [高瞻远瞩] (gāo zhān yuǎn zhǔ 高瞻遠矚) 'far sighted,' [深谋远虑] (shēn móu yuǎn lǜ 深謀遠慮) 'circumspect and far sighted.'

162. 【始终不渝】(始終不渝) shǐ zhōng bù yú

始 means 'beginning,' 终 means 'end,' and 渝 means 'change.' A literal translation of the whole idiom is '(from) beginning to end not change,' with freer translations being 'unswerving, steady, steadfast.'

Example 1: 我们要**始终不渝**地奉行独立自主的和平外交政策。

Wǒmen yào shǐzhōng-bùyú de fèngxíng dúlì zìzhǔ de hépíng wàijiāo zhèngcè.

'We should steadfastly pursue an independent, self-determined, and peaceful foreign policy.'

Example 2: 多年来，他**始终不渝**地坚持为普通人创作诗歌。

Duō nián lái, tā **shǐzhōng-bùyú** de jiānchí wèi pǔtōng rén chuàngzuò shīgē.

'For many years, he persisted steadfastly in creating poetry for the average person.'

Usage: Functions mainly as adverbial, often followed by the adverbial particle 地 (de) and verbs such as 坚持 (jiānchí 堅持) 'persist,' 奉行 (fèngxíng) 'carry out,' and 维护 (wéihù 維護) 'safeguard.'

Note: Complimentary in meaning.

Near Synonym: [一如既往] (yì rú jì wǎng 一如既往) 'exactly the same as in the past.'

Antonyms: [朝三暮四] (zhāo sān mù sì 朝三暮四) 'fickle and inconstant,' [朝秦暮楚] (zhāo Qín mù Chǔ 朝秦暮楚) 'serve Qin in the morning and Chu in the evening – fickle and inconstant,' [见异思迁] (jiàn yì sī qiān 見異思遷) 'see something different and want to change – fickle, capricious.'

163. 【一目了然】（一目瞭然）yí mù liǎo rán

目 here means 'look, glance,' 了 means 'understand,' and 然 means 'in a certain way or manner.' A literal translation of this idiom is 'one glance understanding manner,' with a freer translation being 'at one glance to understand fully.'

Example 1: 总经理把公司的优势和劣势一条条列得清清楚楚，使人**一目了然**。

Zǒngjīnglǐ bǎ gōngsī de yōushì hé lièshì yì tiáo tiáo liède qīngqīngchǔchǔ, shǐ rén yímù-liǎorán.

'The general manager listed the company's favorable and unfavorable conditions one at a time in a crystal clear manner, so that people would be completely clear at one glance.'

Example 2: 超市里的商品都标明总的价格和单价，顾客看了**一目了然**。

Chāoshì lǐ de shāngpǐn dōu biāomíng zǒng de jiàgé hé dānjià, gùkè kànle yímù-liǎorán.

'The goods at the supermarket all indicate the total price and the unit price; when the customers see them they are clear at one glance.'

Usage: Functions mainly as predicate, often used causatively.

Near Synonyms: [了如指掌] (liǎo rú zhǐ zhǎng 瞭如指掌) 'understand as well as one's own fingers and palms – completely clear,' [不言而喻] (bù yán ér yù 不言而喻) 'it goes without saying, obvious.'

Antonyms: [雾里看花] (wù lǐ kàn huā 霧裏看花) 'in the fog to see flowers – see indistinctly,' [管中窥豹] (guǎn zhōng kuī bào 管中窺豹) 'peer at a leopard through a tube – have a limited view of something.'

164. 【量力而行】(量力而行) liàng lì ér xíng

量 here means 'estimate' and 行 means 'act.' A literal translation of the whole idiom is 'estimate one's strength and then carry out some action,' with freer translations being 'act according to one's capacity, do what one can.'

Example 1: 你同时做这么多事，怎么能完成呢？不要贪多，要**量力而行**。

Nǐ tóngshí zuò zhème duō shì, zěnme néng wánchéng ne? Búyào tān duō, yào liànglì-érxíng.

'You are simultaneously doing so many things, how can you complete them? Don't be greedy; you should act according to your ability.'

Example 2: 各地区在发展经济的时候要**量力而行**，抓住重点。

Gè dìqū zài fāzhǎn jīngjì de shíhou yào liànglì-érxíng, zhuāzhù zhòngdiǎn.

'As each region develops the economy, it should act according to its capacity and come to grips with the key points.'

Usage: Functions mainly as predicate.

Near Synonyms: [量体裁衣] (liàng tǐ cái yī 量體裁衣) 'measure body cut clothes – according to the circumstances,' [力所能及] (lì suǒ néng jí 力所能及) 'that which one's ability can reach – within one's power.'

Antonyms: [自不量力] (zì bù liàng lì 自不量力) 'not know one's own limitations,' [好大喜功] (hào dà xǐ gōng 好大喜功) 'love greatness like success – have a fondness for the grandiose.'

165. 【浩浩荡荡】(浩浩蕩蕩) hào hào dàng dàng

浩荡 refers to a 'grand' or 'mighty' flow of water. The meaning of the whole idiom is 'with great strength and vigor, in formidable array, grand.'

Example 1: 结婚的车队从新娘的家**浩浩荡荡**地开向新郎的家。

Jiéhūn de chēduì cóng xīnniáng de jiā hàohào-dàngdàng de kāi xiàng xīnláng de jiā.

'The wedding motorcade drove in a grand procession from the bride's home to the groom's home.'

Example 2: 游行的队伍**浩浩荡荡**地走过了总统府门前。

Yóuxíng de duìwǔ hàohào-dàngdàng de zǒu guò le zǒngtǒngfǔ ménqián.

'With great strength and vigor, the marching troops passed before the gate of the presidential palace.'

Usage: Functions mainly as adverbial, predicate, and attributive.

Near Synonym: [波澜壮阔] (bō lán zhuàng kuò 波瀾壯闊) 'surge forward like mighty waves.'

Antonym: [无声无息] (wú shēng wú xī 無聲無息) 'no sound no breath – silent.'

166. 【雨后春笋】(雨後春筍) yǔ hòu chūn sǔn

笋 means 'bamboo shoot.' The literal meaning of this idiom is '(spring up like) bamboo shoots after spring rain.' Freer translations include 'spring up like mushrooms, emerge rapidly in large numbers.'

Example 1: 私人汽车增加很快，所以加油站也如**雨后春笋**般出现了。

Sīrén qìchē zēngjiā hěn kuài, suǒyǐ jiāyóuzhàn yě rú yǔhòu-chūnsǔn bān chūxiànle.

'Privately owned cars increased very quickly, so gas stations have also appeared, springing up like mushrooms.'

Example 2: 这几年，有关中美贸易的文章如**雨后春笋**，数不过来。

Zhè jǐ nián, yǒuguān Zhōng-Měi màoyì de wénzhāng rú yǔhòu-chūnsǔn, shǔ bú guòlái.

'In the past few years, articles about U.S.-Chinese trade have appeared rapidly in large numbers, too many to count.'

Usage: Functions mainly as adverbial modifier or object. Common collocations include 如～ (rú . . .) and ～般地 (. . . bān de) + verb.

Note: Has a positive connotation.

167. 【一举一动】(一舉一動) yì jǔ yí dòng

举 means 'action' and 动 means 'movement.' The meaning of the whole idiom is 'every action and every movement.'

Example 1: 因为警察怀疑他涉嫌犯罪，所以开始对他进行监视。他的**一举一动**都在警察的监视之下。

Yīnwèi jǐngchá huáiyí tā shèxián fànzuì, suǒyǐ kāishǐ duì tā jìnxíng jiānshì. Tā de yìjǔ-yídòng dōu zài jǐngchá de jiānshì zhīxià.

'Because the police suspected him of having committed a crime, they began to keep him under surveillance; his every move was under surveillance by the police.'

Example 2: 那位明星的**一举一动**都给他的粉丝们很大的影响。

Nà wèi míngxīng de yìjǔ-yídòng dōu gěi tā de fěnsīmen hěn dà de yǐngxiǎng.

'That star's every move has a big influence on his fans.'

Usage: Nominal element, functions as subject and object.

Near Synonyms: [一言一行] (yì yán yì xíng 一言一行) 'every word and every deed,' [举手投足] (jǔ shǒu tóu zú 舉手投足) 'raise hand fling foot – every movement of the body, every action.'

168. 【有目共睹】(有目共睹) yǒu mù gòng dǔ

目 means 'eye' and 睹 means 'see.' A literal translation of the whole idiom is 'have eyes together see,' with a freer translation being 'obvious to all.'

Example 1: 她最近的进步是**有目共睹**的。

Tā zuìjìn de jìnbù shì yǒumù-gòngdǔ de.

'Her recent progress is obvious to all.'

Example 2: 这是**有目共睹**的事实，谁也否认不了。

Zhè shì yǒumù-gòngdǔ de shìshí, shuí yě fǒurèn bùliǎo.

'This is a fact that is obvious to all; nobody can deny it.'

Usage: Functions mainly as predicate and attributive.

Near Synonym: [众目睽睽] (zhòng mù kuí kuí 眾目睽睽) 'all eyes gazing at someone or something.'

Antonym: [视而不见] (shì ér bú jiàn 視而不見) 'look but not see – turn a blind eye to.'

169. 【欣欣向荣】(欣欣向榮) xīn xīn xiàng róng

欣欣 means 'thriving,' 向 here means 'turn toward,' and 荣 means 'flourishing.' A literal translation of the whole idiom is 'thriving and turning toward the flourishing,' with freer translations being 'thriving, flourishing, prosperous.'

Example 1: 经过几十年的发展，全国各地都呈现出**欣欣向荣**的景象。

Jīngguò jǐ shí nián de fāzhǎn, quán guó gè dì dōu chéngxiànchū xīnxīn-xiàngróng de jǐngxiàng.

'After several decades of development, every place in the whole country presents a very thriving picture.'

Example 2: 春天来了，花草树木**欣欣向荣**。

Chūntiān láile, huācǎo shùmù xīnxīn-xiàngróng.

'Spring has come; the flowers, plants, and trees are thriving.'

Usage: Functions mainly as attributive, often followed by nouns such as 景象 (jǐngxiàng) 'scenery,' 局面 (júmiàn) 'condition,' or 气象 (qìxiàng 氣象) 'atmosphere.'

Note: Complimentary in meaning.

Near Synonyms: [朝气蓬勃] (zhāo qì péng bó 朝氣蓬勃) 'full of vigor and vitality,' [方兴未艾] (fāng xīng wèi ài 方興未艾) 'on the rise,' [蒸蒸日上] (zhēng zhēng rì shàng 蒸蒸日上) 'progress day by day.'

Antonyms: [死气沉沉] (sǐ qì chén chén 死氣沉沉) 'lifeless,' [老气横秋] (lǎo qì héng qiū 老氣橫秋) 'lacking vitality,' [日暮穷途] (rì mù qióng tú 日暮窮途) 'in the evening at the end of the road – toward the end of one's days,' [江河日下] (jiāng hé rì xià 江河日下) 'rivers and streams daily decline – deteriorate day by day, go from bad to worse.'

170. 【三顾茅庐】(三顧茅廬) sān gù máo lú

三 means 'three (times),' 顾 means 'pay a visit,' and 茅庐 means 'thatched hut.' A literal translation of the whole idiom is 'make three visits to the thatched cottage (as Liu Bei, prince of Shu, did to visit Zhuge Liang).' By metaphor this means 'repeatedly ask a worthy person to assume an important post' or 'sincerely and repeatedly request something from someone.'

Example 1: 厂长**三顾茅庐**，终于把那位技术高超的退休工人请回了工厂。

Chǎngzhǎng sāngù-máolú, zhōngyú bǎ nà wèi jìshù gāochāo de tuìxiū gōngrén qǐnghuíle gōngchǎng.

'The factory director sincerely and repeatedly entreated him, finally being able to get that retired worker with the superb skills to return to the factory.'

Example 2: 记者**三顾茅庐**，才采访到那起事件的当事人。

Jìzhě sāngù-máolú, cái cǎifǎng dào nà qǐ shìjiàn de dāngshìrén.

'The reporter sincerely asked over and over again; only then was she able to interview the person involved in that incident.'

Usage: Functions mainly as predicate.

Allusion: In the last years of the Eastern Han Dynasty, China was in much turmoil. In 207 C.E., Liu Bei, who was a descendant of the imperial family, heard that Zhuge Liang was a very talented man and wanted to ask him to work for him. At that time, Liu Bei was a high-level local official, somewhat like the governor of a U.S. state, and Zhuge Liang was only a commoner. But Liu Bei lowered his status and personally went to Zhuge Liang's house to visit him. The first two times Zhuge Liang wasn't home; the third time he was home but when Liu Bei came, Zhuge Liang happened to be taking a nap. To express his respect for Zhuge Liang, Liu Bei waited for him until he awoke before speaking with him. Zhuge Liang was very moved, so he made the suggestion to Liu Bei of occupying southwest China and then dividing the empire into three parts. And sure enough, Chinese history later confirmed the correctness of Zhuge Liang's assumptions. (from chapters 37 and 38 of *Romance of the Three Kingdoms*)

Note: Complimentary in meaning.

Near Synonym: [真心实意] (zhēn xīn shí yì 真心實意) 'wholehearted, sincere.'

Antonym: [高高在上] (gāo gāo zài shàng 高高在上) 'up very high, isolated from the masses.'

171. 【五彩缤纷】(五彩繽紛) wǔ cǎi bīn fēn

五彩 means 'five colors, multicolored' and 缤纷 means 'many.' The meaning of the whole idiom is 'a profusion of colors, riot of colors, multicolored.'

Example 1: 节日的时代广场**五彩缤纷**，非常好看。

Jiérì de shídài guǎngchǎng wǔcǎi-bīnfēn, fēicháng hǎokàn.

'During the festival period, the square was filled with colors; it was very beautiful.'

Example 2: 孩子们总是梦想着生活在**五彩缤纷**的世界里。

Háizimen zǒngshì mèngxiǎngzhe shēnghuó zài wǔcǎi-bīnfēn de shìjiè lǐ.

'Children always dream of living in a world of many colors.'

Usage: Functions mainly as attributive and predicate.

Note: Complimentary in meaning.

Near Synonyms: [五光十色] (wǔ guāng shí sè 五光十色), [五颜六色] (wǔ yán liù sè 五顏六色), and [万紫千红] (wàn zǐ qiān hóng 萬紫千紅), all of which mean 'multicolored.'

172. 【一本正经】(一本正經) yì běn zhèng jīng

正经 means 'serious, solemn.' The meaning of the whole idiom is 'serious, solemn, in all seriousness.'

Example 1: 听完汇报以后，领导**一本正经**地说：外交无小事，你们一定要认真处理，不许有任何差错。

Tīngwán huìbào yǐhòu, lǐngdǎo yìběn-zhèngjīng de shuō: "Wàijiāo wú xiǎo shì, nǐmen yídìng yào rènzhēn chǔlǐ, bù xǔ yǒu rèn hé chācuò."

'After hearing the report, the leader said very seriously: "When it comes to diplomacy, there is no such thing as a trivial matter; you definitely must handle this conscientiously, it's not permitted that there be any mistakes."'

Example 2: 看着他**一本正经**的样子，她赶紧说："我是跟你开玩笑呢，别害怕。"

Kànzhe tā yìběn-zhèngjīng de yàngzi, tā gǎnjǐn shuō: "Wǒ shì gēn nǐ kāi wánxiào ne, bié hàipà."

'Looking at his serious manner, she quickly said: "I'm joking with you, don't be afraid."'

Usage: Functions mainly as adverbial and attributive.

Near Synonyms: [不苟言笑] (bù gǒu yán xiào 不苟言笑) 'careful in speech,' [道貌岸然] (dào mào àn rán 道貌岸然) 'sanctimonious' (pejorative).

Antonyms: [油腔滑调] (yóu qiāng huá diào 油腔滑調) 'slick tunes smooth melodies – glib' (pejorative), [嬉皮笑脸] (xī pí xiào liǎn 嬉皮笑臉) 'smilingly, laughingly' (pejorative).

173. 【恍然大悟】(恍然大悟) huǎng rán dà wù

恍然 means 'suddenly' and 悟 means 'come to one's senses, awaken, realize.' A literal translation of the whole idiom is 'suddenly greatly realize,' with freer translations being 'suddenly understand, suddenly see the light, wake up to the facts.'

Example 1: 对方提醒以后，他**恍然大悟**："原来你说的是她啊！"

Duìfāng tíxǐng yǐhòu, tā huǎngrán-dàwù: "Yuánlái nǐ shuō de shì tā a!"

'After the other person reminded him, he suddenly realized: "So the person you were talking about is her!"'

Example 2: 她说出谜底以后，大家才**恍然大悟**。

Tā shuōchū mídǐ yǐhòu, dàjiā cái huǎngrán-dàwù.

'Only after she mentioned the solution to the puzzle did everyone suddenly understand.'

Usage: Functions mainly as predicate; can also serve as adverbial. As adverbial, commonly followed by the verb 说 (shuō 說) 'say.'

Near Synonyms: [豁然开朗] (huō rán kāi lǎng 豁然開朗) 'suddenly see the light,' [茅塞顿开] (máo sè dùn kāi 茅塞頓開) 'suddenly see the light,' [醍醐灌顶] (tí hú guàn dǐng 醍醐灌頂) 'the finest cream from milk and the highest Buddhist doctrine – enlightened.'

Antonyms: [大惑不解] (dà huò bù jiě 大惑不解) 'puzzled, baffled,' [一窍不通] (yí qiào bù tōng 一竅不通) 'one gate not opened – know nothing about something.'

174. 【视而不见】(視而不見) shì ér bú jiàn

视 means 'look' and 见 means 'see.' The literal meaning of this idiom is 'look but not see.' Sometimes this idiom is also used in the sense of 'see but pretend not to see, turn a blind eye to.'

Example 1: 警察怎么能对这类违法活动**视而不见**呢？

Jǐngchá zěnme néng duì zhè lèi wéifǎ huódòng shì'érbújiàn ne?

'How can the police pretend not to see this kind of illegal activity?'

Example 2: 早上我跟他打招呼，可是他却**视而不见**，直接走了过去。

Zǎoshàng wǒ gēn tā dǎ zhāohu, kěshì tā què shì'érbújiàn, zhíjiē zǒule guòqu.

'In the morning I greeted him, but he didn't see me, directly passing by me.'

Usage: Functions mainly as predicate; sometimes followed by 听而不闻 (tīng ér bù wén 聽而不聞) or 充耳不闻 (chōng ěr bù wén 充耳不聞), both meaning 'turn a deaf ear to.'

Note: Derogatory in meaning.

Near Synonyms: [听而不闻] (tīng ér bù wén 聽而不聞) and [充耳不闻] (chōng ěr bù wén 充耳不聞) 'turn a deaf ear to,' [视若无睹] (shì ruò wú dǔ 視若無睹) and [熟视无睹] (shú shì wú dǔ 熟視無睹) 'turn a blind eye to.'

175. 【有条不紊】(有條不紊) yǒu tiáo bù wěn

条 means 'order' and 紊 means 'disorderly.' A literal translation of the whole idiom is 'having order and not disorderly,' with a freer translation being 'orderly, methodical.'

Example 1: 虽然情况相当复杂，但是各项救灾工作还是**有条不紊**地进行着。

Suīrán qíngkuàng xiāngdāng fùzá, dànshì gè xiàng jiùzāi gōngzuò háishì yǒutiáo-bùwěn de jìnxíngzhe.

'Though the situation is fairly complex, each item in the disaster relief work is being carried out in an orderly manner.'

Example 2: 她说话不快不慢，做事**有条不紊**，非常成熟。

Tā shuōhuà bú kuài bú màn, zuòshì yǒutiáo-bùwěn, fēicháng chéngshú.

'She speaks neither fast nor slow and is methodical in her work; she's extremely mature.'

Usage: Functions mainly as adverbial, often followed by verbs such as 进行 (jìnxíng 進行) 'carry out' and 开展 (kāizhǎn 開展) 'develop'; can also serve as predicate.

Note: Complimentary in meaning.

Near Synonyms: [按部就班] (àn bù jiù bān 按部就班) 'do things in an orderly fashion,' [井井有条] (jǐng jǐng yǒu tiáo 井井有條) 'methodical.'

Antonyms: [千头万绪] (qiān tóu wàn xù 千頭萬緒) 'a thousand ends and ten thousand threads – very complicated,' [乱七八糟] (luàn qī bā zāo 亂七八糟) 'in great disorder, a mess' (spoken Chinese).

176. 【别开生面】(別開生面) bié kāi shēng miàn

别 means 'additionally,' 开 means 'open,' and 生面 means 'a new situation.' A literal translation of the whole idiom is 'additionally open up a new situation,' with freer translations being 'start something new, break new ground.'

Example 1: 这种庆祝生日的方式以前从来没见过，可以说是**别开生面**。

Zhè zhǒng qìngzhù shēngrì de fāngshì yǐqián cónglái méi jiànguo, kěyǐ shuō shì biékāi-shēngmiàn.

'This way of celebrating birthdays has never been seen before; one could say that it's breaking new ground.'

Example 2: 会场里正在进行一场**别开生面**的对话，一方是大公司老总，一方是普通小学生。

Huìchǎng lǐ zhèng zài jìnxíng yì cháng biékāi-shēngmiàn de duìhuà, yìfāng shì dà gōngsī lǎozǒng, yìfāng shì pǔtōng xiǎoxuésheng.

'At the conference site there is taking place a ground-breaking dialogue; one side is the head of a major corporation, and the other side is an ordinary elementary school student.'

Usage: Functions mainly as attributive.

Near Synonyms: [耳目一新] (ěr mù yì xīn 耳目一新) 'brand-new sights and sounds,' 别出心裁 (bié chū xīn cái) 'come out with a different plan – have an unconventional idea.'

Antonyms: [千篇一律] (qiān piān yí lǜ 千篇一律) 'a thousand essays uniform – follow the same pattern, stereotyped,' [中规中矩] (zhōng guī zhōng jǔ 中规中矩) 'hit rule hit regulation – by the book,' [一成不变] (yì chéng bú biàn 一成不變) 'fixed and unalterable.'

177. 【锲而不舍】(鍥而不捨) qiè ér bù shě

锲 means 'carve' and 舍 means 'give up, abandon.' The literal meaning is '(keep on) carving without giving up,' this being a metaphor for possessing perseverance and willpower. This idiom can be translated as 'work with perseverance, keep on chipping away at something.'

Example 1: 搞研究就需要这种**锲而不舍**的精神。

Gǎo yánjiū jiù xūyào zhè zhǒng qiè'érbùshě de jīngshen.

'In conducting research, one needs precisely this kind of persevering spirit.'

Example 2: 在国家的基础建设方面必须扎扎实实，**锲而不舍**。

Zài guójiā de jīchǔ jiànshè fāngmiàn bìxū zhā zhā shí shí, qiè'érbùshě.

'In the area of national basic construction, one must be solid and persevering.'

Usage: Functions mainly as attributive; can also serve as predicate.

Allusion: This is a literary allusion to the following line from "Encouraging Learning" by the philosopher Xun Zi: 锲而舍之，朽木不折；锲而不舍，金石可镂 (qiè ér shě zhī, xiǔ mù bù shé; qiè ér bù shě, jīn shí kě lòu) "If when carving one gives up, then rotten wood (which would normally break right away) will not break; but if when carving one doesn't give up, then even metal and stone can be carved." What Xun Zi meant here was that one should persevere in one's studies.

Note: Complimentary in meaning.

Near Synonym: [持之以恒] (chí zhī yǐ héng 持之以恆) 'persevere.'

Antonyms: [半途而废] (bàn tú ér fèi 半途而廢) 'give up halfway,' [浅尝辄止] (qiǎn cháng zhé zhǐ 淺嘗輒止) 'shallowly taste then stop – stop after gaining a little knowledge of something.'

178. 【全神贯注】 (全神貫注) quán shén guàn zhù

全 means 'all,' 神 means 'spirit, energy,' and 贯注 means 'concentrate.' The literal meaning is 'with all one's energy to concentrate on something,' with a freer translation being 'give one's undivided attention to, be absorbed in.'

Example 1: 高水平的比赛中，选手必须**全神贯注**，如果有任何一秒精力不集中，就会失败。

Gāo shuǐpíng de bǐsài zhōng, xuǎnshǒu bìxū quánshén-guànzhù, rúguǒ yǒu rènhé yì miǎo jīnglì bù jízhōng, jiù huì shībài.

'In high-level competition, contestants must concentrate with undivided attention; if they don't concentrate their energy at any time, even just for a second, they will lose.'

Example 2: 她正在**全神贯注**地看书，以至于根本没有听见电话铃声。

Tā zhèngzài quánshén-guànzhù de kànshū, yǐzhìyú gēnběn méiyǒu tīngjiàn diànhuà língshēng.

'She is absorbed in her reading, to the point that she didn't hear the sound of the telephone ringing at all.'

Usage: Functions as adverbial and predicate.

Near Synonyms: [专心致志] (zhuān xīn zhì zhì 專心致志) 'with single-minded devotion,' [聚精会神] (jù jīng huì shén 聚精會神) 'with total concentration.'

Antonym: [心不在焉] (xīn bú zài yān 心不在焉) 'heart is not there – absent-minded, distracted.'

179. 【万无一失】 (萬無一失) wàn wú yì shī

失 means 'mistake.' A literal translation is 'in ten thousand there is not even one mistake,' with a freer translation being 'surefire, cannot go wrong.'

Example 1: 这次活动意义很大，你们一定要好好准备，确保**万无一失**。

Zhè cì huódòng yìyì hěn dà, nǐmen yídìng yào hǎohǎo zhǔnbèi, quèbǎo wànwúyìshī.

'The significance of this activity is great; you must definitely prepare well to ensure that nothing goes wrong.'

Example 2: 为了保证**万无一失**，那位生物学教授同时叫三个学生再做相同的实验。

Wèile bǎozhèng wànwúyìshī, nà wèi shēngwùxué jiàoshòu tóngshí jiào sān ge xuésheng zài zuò xiāngtóng de shíyàn.

'To guarantee that nothing went wrong, the biology professor had three students do the same experiment simultaneously.'

Usage: Occurs mostly after 确保 (quèbǎo 確保) 'ensure,' 保证 (bǎozhèng 保證) 'guarantee' and similar verbs.

Near Synonyms: [十拿九稳] (shí ná jiǔ wěn 十拿九穩) 'ninety percent sure, almost certain,' [板上钉钉] (bǎn shàng dīng dīng 板上釘釘) 'nail nails into a plank – definite, fixed' (used mostly in spoken Chinese).

Antonyms: [百密一疏] (bǎi mì yì shū 百密一疏) 'hundred meticulous things one careless thing – imperfect,' [挂一漏万] (guà yī lòu wàn 掛一漏萬) 'the list is far from complete.'

180. 【按图索骥】 (按圖索驥) àn tú suǒ jì

索 means 'seek' and 骥 means 'thoroughbred horse.' A literal translation of the whole idiom is 'according to a sketch seek a horse.' By analogy, the meaning of the whole idiom is 'search for something based on clues.' The idiom also has an extended meaning of 'do something mechanically' or 'rigid, unimaginative.'

Example 1: 他给了我一张名片，几天后，我**按图索骥**找到了他的公司。

Tā gěile wǒ yì zhāng míngpiàn, jǐ tiān hòu, wǒ àntú-suǒjì zhǎodàole tā de gōngsī.

'He gave me a business card; after several days, by searching based on the clues I had, I located his company.'

Example 2: 吃药得在医生的指导下进行，不能只看电视上广告的片面宣传，**按图索骥**。

Chī yào děi zài yīshēng de zhǐdǎo xià jìnxíng, bù néng zhǐ kàn diànshì shàng guǎnggào de piànmiàn xuānchuán, àntú-suǒjì.

'Taking medicine must be carried out under the guidance of a doctor; you can't just watch the one-sided propaganda of television advertisements and do things mechanically.'

Usage: Functions mainly as predicate and adverbial.

Allusion: During the Spring and Autumn Period (770–476 B.C.E.), there was in the country of Qin a person by the name of Sun Yang. It is said that in all of Chinese history, Sun Yang knew best how to appraise horses, so everyone called him Bo Le, after the god in heaven who was responsible for managing the heavenly horses. Sun Yang wrote a book titled *The Classic of Appraising Horses* in which there is a line that "a good horse has a tall forehead, bulging eyes, and hoofs that appear like medicinal wine pancakes that have been stacked up." Holding this book in his hands, Sun Yang's son went looking for a good horse. On departing his home, he saw a toad that, according to his father's book, had the traits of a good horse, so he brought it home and told his father: "I found a horse that can run a thousand miles a day; its traits are basically the same as those you mentioned in your book. The only thing is its hoofs are not like medicinal wine pancakes that have been stacked up." Knowing that his son was stupid, Sun Yang not only did not get angry but said with humor, "This horse likes to jump, it's hard to control!" (from *Yi Lin Fa Shan* by Yang Shen, Ming Dynasty)

Note: Derogatory in the sense of 'do something mechanically.'

Near Synonyms: [照猫画虎] (zhào māo huà hǔ 照貓畫虎) 'draw a tiger with a cat as a model – follow a model' (sometimes derogatory), [照本宣科] (zhào běn xuān kē 照本宣科) 'go by the book, have no flexibility' (derogatory), [生搬硬套] (shēng bān yìng tào 生搬硬套) 'copy mechanically and force-fit into' (derogatory).

Antonym: [不落窠臼] (bú luò kē jiù 不落窠臼) 'not follow the beaten track, have an original style.'

181. 【诸如此类】(諸如此類) zhū rú cǐ lèi

诸 means 'all,' 如 means 'like,' 此 means 'this,' and 类 means 'type, kind.' A literal translation of the whole idiom is 'all like this kind,' with a freer translation being 'such, such as, and so on.'

Example 1: 不光中国有这样的问题，**诸如此类**的现象在欧美各国也不少见。

Bù guāng Zhōngguó yǒu zhèyàng de wèntí, zhūrú-cǐlèi de xiànxiàng zài Ōu-Měi gè guó yě bù shǎo jiàn.

'Not only China has these kinds of problems; phenomena like these are also not rare in the various countries of Europe and the Americas.'

Example 2: 有时候我们需要说一些善意的谎言，比方说有人问你，她新买的衣服怎么样？你可以说"这件衣服很特别"，"这件衣服你穿着很合适"，**诸如此类**。

Yǒu shíhou wǒmen xūyào shuō yìxiē shànyì de huǎngyán, bǐfāng shuō yǒu rén wèn nǐ, tā xīn mǎi de yīfu zěnmeyàng? Nǐ kěyǐ shuō "Zhè jiàn yīfu hěn tèbié," "Zhè jiàn yīfu nǐ chuānzhe hěn héshì," zhūrú-cǐlèi.

'Sometimes we need to tell some well-intentioned lies; for example, if someone asks you what you think of the new clothes she has bought, you could say "These clothes are very special," or "These clothes fit you very well," or something else like this.'

Usage: Functions mainly as attributive; can also serve as predicate.

Near Synonym: [不一而足] (bù yī ér zú 不一而足) 'mention just a few, not just an isolated example.'

182. 【精益求精】(精益求精) jīng yì qiú jīng

精 means 'perfect' or 'perfection,' 益 means 'even more,' and 求 means 'seek.' A literal translation of the whole idiom is 'perfect even more seek perfection.' Freer translations are 'keep trying to improve, strive for perfection.'

Example 1: 他研制出的机器人已经领先全世界了，但是他仍不满足，**精益求精**，不断地完善它。

Tā yánzhìchū de jīqìrén yǐjīng lǐngxiān quán shìjiè le, dànshì tā réng bù mǎnzú, jīngyì-qiújīng, búduàn de wánshàn tā.

'The robot that he developed and produced is already in the lead in the whole world, but he is still not satisfied, striving for perfection and continuously refining it.'

Example 2: 经理鼓励职员对顾客的服务要**精益求精**，以便吸引更多的顾客。

Jīnglǐ gǔlì zhíyuán duì gùkè de fúwù yào jīngyì-qiújīng, yǐbiàn xīyǐn gèng duō de gùkè.

'The manager encourages employees to keep trying to improve their service to customers, thus attracting even more customers.'

Usage: Functions as predicate and attributive.

Note: Complimentary in meaning.

Near Synonyms: [尽善尽美] (jìn shàn jìn měi 盡善盡美) 'completely perfect,' [锦上添花] (jǐn shàng tiān huā 錦上添花) 'on brocade add flowers – improve to perfection.'

Antonyms: [粗制滥造] (cū zhì làn zào 粗製濫造) 'slapdash and slipshod,' [得过且过] (dé guò qiě guò 得過且過) 'drift or muddle along.'

183. 【一帆风顺】(一帆風順) yì fān fēng shùn

帆 means 'sail' and 顺 means 'favorable, smooth.' A literal translation is 'a sail full of favorable winds,' with a freer translation being 'smooth sailing, unimpeded progress, without a hitch.'

Example 1: 她的一生从来没有遇到过麻烦，**一帆风顺**。

Tā de yìshēng cónglái méiyǒu yùdàoguo máfan, yìfān-fēngshùn.

'Her whole life long she has never encountered trouble; it's been smooth sailing.'

Example 2: 很多事情都不是一**帆风顺**的，你得做好失败的心理准备。

Hěn duō shìqing dōu bú shì yìfān-fēngshùn de, nǐ děi zuòhǎo shībài de xīnlǐ zhǔnbèi.

'Lots of things don't go so smoothly; you must prepare yourself mentally for failure.'

Usage: Functions mainly as predicate; often in negative constructions.

Note: Complimentary in meaning.

Near Synonyms: [风平浪静] (fēng píng làng jìng 風平浪靜) 'wind calm waves still – calm and tranquil,' [一路顺风] (yí lù shùn fēng 一路順風) 'whole road favorable wind – bon voyage, wishing you success,' [无往不利] (wú wǎng bú lì 無往不利) 'there is no place one goes where it is not advantageous – go smoothly everywhere.'

Antonyms: [一波三折] (yì bō sān zhé 一波三折) 'full of obstacles and complications, full of twists and turns,' [惊涛骇浪] (jīng tāo hài làng 驚濤駭浪) 'terrifying storm, perilous situation.'

184. 【审时度势】(審時度勢) shěn shí duó shì

审 means 'examine,' 时 here means 'the times, the current situation,' 度 means 'estimate,' and 势 here means 'trend.' A literal translation of the whole idiom is 'examine the current situation and estimate what the trend is like,' with freer translations being 'judge the hour and size up the situation, observe the times and judge the occasion.'

Example 1: 在经济衰退的情况下，她**审时度势**，大量买入新能源方面的股票，结果赚了大钱。

Zài jīngjì shuāituì de qíngkuàng xià, tā shěnshí-duóshì, dàliàng mǎirù xīn néngyuán fāngmiàn de gǔpiào, jiéguǒ zhuànle dà qián.

'In a situation of economic depression, she examined the current situation and predicted what the trend would be; she bought up large amounts of stocks involving new energy sources, and as a result she made a lot of money.'

Example 2: 那位内阁部长**审时度势**，在总统大选前几天公开支持那位女候选人。

Nà wèi nèigé bùzhǎng shěnshí-duóshì, zài zǒngtǒng dàxuǎn qián jǐ tiān gōngkāi zhīchí nà wèi nǚ hòuxuǎnrén.

'That cabinet minister judged the times and sized up the trend; a few days before the presidential election, he publicly supported that female candidate.'

Usage: Functions as predicate.

Near Synonym: [不失时机] (bù shī shí jī 不失時機) 'not miss an opportunity.'

Antonyms: [刻舟求剑] (kè zhōu qiú jiàn 刻舟求劍) 'carve boat seek sword – not know how to adapt to changed conditions,' [墨守成规] (mò shǒu chéng guī 墨守成規) 'stick to conventions or outmoded practices.'

185. 【谈何容易】(談何容易) tán hé róng yì

何 here means 'how.' The literal meaning is 'to talk about it how is it easy,' with a freer translation being 'easier said than done, not at all easy.'

Example 1: 说可以那样说，但是做起来**谈何容易**！

Shuō kěyǐ nàyàng shuō, dànshì zuòqǐlai **tánhéróngyì**!

'You can talk about it like that, but in doing it, it's not at all easy!'

Example 2: 要想改变一位八十岁的老人的想法**谈何容易**？

Yào xiǎng gǎibiàn yí wèi bāshí suì de lǎorén de xiǎngfǎ **tánhéróngyì**?

'If you want to change the ways of thinking of an older person of eighty years of age, that is easier said than done.'

Usage: Functions as predicate at the end of a sentence; can be followed by a period, question mark, or exclamation mark, depending on the meaning.

Near Synonym: [来之不易] (lái zhī bú yì 來之不易) 'not easily obtained, hard-won.'

Antonym: [轻而易举] (qīng ér yì jǔ 輕而易舉) 'light and easy to lift – easy.'

186. 【大势所趋】(大勢所趨) dà shì suǒ qū

大 means 'overall,' 势 means 'tendency,' and 趋 means 'tend towards.' A literal translation of the whole idiom is 'the direction in which the overall tendency is moving in,' with freer translations being 'the general trend of things' or 'the trend of the times.'

Example 1: 随着人们生活水平的提高，有机蔬菜是**大势所趋**。

Suízhe rénmen shēnghuó shuǐpíng de tígāo, yǒujī shūcài shì dàshì-suǒqū.

'Following along with the rise in people's standard of living, organic vegetables are the trend of the times.'

Example 2: 由于历史和文化比较接近，欧洲各国在政治上和经济上统一是**大势所趋**。

Yóuyú lìshǐ hé wénhuà bǐjiào jiējìn, Ōuzhōu gè guó zài zhèngzhì shàng hé jīngjì shàng tǒngyī shì dàshì-suǒqū.

'Because their history and culture are relatively close, that the various countries of Europe unite politically and economically is the general trend of things.'

Usage: Functions mainly as independent predicate, usually preceded by the verb 是 (shì) 'be.'

Near Synonym: [势在必行] (shì zài bì xíng 势在必行) 'given the circumstances it must be done.'

187. 【潜移默化】(潛移默化) qián yí mò huà

潜 means 'hidden,' 移 means 'move,' 默 means 'silent,' and 化 means 'change.' A literal translation of the whole idiom is 'hidden move and silent change,' with freer translations being 'influence subtly or imperceptibly.'

Example 1: 父母的言行一定会**潜移默化**地影响孩子。

Fùmǔ de yánxíng yídìng huì qiányí-mòhuà de yǐngxiǎng háizi.

'The words and actions of parents are certain to subtly influence children.'

Example 2: 音乐对人的成长有**潜移默化**的作用。

Yīnyuè duì rén de chéngzhǎng yǒu qiányí-mòhuà de zuòyòng.

'Music has an imperceptible effect on the maturation of people.'

Usage: Functions mainly as adverbial and attributive.

Near Synonyms: [耳濡目染] (ěr rú mù rǎn 耳濡目染) 'ears immersed and eyes contaminated – influenced by what one hears and sees,' [近朱者赤] (jìn zhū zhě chì 近朱者赤) 'one who approaches vermilion will become red – the influence of one's surroundings.'

Antonyms: [无动于衷] (wú dòng yú zhōng 無動於衷) 'unmoved, unconcerned,' [刀枪不入] (dāo qiāng bú rù 刀槍不入) 'knife gun not enter – well shielded' (spoken Chinese).

188. 【掉以轻心】(掉以輕心) diào yǐ qīng xīn

掉 here means 'swing' and 轻心 means 'careless, casual.' A literal translation of the whole idiom is 'careless as you swing something.' The meaning is 'treat something lightly, become complacent, lower one's guard.'

Example 1: 虽然我们的对手是个弱队，但是我们也不能**掉以轻心**。

Suīrán wǒmen de duìshǒu shì ge ruò duì, dànshì wǒmen yě bù néng diàoyǐqīngxīn.

'Even though our opponent is a weak team, we must not be complacent.'

Example 2: 首相就职典礼那天，全市所有的警察一律取消放假，没有人敢**掉以轻心**。

Shǒuxiàng jiùzhí diǎnlǐ nà tiān, quán shì suǒyǒu de jǐngchá yílǜ qǔxiāo fàngjià, méiyǒu rén gǎn diàoyǐqīngxīn.

'On the day of the prime minister's inauguration, all of the police in the whole city had their leave cancelled; nobody dared to lower their guard.'

Usage: Functions as predicate, usually preceded by negative auxiliary verb constructions such as 不敢 (bù gǎn) 'dare not' and 不能 (bù néng) or 不可 (bù kě), both of which mean 'can not, should not, must not.'

Near Synonyms: [麻痹大意] (má bì dà yì 麻痹大意) 'careless and inattentive,' [不屑一顾] (bú xiè yí gù 不屑一顧) 'not deign to look.'

Antonyms: [郑重其事] (zhèng zhòng qí shì 鄭重其事) 'treat a matter seriously,' [全神贯注] (quán shén guàn zhù 全神貫注) 'give one's undivided attention to,' [一丝不苟] (yì sī bù gǒu 一絲不苟) 'not the least bit negligent.'

189. 【此起彼伏】(此起彼伏) cǐ qǐ bǐ fú

此 means 'this one,' 起 means 'rise,' 彼 means 'that one,' and 伏 means 'go down.' A literal translation of the whole idiom is 'this one rises that one goes down,' with freer translations including 'one rises while another falls,' 'in rapid succession,' and 'continuously.'

Example 1: 游行示威活动**此起彼伏**，全国乱成了一锅粥。

Yóuxíng shìwēi huódòng cǐqǐ-bǐfú, quán guó luànchéngle yìguōzhōu.

'The demonstrations continued in rapid succession, the whole country ending up in one great disorderly mess.'

Example 2: 表演太精彩了，掌声和欢呼声**此起彼伏**。

Biǎoyǎn tài jīngcǎi le, zhǎngshēng hé huānhū shēng cǐqǐ-bǐfú.

'The performance was absolutely brilliant, applause and cheers continuing in rapid succession.'

Usage: Functions mainly as predicate and attributive.

Near Synonym: [一波未平，一波又起] (yì bō wèi píng, yì bō yòu qǐ 一波未平，一波又起) 'one wave has not yet leveled, another wave rises again.'

Antonym: [风平浪静] (fēng píng làng jìng 風平浪靜) 'wind calm waves still – calm and tranquil.'

190. 【名落孙山】(名落孫山) míng luò Sūn Shān

名 means 'name, rank,' 落 means 'fall behind,' and 孙山 is the name of a person. A literal translation of the whole idiom is 'one's name falls behind Sun Shan,' with freer translations being 'fail to pass an examination, fail to be a successful candidate.'

Example 1: 虽然她参加过三次奥运会，可是每次都**名落孙山**。

Suīrán tā cānjiāguo sān cì Àoyùnhuì, kěshì měi cì dōu míngluò-Sūn Shān.

'Although she participated in the Olympics three times, each time she was unsuccessful.'

Example 2: 在这次选举中，他以两票之差**名落孙山**，令人感到十分可惜。

Zài zhè cì xuǎnjǔ zhōng, tā yǐ liǎng piào zhī chā míngluò-Sūn Shān, lìng rén gǎndào shífēn kěxī.

'In this election, he lost by two votes, making others feel it was a great pity.'

Usage: Functions mainly as predicate.

Allusion: Sun Shan was considered very talented by the people in his hometown. One day he went to another county to take an imperial examination. One of his fellow-townsmen asked Sun Shan to let his son go and take the examination together with him, hoping that his son would get lucky by association with Sun Shan. Unfortunately, the son failed the examination, whereas Sun Shan ranked last on the list of successful candidates. When Sun Shan returned home, his fellow-townsman asked him how his son had done. Sun Shan answered: 解名尽处是孙山，贤郎更在孙山外 (xiè míng jìn chù shì Sūn Shān, xián láng gèng zài Sūn Shān wài) "I was the last successful candidate, and your son fell behind even me."

Near Synonym: [一败涂地] (yí bài tú dì 一败涂地) 'collapse completely, suffer a crushing defeat.'

Antonyms: [金榜题名] (jīn bǎng tí míng 金榜题名) 'golden noticeboard write (one's) name – succeed on the imperial examination,' [名列前茅] (míng liè qián máo 名列前茅) 'at the top of the list.'

191. 【引人入胜】(引人入勝) yǐn rén rù shèng

引 means 'lead' and 胜 means 'beautiful, wonderful.' A literal translation of this idiom is 'lead people to enter a beautiful place.' The meaning of the whole idiom as now used is usually 'fascinating, absorbing, mesmerizing.'

Example 1: 美国电视上的幼儿节目内容丰富多彩，**引人入胜**。

Měiguó diànshì shàng de yòu'ér jiémù nèiróng fēngfù duōcǎi, yǐnrén-rùshèng.

'Children's programs on U.S. television are rich and varied in content; they are fascinating and absorbing.'

Example 2: 欧洲十八、十九世纪产生了大量的优秀的、**引人入胜**的作品。

Ōuzhōu shíbā, shíjiǔ shìjì chǎnshēngle dàliàng de yōuxiù de yǐnrén-rùshèng de zuòpǐn.

'Europe in the 18th and 19th centuries produced a great amount of outstanding and mesmerizing literary and artistic works.'

Usage: Functions mainly as predicate and attributive.

Note: Complimentary in meaning.

Near Synonym: [令人神往] (lìng rén shén wǎng 令人神往) 'let one's spirit go there – fire up one's imagination.'

Antonyms: [味同嚼蜡] (wèi tóng jiáo là 味同嚼蠟) 'taste like chewing wax – without taste,' [索然无味] (suǒ rán wú wèi 索然無味) 'dull and without flavor – insipid.'

192. 【不堪设想】(不堪設想) bù kān shè xiǎng

堪 means 'can' and 设想 means 'imagine.' The whole idiom means 'unbearable to contemplate, unthinkable, inconceivable.'

Example 1: 如果地球的平均温度升高两度，那么后果**不堪设想**。

Rúguǒ dìqiú de píngjūn wēndù shēnggāo liǎng dù， nàme hòuguǒ bùkān-shèxiǎng.

'If the average earth temperature were to rise by two degrees, the consequences would be unimaginable.'

Example 2: 因为很多国家有核武器，万一再发生世界大战，结果**不堪设想**。

Yīnwèi hěn duō guójiā yǒu héwǔqì, wànyī zài fāshēng shìjiè dàzhàn, jiéguǒ bùkān-shèxiǎng.

'Because many countries possess nuclear weapons, if by some chance another world war were to occur, the results would be inconceivable.'

Usage: Functions as predicate; usually preceded by subject meaning "result."

Near Synonym: [凶多吉少] (xiōng duō jí shǎo 凶多吉少) 'bad luck much, good luck little – bode ill rather than well.'

Antonym: [安然无恙] (ān rán wú yàng 安然無恙) 'safe and without illness, safe and sound.'

193. 【义无反顾】(義無反顧) yì wú fǎn gù

义 means 'obligation' and 反顾 means 'look back, change one's mind.' The meaning of the whole idiom is 'duty-bound not to turn back, one should not hesitate concerning one's obligations.'

Example 1: 大学毕业以后，他**义无反顾**地去了西藏工作。

Dàxué bìyè yǐhòu, tā yìwúfǎngù de qùle Xīzàng gōngzuò.

'After graduating from college, without hesitating concerning his obligations, he went to Tibet to work.'

Example 2: 他坚信，只要是正义的事情，就**义无反顾**。

Tā jiānxìn, zhǐyào shì zhèngyì de shìqing, jiù yìwúfǎngù.

'He firmly believes that so long as it is a matter that involves righteousness, then one is duty-bound not to turn back.'

Usage: Functions mainly as adverbial; can also serve as predicate.

Note: Complimentary in meaning.

Near Synonyms: [义不容辞] (yì bù róng cí 義不容辭) 'duty-bound not to refuse,' [破釜沉舟] (pò fǔ chén zhōu 破釜沉舟) 'break kettles sink boats – burn one's bridges.'

Antonyms: [畏首畏尾] (wèi shǒu wèi wěi 畏首畏尾) 'fear head fear tail – fraught with uncertainty, overcautious,' [畏缩不前] (wèi suō bù qián 畏縮不前) 'afraid to advance.'

194. 【焕然一新】(煥然一新) huàn rán yì xīn

焕然 means 'bright, shining.' A literal translation of the whole idiom is 'in a bright and shining manner and completely new,' with freer translations being 'look brand-new, change beyond recognition.'

Example 1: 装修以后，原来黑暗狭窄的小屋**焕然一新**，显得宽敞明亮。

Zhuāngxiū yǐhòu, yuánlái hēi'àn xiázhǎi de xiǎowū huànrán-yìxīn, xiǎnde kuānchǎng míngliàng.

'After renovation, the small room that originally had been dark and narrow appeared spacious and bright.'

Example 2: 经过十年发展，那座小城市**焕然一新**，简直让人难以相信。

Jīngguò shí nián fāzhǎn, nà zuò xiǎo chéngshì huànrán-yìxīn, jiǎnzhí ràng rén nán yǐ xiāngxìn.

'After ten years of development, that little city changed beyond recognition; it was simply hard for a person to believe.'

Usage: Functions as predicate.

Note: Complimentary in meaning.

Near Synonyms: [日新月异] (rì xīn yuè yì 日新月異) 'change rapidly with each new day,' [耳目一新] (ěr mù yì xīn 耳目一新) 'brand-new sights and sounds.'

Antonyms: [依然如故] (yī rán rú gù 依然如故) 'still the same as before,' [一成不变] (yì chéng bú biàn 一成不變) 'fixed and unalterable.'

195. 【一视同仁】(一視同仁) yí shì tóng rén

视 here means 'look upon as, treat as,' 同 means 'same,' and 仁 means 'benevolence, kindheartedness.' A literal translation of the whole idiom is 'all treat same kindheartedness,' with a freer translation being 'give equal or impartial treatment to all.'

Example 1: 大学对所有申请的学生一**视同仁**，不管学生的家庭经济情况怎么样，学生只要达到要求就可以被录取。

Dàxué duì suǒyǒu shēnqǐng de xuésheng yíshì-tóngrén, bùguǎn xuésheng de jiātíng jīngjì qíngkuàng zěnmeyàng, xuésheng zhǐyào dádào yāoqiú jiù kěyǐ bèi lùqǔ.

'Universities give impartial treatment to all students who apply; no matter what the students' family financial situation is like; so long as students meet the requirements, they can be enrolled.'

Example 2: 政府对于本国的企业和外国的企业应该一**视同仁**。

Zhèngfǔ duìyú běn guó de qǐyè hé wàiguó de qǐyè yīnggāi yíshì-tóngrén.

'The government should give equal treatment to domestic businesses and foreign businesses.'

Usage: Functions mainly as predicate; can also serve as adverbial.

Near Synonym: [等量齐观] (děng liàng qí guān 等量齊觀) 'consider as equal.'

Antonyms: [厚此薄彼] (hòu cǐ bó bǐ 厚此薄彼) 'favor this one and slight that one,' [另眼相看] (lìng yǎn xiāng kàn 另眼相看) 'have a different view about something.'

196. 【五颜六色】 (五顏六色) wǔ yán liù sè

颜 means 'color' and 色 means 'color.' The meaning of the whole idiom is 'all kinds of colors, a variety of colors, multicolored.'

Example 1: 节日的时候，人们穿上**五颜六色**的衣服在街上游行。

Jiérì de shíhou, rénmen chuānshàng wǔyán-liùsè de yīfu zài jiē shàng yóuxíng.

'On holidays, people wear brightly colored clothes and parade around on the streets.'

Example 2: 植物园里开满了**五颜六色**的花草。

Zhíwùyuán lǐ kāimǎnle wǔyán-liùsè de huācǎo.

'The botanical gardens were all abloom with multicolored flowering plants.'

Usage: Functions mainly as attributive.

Near Synonym: [五彩缤纷] (wǔ cǎi bīn fēn 五彩繽紛) 'multicolored.'

197. 【束手无策】 (束手無策) shù shǒu wú cè

束 means 'bind, tie up' and 策 means 'plan.' The literal meaning is 'bind up one's hands and be without a strategy,' with a freer translation being 'at a complete loss about what to do.'

Example 1: 这是突发的情况，大家都显得**束手无策**。

Zhè shì tūfā de qíngkuàng, dàjiā dōu xiǎnde shùshǒu-wúcè.

'This was a situation that occurred suddenly, everyone seeming to be at a complete loss.'

Example 2: 眼看着华尔街股票市场道琼斯指数不断下跌，美联储主席也**束手无策**。

Yǎn kànzhe Huá'ěr Jiē gǔpiào shìchǎng Dàoqióngsī zhǐshù búduàn xiàdiē, Měiliánchǔ zhǔxí yě shùshǒu-wúcè.

'With his own eyes watching the Dow Jones index of the Wall Street stock market continuously dropping, the chairman of the U.S. Federal Reserve Board also was at a total loss.'

Usage: Functions mainly as predicate.

Note: Derogatory in meaning.

Near Synonym: [无能为力] (wú néng wéi lì 無能為力) 'powerless, helpless.'

Antonyms: [得心应手] (dé xīn yìng shǒu 得心應手) 'do or handle expertly,' [左右逢源] (zuǒ yòu féng yuán 左右逢源) 'resourceful and successful.'

198. 【十字路口】(十字路口) shí zì lù kǒu

The literal meaning is 'a street intersection shaped like the character 十 "ten" (i.e, like a cross or an X-shape).' This idiom is frequently used in the literal sense. However, it has gained an extended meaning of 'crossroads,' i.e., a situation of having arrived at a time or place where one must make an important choice.

Example 1: 高中毕业后，一个人就会处在人生和事业的**十字路口**，该何去何从得好好思考。

Gāozhōng bìyè hòu, yí ge rén jiù huì chǔ zài rénshēng hé shìyè de shízì-lùkǒu, gāi héqù-hécóng děi hǎohǎo sīkǎo.

'After high school graduation, a person will be at a crossroads as regards his or her life and career; what path he or she should take is something they must think through well.'

Example 2: 中欧关系现在正处在**十字路口**，双方都小心翼翼，避免关系恶化。

Zhōng-Ōu guānxi xiànzài zhèng chǔ zài shízì-lùkǒu, shuāngfāng dōu xiǎoxīn-yìyì, bìmiǎn guānxi èhuà.

'Chinese-European relations now are just at a crossroads, both sides being extremely cautious to avoid relations deteriorating.'

Usage: Often functions as object of the verbs 处于(chǔ yú 處於) 'be at,' 处在 (chǔ zài 處在) 'be at,' and 到了(dàole) 'arrived at.'

Near Synonym: [十字街头] (shí zì jiē tóu 十字街頭) 'cross streets, busy streets.'

Antonym: [阳关大道] (yáng guān dà dào 陽關大道) 'open road, bright future.'

199. 【与日俱增】(與日俱增) yǔ rì jù zēng

与 means 'with,' 日 means 'days,' 俱 means 'together,' and 增 means 'increase.' A literal translation of the whole idiom is 'with the days together increase,' with a freer translation being 'grow day by day, be on the increase.'

Example 1: 多年来，两国的友好交往**与日俱增**。

Duō nián lái, liǎng guó de yǒuhǎo jiāowǎng yǔrì-jùzēng.

'For many years, the friendly relationship between the two countries has been growing day by day.'

Example 2: 面对**与日俱增**的人口增长压力，中国政府决定实行计划生育政策。

Miànduì yǔrì-jùzēng de rénkǒu zēngzhǎng yālì, Zhōngguó zhèngfǔ juédìng shíxíng jìhuà shēngyù zhèngcè.

'Facing the daily increasing pressure of population growth, the Chinese government decided to implement family planning policies.'

Usage: Functions mainly as predicate at the end of a sentence; can also serve as attributive.

Near Synonyms: [与时俱进] (yǔ shí jù jìn 與時俱進) 'keep pace with the times,' [日积月累] (rì jī yuè lěi 日積月累) 'accumulate day by day and month by month.'

Antonym: [每况愈下] (měi kuàng yù xià 每况愈下) 'go from bad to worse.'

200. 【拔苗助长】(拔苗助長) bá miáo zhù zhǎng

拔 means 'pull up,' 苗 means 'seedling, shoot,' 助 means 'help,' and 长 means 'grow.' The literal meaning of this idiom is 'pull up shoots to help them grow,' with freer translations including 'spoil things by trying to be too helpful, spoil by undue haste, haste makes waste.'

Example 1: 家长对孩子的期望都比较高，但是不能**拔苗助长**，孩子的成长需要时间。

Jiāzhǎng duì háizi de qīwàng dōu bǐjiào gāo, dànshì bù néng bámiáo-zhùzhǎng, háizi de chéngzhǎng xūyào shíjiān.

'Parents all have relatively high hopes for their children, but one cannot try to help young shoots grow by pulling them up; children's maturation takes time.'

Example 2: 我们反对这种**拔苗助长**的做法。

Wǒmen fǎnduì zhè zhǒng bámiáo-zhùzhǎng de zuòfǎ.

'We are opposed to this kind of method that spoils things through undue haste.'

Usage: Functions mainly as predicate at the end of a sentence; can also serve as attributive.

Allusion: There was a farmer who was very worried that the seedlings for his next crop were not growing quickly enough, so he pulled them up high. After he had finished pulling them out, he was very tired, so he went home. When he saw other people, he said, "I'm exhausted; I helped the rice seedlings grow tall." His son immediately ran to the field; all the rice seedlings had withered and died. (from "Gong Sun Chou" in *Mencius*)

Note: Has a negative connotation. There is an alternative form 揠苗助长 (yà miáo zhù zhǎng 揠苗助長).

201. 【博大精深】(博大精深) bó dà jīng shēn

博 means 'broad,' 精 means 'proficient,' and 深 means 'deep.' The whole idiom means 'broad and profound, vast and profound.'

Example 1: 佛教文化**博大精深**，不是一两句话就解释得清的。

Fójiào wénhuà **bódà-jīngshēn**, bú shì yì liǎng jù huà jiù jiěshìdeqīng de.

'Buddhist culture is vast and profound; it's not something that could be explained clearly in just a sentence or two.'

Example 2: 他在少林寺领略到了**博大精深**的中华武术。

Tā zài Shàolín Sì lǐnglüèdàole **bódà-jīngshēn** de Zhōnghuá wǔshù.

'At the Shaolin Temple, he came to appreciate the vast and profound martial arts of China.'

Usage: Functions mainly as predicate and attributive.

Note: Complimentary in meaning.

Near Synonym: [包罗万象] (bāo luó wàn xiàng 包羅萬象) 'covering ten thousand phenomena – all-inclusive, comprehensive' (neutral in meaning).

Antonym: [鸡毛蒜皮] (jī máo suàn pí 雞毛蒜皮) 'chicken feathers garlic peels – trivial things.'

202. 【喜气洋洋】(喜氣洋洋) xǐ qì yáng yáng

喜气 means 'happy mood or atmosphere' and 洋洋 means 'content.' The meaning of the whole idiom is 'very cheerful and joyful, jubilant.'

Example 1: 春节来了，全国上下充满了**喜气洋洋**的气氛。

Chūnjié láile, quánguó shàngxià chōngmǎnle **xǐqì-yángyáng** de qìfēn.

'Chinese New Year came, and the entire country, high and low, was permeated with a jubilant atmosphere.'

Example 2: 卫星发射成功，在场的人都**喜气洋洋**。

Wèixīng fāshè chénggōng, zài chǎng de rén dōu **xǐqì-yángyáng**.

'When the satellite was launched successfully, all the people present were jubilant.'

Usage: Functions mainly as predicate, attributive, and adverbial.

Note: Complimentary in meaning.

Near Synonyms: [欢天喜地] (huān tiān xǐ dì 歡天喜地) 'overjoyed,' [其乐融融] (qí lè róng róng 其樂融融) 'harmonious happiness.'

Antonym: [愁眉苦脸] (chóu méi kǔ liǎn 愁眉苦臉) 'worried eyebrows bitter face – distressed.'

203. 【不可或缺】(不可或缺) bù kě huò quē

或 means 'a little' and 缺 means 'lack.' A literal translation of the whole idiom is 'not can even a little lack,' with freer translations being 'indispensable, absolutely essential.'

Example 1: 实习是大学生活中**不可或缺**的一项内容。

Shíxí shì dàxué shēnghuó zhōng bùkě-huòquē de yí xiàng nèiróng.

'Internships are a kind of content that is absolutely essential in college life.'

Example 2: "礼"是儒家思想中**不可或缺**的一个方面。

"Lǐ" shì Rújiā sīxiǎng zhōng bùkě-huòquē de yí ge fāngmiàn.

'The *li* (rites) are an indispensable aspect in Confucian thought.'

Usage: Functions mainly as attributive.

Near Synonyms: [必不可少] (bì bù kě shǎo 必不可少) and [缺一不可] (quē yī bù kě 缺一不可) , both 'indispensable.'

Antonyms: [无关紧要] (wú guān jǐn yào 無關緊要) 'immaterial, unimportant,' [无关大局] (wú guān dà jú 無關大局) 'have no bearing on the general situation – unimportant.'

204. 【顺理成章】(順理成章) shùn lǐ chéng zhāng

顺 means 'according to,' 理 means 'reason,' and 章 means 'order.' A literal translation is 'according to reason achieve order.' A freer translation of this idiom would be 'do something in a reasonable and orderly manner, logical, rational.'

Example 1: 他是副总裁，为公司做出过很多贡献，现在总裁退休了，他当选总裁是**顺理成章**的事。

Tā shì fùzǒngcái, wèi gōngsī zuòchūguo hěn duō gòngxiàn, xiànzài zǒngcái tuìxiūle, tā dāngxuǎn zǒngcái shì shùnlǐ-chéngzhāng de shì.

'He's the deputy director general and has made a lot of contributions to the company; now the director general is about to retire, so his being elected director general is the logical thing.'

Example 2: 中国开放了保险业，外国保险公司**顺理成章**地进入了中国市场。

Zhōngguó kāifàngle bǎoxiǎnyè, wàiguó bǎoxiǎn gōngsī shùnlǐ-chéngzhāng de jìnrùle Zhōngguó shìchǎng.

'China has opened up the insurance industry, so foreign insurance firms have quite understandably entered the Chinese market.'

Usage: Functions mainly as attributive and predicate.

Near Synonyms: [自然而然] (zì rán ér rán 自然而然) 'naturally,' [水到渠成] (shuǐ dào qú chéng 水到渠成) 'water arrives and channel is formed – when conditions are ripe success is achieved; achieved naturally and without effort,' [马到成功] (mǎ dào chéng gōng 馬到成功) 'horse arrives achieve success – imminent success.'

Antonym: [名不正言不顺] (míng bú zhèng yán bú shùn 名不正言不順) 'If the names of things are not correct, then language is not in accordance with the truth of things.'

205. 【大刀阔斧】(大刀闊斧) dà dāo kuò fǔ

阔 means 'wide' and 斧 means 'axe.' The literal meaning of the whole idiom is 'big knife and wide axe.' A freer translation is 'bold and resolute.'

Example 1: 他当了领导之后，对这个公司进行了**大刀阔斧**的改革，取得了很大的成绩。

Tā dāngle lǐngdǎo zhīhòu, duì zhège gōngsī jìnxíngle dàdāo-kuòfǔ de gǎigé, qǔdéle hěn dà de chéngjì.

'After he became leader, he undertook bold and resolute reforms in the company, attaining great results.'

Example 2: 新总统**大刀阔斧**地推行他的新经济政策。

Xīn zǒngtǒng dàdāo-kuòfǔ de tuīxíng tā de xīn jīngjì zhèngcè.

'The new president is implementing his new economic policies boldly and resolutely.'

Usage: Functions mainly as adverbial and attributive.

Note: Complimentary in meaning.

Near Synonym: [雷厉风行] (léi lì fēng xíng 雷厲風行) 'vigorous and resolute.'

Antonym: [缩手缩脚] (suō shǒu suō jiǎo 縮手縮腳) 'draw in one's hands and feet – overcautious.'

206. 【不遗余力】(不遺餘力) bù yí yú lì

遗 means 'hold back' and 余 means 'surplus, remaining.' A literal translation is 'not hold back surplus effort,' with freer translations of the whole idiom being 'spare no efforts, do one's utmost.'

Example 1: 她一生**不遗余力**地宣传中国传统文化。

Tā yìshēng bùyí-yúlì de xuānchuán Zhōngguó chuántǒng wénhuà.

'Her whole life long she did her utmost to popularize traditional Chinese culture.'

Example 2: 国际奥委会在反兴奋剂问题上**不遗余力**。

Guójì Àowěihuì zài fǎn xīngfènjì wèntí shàng bùyí-yúlì.

'The International Olympic Committee spared no efforts on the issue of opposing stimulants.'

Usage: Functions mainly as adverbial; can also serve as predicate.

Near Synonyms: [竭尽全力] (jié jìn quán lì 竭盡全力) 'do one's utmost,' [全力以赴] (quán lì yǐ fù 全力以赴) 'spare no effort.'

Antonyms: [留有余地] (liú yǒu yú dì 留有餘地) 'leave room – allow for the unexpected,' [明哲保身] (míng zhé bǎo shēn 明哲保身) 'wise people protect their person – don't stick one's neck out.'

207. 【字里行间】 (字裏行間) zì lǐ háng jiān

行 means 'line.' The meaning of the whole idiom is 'between the lines.'

Example 1: 她给丈夫的信**字里行间**都充满着深深的爱。

Tā gěi zhàngfu de xìn zìlǐ-hángjiān dōu chōngmǎnzhe shēnshēn de ài.

'As for the letters she sends her husband, between the lines they are all imbued with the deepest love.'

Example 2: 他的演讲**字里行间**透露出想退休的意思。

Tā de yǎnjiǎng zìlǐ-hángjiān tòulùchū xiǎng tuìxiū de yìsi.

'Between the lines, his lecture divulged his intention to retire.'

Usage: Functions mainly as subject; can also serve as object. Often followed by verbs such as 充满 (chōngmǎn 充滿) 'full of,' 流露 (liúlù 流露) 'reveal,' 透露 (tòulù 透露) 'divulge,' 渗透 (shèntòu 滲透) 'permeate,' and 饱含 (bǎohán 飽含) 'full of.'

Near Synonyms: [言外之意] (yán wài zhī yì 言外之意) 'implied meaning, implication,' [弦外之音] (xián wài zhī yīn 弦外之音) 'implication, overtone.'

Antonym: [直抒胸臆] (zhí shū xiōng yì 直抒胸臆) 'express one's feelings directly.'

208. 【不解之缘】 (不解之緣) bù jiě zhī yuán

解 means 'untie, dissolve' and 缘 means 'predestined relationship, fate.' A literal translation of the whole idiom is 'a predestined relationship that one cannot dissolve.' Freer translations of the idiom include 'indissoluble bond, very close connection.'

Example 1: 自从听了那位僧人演讲之后，他就与佛教结下了**不解之缘**。

Zìcóng tīngle nà wèi sēngrén yǎnjiǎng zhīhòu, tā jiù yǔ fójiào jiéxiàle bùjiě-zhīyuán.

'From the time he heard that Buddhist monk lecture, he formed an indissoluble bond with Buddhism.'

Example 2: 一次偶然的相遇使他们结下了**不解之缘**。

Yí cì ǒurán de xiàngyù shǐ tāmen jiéxiàle bùjiě-zhīyuán.

'A fortuitous encounter made them form an indissoluble bond.'

Usage: Functions as object, mainly in the pattern A 与 B 结下了～ (A yǔ B jié xià le . . . A 與 B 結下了～) 'A and B have formed. . . .'

Near Synonym: [难解难分] (nán jiě nán fēn 難解難分) 'hard to divide hard to separate – inextricably involved.'

Antonym: [一刀两断] (yì dāo liǎng duàn 一刀兩斷) 'one (blow of a) knife two severed portions – make a clean break with.'

209. 【一无所有】(一無所有) yì wú suǒ yǒu

The meaning of this idiom is 'have absolutely nothing, penniless, destitute.'

Example 1: 他们结婚的时候，除了一身红色的新衣服，其他的**一无所有**。

Tāmen jiéhūn de shíhou, chúle yì shēn hóngsè de xīn yīfu, qítā de yìwúsuǒyǒu.

'When they married, except for a new suit of red clothes, they had absolutely nothing else.'

Example 2: 他觉得自己成了除了钱以外一**无所有**的可怜虫了。

Tā juéde zìjǐ chéngle chúle qián yǐwài yìwúsuǒyǒu de kěliánchóng le.

'He felt that he had become a pitiful thing who had nothing aside from money.'

Usage: Functions mainly as predicate; can also serve as attributive.

Near Synonyms: [身无长物] (shēn wú cháng wù 身無長物) 'have no surplus things on you – have nothing but the necessities of life,' [空空如也] (kōng kōng rú yě 空空如也) 'completely empty,' [家徒四壁] (jiā tú sì bì 家徒四壁) 'home only has four walls – completely destitute.'

Antonyms: [应有尽有] (yīng yǒu jìn yǒu 應有盡有) 'have everything that should be had,' [无所不有] (wú suǒ bù yǒu 無所不有) 'there is nothing one doesn't have – have everything,' [一应俱全] (yì yīng jù quán 一應俱全) 'complete with everything.'

210. 【守株待兔】(守株待兔) shǒu zhū dài tù

守 means 'guard or keep watch over,' 株 means 'tree stump,' 待 means 'await,' and 兔 means 'hare, rabbit,' The literal meaning is 'keep watch over a tree stump waiting for hares (to come and dash themselves against it).' A freer translation is 'wait passively for a windfall, wait for gains without pains, trust chance and windfalls.'

Example 1: 要想吸引外资，就要主动跟外资企业联系，不能**守株待兔**。

Yào xiǎng xīyǐn wàizī, jiù yào zhǔdòng gēn wàizī qǐyè liánxì, bù néng shǒuzhū-dàitù.

'If you want to attract foreign investment, then you have to take the initiative and contact foreign enterprises; you can't just wait for a windfall.'

Example 2: 美国是一个竞争激烈的社会，**守株待兔**的思想是不行的。

Měiguó shì yí ge jìngzhēng jīliè de shèhuì, shǒuzhū-dàitù de sīxiǎng shì bù xíng de.

'The U.S. is a society of intense competition; the kind of thinking where one "waits for gains without pains" will not do.'

Usage: Functions mainly as predicate or attributive.

Allusion: There was a farmer who made his living on the land. One day a rabbit was running too quickly; all of a sudden, it ran into a wooden post in the ground, snapped its neck, and died. The farmer got a rabbit for nothing and was very happy. So he stopped doing work and every day waited next to the wooden post, hoping more rabbits would run into it, but no more rabbits came. His land became uncultivated, but he also became mocked by everyone. (from "Wu Du" in *Han Feizi*)

Note: Has a negative connotation.

Near Synonyms: [刻舟求剑] (kè zhōu qiú jiàn 刻舟求劍) 'carve boat seek sword – not know how to adapt to changed conditions,' [坐吃山空] (zuò chī shān kōng 坐吃山空) 'only to sit and eat will wear even a mountain away – only expenditures without any income will deplete even the greatest fortune.'

Antonym: [八面玲珑] (bā miàn líng lóng 八面玲瓏) 'smooth and slick, get along well with everyone.'

211. 【百花齐放】(百花齊放) bǎi huā qí fàng

百花 means 'all kinds of flowers,' 齐 means 'together,' 放 means 'bloom.' The literal meaning is 'all kinds of flowers bloom at the same time.' An extended meaning is 'different points of view exist simultaneously.'

Example 1: 春天来了，公园里**百花齐放**，非常漂亮。

Chūntiān láile, gōngyuán lǐ bǎihuā-qífàng, fēicháng piàoliàng.

'Spring has come, in the park all kinds of flowers are blooming at the same time, it's very pretty.'

Example 2: 不论是文学界、艺术界，还是政治界、思想界，都应该坚持**百花齐放**、百家争鸣的原则，不能认为只有一种观点是正确的。

Búlùn shì wénxué jiè yìshùjiè, háishì zhèngzhìjiè sīxiǎngjiè, dōu yīnggāi jiānchí bǎihuā-qífàng bǎijiā-zhēngmíng de yuánzé, bù néng rènwéi zhǐyǒu yì zhǒng guāndiǎn shì zhèngquè de.

'Whether in literary and artistic circles or in political and ideological circles, one should insist on the principle of "let a hundred flowers bloom, let a hundred schools of thought contend"; one should not hold that only one point of view is correct.'

Usage: Functions mainly as attributive; can also serve as predicate. Often co-occurs with 百家争鸣 (bǎijiā-zhēngmíng 百家爭鳴).

Note: The extended meaning is now most common. This idiom came to be widely used after a 1942 lecture by Mao Zedong titled 关于正确处理人民内部矛盾的问题 (Guānyú zhèngquè chǔlǐ rénmín nèibù máodùn de wèntí 關於正確處理人民內部矛盾的問題) *"On the Correct Handling of Contradictions Among the People."*

Antonyms: [一枝独秀] (yì zhī dú xiù 一枝獨秀) 'one branch of a tree alone is excellent – outshine others' (complimentary); [一花独放] (yì huā dú fàng 一花獨放) 'one flower alone blooms' (somewhat derogatory).

212. 【力不从心】(力不從心) lì bù cóng xīn

从 here means 'follow.' A literal translation of the whole idiom is 'one's strength does not follow one's heart,' with freer translations being 'lack the ability to do what one would like to do.'

Example 1: 他想像十年前那样工作，但是毕竟是四十岁的人了，有些**力不从心**了。

Tā xiǎng xiàng shí nián qián nàyàng gōngzuò, dànshì bìjìng shì sìshí suì de rén le, yǒuxiē lìbùcóngxīn le.

'He wants to work like ten years ago, but after all, he's now a man of forty; to a certain extent, he now lacks the ability to do as he would like to do.'

Example 2: 总统想改革，但是国会不支持，总统显得**力不从心**。

Zǒngtǒng xiǎng gǎigé, dànshì guóhuì bù zhīchí, zǒngtǒng xiǎnde lìbùcóngxīn.

'The president wants to implement reforms, but Congress doesn't support him; the president appears to lack the ability to do what he would like to do.'

Usage: Functions mainly as predicate and object.

Near Synonyms: [有心无力] (yǒu xīn wú lì 有心無力) 'intend to but be unable,' [无能为力] (wú néng wéi lì 無能為力) 'powerless, helpless.'

Antonyms: [游刃有余] (yóu rèn yǒu yú 游刃有餘) 'more than capable of doing something,' [得心应手] (dé xīn yìng shǒu 得心應手) 'do or handle expertly.'

213. 【异口同声】(異口同聲) yì kǒu tóng shēng

异 means 'different,' 口 means 'mouth,' and 声 means 'voice.' A literal translation of this idiom is 'different mouths same sound.' A freer translation is 'with one voice, in unison, in concert.'

Example 1: 大家**异口同声**地说："不可能。"

Dàjiā **yìkǒu-tóngshēng** de shuō: "Bù kěnéng."

'Everyone said in unison: "Impossible."'

Example 2: 不论是共和党人还是民主党人，大家都**异口同声**地称赞他是位伟大的总统。

Búlùn shì Gònghédǎng rén háishì Mínzhǔdǎng rén, dàjiā dōu **yìkǒu-tóngshēng** de chēngzàn tā shì wèi wěidà de zǒngtǒng.

'No matter whether they are Republicans or Democrats, everyone unanimously praises him as having been a great president.'

Usage: Functions as adverbial, followed by verbs meaning 'say.'

Near Synonym: [不约而同] (bù yuē ér tóng 不約而同) 'take the same action or have the same view without prior consultation.'

Antonym: [众说纷纭] (zhòng shuō fēn yún 眾說紛紜) 'opinions vary greatly.'

214. 【背道而驰】(背道而馳) bèi dào ér chí

背 here means 'opposing,' 道 means 'road,' and 驰 means 'run.' A literal translation of the whole idiom is 'run on the opposing road,' with freer translations being 'run counter to, diametrically opposed to.'

Example 1: 他的做法和他的诺言显然是**背道而驰**的。

Tā de zuòfǎ hé tā de nuòyán xiǎnrán shì **bèidào-érchí** de.

'His practices are obviously the exact opposite of his promises.'

Example 2: 这项新政策实际上与宪法的精神**背道而驰**。

Zhè xiàng xīn zhèngcè shíjìshàng yǔ xiànfǎ de jīngshen **bèidào-érchí**.

'This new policy actually runs counter to the spirit of the constitution.'

Usage: Functions mainly as predicate.

Note: Derogatory in meaning.

Near Synonym: [南辕北辙] (nán yuán běi zhé 南轅北轍) 'one's goal and one's actions are exactly opposite, diametrically opposed.'

Antonyms: [如出一辙] (rú chū yì zhé 如出一轍) 'as if emerging from the same track – one and the same, cut from the same cloth,' [并驾齐驱] (bìng jià qí qū 並駕齊驅) 'run neck and neck with, be on equal terms.'

215. 【势在必行】(勢在必行) shì zài bì xíng

The literal meaning is 'imperative under the situation.'

Example 1: 文化大革命以后，经济改革**势在必行**。

Wénhuàdàgémìng yǐhòu, jīngjì gǎigé **shìzàibìxíng**.

'After the Cultural Revolution, economic reform was imperative under the situation.'

Example 2: 因为全世界的石油资源只能再用三十年，所以寻找新的能源**势在必行**。

Yīnwèi quán shìjiè de shíyóu zīyuán zhǐ néng zài yòng sānshí nián, suǒyǐ xúnzhǎo xīnde néngyuán **shìzàibìxíng**.

'Because the entire world's oil resources can only be used for thirty more years, searching for new energy sources is imperative under the situation.'

Usage: Functions mainly as predicate at the end of a sentence.

Near Synonym: [大势所趋] (dà shì suǒ qū 大勢所趨) 'the general trend of things, the trend of the times.'

Antonym: [随心所欲] (suí xīn suǒ yù 隨心所欲) 'do exactly as one pleases, at will.'

216. 【当之无愧】(當之無愧) dāng zhī wú kuì

当 means 'take on, accept,' 之 means 'it,' and 愧 means 'shame.' A literal translation of the whole idiom is 'accept it not have shame.' Freer translations of the idiom include 'deserve, merit, be worthy of.'

Example 1: 费德勒是网坛**当之无愧**的第一人。

Fèidélè shì wǎngtán **dāngzhī-wúkuì** de dìyī rén.

'Federer deserves to be the number one person of the tennis world.'

Example 2: 泰山**当之无愧**地入选了世界自然与文化双重遗产。

Tài Shān **dāngzhī-wúkuì** de rùxuǎnle shìjiè zìrán yǔ wénhuà shuāngchóng yíchǎn.

'Mount Tai fully deserves having been selected as a world natural and cultural double heritage site.'

Usage: Functions mainly as attributive and predicate; can also serve as adverbial.

Note: Complimentary in meaning.

Near Synonyms: [名副其实] (míng fù qí shí 名副其實) 'worthy of the name or reputation,' [实至名归] (shí zhì míng guī 實至名歸) 'a good reputation will come if there is real achievement.'

Antonyms: [名不副实] (míng bú fù shí 名不副實) 'unworthy of the name,' [欺世盗名] (qī shì dào míng 欺世盜名) 'deceive the generations and steal a name – gain fame by deceiving people,' [徒有其表] (tú yǒu qí biǎo 徒有其表) 'only have its surface – only have external appearances without real substance,' [徒有虚名] (tú yǒu xū míng 徒有虚名) 'enjoy unwarranted fame, in name only,' [当之有愧] (dāng zhī yǒu kuì 當之有愧) 'not deserve or be worthy of something.'

217. 【咄咄逼人】(咄咄逼人) duō duō bī rén

咄咄 is an interjection indicating surprise, 逼 means 'force,' and 逼人 means 'threatening.' The meaning of the whole idiom is 'threatening and overbearing.'

Example 1: 他说话的声音很大，**咄咄逼人**，没理好象也有三分理了。

Tā shuōhuà de shēngyīn hěn dà, duōduō-bīrén, méi lǐ hǎoxiàng yě yǒu sān fēn lǐ le.

'He speaks with a loud voice, quite threatening and overbearing, so that even when he's wrong, it appears as though he's somewhat right.'

Example 2: 面对中国经济上**咄咄逼人**的威胁，我们应该怎么办呢？

Miànduì Zhōngguó jīngjì shàng duōduō-bīrén de wēixié, wǒmen yīnggāi zěnme bàn ne?

'What should we do in the face of the aggressive and overbearing threat of China's economy?'

Usage: Functions mainly as attributive, adverbial, and predicate.

Note: Sometimes slightly derogatory in meaning.

Near Synonyms: [气势汹汹] (qì shì xiōng xiōng 氣勢洶洶) 'fierce or agitated manner,' [盛气凌人] (shèng qì líng rén 盛氣凌人) 'arrogant, overbearing.'

Antonym: [温文尔雅] (wēn wén ěr yǎ 溫文爾雅) 'mild-mannered and cultivated.'

218. 【四通八达】(四通八達) sì tōng bā dá

通 means 'pass through freely without impediment' and 达 means 'reach or extend to without obstruction.' A literal translation of the whole idiom is 'four (sides) pass through freely and eight (directions) extend to without obstruction.' This usually describes very convenient transportation networks. A possible English translation is 'extend or radiate in all directions.'

Example 1: 亚特兰大位于美国东南部，是一个交通**四通八达**的大城市。

Yàtèlándà wèiyú Měiguó dōngnán bù, shì yí ge jiāotōng sìtōng-bādá de dà chéngshì.

'Atlanta is located in the southeast of the U.S.; it's a major city with a transportation network that radiates in all directions.'

Example 2: 伦敦的地铁**四通八达**，十分方便。

Lúndūn de dìtiě sìtōng-bādá, shífēn fāngbiàn.

'The London underground railway system extends in all directions; it's very convenient.'

Usage: Functions as attributive and predicate.

Near Synonym: [畅通无阻] (chàng tōng wú zǔ 暢通無阻) 'unimpeded and unobstructed.'

Antonyms: [水泄不通] (shuǐ xiè bù tōng 水泄不通) 'not even a drop of water could get through,' [四面碰壁] (sì miàn pèng bì 四面碰壁) 'on four sides collide with a wall.'

219. 【可歌可泣】(可歌可泣) kě gē kě qì

泣 means 'shed tears.' The literal meaning of this idiom is 'can sing can cry – moving people to songs and tears,' with a freer translation being 'inspiring, heroic and moving.'

Example 1: 在抗日战争中，涌现出了许多**可歌可泣**的英雄人物和事迹。

Zài Kàngrì zhànzhēng zhōng, yǒngxiàn chūle xǔduō kěgē-kěqì de yīngxióng rénwù hé shìjì.

'In the Sino-Japanese War, there emerged many heroic and moving heroes and deeds.'

Example 2: 罗密欧与朱丽叶反映的是一个**可歌可泣**的爱情故事。

Luómì'ōu yǔ Zhūlìyè fǎnyìng de shì yí ge kěgē-kěqì de àiqíng gùshi.

'What Romeo and Juliet reflects is a heroic and moving love story.'

Usage: Functions mainly as attributive; can also serve as predicate.

Note: Complimentary in meaning. Even stronger and more literary is the idiom 惊天地，泣鬼神 (jīng tiāndì, qì guǐshén) 'shocking and tragic.'

Near Synonym: [气壮山河] (qì zhuàng shān hé 氣壯山河) 'magnificent, inspiring.'

Antonym: [令人作呕] (lìng rén zuò ǒu 令人作嘔) 'make one feel nauseated – repulsive.'

220. 【惊弓之鸟】(驚弓之鳥) jīng gōng zhī niǎo

惊 means 'frightened of' and 弓 means 'bow (as in bow and arrow).' A literal translation of the whole idiom is 'a bird that is frightened of a bow.' This is a metaphor for someone who is frightened because of past experience. A possible translation is 'once bitten twice shy.'

Example 1: 因为股票市场连续几天下跌，股民们成了**惊弓之鸟**，生怕再听到不利股市的消息。

Yīnwèi gǔpiào shìchǎng liánxù jǐ tiān xiàdiē, gǔmínmen chéngle jīnggōng-zhīniǎo, shēngpà zài tīngdào búlì gǔshì de xiāoxi.

'Because the stock market fell continuously for several days, speculators in stocks have become like "birds that are frightened of a bow" due to bad experiences in the past, afraid of again hearing unfavorable news about the stock market.'

Example 2: 头顶上的地板震动了一下，下面的人就像**惊弓之鸟**，赶快往门外跑，以为发生了地震。

Tóudǐng shàng de dìbǎn zhèndòngle yíxià, xiàmiàn de rén jiù xiàng jīnggōng-zhīniǎo, gǎnkuài wǎng mén wài pǎo, yǐwéi fāshēngle dìzhèn.

'When the floorboards above their heads vibrated, the people underneath were just like "birds that are frightened of a bow" due to bad experiences in the past and quickly ran outside the door, mistakenly thinking that an earthquake had taken place.'

Usage: Functions mainly as object, often preceded by verbs such as 成了(chéngle) 'have become,' or 像 (xiàng) or 如 (rú), both of which mean 'be like.'

Allusion: Two people were standing on a high platform when they saw a bird in the distance that was flying in their direction. One of them said, "I need only draw the bowstring of my bow and I can shoot that bird; I needn't put in an arrow." The second person was very surprised at that and said, "Is your skill really that outstanding?" The first person said, "Yes, I can do that." After a while, a wild goose flew above their heads. The first person drew the bowstring, without putting in an arrow, and there was a loud "bang." And so that goose dropped down in an instant. Astonished, the second person asked how this had happened. The first person answered: "The goose was wounded." The second person asked: "It was so far away; how did you know?" The first person replied: "The goose was flying very slowly, calling sadly as it flew. That it flew so slowly showed that it had an internal injury. That it called so sadly showed that it had already left its flock for a long time. The goose heard the sound of my bowstring and got scared, instinctively trying to fly higher with all its might. As a result, its wound burst open, and so it dropped from the sky." (from "Stratagems of Chu," No. 4, in *Stratagems of the Warring States*)

Note: Derogatory in meaning.

Near Synonym: [漏网之鱼] (lòu wǎng zhī yú 漏網之魚) 'a fish that has slipped through the net – fugitive, runaway.'

Antonym: [初生牛犊] (chū shēng niú dú 初生牛犢) 'newborn calf.'

221. 【真心实意】(真心實意) zhēn xīn shí yì

真心 means 'true heart' and 实意 means 'real intention.' A literal translation of this idiom is 'true heart real intention,' with a freer translation being 'sincere, wholehearted.'

Example 1: 只有**真心实意**地为老百姓着想才能得到老百姓的拥护。

Zhǐyǒu zhēnxīn-shíyì de wèi lǎobǎixìng zháoxiǎng cái néng dédào lǎobǎixìng de yōnghù.

'Only if one sincerely takes the common people's interests into consideration can one obtain the common people's support.'

Example 2: 我知道您是**真心实意**的，但是您的好意我不能接受。

Wǒ zhīdao nín shì zhēnxīn-shíyì de, dànshì nín de hǎoyì wǒ bù néng jiēshòu.

'I know you're being sincere, but I can't accept your good intentions.'

Usage: Functions mainly as adverbial; can also serve as predicate.

Note: Complimentary in meaning.

Near Synonym: [诚心诚意] (chéng xīn chéng yì 誠心誠意) 'earnestly and sincerely.'

Antonym: [虚情假意] (xū qíng jiǎ yì 虛情假意) 'hypocritical, insincere.'

222. 【恰到好处】(恰到好處) qià dào hǎo chù

恰 means 'just, exactly' and 好处 here means 'good place, best situation.' The meaning of the whole idiom is 'just right.'

Example 1: 她很会说话，不多不少，**恰到好处**。

Tā hěn huì shuōhuà, bù duō bù shǎo, qiàdào-hǎochù.

'She is good with words, saying neither too much nor too little – just right.'

Example 2: 这个裁判很有经验，**恰到好处**地终止了比赛。

Zhège cáipàn hěn yǒu jīngyàn, qiàdào-hǎochù de zhōngzhǐle bǐsài.

'This umpire is very experienced, ending the match in just the right way.'

Usage: Functions mainly as predicate and adverbial.

Note: Somewhat complimentary in meaning.

Antonym: [过犹不及] (guò yóu bù jí 過猶不及) 'going too far is as bad as not going far enough.'

223. 【津津乐道】(津津樂道) jīn jīn lè dào

津 means 'saliva,' 津津 means 'succulent, tasty,' 乐 means 'happy to, love to,' and 道 means 'say, talk about.' The meaning of the whole idiom is 'love to talk about, dwell on.'

Example 1: 这个故事流传了上千年了，人们到今天仍然**津津乐道**。

Zhège gùshi liúchuánle shàng qiān nián le, rénmen dào jīntiān réngrán jīnjīn-lèdào.

'This story has been handed down for thousands of years; people up until today still love to talk about it.'

Example 2: 她**津津乐道**地向朋友们介绍她收藏的艺术品。

Tā jīnjīn-lèdào de xiàng péngyoumen jièshào tā shōucáng de yìshùpǐn.

'With great pleasure, she introduced to her friends the works of art she had collected.'

Usage: Functions mainly as predicate, adverbial, and attributive.

Near Synonyms: [脍炙人口] (kuài zhì rén kǒu 膾炙人口) 'on everyone's lips,' [乐此不疲] (lè cǐ bù pí 樂此不疲) 'never tire of.'

Antonym: [兴味索然] (xìng wèi suǒ rán 興味索然) 'uninterested.'

224. 【取长补短】(取長補短) qǔ cháng bǔ duǎn

取 means 'take,' 长 means 'strong point,' 补 means 'make up for,' and 短 means 'shortcoming.' A literal translation of the whole idiom is 'take strong points make up for shortcomings,' with a freer translation being 'draw on the strong points of others to make up for one's own deficiencies.'

Example 1: 两家大公司虽然不在同一个领域，但是合并以后能够**取长补短**，发挥各自的优势。

Liǎng jiā dà gōngsī suīrán bú zài tóng yí ge lǐngyù, dànshì hébìng yǐhòu nénggòu qǔcháng-bǔduǎn, fāhuī gèzì de yōushì.

'Even though the two large companies were not in the same domain, after they merged they were able to draw on each other's strengths to make up for deficiencies, and develop their individual advantages.'

Example 2: 今后我们应该互相学习，**取长补短**，加强合作。

Jīnhòu wǒmen yīnggāi hùxiāng xuéxí, qǔcháng-bǔduǎn, jiāqiáng hézuò.

'Hereafter we should learn from each other, draw on each other's strong points to make up for our own weaknesses, and strengthen cooperation.'

Usage: Functions as predicate. Often preceded by words such as 借鉴 (jièjiàn 借鑒) 'profit from another's experience,' 交流 (jiāoliú) 'interact,' 学习 (xuéxí 學習) 'learn,' and 合作 (hézuò) 'cooperate.'

Note: Complimentary in meaning.

Near Synonyms: [扬长避短] (yáng cháng bì duǎn 揚長避短) 'enhance strong points and avoid weaknesses,' [相得益彰] (xiàng dé yì zhāng 相得益彰) 'each improves by association with the other.'

Antonym: [固步自封] (gù bù zì fēng 固步自封) 'complacent and conservative.'

225. 【喜出望外】(喜出望外) xǐ chū wàng wài

望 means 'one's hopes.' A literal translation of this idiom is 'one's happiness exceeds outside of one's hopes,' with a freer translation being 'overjoyed at unexpected good luck, pleasantly surprised.'

Example 1: 听到女儿考上清华大学的消息，父亲**喜出望外**，马上拿出一瓶好酒请大家喝。

Tīngdào nǚ'ér kǎoshàng Qīnghuá Dàxué de xiāoxi, fùqin xǐchūwàngwài, mǎshàng náchū yì píng hǎo jiǔ qǐng dàjiā hē.

'When he heard the news that his daughter had passed the entrance examination to and been accepted by Tsinghua University, the father was overjoyed, immediately taking out a bottle of fine wine and inviting everyone to drink.'

Example 2: 他不但得到了一张免费的来回机票，还有一个星期的免费旅馆，这真让他**喜出望外**。

Tā búdàn dédàole yì zhāng miǎnfèi de láihuí jīpiào, hái yǒu yí ge xīngqī de miǎnfèi lǚguǎn, zhè zhēn ràng tā xǐchūwàngwài.

'He not only received a free round-trip ticket, but also one week's free hotel accommodations, which really made him overjoyed at his good fortune.'

Usage: Functions mainly as predicate; can also serve as adverbial and attributive.

Note: Complimentary in meaning.

Near Synonyms: [大喜过望] (dà xǐ guò wàng 大喜過望) 'overjoyed that things went even better than hoped for,' [喜从天降] (xǐ cóng tiān jiàng 喜從天降) 'unexpected joy.'

Antonyms: [雪上加霜] (xuě shàng jiā shuāng 雪上加霜) 'on top of snow to add frost – make a bad situation even worse,' [祸不单行] (huò bù dān xíng 禍不單行) 'misfortune never comes alone, misery loves company.'

226. 【本来面目】（本來面目）bĕn lái miàn mù

本来 means 'original,' while 面目 means 'appearance.' The whole idiom means 'true colors' or 'true qualities.'

Example 1: 记者做了很多调查，终于发现了这位"明星"的**本来面目**。

Jìzhě zuòle hěn duō diàochá, zhōngyú fāxiànle zhè wèi míngxīng de běnlái-miànmù.

'The reporter did much investigation and in the end discovered the true colors of this "star."'

Example 2: 历史学就是要还原历史事件的**本来面目**。

Lìshǐxué jiùshì yào huányuán lìshǐ shìjiàn de běnlái-miànmù.

'What historians need to do is precisely restore the original appearance of historical incidents.'

Usage: Functions mainly as object.

Note: When it refers to people, it has a derogatory meaning.

Near Synonym: [真相大白] (zhēn xiàng dà bái 真相大白) 'everything is now clear, the whole truth is out.'

227. 【脍炙人口】(膾炙人口) kuài zhì rén kǒu

脍 means 'minced meat,' 炙 means 'roasted meat,' and 人口 here means 'people's mouths.' A literal translation of the whole idiom is 'minced meat and roasted meat in people's mouths.' The original meaning was 'having a delicious taste,' but the idiom nowadays means 'liked by all, very popular, praised by all, on everyone's lips.'

Example 1: 她创作了大量**脍炙人口**的歌曲。

Tā chuàngzuòle dàliàng kuàizhì-rénkǒu de gēqǔ.

'She produced a large number of highly praised songs.'

Example 2: 他为后人留下了一部**脍炙人口**的作品。

Tā wèi hòurén liúxiàle yí bù kuàizhì-rénkǒu de zuòpǐn.

'He left behind for later generations a very popular work.'

Usage: Functions mainly as attributive; can also serve as predicate.

Note: Complimentary in meaning.

Near Synonyms: [交口称誉] (jiāo kǒu chēng yù 交口稱譽) 'praise unanimously,' [喜闻乐见] (xǐ wén lè jiàn 喜聞樂見) 'love to see and hear.'

Antonyms: [平淡无味] (píng dàn wú wèi 平淡無味) 'insipid, flat,' [味同嚼蜡] (wèi tóng jiáo là 味同嚼蠟) 'taste like chewing wax – without taste.'

228. 【自由自在】(自由自在) zì yóu zì zài

Since 自由 means 'free' and 自在 means 'unrestrained,' this idiom means 'free and unrestrained.'

Example 1: 他只想过**自由自在**的生活，所以不愿意结婚。

Tā zhǐ xiǎng guò zìyóu-zìzài de shēnghuó, suǒyǐ bú yuànyi jiéhūn.

'He only wants to have a free and unrestrained life, so he's unwilling to get married.'

Example 2: 孩子们在草地上**自由自在**地玩耍。

Háizimen zài cǎodì shàng zìyóu-zìzài de wánshuǎ.

'The children played freely and unrestrained on the grass.'

Usage: Functions mainly as attributive, adverbial, and predicate.

Near Synonyms: [无拘无束] (wú jū wú shù 無拘無束) 'unrestrained,' [逍遥自在] (xiāo yáo zì zài 逍遙自在) 'free and unrestrained.'

Antonyms: [束手束脚] (shù shǒu shù jiǎo 束手束腳) 'tied hand and foot,' [身不由己] (shēn bù yóu jǐ 身不由己) 'having no control over one's body or actions.'

229. 【气喘吁吁】(氣喘吁吁) qì chuǎn xū xū

喘 means 'gasp for breath, pant' and 吁吁 is the sound of panting. The meaning of the whole idiom is 'gasp for breath, pant.'

Example 1: 爸爸**气喘吁吁**地跟着儿子爬到山顶，对儿子说："我老了。"

Bàba **qìchuǎn-xūxū** de gēnzhe érzi pádào shāndǐng, duì érzi shuō: "Wǒ lǎo le."

'Gasping for breath, the father followed his son in climbing to the summit, and said to his son: "I've gotten old."'

Example 2: 他不常锻炼身体，所以只打了十分钟篮球就累得**气喘吁吁**的了。

Tā bù cháng duànliàn shēntǐ, suǒyǐ zhǐ dǎle shí fēn zhōng lánqiú jiù lèi de **qìchuǎn-xūxū** de le.

'He doesn't often exercise, so he was tired to the point of panting after playing basketball for only ten minutes.'

Usage: Functions mainly as adverbial; can also serve as predicate and complement.

Note: A more colloquial way of expressing about the same meaning is 上气不接下气 (shàng qì bù jiē xià qì 上氣不接下氣).

Antonym: [平心静气] (píng xīn jìng qì 平心靜氣) 'calmly and patiently.'

230. 【画蛇添足】(畫蛇添足) huà shé tiān zú

画 means 'draw,' 蛇 means 'snake,' 添 means 'add,' and 足 means 'foot.' The literal meaning of this idiom is 'draw a snake and add feet.' The meaning is 'add something superfluous and thereby ruin the effect.'

Example 1: 这句话没有什么意思，简直是**画蛇添足**。

Zhè jù huà méiyǒu shénme yìsi, jiǎnzhí shì **huàshé-tiānzú**.

'This sentence doesn't have any meaning; it simply ruins the effect by adding something superfluous.'

Example 2: 那个故事的结尾没有必要，给人**画蛇添足**的感觉。

Nàge gùshi de jiéwěi méiyǒu bìyào, gěi rén **huàshé-tiānzú** de gǎnjué.

'That story's ending is unnecessary; it gives one a feeling of the effect being ruined by the addition of something superfluous.'

Usage: Functions mainly as predicate at the end of a sentence; also serves as attributive.

Allusion: There were once several servants. One day their master gave them a jug of wine. After consulting among themselves, they decided that, with only one jug of wine for several people to drink, there would not be enough for everyone. Therefore, they decided to have a competition. So they drew pictures of snakes on the ground; whoever finished drawing first would get to drink all of the wine. One man finished drawing first and grabbed the wine, but then said he could draw feet for the snake. Thus, he held the jug of wine in his left hand and drew feet for the snake with his right hand. However, before he had finished drawing feet for the snake, another man finished drawing his snake. This man snatched the jug of wine away from the first man, saying: "Snakes have never had feet. How can you draw feet on a snake?" The second man drank all the wine. In the end, the first person to finish drawing the snake didn't get to drink the wine. (from *Stratagems of the Warring States*)

Note: Has a negative connotation.

Near Synonyms: [多此一举] (duō cǐ yì jǔ 多此一舉) 'make an unnecessary move,' [徒劳无功] (tú láo wú gōng 徒勞無功) 'work in vain.'

Antonyms: [画龙点睛] (huà lóng diǎn jīng 畫龍點睛) 'add the perfect finishing touch,' [恰到好处] (qià dào hǎo chù 恰到好處) 'just right.'

231. 【座无虚席】(座無虛席) zuò wú xū xí

座 means 'seat,' 虚 means 'empty,' and 席 also means 'seat, place.' A literal translation of the whole idiom is 'as regards seats there are no empty seats,' with freer translations being 'a packed house, standing room only.'

Example 1: 诺贝尔文学奖得主正在演讲，礼堂里**座无虚席**。

Nuòbèi'ěr wénxué jiǎng dézhǔ zhèng zài yǎnjiǎng, lǐtáng lǐ zuòwúxūxí.

'When the recipient of the Nobel Prize in literature was lecturing, there were no empty seats in the auditorium.'

Example 2: 周末的圣保罗大教堂**座无虚席**，教皇正在布道。

Zhōumò de Shèng Bǎoluó dà jiàotáng zuòwúxūxí, jiàohuáng zhèng zài bùdào.

'On the weekend in St. Paul's cathedral there were no empty seats, as the pope was giving a sermon.'

Usage: Functions as predicate.

Near Synonym: [济济一堂] (jǐ jǐ yì táng 濟濟一堂) 'a large assembly.'

Antonyms: [门可罗雀] (mén kě luó què 門可羅雀) 'at the doorway one can snare sparrows – an infrequently visited place,' [寥寥无几] (liáo liáo wú jǐ 寥寥無幾) 'very few,' [一无所有] (yì wú suǒ yǒu 一無所有) 'have absolutely nothing, destitute.'

232. 【夜以继日】(夜以繼日) yè yǐ jì rì

以 means 'use' and 继 means 'continue.' A literal translation of the whole idiom is 'using night to continue the day,' with a freer translation being 'day and night.'

Example 1: 经过五天**夜以继日**的谈判，双方最终达成了协议。

Jīngguò wǔ tiān yèyǐjìrì de tánpàn, shuāngfāng zuìzhōng dáchéngle xiéyì.

'After five days of day-and-night negotiations, both sides finally reached an agreement.'

Example 2: 科研人员**夜以继日**地工作，期望能够在最后期限到达之前完成那项任务。

Kēyán rényuán yèyǐjìrì de gōngzuò, qīwàng nénggòu zài zuìhòu qīxiàn dàodá zhīqián wánchéng nà xiàng rènwù.

'The scientific research personnel worked day and night, hoping that they could before the arrival of the final deadline complete that task.'

Usage: Functions mainly as adverbial and attributive; can also serve as predicate.

Near Synonyms: [通宵达旦] (tōng xiāo dá dàn 通宵達旦) 'all night long until the dawn,' [废寝忘食] (fèi qǐn wàng shí 廢寢忘食) 'abandon sleeping and forget eating.'

Antonym: [悠哉游哉] (yōu zāi yóu zāi 悠哉游哉) 'free from restraint' (colloquial).

233. 【持之以恒】(持之以恆) chí zhī yǐ héng

持 means 'hold,' 之 means 'it,' 以 means 'take, use,' and 恒 means 'permanence.' A literal translation of the whole idiom is 'hold it with permanence.' This idiom is used with the meaning 'persevere, persist.'

Example 1: 学习任何外语都要**持之以恒**，一两天是学不会的。

Xuéxí rènhé wàiyǔ dōu yào chízhī-yǐhéng, yì liǎng tiān shì xué bú huì de.

'In learning any foreign language, you must persevere; you can't learn it in just a day or two.'

Example 2: 政府决心**持之以恒**地反对贪污和受贿行为。

Zhèngfǔ juéxīn chízhī-yǐhéng de fǎnduì tānwū hé shòuhuì xíngwéi.

'The government determined to persevere in opposing corruption and bribery.'

Usage: Functions mainly as adverbial and predicate.

Note: Complimentary in meaning.

Near Synonyms: [锲而不舍] (qiè ér bù shě 鍥而不捨) 'work with perseverance,' [孜孜不倦] (zī zī bú juàn 孜孜不倦) 'diligently,' [坚持不懈] (jiān chí bú xiè 堅持不懈) 'unremitting.'

Antonyms: [浅尝辄止] (qiǎn cháng zhé zhǐ 淺嘗輒止) 'shallowly taste then stop – stop after gaining a little knowledge of something,' [半途而废] (bàn tú ér fèi 半途而廢) 'give up halfway,' [三天打鱼，两天晒网] (sān tiān dǎ yú, liǎng tiān shài wǎng 三天打鱼，兩天曬網) 'go fishing for three days, dry the nets for two days – lack of perseverance; work by fits and starts.'

234. 【针锋相对】(針鋒相對) zhēn fēng xiāng duì

针锋 means 'pinpoint' and 相对 means 'diametrically opposed, opposite.' A literal translation of this idiom is 'pinpoints diametrically opposed,' that is, the point of one pin being precisely against the point of another pin. A freer translation is 'in sharp opposition, give tit for tat.'

Example 1: 在最高法院大法官的人选上，保守派与改革派**针锋相对**，也提出了自己的候选人。

Zài zuìgāo fǎyuàn dàfǎguān de rénxuǎn shàng, bǎoshǒupài yǔ gǎigépài zhēnfēng-xiāngduì, yě tíchūle zìjǐ de hòuxuǎnrén.

'In the choosing of a Chief Justice for the Supreme Court, the conservative faction stood in sharp opposition to the reformist faction, putting forward its own candidate.'

Example 2: 针对对手的恶意攻击，他进行了**针锋相对**的反击。

Zhēnduì duìshǒu de èyì gōngjī, tā jìnxíngle zhēnfēng-xiāngduì de fǎnjī.

'In light of his adversary's malicious attack, he carried out a counterattack where he gave tit for tat.'

Usage: Functions mainly as predicate, adverbial, and attributive. Often occurs in debates and political campaigns.

Near Synonym: [寸步不让] (cùn bù bú ràng 寸步不讓) 'not yield an inch.'

Antonym: [退避三舍] (tuì bì sān shè 退避三舍) 'make concessions to avoid conflict.'

235. 【相得益彰】(相得益彰) xiāng dé yì zhāng

相 means 'mutually,' 得 means 'obtain,' 益 means 'even more,' and 彰 means 'clear, obvious.' The meaning of the whole idiom is 'mutual coordination makes the results even better' or 'each improves by association with the other.' In freer translation, this can be rendered as 'bring out the best in each other, complement each other.'

Example 1: 这对夫妻，一个善于在外面谈生意，一个喜欢在家里做家务，两个人**相得益彰**。

Zhè duì fūqī, yí ge shànyú zài wàimiàn tán shēngyi, yí ge xǐhuan zài jiā lǐ zuò jiāwù, liǎng ge rén xiāngdé-yìzhāng.

'This husband and wife, one of them is good at doing business on the outside, the other likes doing housework at home, the two of them complement each other very well.'

Example 2: 中国古代的画家一般来说书法和诗词都很好，因此，诗、书、画**相得益彰**。

Zhōngguó gǔdài de huàjiā yìbān lái shuō shūfǎ hé shīcí dōu hěn hǎo, yīncǐ, shī, shū, huà xiāngdé-yìzhāng.

'In general, ancient Chinese painters were good both at calligraphy and in poetry; therefore, poetry, calligraphy, and painting complemented and brought out the best in each other.'

Usage: Functions as predicate.

Note: Complimentary in meaning.

Near Synonyms: [取长补短] (qǔ cháng bǔ duǎn 取長補短) 'draw on the strong points of others to make up for one's own deficiencies,' [珠联璧合] (zhū lián bì hé 珠聯璧合) 'perfect match,' [相辅相成] (xiāng fǔ xiāng chéng 相輔相成) 'complement each other,' [交相辉映] (jiāo xiāng huī yìng 交相輝映) 'enhance one another's beauty.'

Antonyms: [势不两立] (shì bù liǎng lì 勢不兩立) 'irreconcilable, incompatible,' [两败俱伤] (liǎng bài jù shāng 兩敗俱傷) 'both sides lose and are equally wounded.'

236. 【念念不忘】(念念不忘) niàn niàn bú wàng

念 here means 'think of.' The meaning of the whole idiom is 'never forget, constantly bear in mind.'

Example 1: 他**念念不忘**父亲对他的教诲，"为国家多做一些事。"

Tā niànniàn-búwàng fùqīn duì tā de jiàohuì, "Wèi guójiā duō zuò yìxiē shì."

'He constantly bore in mind his father's teaching, "Do more for your country."'

Example 2: 三年过去了，她仍**念念不忘**她的初恋情人。

Sān nián guòqùle, tā réng niànniàn-búwàng tā de chūliàn qíngrén.

'Three years had passed, but she still constantly kept in mind her first love.'

Usage: Functions mainly as adverbial; can also serve as predicate.

Near Synonym: [朝思暮想] (zhāo sī mù xiǎng 朝思暮想) 'think of from dawn to dusk.'

Antonym: [抛在脑后] (pāo zài nǎo hòu 拋在腦後) 'throw to the back of one's mind – not remember.'

237. 【深思熟虑】 (深思熟慮) shēn sī shú lǜ

熟 means 'mature, thorough' and 虑 means 'consider.' The literal meaning is 'deeply think thoroughly consider,' with a freer translation being 'careful deliberation or consideration.'

Example 1: 经过**深思熟虑**，他提出了自己的建议。

Jīngguò shēnsī-shúlǜ, tā tíchūle zìjǐ de jiànyì.

'After careful consideration, he raised his suggestion.'

Example 2: 总统**深思熟虑**之后，决定对全体公民的医疗保险进行改革。

Zǒngtǒng shēnsī-shúlǜ zhīhòu, juédìng duì quántǐ gōngmín de yīliáo bǎoxiǎn jìnxíng gǎigé.

'After careful deliberation, the president decided to undertake reforms of all citizens' health insurance.'

Usage: Often functions as object of the verb 经过 (jīngguò 經過) 'undergo, experience.'

Note: Complimentary in meaning.

Near Synonym: [深谋远虑] (shēn móu yuǎn lǜ 深謀遠慮) 'circumspect and far sighted.'

Antonym: [不假思索] (bù jiǎ sī suǒ 不假思索) 'without stopping to think.'

238. 【独树一帜】 (獨樹一幟) dú shù yí zhì

独 means 'alone,' 树 here means 'set up,' and 帜 means 'flag.'

A literal translation of the idiom is 'a single individual raises a flag.' A freer translation would be 'have one's own style, fly one's own colors, create one's own school of thought, be unique.'

Example 1: 她的绘画风格在整个艺术界**独树一帜**。

Tā de huìhuà fēnggé zài zhěnggè yìshùjiè dúshù-yízhì.

'Her brushwork style is unique in the entire art world.'

Example 2: 几十年之后，他建立起了**独树一帜**的理论体系。

Jǐ shí nián zhīhòu, tā jiànlì qǐ le dúshù-yízhì de lǐlùn tǐxì.

'A few decades later, he established his own unique theoretical system.'

Usage: Functions mainly as predicate; can also serve as adverbial.

Note: Complimentary in meaning.

Near Synonyms: [自成一家] (zì chéng yì jiā 自成一家) 'personally create a school – unique in one's style,' [独辟蹊径] (dú pì xī jìng 獨闢蹊徑) 'alone open a road for oneself – develop one's own style or method,' [标新立异] (biāo xīn lì yì 標新立異) 'create something new and different.'

Antonyms: [如出一辙] (rú chū yì zhé 如出一轍) 'as if emerging from the same track – one and the same, cut from the same cloth,' [墨守成规] (mò shǒu chéng guī 墨守成規) 'stick to conventions or outmoded practices,' [人云亦云] (rén yún yì yún 人云亦云) 'repeat other's ideas – say and do exactly as others,' [萧规曹随] (Xiāo guī Cáo suí 蕭規曹隨) 'Xiao's rules Cao (the famous general) follows – abide by the rules laid down by one's predecessor, follow in someone's footsteps.'

239. 【惊天动地】(驚天動地) jīng tiān dòng dì

惊天 means 'startle or surprise the heavens' and 动地 means 'move the earth.' The meaning of the whole idiom is 'earthshaking, resounding.'

Example 1: 闪电之后是**惊天动地**的巨响。

Shǎndiàn zhīhòu shì jīngtiān-dòngdì de jùxiǎng.

'After the lightning struck there was an earthshaking loud sound.'

Example 2: 有人在毛泽东小时候就看出他将来会做出一番**惊天动地**的事业。

Yǒu rén zài Máo Zédōng xiǎoshíhou jiù kànchū tā jiānglái huì zuòchū yì fān jīngtiān-dòngdì de shìyè.

'There are people who, when Mao Zedong was a child, already were able to tell that in the future he would accomplish earthshaking feats.'

Usage: Functions mainly as attributive; can also serve as predicate.

Near Synonyms: [地动山摇] (dì dòng shān yáo 地動山搖) 'earthshaking,' [天崩地裂] (tiān bēng dì liè 天崩地裂) 'earth-shattering.'

Antonyms: [万籁俱寂] (wàn lài jù jì 萬籟俱寂) 'the sounds of nature are all quiet,' [波澜不惊] (bō lán bù jīng 波澜不驚) 'mighty waves not risen – uneventful.'

240. 【东窗事发】(東窗事發) dōng chuāng shì fā

窗 means 'window' and 发 means 'discovered.' A literal translation of the whole idiom is 'the matter by the east window has been discovered.' This is a metaphor for intrigue that has failed and been exposed. English equivalents include 'the plot has come to light' and 'the secret is out.'

Example 1: 那位高官跟开发商有背后交易，后来**东窗事发**，他被迫辞去了职务。

Nà wèi gāoguān gēn kāifāshāng yǒu bèihòu jiāoyì, hòulái dōngchuāng-shìfā, tā bèipò cíqùle zhíwù.

'That high official had a secret business deal with a commercial developer; later their plot came to light and he was forced to resign his post.'

Example 2: 钱权交易要冒着很大的风险，一旦**东窗事发**，只好去坐牢了。

Qián quán jiāoyì yào màozhe hěndà de fēngxiǎn, yídàn dōngchuāng-shìfā, zhǐ hǎo qù zuòláo le.

'Trading money for power involves a great amount of risk; once you have been discovered, the only alternative is to go to jail.'

Usage: Functions mainly as predicate.

Allusion: During the Southern Song Dynasty, the traitor Qin Hui wanted to kill Yue Fei (1103–1142 C.E.), the most famous national hero in Chinese history, but many righteous officials were opposed. Qin Hui and his wife plotted by the east window, discussing what they should do. His wife said: "The tiger has now already been caught; to let the tiger go would be easy. But after you let it go, to then try to catch it again, that would be hard." And so Qin Hui killed Yue Fei on trumped up charges. Thirteen years later, Qin Hui died. His wife had a Taoist priest come to drive out the demons. The Taoist priest saw Qin Hui in hell receiving all kinds of cruel punishments. Qin Hui told the Buddhist priest: "Please convey to my wife that our intrigue by the east window has been discovered."

Note: Derogatory in meaning.

Near Synonyms: [真相大白] (zhēn xiàng dà bái 真相大白) 'everything is now clear, the whole truth is out,' [原形毕露] (yuán xíng bì lù 原形畢露) 'reveal one's true colors.'

Antonyms: [蒙在鼓里] (méng zài gǔ lǐ 蒙在鼓裏) 'keep inside a drum – keep in the dark, keep ignorant,' [秘而不宣] (mì ér bù xuān 秘而不宣) 'secret and not announce – keep secret.'

241. 【铺天盖地】(鋪天蓋地) pū tiān gài dì

铺 means 'spread out' and 盖 means 'cover.' The meaning of the whole idiom is 'cover the earth, omnipresent.'

Example 1: 当一位八十二岁的老人与一位二十八岁的女人结婚的时候，媒体上批评的声浪**铺天盖地**而来。

Dāng yí wèi bāshí'èr suì de lǎorén yǔ yí wèi èrshíbā suì de nǚrén jiéhūn de shíhou, méitǐ shàng pīpíng de shēnglàng pūtiān-gàidì ér lái.

'When an 82-year-old man and a 28-year-old woman got married, the uproar of criticism in the media came from everywhere.'

Example 2: 在北欧，**铺天盖地**的大雪常常一下就是一天。

Zài Běi'ōu, pūtiān-gàidì de dà xuě chángcháng yí xià jiù shì yì tiān.

'In Scandinavia, there is omnipresent heavy snow; it often snows for the whole day.'

Usage: Functions as adverbial, predicate, and attributive.

Near Synonym: [遮天蔽日] (zhē tiān bì rì 遮天蔽日) 'blot out the sky and cover the sun – cover all the sky.'

Antonym: [蜻蜓点水] (qīng tíng diǎn shuǐ 蜻蜓點水) 'dragonfly skims surface of water – just scratch the surface of something without going into it deeply.'

242. 【大张旗鼓】(大張旗鼓) dà zhāng qí gǔ

张 means 'open' and 旗鼓 means 'banners and drums.' The literal meaning of the idiom is 'open up banners and drums on a large scale (as in war)'; a freer translation is 'with a lot of fanfare, on a grand scale.'

Example 1: 我们要**大张旗鼓**地宣传和表扬那些为国家的利益做出贡献的人。

Wǒmen yào dàzhāng-qígǔ de xuānchuán hé biǎoyáng nàxiē wèi guójiā de lìyì zuòchū gòngxiàn de rén.

'We should with a lot of fanfare publicize and praise those who have made contributions for the benefit of the country.'

Example 2: 我们的研究方法还不太完善，所以对于结果先不要**大张旗鼓**地宣传。

Wǒmen de yánjiū fāngfǎ hái bú tài wánshàn, suǒyǐ duìyú jiéguǒ xiān búyào dàzhāng-qígǔ de xuānchuán.

'Our research method is not yet refined enough, so let's not yet publicize our results with a lot of fanfare.'

Usage: Functions as adverbial, followed mainly by the verb 宣传 (xuānchuán 宣傳) 'publicize.'

Near Synonym: [兴师动众] (xīng shī dòng zhòng 興師動眾) 'drag a lot of people in, make a big fuss over a small job.'

Antonym: [悄无声息] (qiāo wú shēng xī 悄無聲息) 'quiet and without a sound.'

243. 【彬彬有礼】(彬彬有禮) bīn bīn yǒu lǐ

彬彬 means 'refined, elegant' and 有礼 means 'courteous.' The whole idiom means 'refined and well-mannered.'

Example 1: 高级饭店的服务员总是**彬彬有礼**，让客人感觉很舒服。

Gāojí fàndiàn de fúwùyuán zǒngshì bīnbīn-yǒulǐ, ràng kèrén gǎnjué hěn shūfu.

'The service personnel in high-class hotels are always refined and well-mannered, allowing guests to feel comfortable.'

Example 2: 她**彬彬有礼**地回答记者提出的各种各样的问题。

Tā bīnbīn-yǒulǐ de huídá jìzhě tíchū de gèzhǒng-gèyàng de wèntí.

'She answered all the questions that the reporters asked with great courtesy.'

Usage: Functions mainly as predicate, can also serve as attributive and adverbial.

Note: Complimentary in meaning.

Near Synonyms: [落落大方] (luò luò dà fāng 落落大方) 'natural and dignified,' [文质彬彬] (wén zhì bīn bīn 文質彬彬) 'refined and courteous.'

Antonym: [蛮横无理] (mán hèng wú lǐ 蠻橫無理) 'unreasonable.'

244. 【熙熙攘攘】(熙熙攘攘) xī xī rǎng rǎng

熙熙 means 'gentle, happy' and 攘攘 means 'disorderly, chaotic.' The meaning of the whole idiom is 'crowded, bustling, busy.'

Example 1: 夏季，巴黎街头游客**熙熙攘攘**，非常热闹，不过本地人都到外地去度假了。

Xiàjì, Bālí jiētóu yóukè xīxī-rǎngrǎng, fēicháng rè'nao, búguò běndì rén dōu dào wàidì qù dùjiàle.

'In the summertime, the streets of Paris are bustling with tourists; it's very lively, but the locals have all gone out of town on vacation.'

Example 2: 在**熙熙攘攘**的人群中，有位身高两米二的大个子格外引人注目。

Zài xīxī-rǎngrǎng de rénqún zhōng, yǒu wèi shēn'gāo liǎng mǐ èr de dà gèzi géwài yǐnrén-zhùmù.

'In the bustling crowd, there was a tall fellow of two meters twenty who especially attracted people's attention.'

Usage: Functions as attributive and predicate.

Near Synonyms: [人山人海] (rén shān rén hǎi 人山人海) 'people mountain people sea – huge crowds,' [水泄不通] (shuǐ xiè bù tōng 水泄不通) 'not even a drop of water could get through – crowded with people, heavy traffic.'

Antonym: [门可罗雀] (mén kě luó què 門可羅雀) 'at the doorway one can snare sparrows – an infrequently visited place.'

245. 【无影无踪】(無影無蹤) wú yǐng wú zōng

影 means 'shadow' and 踪 means 'track, trace.' A literal translation is 'there is no shadow and there is no trace.' A freer translation of this idiom is 'vanish without a trace' or simply 'without a trace.'

Example 1: 等警察赶到现场的时候，凶手早已消失得**无影无踪**。

Děng jǐngchá gǎndào xiànchǎng de shíhou, xiōngshǒu zǎoyǐ xiāoshīde wúyǐng-wúzōng.

'By the time the police had rushed to the scene, the assailant had long since disappeared without a trace.'

Example 2: 学期末的时候，学生已经把老师在学期初说的话忘得**无影无踪**了。

Xuéqīmò de shíhou, xuésheng yǐjīng bǎ lǎoshī zài xuéqīchū shuō de huà wàngde wúyǐng-wúzōng le.

'By the end of the term, the students had already completely forgotten what the instructor had said at the beginning of the term.'

Usage: Functions mainly as complement for verbs such as 消失 (xiāoshī) 'disappear,' 跑 (pǎo) 'run,' and 逃 (táo) 'flee.'

Near Synonym: [荡然无存] (dàng rán wú cún 蕩然無存) 'vanish without a trace.'

Antonyms: [有迹可寻] (yǒu jì kě xún 有跡可尋) 'there are signs that can be traced,' [如影随形] (rú yǐng suí xíng 如影隨形) 'like the shadow following a person – intimate pair,' [挥之不去] (huī zhī bú qù 揮之不去) 'cannot be brushed away – will not go away, lingering.'

246. 【至高无上】(至高無上) zhì gāo wú shàng

至 means 'most.' A literal translation of this idiom is 'most high there is not higher,' with freer translations including 'highest' and 'supreme.'

Example 1: 在天主教里，教皇拥有**至高无上**的权力。

Zài Tiānzhǔjiào lǐ, Jiàohuáng yōngyǒu zhìgāo-wúshàng de quánlì.

'In Catholicism, the Pope possesses supreme authority.'

Example 2: 在一个传统家庭里，父亲的地位是**至高无上**的。

Zài yí ge chuántǒng jiātíng lǐ, fùqin de dìwèi shì zhìgāo-wúshàng de.

'In a traditional family, the father's position is the highest.'

Usage: Functions mainly as attributive; can also serve as predicate.

Near Synonyms: [无出其右] (wú chū qí yòu 無出其右) 'second to none,' [无与伦比] (wú yǔ lún bǐ 無與倫比) 'unequaled, peerless.'

Antonym: [等而下之] (děng ér xià zhī 等而下之) 'from this point down.'

247. 【司空见惯】(司空見慣) sī kōng jiàn guàn

司空 was the title of an official in ancient China; 惯 means 'become accustomed to.' The literal meaning is 'the Sikong official has gotten used to seeing things,' with a freer translation being 'to see so many things that you have gotten used to seeing almost anything and find nothing strange anymore.'

Example 1: 在当代社会里，老夫少妻的现象已经**司空见惯**了，大家不再像以前那样奇怪。

Zài dāngdài shèhuì lǐ, lǎo fū shǎo qī de xiànxiàng yǐjīng sīkōng-jiànguàn le, dàjiā bú zài xiàng yǐqián nàyàng qíguài.

'In contemporary society, the phenomenon of an older husband with a young wife is no longer anything unusual, everyone no longer finds it strange as in the past.'

Example 2: 在那个国家，踢假球是**司空见惯**的事情。

Zài nàge guójiā, tī jiǎ qiú shì sīkōng-jiànguàn de shìqing.

'In that country, kicking fake balls is nothing out of the ordinary.'

Usage: Functions mainly as predicate and attributive.

Near Synonyms: [屡见不鲜] (lǚ jiàn bù xiān 屢見不鮮) 'often seen and nothing remarkable,' [习以为常] (xí yǐ wéi cháng 習以為常) 'accustomed to something and think it's always like that,' [见怪不怪] (jiàn guài bú guài 見怪不怪) 'see strange things but not find them strange.'

Antonym: [少见多怪] (shǎo jiàn duō guài 少見多怪) 'a person who has seen little marvels much.'

248. 【接二连三】(接二連三) jiē èr lián sān

A literal translation of this idiom is 'join two link three' (the numbers 二 and 三 here have no particular meaning). The meaning of the whole idiom is 'one after another, repeatedly, in rapid succession.'

Example 1: 令大家恐怖的是，这种事情**接二连**三地发生了。

Lìng dàjiā kǒngbù de shì, zhè zhǒng shìqing jiē'èr-liánsān de fāshēng le.

'What has horrified everyone is that this kind of thing has happened repeatedly in rapid succession.'

Example 2: 他的小说**接二连**三地出版，给他带来了巨大的声誉和收入。

Tā de xiǎoshuō jiē'èr-liánsān de chūbǎn, gěi tā dàiláile jùdà de shēngyù hé shōurù.

'His novels are published one after another, which has brought him an enormous reputation and income.'

Usage: Functions mainly as attributive.

Near Synonyms: [络绎不绝] (luò yì bù jué 絡繹不絕) 'continuous flow,' [隔三差五] (gé sān chà wǔ 隔三差五) 'at intervals of three and differing by five – at short intervals, regularly' (limited mostly to spoken Chinese).

Antonym: [稀稀落落] (xī xī luò luò 稀稀落落) 'sparse, scattered.'

249. 【斩钉截铁】(斬釘截鐵) zhǎn dīng jié tiě

斩 means 'cut, chop,' 钉 means 'nail,' 截 means 'cut, sever,' and 铁 means 'iron.' A literal translation of this idiom is 'cut a nail and sever iron,' which by metaphor means 'firm and resolute, decisive.'

Example 1: 孩子跟父亲要一辆新汽车，父亲**斩钉截铁**地回答，"没门！"

Háizi gēn fùqin yào yí liàng xīn qìchē, fùqin zhǎndīng-jiétiě de huídá, "Méi mén!"

'When the child wanted a new car from the father, the father answered very firmly, "No way!"'

Example 2: 公安局长**斩钉截铁**地说："我们要不惜任何代价抓住凶手。"

Gōngānjúzhǎng zhǎndīng-jiétiě de shuō: "Wǒmen yào bù xī rènhé dàijià zhuāzhù xiōngshǒu."

'The head of the Public Security Bureau said resolutely: "No matter what the cost, we must capture the assailant."'

Usage: Functions as adverbial followed by verbs such as 说 (shuō 說) 'say' and 回答 (huídá) 'answer.'

Note: Complimentary in meaning.

Near Synonyms: [落地有声] (luò dì yǒu shēng 落地有聲) 'fall on the ground and have a sound – firm, resolute, trustworthy,' [掷地有声] (zhì dì yǒu shēng 擲地有聲) 'throw on the ground and have a sound – firm, resolute, trustworthy.'

Antonyms: [拖泥带水] (tuō ní dài shuǐ 拖泥帶水) 'drag through mud and water – do things sloppily,' [优柔寡断] (yōu róu guǎ duàn 優柔寡斷) 'irresolute and hesitant, indecisive.'

250. 【滥竽充数】(濫竽充數) làn yú chōng shù

滥 means 'excess,' 竽 is the name for a musical instrument somewhat like a flute, and 充数 means 'make up a number.' A literal translation of the whole idiom is 'excess *yu* makes up a number' or, more freely, 'someone who does not know how to play the *yu* pretends to play and becomes a member of the band.' This is a metaphor for 'people who have no talent but pretend they do,' 'inferior but pose as superior,' or 'contribute no work but go undetected because of the work of others.'

Example 1: 现在很多有钱的商人都在高校里兼任教授，简直是**滥竽充数**。

Xiànzài hěn duō yǒu qián de shāngrén dōu zài gāoxiào lǐ jiānrèn jiàoshòu, jiǎnzhí shì lànyú-chōngshù.

'Nowadays many wealthy business people teach as part-time professors at institutes of higher education; this is simply amateurs pretending to be experts.'

Example 2: 市场上有很多假名牌，一些人穿上这些所谓的名牌**滥竽充数**。

Shìchǎng shàng yǒu hěn duō jiǎ míngpái, yìxiē rén chuānshàng zhèxiē suǒwèi de míngpái lànyú-chōngshù.

'On the market there are many famous brands; some people wear these so-called famous brands to pretend they are something they are not.'

Usage: Functions mainly as predicate and attributive.

Allusion: When King Xuan of the country of Qi had musicians play the *yu* flute, he insisted on having 300 people play together. Now, there was a man by the name of Nanguo who didn't know how to play the *yu*; but he pretended to know and asked to play for King Xuan. King Xuan was very pleased and paid him the same salary as the other players. Later King Xuan died and his son became king. The son liked solo performances, so Nanguo had no choice but to flee. (from "Nei Chu Shuo Shang" in *Han Feizi*)

Note: Derogatory in meaning. Occasionally used in a self-depreciatory manner.

Near Synonyms: [名不副实] (míng bú fù shí 名不副實) 'unworthy of the name,' [鱼目混珠] (yú mù hùn zhū 魚目混珠) 'confuse fish eggs and pearls – pass off fake articles for the real thing.'

Antonyms: [名副其实] (míng fù qí shí 名副其實) 'worthy of the name or reputation,' [货真价实] (huò zhēn jià shí 貨真價實) 'genuine goods at reasonable prices.'

251. 【不择手段】(不擇手段) bù zé shǒu duàn

择 means 'choose' and 手段 means 'method, means.' The meaning of the whole idiom is 'resort to any means, stop at nothing.'

Example 1: 有的人为了达到目的而**不择手段**。

Yǒude rén wèile dádào mùdì ér bùzé-shǒuduàn.

'Some people will stop at nothing in order to attain their goal.'

Example 2: 他**不择手段**地攻击对手。

Tā bùzé-shǒuduàn de gōngjī duìshǒu.

'He resorted to any means to attack his adversary.'

Usage: Functions mainly as predicate and adverbial.

Note: Derogatory in meaning.

Near Synonym: [心狠手辣] (xīn hěn shǒu là 心狠手辣) 'extremely cruel and merciless.'

252. 【津津有味】(津津有味) jīn jīn yǒu wèi

津 means 'saliva,' 津津 means 'succulent, tasty,' and 有味 means 'have flavor, tasty.' The meaning of the whole idiom is '(do something) with gusto.'

Example 1: 他**津津有味**地吃鸡爪子。

Tā jīnjīn-yǒuwèi de chī jīzhuǎzi.

'He ate the chicken feet with great gusto.'

Example 2: 这个故事太吸引人了，大家听得**津津有味**。

Zhège gùshi tài xīyǐn rén le, dàjiā tīng de jīnjīn-yǒuwèi.

'This story very much attracted people's attention, everyone listening with gusto.'

Usage: Functions mainly as predicate and adverbial.

Near Synonym: [兴致勃勃] (xìng zhì bó bó 興致勃勃) 'full of enthusiasm.'

Antonyms: [味同嚼蜡] (wèi tóng jiáo là 味同嚼蠟) 'taste like chewing wax – without taste,' [索然无味] (suǒ rán wú wèi 索然無味) 'dull and without flavor – insipid.'

253. 【深入浅出】(深入淺出) shēn rù qiǎn chū

深 means 'deep' and 浅 means 'shallow.' The literal translation is 'deeply enter and shallowly come out.' This idiom refers to speech or writing with deep content that is expressed in a way that is easy to understand. The idiom can be translated as 'explain profound things in simple language, make something complicated sound simple.'

Example 1: 她**深入浅出**地向听众介绍了这个方面的最新理论。

Tā shēnrù-qiǎnchū de xiàng tīngzhòng jièshàole zhège fāngmiàn de zuì xīn lǐlùn.

'She introduced the newest theories in this area to the audience in a way that made them seem simple.'

Example 2: 他讲课的时候生动幽默、**深入浅出**，深受学生喜欢。

Tā jiǎngkè de shíhou shēngdòng yōumò, shēnrù-qiǎnchū, shēnshòu xuésheng xǐhuan.

'When he lectured, he was lively and humorous, with the ability to explain complicated matters in an easy-to-understand manner, so he was much liked by his students.'

Usage: Functions mainly as adverbial, predicate, and attributive.

Note: Complimentary in meaning.

Near Synonym: [通俗易懂] (tōng sú yì dǒng 通俗易懂) 'in a colloquial and easy to understand manner' (used mostly in speech).

254. 【相提并论】(相提並論) xiāng tí bìng lùn

相 means 'mutually,' 提 means 'mention,' 并 means 'simultaneously,' and 论 means 'discuss.' The meaning of the whole idiom is 'talk about two different people or things at the same time, mention in the same breath.'

Example 1: 有的人把德州与美国的关系跟新西兰与英国的关系**相提并论**，其实这是不了解历史。

Yǒu de rén bǎ Dézhōu yǔ Měiguó de guānxi gēn Xīnxīlán yǔ Yīngguó de guānxi xiāngtí-bìnglùn, qíshí zhè shì bù liǎojiě lìshǐ.

'Some people talk about the relationship of Texas to the U.S. in the same breath as the relationship of New Zealand to England; actually, this is not understanding history.'

Example 2: 他们两个人的贡献一大一小，根本不能**相提并论**。

Tāmen liǎng ge rén de gòngxiàn yí dà yì xiǎo, gēnběn bù néng xiāngtí-bìnglùn.

'As far as the contributions of the two of them are concerned, one was great and one was small; they absolutely cannot be mentioned in the same breath.'

Usage: Functions as predicate.

Near Synonym: [同日而语] (tóng rì ér yǔ 同日而語) 'speak about on the same day – mention in the same breath.'

Antonym: [一分为二] (yì fēn wéi èr 一分為二) 'one divides into two' (refers to Mao Zedong's theory of dialectics whereby every phenomenon, throughout all stages of its development, encompasses two mutually opposing and at the same time mutually united antitheses that are simultaneously in a state of unity and in a state of struggle).

255. 【深恶痛绝】(深惡痛絕) shēn wù tòng jué

深 means 'deeply,' 恶 means 'hate,' 痛 also means 'hate,' and 绝 means 'extremely.' A literal translation of the whole idiom is 'deeply hate and hate extremely,' with freer translations being 'abhor, detest.'

Example 1: 她对说谎的人**深恶痛绝**。

Tā duì shuōhuǎng de rén shēnwù-tòngjué.

'She loathes liars.'

Example 2: 毒品令人**深恶痛绝**。

Dúpǐn lìng rén shēnwù-tòngjué.

'Narcotics make one detest them.'

Usage: Functions mainly as predicate.

Near Synonyms: [恨之入骨] (hèn zhī rù gǔ 恨之入骨) 'hate someone so much that the hate enters the marrow of one's bones,' [疾恶如仇] (jí è rú chóu 疾惡如仇) 'hate the evil like personal enemies.'

Antonym: [爱不释手] (ài bú shì shǒu 愛不釋手) 'love something so much that one can't let go of it.'

256. 【不可多得】(不可多得) bù kě duō dé

可 means 'can' and 得 means 'obtain, get.' The whole idiom means 'hard to come by, uncommon.'

Example 1: 他又年轻又有能力，是个**不可多得**的人才。

Tā yòu niánqīng yòu yǒu nénglì, shì gè bùkě-duōdé de réncái.

'He is both young and capable, a person of uncommon talent.'

Example 2: 这种瓷器是三百年前的，已经非常少了，**不可多得**。

Zhè zhǒng cíqì shì sān bǎi nián qián de, yǐjīng fēicháng shǎole, bùkě-duōdé.

'This type of porcelain is from 300 years ago; there isn't much of it around anymore, and it is very hard to come by.'

Usage: Functions mainly as attributive and predicate. As attributive, often co-occurs with words referring to 'talent.'

Note: Complimentary in meaning.

Near Synonym: [屈指可数] (qū zhǐ kě shǔ 屈指可數) 'can be counted on the fingers, very few.'

Antonyms: [多如牛毛] (duō rú niú máo 多如牛毛) 'as numerous as the hairs of an ox, countless,' [比比皆是] (bǐ bǐ jiē shì 比比皆是) 'can be found everywhere.'

257. 【沸沸扬扬】(沸沸揚揚) fèi fèi yáng yáng

沸沸 describes the appearance of boiling water and 扬 means 'rise.' The meaning of the whole idiom is 'noisy, tumultuous, raging.'

Example 1: 他们的婚外恋闹得**沸沸扬扬**的，全城人都知道了。

Tāmen de hūnwàiliàn nào de fèifèi-yángyáng de, quán chéng rén dōu zhīdao le.

'Their extramarital affair noisily raged on and on, everyone in the city finding out about it.'

Example 2: **沸沸扬扬**的选美活动结束了，又是委内瑞拉小姐当选世界小姐。

Fèifèi-yángyáng de xuǎnměi huódòng jiéshùle, yòu shì Wěinèiruìlā xiǎojiě dāngxuǎn shìjiè xiǎojiě.

'The tumultuous beauty contest activities concluded, with Miss Venezuela once again having been elected Miss World.'

Usage: Functions mainly as predicate and attributive.

Near Synonym: [满城风雨] (mǎn chéng fēng yǔ 滿城風雨) 'whole city wind and rain – become the talk of the town.'

Antonym: [鸦雀无声] (yā què wú shēng 鴉雀無聲) 'crow sparrow no sound – complete silence.'

258. 【雪上加霜】(雪上加霜) xuě shàng jiā shuāng

雪 means 'snow,' 加 means 'add,' 霜 means 'frost.' A literal translation of the whole idiom is 'on top of snow to add frost,' with freer translations being 'make a bad situation even worse, exacerbate.'

Example 1: 在经济危机中，飞机乘客减少，这对于航空业已经是不小的打击了；现在燃油价格又大幅上涨，这无疑是**雪上加霜**。

Zài jīngjì wēijī zhōng, fēijī chéngkè jiǎnshǎo, zhè duìyú hángkōngyè yǐjīng shì bùxiǎo de dǎjī le; xiànzài rányóu jiàgé yòu dàfú shàngzhǎng, zhè wúyí shì xuěshàng-jiāshuāng.

'In the economic crisis, airplane passengers have reduced; this is already a big blow to the aviation industry; now the price of fuel has risen substantially; this without a doubt is exacerbating the situation.'

Example 2: 本来保守党在民意调查中就已经落后于对手了，最近一位重量级人物又爆出性丑闻，这对于保守党来说是**雪上加霜**。

Běnlái bǎoshǒudǎng zài mínyì diàochá zhōng jiù yǐjīng luòhòu yú duìshǒu le, zuìjìn yí wèi zhòngliàngjí rénwù yòu bàochū xìngchǒuwén, zhè duìyú bǎoshǒudǎng láishuō shì xuěshàng-jiāshuāng.

'In the opinion poll, the conservative party was already lagging behind its adversary; recently a scandal erupted about a major figure; for the conservative party this is making a bad situation even worse.'

Usage: Functions as object, usually preceded by verbs and verbal constructions such as 是 'be a situation of,' 犹如 (yóurú 猶如) 'as if,' and 无异于 (wúyìyú 無異於) 'be tantamount to.'

Near Synonym: [祸不单行] (huò bù dān háng 禍不單行) 'misfortune never comes alone, misery loves company.'

Antonyms: [锦上添花] (jǐn shàng tiān huā 錦上添花) 'on brocade add flowers – improve to perfection,' [雪中送炭] (xuě zhōng sòng tàn 雪中送炭) 'deliver charcoal in snowy weather – offer timely assistance,' [双喜临门] (shuāng xǐ lín mén 雙喜臨門) 'double happiness descends on the house.'

259. 【风尘仆仆】(風塵僕僕) fēng chén pú pú

风尘 means 'wind and dust – travel' and 仆仆 means 'fatigue from travel.' The meaning of the whole idiom is 'fatigued from travel.'

Example 1: 总理**风尘仆仆**地赶到地震最严重的地区。

Zǒnglǐ fēngchén-púpú de gǎn dào dìzhèn zuì yánzhòng de dìqū.

'The premier, fatigued from travel, rushed to the area where the earthquake had been the most severe.'

Example 2: 你坐了一天的火车，刚下车，**风尘仆仆**的，先去休息吧。

Nǐ zuòle yì tiān de huǒchē, gāng xiàchē, fēngchén-púpú de, xiān qù xiūxi ba.

'You just got off the train after riding the whole day, you must be tired from your travels, why don't you first go rest.'

Usage: Functions mainly as adverbial; can also serve as predicate.

Note: Slightly complimentary in meaning.

Near Synonyms: [舟车劳顿] (zhōu chē láo dùn 舟車勞頓) 'fatigued from travel,' [栉风沐雨] (zhì fēng mù yǔ 櫛風沐雨) 'exposed to the elements.'

260. 【朝三暮四】(朝三暮四) zhāo sān mù sì

朝 means 'morning' and 暮 means 'evening, dusk.' The literal meaning is 'in the morning three and in the evening four.' English translations include 'fickle and inconstant, change one's mind frequently, six of one and half a dozen of the other.'

Example 1: 他对爱情太不认真，**朝三暮四**的，经常换女朋友。

Tā duì àiqíng tài bú rènzhēn, zhāosān-mùsì de, jīngcháng huàn nǚpéngyou.

'He's not the least bit serious about love, being fickle and inconstant, and frequently changing girlfriends.'

Example 2: 她是那种**朝三暮四**的人，别跟她交朋友。

Tā shì nà zhǒng zhāosān-mùsì de rén, bié gēn tā jiāo péngyou.

'She is that kind of very fickle person; don't make friends with her.'

Usage: Functions mainly as predicate or attributive.

Allusion: There was a man who raised monkeys but needed to reduce the amount of food fed to them due to his family's economic difficulties. Fearing his monkeys would be displeased, he purposely deceived them by saying he would feed them three acorns in the morning and four in the evening. The monkeys were very angry. Then he told them he would feed them four acorns in the morning and three in the evening, resulting in a group of happy monkeys.

Note: Can be used in speech as well as in writing. Has a negative connotation; often used to criticize people for not being constant in their love or for changing back and forth in other ways. Note that the character 朝, which is most commonly pronounced cháo, is here pronounced zhāo.

Near Synonyms: [朝秦暮楚] (zhāo Qín mù Chǔ 朝秦暮楚) 'serve Qin in the morning and Chu in the evening – fickle and inconstant,' [反复无常] (fǎn fù wú cháng 反復無常) 'unsteady.'

Antonyms: [萧规曹随] (Xiāo guī Cáo suí 蕭規曹隨) 'Xiao's rules Cao (the famous general) follows – abide by the rules laid down by one's predecessor,' [一成不变] (yì chéng bú biàn 一成不變) 'fixed and unalterable.'

261. 【心平气和】(心平氣和) xīn píng qì hé

平 means 'peaceful,' 气 means 'spirit,' and 和 means 'harmonious.' A literal translation of this idiom is therefore 'heart peaceful spirit harmonious.' A freer translation is 'in a calm mood, with a gentle disposition, in an even-tempered manner.'

Example 1: 我们能不能**心平气和**地坐下来谈一谈？

Wǒmen néng bù néng xīnpíng-qìhé de zuòxiàlái tán yi tán?

'Could we sit down calmly and talk?'

Example 2: 即使孩子错了，你也不能急躁，要**心平气和**地跟他讲道理。

Jíshǐ háizi cuòle, nǐ yě bù néng jízào, yào xīnpíng-qìhé de gēn tā jiǎng dàolǐ.

'Even if the child was wrong, you still mustn't be impatient; you should in an even-tempered manner reason things out with him.'

Usage: Functions mainly as adverbial.

Note: Complimentary in meaning.

Near Synonym: [平心静气] (píng xīn jìng qì 平心靜氣) 'calmly and patiently.'

Antonym: [暴跳如雷] (bào tiào rú léi 暴跳如雷) 'violent, jump about like thunder – fly into a rage.'

262. 【德高望重】(德高望重) dé gāo wàng zhòng

德 means 'moral character,' 望 means 'prestige,' and 重 here means 'weighty, heavy, considerable.' A literal translation of the whole idiom is 'character high prestige considerable,' with a freer translation being 'of noble character and high prestige.'

Example 1: 在电影界，他是一位**德高望重**的老前辈。

Zài diànyǐng jiè, tā shì yí wèi dégāo-wàngzhòng de lǎoqiánbèi.

'In film circles, he is a doyen of noble character and high prestige.'

Example 2: 每个春节，弟子们都会去看望他们**德高望重**的导师。

Měi gè chūnjié, dìzǐmen dōu huì qù kànwàng tāmen dégāo-wàngzhòng de dǎoshī.

'Every Chinese New Year, the disciples will all call on their teacher, who is of noble character and high prestige.'

Usage: Functions mainly as attributive; can also serve as predicate.

Note: Complimentary in meaning.

Antonyms: [无名小辈] (wú míng xiǎo bèi 無名小輩) 'anonymous incapable people,' [无名鼠辈] (wú míng shǔ bèi 無名鼠輩) 'anonymous and worthless people; unknown scoundrels.'

263. 【燃眉之急】(燃眉之急) rán méi zhī jí

燃 means 'burn,' 眉 means 'eyebrow,' and 急 means 'urgency.' A literal translation of the whole idiom is 'the urgency of fire singeing the eyebrows,' with a freer translation being 'a matter of great urgency.'

Example 1: 救援人员用直升飞机运来了饮用水，解决了灾区人民的**燃眉之急**。

Jiùyuán rényuán yòng zhíshēngfēijī yùnláile yǐnyòngshuǐ, jiějuéle zāiqū rénmín de ránméi-zhījí.

'The rescue workers used helicopters to bring in drinking water; they solved the urgent problems of the people in the disaster area.'

Example 2: 中央政府特别贷款一百亿美元，解了那家大银行的**燃眉之急**。

Zhōngyāng zhèngfǔ tèbié dàikuǎn yī bǎi yì měiyuán, jiěle nà jiā dà yínháng de ránméi-zhījí.

'The central government made a special loan of 10 billion U.S. dollars, relieving the urgent problems of that large bank.'

Usage: Functions as object, usually preceded by verbs such as 解决 (jiějué 解决) 'solve' or 解 (jiě) 'relieve.'

Near Synonyms: [迫在眉睫] (pò zài méi jié 迫在眉睫) 'very urgent,' [当务之急] (dāng wù zhī jí 當務之急) 'a matter of great urgency.'

264. 【不厌其烦】(不厭其煩) bú yàn qí fán

厌 means 'dislike,' 其 means 'its,' and 烦 means 'trouble.' The whole idiom means 'not mind the trouble, with great patience, tirelessly.'

Example 1: 父母**不厌其烦**地回答女儿提出的一个又一个 "简单" 的问题。

Fùmǔ búyàn-qífán de huídá nǚ'ér tíchū de yí ge yòu yí ge jiǎndān de wèntí.

'Her parents tirelessly answered the "simple" questions their daughter raised one after another.'

Example 2: 每次大会上，领导总是**不厌其烦**地强调稳定的重要性。

Měi cì dàhuì shàng, lǐngdǎo zǒngshì búyàn-qífán de qiángdiào wěndìng de zhòngyàoxìng.

'At each mass meeting, the leader with great patience stressed the importance of stability.'

Usage: Functions mainly as adverbial.

Near Synonym: [苦口婆心] (kǔ kǒu pó xīn 苦口婆心) 'admonish over and over with good intentions.'

Antonym: [不胜其烦] (bú shèng qí fán 不勝其煩) 'burdensome, boring.'

265.【别出心裁】(别出心裁) bié chū xīn cái

别 means 'another, different,' 出 means 'come out with, produce,' and 心裁 means 'idea, concept.' A literal translation of the whole idiom is 'come out with a different plan or concept,' with freer translations being 'have an unconventional idea, adopt an original approach.'

Example 1: 她**别出心裁**地在指甲上纹了几朵小花。

Tā biéchū-xīncái de zài zhǐjiǎ shàng wénle jǐ duǒ xiǎo huā.

'Adopting an original approach, she drew a few small flowers on her nails.'

Example 2: 贝聿铭为法国巴黎罗浮宫设计了一个**别出心裁**的玻璃金字塔入口。

Bèi Yùmíng wèi Fǎguó Bālí Luófú Gōng shèjìle yí ge biéchū-xīncái de bōlí jīnzìtǎ rùkǒu.

'I. M. Pei created a very original glass pyramid entrance for the Louvre museum in Paris, France.'

Usage: Functions mainly as adverbial and attributive; can also serve as predicate.

Note: Complimentary in meaning.

Near Synonyms: [独出机杼] (dú chū jī zhù 獨出機杼) 'on one's own come up with the idea for something (usually refers to a writer),' [独具匠心] (dú jù jiàng xīn 獨具匠心) 'show ingenuity,' [别开生面] (bié kāi shēng miàn 別開生面) 'start something new.'

Antonyms: [千篇一律] (qiān piān yí lǜ 千篇一律) 'a thousand essays uniform – follow the same pattern, stereotyped,' [如法炮制] (rú fǎ páo zhì 如法炮制) 'follow a set pattern,' [照猫画虎] (zhào māo huà hǔ 照貓畫虎) 'draw a tiger with a cat as a model – follow a model' (spoken style).

266.【不见经传】(不見經傳) bú jiàn jīng zhuàn

经传 means 'classics.' A literal translation is 'something not seen in the classics.' A freer translation is 'unattested by historical records, unknown.'

Example 1: 就是这样一位此前**不见经传**的小人物改写了整个历史。

Jiùshì zhèyàng yí wèi cǐqián bújiàn-jīngzhuàn de xiǎorénwù gǎixiěle zhěnggè lìshǐ.

'It was precisely a heretofore unknown "nobody" like this who rewrote all of history.'

Example 2: 京剧曾经名**不见经传**，只是到了清朝以后才流行起来。

Jīngjù céngjīng míngbújiànjīngzhuàn, zhǐshì dàole Qīngcháo yǐhòu cái liúxíng qǐlai.

'Beijing Opera used to be unknown; it was only with the advent of the Qing Dynasty that it came into fashion.'

Usage: Functions as attributive

Note: A common alternate form of this idiom is 名不见经传 (míng bú jiàn jīng zhuàn 名不見經傳).

Near Synonyms: [默默无闻] (mò mò wú wén 默默無聞) 'unknown to the public,' [无名鼠辈] (wú míng shǔ bèi 無名鼠輩) 'anonymous and worthless people; unknown scoundrels.'

Antonyms: [大名鼎鼎] (dà míng dǐng dǐng 大名鼎鼎) 'famous; well known,' [众所周知] (zhòng suǒ zhōu zhī 眾所周知) 'as is known to all,' [家喻户晓] (jiā yù hù xiǎo 家喻戶曉) 'known to every family, widely known.'

267. 【蔚然成风】(蔚然成風) wèi rán chéng fēng

蔚然 means 'luxuriant, magnificent' and 风 here means 'established practice or custom.' A literal translation of the whole idiom is 'magnificently become the custom.' A freer translation of the idiom is 'become common practice.'

Example 1: 最近几年，食疗**蔚然成风**。

Zuìjìn jǐ nián, shíliáo wèirán-chéngfēng.

'The last few years, nutritional therapy has become common practice.'

Example 2: 在他的号召下，减少浪费、保护环境**蔚然成风**。

Zài tā de hàozhào xià, jiǎnshǎo làngfèi, bǎohù huánjìng wèirán-chéngfēng.

'As a result of his appeal, reducing waste and protecting the environment have become common practice.'

Usage: Functions as predicate.

Near Synonyms: [蔚为大观] (wèi wéi dà guān 蔚為大觀) 'present an impressive sight,' [风靡一时] (fēng mí yì shí 風靡一時) 'fashionable for a period of time.'

268. 【大惊小怪】(大驚小怪) dà jīng xiǎo guài

The meaning of this idiom is 'get excited over little things, make a big fuss about nothing.'

Example 1: 这没什么了不起的，别**大惊小怪**的。

Zhè méishénme liǎobùqǐ de, bié dàjīng-xiǎoguài de.

'This is nothing unusual, don't make such a big deal about it.'

Example 2: 妹妹**大惊小怪**地说："哎呀，你们看！这么多蚂蚁！"

Mèimei dàjīng-xiǎoguài de shuō: "Āiya, nǐmen kàn! Zhème duō mǎyǐ!"

'Making a big fuss over nothing, younger sister said: "Oh, look! So many ants!"'

Usage: Functions mainly as predicate and adverbial.

Near Synonym: [少见多怪] (shǎo jiàn duō guài 少見多怪) 'a person who has seen little marvels much.'

Antonyms: [司空见惯] (sī kōng jiàn guàn 司空見慣) 'get used to seeing and no longer think it strange,' [不足为奇] (bù zú wéi qí 不足為奇) 'not at all surprising.'

269. 【千辛万苦】(千辛萬苦) qiān xīn wàn kǔ

The literal meaning is 'a thousand pains and ten thousand bitternesses.' The meaning of the idiom is 'countless sufferings, innumerable hardships.'

Example 1: 他历尽**千辛万苦**，才把这个公司发展成为世界有名的大公司。

Tā lìjìn qiānxīn-wànkǔ, cái bǎ zhège gōngsī fāzhǎn chéngwéi shìjiè yǒumíng de dà gōngsī.

'He experienced countless hardships; only after that did he develop this company into a world-famous major firm.'

Example 2: 那个年代，生活条件很差，父母**千辛万苦**地把一家孩子养大。

Nàge niándài, shēnghuó tiáojiàn hěn chà, fùmǔ qiānxīn-wànkǔ de bǎ yì jiā háizi yǎngdà.

'In those years, living conditions were very bad; the parents endured innumerable sufferings and hardships in raising their children.'

Usage: Functions mainly as object, often preceded by verbs meaning 'experience,' such as 历尽 (lìjìn 歷盡), 经历 (jīnglì 經歷), 经过 (jīngguò 經過), etc.

Near Synonym: [千难万险] (qiān nán wàn xiǎn 千難萬險) 'numerous difficulties and dangers.'

Antonym: [一帆风顺] (yì fān fēng shùn 一帆風順) 'smooth sailing, unimpeded progress.'

270. 【东施效颦】(東施效顰) Dōng Shī xiào pín

东施 is the name of a fictional person in the Spring and Autumn Period in Chinese history, 效 means 'imitate,' and 颦 means 'knit the brows, frown.' A literal translation of the whole idiom is 'Dong Shi imitates (the famous beauty Xi Shi) in knitting her eyebrows (and ends up looking even uglier).' This is a metaphor for 'imitate others only to make a fool of oneself.'

Example 1: 模特的身材棒，所以穿那样的衣服好看；而你的身材那么差，穿那样的衣服可就**东施效颦**了。

Mótè de shēncái bàng, suǒyǐ chuān nàyàng de yīfú hǎokàn; ér nǐ de shēncái nàme chà, chuān nàyàng de yīfú kě jiù Dōng Shī-xiàopín le.

'The model had a great figure, so when she wore that kind of clothes, it looked good; but your figure is so bad that if you wear that kind of clothes, it will be just like when Dong Shi tried to imitate Xi Shi in knitting her eyebrows but only ended up making a fool of herself.'

Example 2: 你的发音那么差，却要模仿别人的腔调，真是**东施效颦**。

Nǐ de fāyīn nàme chà, què yào mófǎng biérén de qiāngdiào, zhēn shì Dōng Shī-xiàopín.

'Your pronunciation is so bad, and yet you want to imitate other people's accents; it's really like the time when Dong Shi tried to imitate Xi Shi in knitting her eyebrows but only ended up making a fool of herself.'

Usage: Functions mainly as predicate.

Allusion: Of the four great beauties of ancient China, Xi Shi was the most beautiful. There was a time when Xi Shi's stomach hurt and so, as she walked, she held her hand to her stomach and knit her eyebrows. Now, among Xi Shi's fellow townspeople there was a woman by the name of Dong Shi who was especially ugly. Seeing Xi Shi like that, she thought that was also very beautiful, so she imitated Xi Shi in the way she held her hand to her stomach and knit her eyebrows. When they saw her, those among Dong Shi's fellow townspeople who were rich closed their front doors tightly and wouldn't come out; those who weren't rich hurriedly pulled their wives and children with them and hid far away. Dong Shi knew that the way Xi Shi knit her eyebrows was beautiful, but she didn't know why it was beautiful. (from "Tian Yun" in *Zhuangzi*)

Note: Derogatory in meaning.

Near Synonyms: [照猫画虎] (zhào māo huà hǔ 照貓畫虎) 'draw a tiger with a cat as a model – follow a model,' [生搬硬套] (shēng bān yìng tào 生搬硬套) 'copy mechanically and force-fit into.'

Antonyms: [标新立异] (biāo xīn lì yì 標新立異) 'create something new and different,' [择善而从] (zé shàn ér cóng 擇善而從) 'select the good and follow it.'

271. 【因势利导】(因勢利導) yīn shì lì dǎo

因 here means 'according to,' 势 means 'situation,' and 利导 means 'skillfully guide.' A literal translation of the whole idiom is 'according to the situation skillfully guide (action),' with a freer translation being 'guided by the circumstances.'

Example 1: 在农村的改革取得成功后，邓小平**因势利导**，在城市以及其他行业也进行了全面的改革。

Zài nóngcūn de gǎigé qǔdé chénggōng hòu, Dèng Xiǎopíng yīnshì-lìdǎo, zài chéngshì yǐjí qítā hángyè yě jìnxíngle quánmiàn de gǎigé.

'After the reforms in the countryside achieved success, Deng Xiaoping was guided by the circumstances, and in the cities and in other professions also carried out comprehensive reforms.'

Example 2: 市政府抓住机遇，**因势利导**，建立了一批出口企业。

Shì zhèngfǔ zhuāzhù jīyù, yīnshì-lìdǎo, jiànlìle yì pī chūkǒu qǐyè.

'The municipal government seized the opportunity, skillfully guiding their action according to the situation, and set up a number of export enterprises.'

Usage: Functions as predicate.

Near Synonym: [顺水推舟] (shùn shuǐ tuī zhōu 順水推舟) 'push one's boat along with a favorable current – go with the tide.'

Antonym: [倒行逆施] (dǎo xíng nì shī 倒行逆施) 'go against the tide of history, try to push the clock back.'

272. 【千里迢迢】(千里迢迢) qiān lǐ tiáo tiáo

迢迢 means 'far away.' The meaning of the whole idiom is 'thousands of miles away, far away.'

Example 1: 那位记者**千里迢迢**地跑到偏远的边疆的农村采访当地人的真实生活。

Nà wèi jìzhě qiānlǐ-tiáotiáo de pǎodào piānyuǎn de biānjiāng de nóngcūn cǎifǎng dāngdì rén de zhēnshí shēnghuó.

'That reporter went far away to the remote countryside in the border region to interview local people about their true lives.'

Example 2: 病人**千里迢迢**地来到北京治病。

Bìngrén qiānlǐ-tiáotiáo de láidào Běijīng zhìbìng.

'Patients came to Beijing from far away to seek treatment for their illnesses.'

Usage: Functions mainly as adverbial.

Near Synonym: [不远千里] (bù yuǎn qiān lǐ 不遠千里) 'not consider a thousand miles as far' (used mostly in speech).

273. 【格格不入】(格格不入) gé gé bú rù

格格 means 'obstruct.' The meaning of the whole idiom is 'incompatible with, incongruous with.'

Example 1: 这种观念跟中国的实际情况**格格不入**。

Zhè zhǒng guānniàn gēn Zhōngguó de shíjì qíngkuàng gégé-búrù.

'Such an attitude is incompatible with the actual situation in China.'

Example 2: 跟豪华的宫殿**格格不入**的是，门口站着一群乞丐。

Gēn háohuá de gōngdiàn gégé-búrù de shì, ménkǒu zhànzhe yì qún qǐgài.

'What was incongruous with the lavish palace was that, at the entrance, there was standing a group of beggars.'

Usage: Functions mainly as predicate; can also serve as attributive.

Near Synonyms: [水火不容] (shuǐ huǒ bù róng 水火不容) 'as incompatible as fire and water,' [方枘圆凿] (fāng ruì yuán záo 方枘圓鑿) 'like a square peg in a round hole.'

Antonym: [水乳交融] (shuǐ rǔ jiāo róng 水乳交融) 'water and milk blended together – in perfect harmony.'

274. 【如火如荼】(如火如荼) rú huǒ rú tú

荼 means 'the white flowers of cogon grass.' The literal meaning of this idiom is 'as (red as) fire and as (white as) cogon grass flowers,' with freer translations being 'like a raging fire, with great fervor, flourishing.'

Example 1: 国家正在重点建设这个地区，所以各种建设项目**如火如荼**地展开了。

Guójiā zhèngzài zhòngdiǎn jiànshè zhège dìqū, suǒyǐ gè zhǒng jiànshè xiàngmù rúhuǒ-rútú de zhǎnkāile.

'The country is giving priority to reconstructing this district, so all kinds of construction projects have been launched with great fervor.'

Example 2: 在**如火如荼**的文化大革命里，知识分子受到的影响最大。

Zài rúhuǒ-rútú de wénhuà dà gémìng lǐ, zhīshi fènzǐ shòudào de yǐngxiǎng zuì dà.

'During the conflagration that was the Cultural Revolution, intellectuals were the most affected.'

Usage: Functions mainly as attributive, adverbial, and predicate. Used mostly in connection with political campaigns or activities.

Note: Complimentary in meaning.

Near Synonym: [轰轰烈烈] (hōng hōng liè liè 轟轟烈烈) 'grand and gigantic.'

Antonym: [无声无息] (wú shēng wú xī 無聲無息) 'no sound no breath – silent.'

275. 【肃然起敬】(肅然起敬) sù rán qǐ jìng

肃然 means 'with great respect,' 起 means 'give rise to,' and 敬 means 'respect.' The meaning of the whole idiom is 'suddenly have great respect or reverence for.'

Example 1: 她冒着危险从河里救上来一个小孩儿，这样的行为让人**肃然起敬**。

Tā màozhe wēixiǎn cóng hé lǐ jiùshànglái yí ge xiǎoháir, zhèyàng de xíngwéi ràng rén sùrán-qǐjìng.

'She risked danger in rescuing a child from the river; this kind of conduct makes one suddenly feel great respect.'

Example 2: 听了他的故事以后，我不禁**肃然起敬**。

Tīngle tā de gùshi yǐhòu, wǒ bù jīn sùrán-qǐjìng.

'After hearing his story, I couldn't help suddenly having great respect for him.'

Usage: Functions mainly as predicate after 令人 (lìng rén), 让人 (ràng rén 讓人), or 使人 (shǐ rén), all of which mean 'make someone . . .' or 'make people. . . .'

Note: Complimentary in meaning.

Near Synonym: [奉若神明] (fèng ruò shén míng 奉若神明) 'revere something as sacred.'

Antonym: [嗤之以鼻] (chī zhī yǐ bí 嗤之以鼻) 'snort at contemptuously with one's nose.'

276. 【扬长避短】(揚長避短) yáng cháng bì duǎn

扬 means 'raise,' 长 means 'strong point,' 避 means 'avoid,' and 短 means 'shortcoming.' A literal translation of the whole idiom is 'raise strong points avoid shortcomings,' with a freer translation being 'enhance one's strong points and avoid any weaknesses.'

Example 1: 那支球队的长处是防守，于是他们**扬长避短**，避免跟对手对攻。

Nà zhī qiúduì de chángchù shì fángshǒu, yúshì tāmen yángcháng-bìduǎn, bìmiǎn gēn duìshǒu duìgōng.

'That team's strong point is defense, and so they took advantage of their strong points and avoided their shortcomings, avoiding going on the offensive against their opponent.'

Example 2: 日本领土狭小，资源相对缺乏，但是日本人**扬长避短**，大力发展高科技产品，例如照相机和汽车等产品。

Rìběn lǐngtǔ xiáxiǎo, zīyuán xiāngduì quēfá, dànshì Rìběnrén yángcháng-bìduǎn, dàlì fāzhǎn gāokējì chǎnpǐn, lìrú zhàoxiàngjī hé qìchē děng chǎnpǐn.

'Japanese territory is narrow and small, and resources are relatively lacking; but the Japanese enhance their strong points and avoid their weaknesses, vigorously developing high-tech products, for instance, products such as cameras and cars.'

Usage: Functions mainly as predicate.

Note: Complimentary in meaning.

Near Synonyms: [取长补短] (qǔ cháng bǔ duǎn 取長補短) 'draw on the strong points of others to make up for one's own deficiencies,' [避实击虚] (bì shí jī xū 避實擊虛) 'avoid the enemy's strength and hit its weaknesses.'

Antonym: [自不量力] (zì bú liàng lì 自不量力) 'not know one's own limitations.'

277. 【蒸蒸日上】(蒸蒸日上) zhēng zhēng rì shàng

蒸蒸 means 'thriving' and 日上 means 'improving day by day.' The meaning of the whole idiom is 'become more thriving and flourishing each day, progress day by day.'

Example 1: 自从他当市长以来，市里的各项事业**蒸蒸日上**。

Zìcóng tā dāng shìzhǎng yǐlái, shì lǐ de gè xiàng shìyè zhēngzhēng-rìshàng.

'Ever since he became mayor, all kinds of businesses in the city have been flourishing.'

Example 2: 国有企业困难重重的时候，私营企业呈现出**蒸蒸日上**的景象。

Guóyǒu qǐyè kùnnán chóngchóng de shíhou, sīyíng qǐyè chéngxiànchū zhēngzhēng-rìshàng de jǐngxiàng.

'While state-owned enterprises have been beset with difficulties, private enterprises have been revealing a picture of being more thriving and flourishing by the day.'

Usage: Functions mainly as predicate; can also serve as attributive.

Note: Complimentary in meaning.

Near Synonym: [欣欣向荣] (xīn xīn xiàng róng 欣欣向榮) 'thriving, flourishing.'

Antonyms: [江河日下] (jiāng hé rì xià 江河日下) 'rivers and streams daily decline – deteriorate day by day, go from bad to worse,' [每况愈下] (měi kuàng yù xià 每况愈下) 'go from bad to worse.'

278. 【胸有成竹】(胸有成竹) xiōng yǒu chéng zhú

胸 means 'chest, thorax,' 成 means 'fully developed,' and 竹 means 'bamboo.' The literal meaning is '(when about to draw bamboo,) in the chest there is fully developed bamboo.' English translations include 'have a well thought out plan, have a whole idea in one's mind, have a card up one's sleeve.'

Example 1: 至于下一步应该怎么做，她已经**胸有成竹**了。

Zhìyú xià yí bù yīnggāi zěnme zuò, tā yǐjīng xiōngyǒuchéngzhú le.

'As for what she should do as the next step, she already has a well thought out plan.'

Example 2: 他**胸有成竹**地回答："这件事绝对没问题。"

Tā xiōng yǒu chéng zhú de huídá: "Zhè jiàn shì juéduì méi wèntí."

'With a well thought out plan in mind, he answered, "There are absolutely no problems concerning this matter."'

Explanation: When painting bamboo, if you draw it slowly, one section or leaf at a time, then you will certainly not be able to draw the bamboo well. Before painting the bamboo, you should already have a preconceived notion in your mind. That way, when you paint it, you can do so quickly.

Usage: Functions mainly as predicate at the end of a sentence; also serves as adverbial modifier after verbs such as 说 (shuō 說) 'say' and 回答 (huídá) 'answer.'

Note: Written-style usage. Has a positive connotation. There is an alternate form 成竹在胸 (chéng zhú zài xiōng).

Near Synonyms: [胸中有数] (xiōng zhōng yǒu shù 胸中有數) 'have a good idea of how things stand,' [胜券在握] (shèng quàn zài wò 勝券在握) 'have the game in one's hands, certain of winning.'

Antonyms: [胸中无数] (xiōng zhōng wú shù 胸中無數) 'ignorant of how things stand,' [胸无点墨] (xiōng wú diǎn mò 胸無點墨) 'not a bit of ink in one's chest – without much learning or knowledge.'

279. 【肆无忌惮】(肆無忌憚) sì wú jì dàn

肆 means 'unrestrained,' 忌 means 'scruples, misgivings,' and 惮 means 'fear.' The literal meaning is 'unrestrained and not have any scruples or fear,' with a freer translation being 'unscrupulous, unbridled.'

Example 1: 他仗着他爸爸是县长，因此在那个县里到处做坏事，**肆无忌惮**。

Tā zhàngzhe tā bàba shì xiànzhǎng, yīncǐ zài nàge xiàn lǐ dàochù zuò huài shì, sìwújìdàn.

'He was relying on his father's being county magistrate, and therefore did bad things everywhere in that county, completely without scruples.'

Example 2: 开发商**肆无忌惮**地砍伐巴西亚马逊河流域的森林。

Kāifāshāng sìwújìdàn de kǎnfá Bāxī Yàmǎxùn Hé liúyù de sēnlín.

'Commercial developers, completely without scruples, are felling the forests in the Amazon River basin.'

Usage: Functions mainly as adverbial and predicate.

Note: Derogatory in meaning.

Near Synonyms: [有恃无恐] (yǒu shì wú kǒng 有恃無恐) 'have someone one can rely on and not have fear – feel secure because one has strong backing,' [无所顾忌] (wú suǒ gù jì 無所顧忌) 'have no scruples or misgivings.'

Antonyms: [小心翼翼] (xiǎo xīn yì yì 小心翼翼) 'cautiously,' [循规蹈矩] (xún guī dǎo jǔ 循規蹈矩) 'toe the line, stick to convention.'

280. 【囫囵吞枣】(囫圇吞棗) hú lún tūn zǎo

囫囵 means 'whole, complete,' 吞 means 'swallow,' and 枣 means 'date.' A literal translation is 'swallow a date whole,' with a freer translation being 'study or read something without thinking it through carefully' or 'accept something uncritically without careful consideration.'

Example 1: 对于英语不是母语的人来说，看莎士比亚的剧本有时候未免**囫囵吞枣**，理解得不一定完全准确。

Duìyú Yīngyǔ bú shì mǔyǔ de rén lái shuō, kàn Shāshìbǐyà de jùběn yǒu shíhou wèimiǎn húlún-tūnzǎo, lǐjiěde bù yídìng wánquán zhǔnquè.

'For non-native speakers of English, reading Shakespeare's plays sometimes inevitably involves "swallowing a date whole" without being able completely to digest it; they don't necessarily understand everything completely accurately.'

Example 2: 学习外国经验的时候要结合本国的国情，千万不能**囫囵吞枣**，生搬硬套。

Xuéxí wàiguó jīngyàn de shíhou yào jiéhé běnguó de guóqíng, qiānwàn bù néng húlún-tūnzǎo, shēngbān-yìngtào.

'When one is studying foreign experience one should integrate it with the national conditions of one's own country; one absolutely must not swallow something whole without careful consideration, or copy others mechanically and slavishly.'

Usage: Functions mainly as predicate and adverbial.

Allusion: It is said that pears are good for the teeth but harm the spleen; and that dates are good for the spleen but harm the teeth. There was once a stupid student who, after thinking for a long time, said: "When I eat pears, I only chew without swallowing; this way it won't harm my spleen. And when I eat dates, I swallow them whole without chewing; this way it won't harm my teeth." Someone joked: "You're that date that was swallowed whole!" Immediately everyone fell over laughing. (from *Zhan Yuan Jing Yu* by Bai Wangting, Yuan Dynasty)

Note: Derogatory in meaning.

Near Synonyms: [生搬硬套] (shēng bān yìng tào 生搬硬套) 'copy mechanically and force-fit into' (derogatory), [生吞活剥] (shēng tūn huó bō 生吞活剥) 'swallow raw and skin alive – accept uncritically,' [不求甚解] (bù qiú shèn jiě 不求甚解) 'not seek deep understanding.'

Antonyms: [细嚼慢咽] (xì jiáo màn yàn 細嚼慢嚥) 'chew carefully and swallow slowly,' [融会贯通] (róng huì guàn tōng 融會貫通) 'gain a thorough understanding after comprehensive study,' [含英咀华] (hán yīng jǔ huá 含英咀華) 'enjoy the beauty of words.'

281. 【异乎寻常】 (異乎尋常) yì hū xún cháng

异 means 'different,' 乎 here means 'from,' and 寻常 means 'ordinary, common.' A literal translation is 'different from the ordinary,' with a freer translation being 'unusual, uncommon, extraordinary.'

Example 1: 他突然对国际关系表现出**异乎寻常**的热情。

Tā tūrán duì guójì guānxi biǎoxiànchū yìhū-xúncháng de rèqíng.

'He suddenly showed unusual enthusiasm for international relations.'

Example 2: 今年的冬天**异乎寻常**地冷，是近二十年来最冷的冬天。

Jīnnián de dōngtiān yìhū-xúncháng de lěng, shì jìn èrshí nián lái zuì lěng de dōngtiān.

'Winter this year has been uncommonly cold; it's the coldest winter in the last twenty years.'

Usage: Functions mainly as attributive and adverbial.

Near Synonyms: [一反常态] (yì fǎn cháng tài 一反常態) 'depart from one's normal behavior,' [出人意料] (chū rén yì liào 出人意料) 'beyond one's expectations.'

Antonym: [意料之中] (yì liào zhī zhōng 意料之中) 'as might be expected.'

282. 【赏心悦目】(賞心悅目) shǎng xīn yuè mù

赏心 here means 'please the mind' and 悦目 means 'please the eye.' The whole idiom means 'pleasing to the mind and the eye.'

Example 1: 巴西球员的足球技术很华丽，他们的比赛令人**赏心悦目**。

Bāxī qiúyuán de zúqiú jìshù hěn huálì, tāmen de bǐsài lìng rén shǎngxīn-yuèmù.

'The Brazil players' soccer technique is magnificent; their matches are pleasing to the eye and to the mind.'

Example 2: 新年那天，她看了一场**赏心悦目**的演出。

Xīnnián nà tiān, tā kànle yì chǎng shǎngxīn-yuèmù de yǎnchū.

'On New Year's Day, she saw a very pleasing performance.'

Usage: Functions mainly as predicate, often preceded by 令人 (lìng rén) or 让人 (ràng rén 讓人), both of which mean 'make someone. . . .' Also frequently serves as attributive.

Note: Complimentary in meaning.

Near Synonym: [心旷神怡] (xīn kuàng shén yí 心曠神怡) 'cheerful and happy.'

Antonym: [怵目惊心] (chù mù jīng xīn 怵目驚心) 'alarmed at the sight of something.'

283. 【古往今来】(古往今來) gǔ wǎng jīn lái

The meaning of this idiom is 'through the ages, since time immemorial.'

Example 1: **古往今来**，哪个成功的人没有付出艰辛的努力？

Gǔwǎng-jīnlái, nǎge chénggōng de rén méiyǒu fùchū jiānxīn de nǔlì?

'Since time immemorial, what successful person has not had to make hard efforts?'

Example 2: 博物馆员给大家一一介绍了**古往今来**的名画。

Bówùguǎnyuán gěi dàjiā yī yī jièshàole gǔwǎng-jīnlái de mínghuà.

'The museum docent introduced to everyone the famous paintings from through the ages, one after another.'

Usage: Functions mainly as adverbial; can also serve as attributive. Frequently occurs by itself and set off from the rest of a sentence, as in Example 1.

Near Synonym: [有史以来] (yǒu shǐ yǐ lái 有史以來) 'since the beginning of history.'

Antonym: [史无前例] (shǐ wú qián lì 史無前例) 'in history there is no precedent, unprecedented.'

284. 【大有作为】(大有作為) dà yǒu zuò wéi

大 here means 'greatly, very much' and 作为 means 'achievements, contributions.' A literal translation of the whole idiom is 'greatly have contributions.' Freer translations include 'able to develop one's ability to the fullest, have great prospects, have great potential.'

Example 1: 在毕业典礼上，校长祝所有的毕业生在社会上**大有作为**。

Zài bìyè diǎnlǐ shàng, xiàozhǎng zhù suǒyǒu de bìyèshēng zài shèhuì shàng dàyǒuzuòwéi.

'At the graduation ceremony, the president wished all the graduates that in society they might have great contributions.'

Example 2: 这两家大公司强强联手，是可以**大有作为**的。

Zhè liǎng jiā dà gōngsī qiáng qiáng liánshǒu, shì kěyǐ dàyǒu zuòwéi de.

'If these two major companies join forces, they could have great prospects.'

Usage: Functions mainly as predicate; can also serve as attributive.

Near Synonyms: [大显身手] (dà xiǎn shēn shǒu 大顯身手) 'display one's skills to the fullest,' [大展宏图] (dà zhǎn hóng tú 大展宏圖) 'fulfill one's great aspirations.'

Antonyms: [无所作为] (wú suǒ zuò wéi 無所作為) 'do or accomplish nothing,' [碌碌无为] (lù lù wú wéi 碌碌無為) 'ordinary and devoid of ability,' [一事无成] (yí shì wú chéng 一事無成) 'accomplish nothing,' [庸庸碌碌] (yōng yōng lù lù 庸庸碌碌) 'mediocre and ordinary.'

285. 【集思广益】(集思廣益) jí sī guǎng yì

集 means 'concentrate,' 思 means 'thought,' 广 means 'make wide,' and 益 means 'benefit.' A literal translation of the whole idiom is 'concentrate thoughts and enlarge the benefits,' with freer translations including 'benefit from a wide range of opinions' and 'profit by soliciting opinions from various sources.'

Example 1: 有关部门**集思广益**，充分吸收专家和群众的意见。

Yǒuguān bùmén jísī-guǎngyì, chōngfèn xīshōu zhuānjiā hé qúnzhòng de yìjiàn.

'The concerned departments benefited from a wide range of opinions, to the fullest extent possible soliciting opinions from experts and the masses.'

Example 2: 我们应该**集思广益**，听取各方面的声音，以便完善我们的政策。

Wǒmen yīnggāi jísī-guǎngyì, tīngqǔ gè fāngmiàn de shēngyīn, yǐbiàn wánshàn wǒmen de zhèngcè.

'We should profit by soliciting opinions from various sources, and listen to the voices from all quarters, so as to perfect our policies.'

Usage: Functions mainly as predicate.

Note: Complimentary in meaning.

Near Synonyms: [集腋成裘] (jí yè chéng qiú 集腋成裘) 'collect together many little pieces of fur to make a fur coat,' [群策群力] (qún cè qún lì 群策群力) 'pool together everyone's wisdom and strength.'

Antonyms: [独断专行] (dú duàn zhuān xíng 獨斷專行) 'act arbitrarily,' [一意孤行] (yí yì gū xíng 一意孤行) 'cling obstinately to a reckless course.'

286. 【一应俱全】(一應俱全) yì yīng jù quán

一应 means 'all, everything' and 俱全 means 'complete.' The meaning of the whole idiom is 'amply supplied with everything needed, complete with everything.'

Example 1: 赌场里旅馆、饭馆、商店、邮局等**一应俱全**，简直就是一个社区。

Dǔchǎng lǐ lǚguǎn, fànguǎn, shāngdiàn, yóujú děng yìyīng-jùquán, jiǎnzhí jiùshì yí ge shèqū.

'In the casino, everything – hotel, restaurants, shops, post office, and so on – is amply provided; it's virtually a community.'

Example 2: 农民工在城里卖东西要具备四个证，只有这四个证**一应俱全**了，有关部门才批准你可以合法地卖东西。

Nóngmíngōng zài chéng lǐ mài dōngxi yào jùbèi sì ge zhèng, zhǐ yǒu zhè sì ge zhèng yìyīng-jùquán le, yǒuguān bùmén cái pīzhǔn nǐ kěyǐ héfǎ de mài dōngxi.

'Peasant workers who sell things in the city must possess four permits; only when these four permits are all complete do the concerned authorities authorize you so you can legally sell things.'

Usage: Functions mainly as predicate; can also serve as attributive.

Near Synonyms: [无所不有] (wú suǒ bù yǒu 無所不有) 'there is nothing one doesn't have – have everything,' [面面俱到] (miàn miàn jù dào 面面俱到) 'complete and thorough,' [万事俱备] (wàn shì jù bèi 萬事俱備) 'everything is ready, all is in place.'

Antonym: [一无所有] (yì wú suǒ yǒu 一無所有) 'have absolutely nothing, destitute.'

287. 【不得而知】(不得而知) bù dé ér zhī

得 means 'can' while 知 means 'know.' 而 here has no meaning, only contributing a syllable so that the idiom can have the standard four syllables. The meaning of the whole idiom is 'cannot be known, unable to ascertain.'

Example 1: 至于他心里是怎么想的，那就**不得而知**了。

Zhìyú tā xīnlǐ shì zěnme xiǎng de, nà jiù bùdé'érzhī le.

'As for how he thought in his mind, that cannot be known.'

Example 2: 这种快餐的热量到底有多少，消费者仍然**不得而知**。

Zhè zhǒng kuàicān de rèliàng dàodǐ yǒu duōshǎo, xiāofèizhě réngrán bùdé'érzhī.

'Consumers are still unable to ascertain how many calories this kind of fast food really has.'

Usage: Functions as predicate, occurring at the end of a sentence.

Note: Somewhat derogatory in meaning.

Antonym: [了如指掌] (liǎo rú zhǐ zhǎng 瞭如指掌) 'understand as well as one's own fingers and palms – completely clear.'

288. 【提心吊胆】(提心吊膽) tí xīn diào dǎn

提 here means 'carry,' 吊 means 'hang,' and 胆 means 'gallbladder.' The literal meaning is 'carry one's heart and hang one's gallbladder,' which can be translated as 'very worried, very much afraid.'

Example 1: 那个街区不安全，附近的居民**提心吊胆**的，一到天黑就不敢上街。

Nàge jiēqū bù ānquán, fùjìn de jūmín tíxīn-diàodǎn de, yí dào tiānhēi jiù bù gǎn shàngjiē.

'That area is not safe, the residents nearby being very much afraid; as soon as it gets dark, they don't dare to go on the streets.'

Example 2: 他贪污了国家的钱，**提心吊胆**地生活了一年后，最终自己找警察承认了。

Tā tānwūle guójiā de qián, tíxīn-diàodǎn de shēnghuóle yì nián hòu, zuìzhōng zìjǐ zhǎo jǐngchá chéngrènle.

'He embezzled the country's money; after living in great fear for a year, in the end he went to the police himself and confessed.'

Usage: Functions mainly as predicate and adverbial.

Note: Derogatory in meaning.

Near Synonym: [心惊胆战] (xīn jīng dǎn zhàn 心驚膽戰) (also written as [心惊胆颤] (xīn jīng dǎn chàn 心驚膽顫)) 'terror-stricken.'

Antonym: [心安理得] (xīn ān lǐ dé 心安理得) 'have peace of mind.'

289. 【货真价实】(貨真價實) huò zhēn jià shí

货 means 'goods, merchandise,' 价 means 'price,' and 实 means 'honest, solid, reasonable.' The meaning of the whole idiom is 'genuine goods at reasonable prices.'

Example 1: 这家商店卖的商品**货真价实**，深受消费者欢迎。

Zhè jiā shāngdiàn mài de shāngpǐn huòzhēn-jiàshí, shēnshòu xiāofèizhě huānyíng.

'The merchandise this store sells is genuine and prices are reasonable, so it is very favorably received by consumers.'

Example 2: 她是实力派，不是靠炒作成名的，是**货真价实**的明星。

Tā shì shílìpài, bú shì kào chǎozuò chéngmíng de, shì huòzhēn-jiàshí de míngxīng.

'She has real power and she didn't gain fame through hype; she's a genuine star.'

Usage: Functions mainly as attributive and predicate.

Note: Complimentary in meaning.

Near Synonyms: [名副其实] (míng fù qí shí 名副其實) 'worthy of the name or reputation,' [名不虚传] (míng bù xū chuán 名不虚傳) 'live up to one's reputation.'

Antonyms: [华而不实] (huá ér bù shí 華而不實) 'flowers but no fruit – flashy but lacking substance,' [徒有虚名] (tú yǒu xū míng 徒有虚名) 'enjoy unwarranted fame, in name only.'

290. 【鸡犬升天】(雞犬升天) jī quǎn shēng tiān

鸡 means 'chicken,' 犬 means 'dog,' and 升 means 'rise up to.' A literal translation of the whole idiom is '(his) chickens and dogs rise to heaven (with him).' By metaphor, this means that if someone becomes an official, the people who have a connection with him will also gain power, or that followers benefit when their leader gains power.

Example 1: 不管古代的官场还是现代的官场，都是一人得道，**鸡犬升天**。

Bùguǎn gǔdài de guānchǎng háishì xiàndài de guānchǎng, dōu shì yìrén-dédào, jīquǎn-shēngtiān.

'No matter whether it's officialdom in ancient times or officialdom nowadays, it's always been the case that "when one person attains enlightenment, his chickens and dogs will rise to heaven with him" – in other words, nepotism is a very common phenomenon.'

Example 2: 他当了总统，兄弟姐妹都当了高官，这不是一人得道，**鸡犬升天**吗？

Tā dāngle zǒngtǒng, xiōngdìjiěmèi dōu dāngle gāoguān, zhè búshì yìrén-dédào, jīquǎn-shēngtiān ma?

'When he became president, his siblings became high officials; is this not an example of nepotism?'

Usage: Functions mainly as predicate, usually used with 一人得道 (yì rén dé dào) 'one person attains enlightenment' or 一人得势 (yì rén dé shì 一人得勢) 'one person gains power.'

Allusion: It is said that during Western Han times, Liu An, the king of Huainan, became an immortal through alchemy. He threw the remaining potions into the courtyard, and after the chickens and dogs in the courtyard had eaten them, they also rose to heaven and became immortals.

Note: Derogatory in meaning.

Near Synonym: [一荣俱荣] (yì róng jù róng 一榮俱榮) 'if one flourishes, all flourish; honor one, honor them all.'

Antonym: [株连九族] (zhū lián jiǔ zú 株連九族) 'implicate the nine generations of a family.'

291. 【奋不顾身】(奮不顧身) fèn bú gù shēn

奋 here means 'courageous,' 顾 means 'consider,' and 身 means 'one's own body.' A literal translation of the whole idiom is 'courageously not consider one's own body,' with a freer translation being 'act boldly without regard for one's own life.'

Example 1: 就在歹徒行凶的一刹那，他**奋不顾身**地冲了上去，紧紧地抓住了歹徒的手。

Jiù zài dǎitú hángxiōng de yíchà'nà, tā fènbúgùshēn de chōngle shàngqù, jǐnjǐn de zhuāzhùle dǎitú de shǒu.

'Just at the instant that the evildoer was committing the crime, he boldly and without regard for his own life rushed forward and tightly grabbed the evildoer's arm.'

Example 2: 有个孩子掉进了河里，她**奋不顾身**地跳了下去，去救那个孩子。

Yǒu ge háizi diàojìnle hé lǐ, tā fènbúgùshēn de tiàole xiàqù, qù jiù nàge háizi.

'There was a child that fell into the river; boldly and disregarding her own life, she jumped in to go save the child.'

Usage: Functions mainly as adverbial.

Note: Complimentary in meaning.

Near Synonyms: [舍生忘死] (shě shēng wàng sǐ 捨生忘死) 'abandon one's life and forget death,' [万死不辞] (wàn sǐ bù cí 萬死不辭) 'despite ten thousand deaths not decline to do something.'

Antonym: [贪生怕死] (tān shēng pà sǐ 貪生怕死) 'covet life and fear death.'

292. 【精打细算】(精打細算) jīng dǎ xì suàn

精 means 'skilled,' 细 means 'meticulous,' and 打算 means 'plan.' The meaning of the whole idiom is 'careful planning and calculations.'

Example 1: 普通人的收入不高，过日子就得**精打细算**，花好每一块钱。

Pǔtōngrén de shōurù bù gāo, guò rìzi jiù děi jīngdǎ-xìsuàn, huā hǎo měi yí kuài qián.

'The income of ordinary people is not high; to live they must plan and calculate carefully, spending every dollar well.'

Example 2: 油价下跌了，严重影响了人们的日常生活，过惯了大手大脚的生活的沙特人也开始**精打细算**了。

Yóujià xiàdiēle, yánzhòng yǐngxiǎngle rénmen de rìcháng shēnghuó, guòguànle dàshǒu-dàjiǎo de shēnghuó de Shātèrén yě kāishǐ jīngdǎ-xìsuàn le.

'The price of oil has dropped, which has seriously affected people's everyday lives; even Saudi Arabians, who are used to extravagant lives, have begun carefully planning and calculating.'

Usage: Functions mainly as predicate.

Near Synonyms: [克勤克俭] (kè qín kè jiǎn 克勤克儉) 'hardworking and thrifty,' [一丝不苟] (yì sī bù gǒu 一絲不苟) 'not the least bit negligent.'

Antonyms: [大手大脚] (dà shǒu dà jiǎo 大手大腳) 'big hands big feet – extravagant,' [粗心大意] (cū xīn dà yì 粗心大意) 'careless, negligent.'

293. 【目不转睛】(目不轉睛) mù bù zhuǎn jīng

目 here means 'look at,' 转 means 'turn,' and 睛 means 'eyeballs.' A literal translation of the whole idiom is 'look at but not turn the eyeballs,' with freer translations being 'fix the eyes on, look at with great concentration and attention.'

Example 1: 孩子**目不转睛**地盯着电视画面。

Háizi mùbùzhuǎnjīng de dīngzhe diànshì huàmiàn.

'The child with great concentration stared at the televised image.'

Example 2: 那对情人**目不转睛**地看着对方，眼睛里传递了多少爱！

Nà duì qíngrén mùbùzhuǎnjīng de kànzhe duìfāng, yǎnjing lǐ chuándìle duōshǎo ài!

'That pair of sweethearts gazed at each other without moving an eyeball; how much love was transmitted in the eyes!'

Usage: Functions mainly as adverbial, modifying words meaning 'see.'

Near Synonym: [目不斜视] (mù bù xié shì 目不斜視) 'not look to either side, not be distracted.'

Antonyms: [左顾右盼] (zuǒ gù yòu pàn 左顧右盼) 'glance this way and that,' [东张西望] (dōng zhāng xī wàng 東張西望) 'east look west gaze – look around in all directions.'

294. 【车水马龙】(車水馬龍) chē shuǐ mǎ lóng

The 车 or 'vehicles' (originally horse carriages) are like 流水 'flowing water,' and the 马 or 'horses' are like playing dragons. The meaning of the whole idiom is 'a steady stream of.'

Example 1: 大街上**车水马龙**，热闹得很。

Dàjiē shàng chēshuǐ-mǎlóng, rènào de hěn.

'On the streets there was heavy traffic and it was very lively.'

Example 2: 开学的时候，北京大学门前**车水马龙**，很多家长都来送自己的孩子上学。

Kāixué de shíhou, Běijing Dàxué ménqián chēshuǐ-mǎlóng, hěn duō jiāzhǎng dōu lái sòng zìjǐ de háizi shàngxué.

'At the start of the school year, there was a steady stream of people in front of the gates of Peking University, many parents having come to bring their children to school.'

Usage: Functions mainly as predicate, usually referring to traffic or people.

Near Synonym: [络绎不绝] (luò yì bù jué 絡繹不絕) 'continuous flow.'

Antonym: [稀稀落落] (xī xī luò luò 稀稀落落) 'sparse, scattered.'

295. 【一望无际】(一望無際) yí wàng wú jì

望 means 'see, gaze' and 际 means 'border, boundary.' A literal translation of this idiom is 'once you gaze there are no boundaries,' with a freer translation being 'stretch as far as the eye can see, boundless, vast.'

Example 1: 俄罗斯的东部到处是**一望无际**的森林和草原。

Éluósī de dōngbù dàochù shì yíwàng-wújì de sēnlín hé cǎoyuán.

'In the eastern part of Russia, there are everywhere forests and prairies that stretch as far as the eye can see.'

Example 2: 美国很多农场非常大，**一望无际**。

Měiguó hěn duō nóngchǎng fēicháng dà, yíwàng-wújì.

'Many U.S. farms are extremely large, stretching as far as the eye can see.'

Usage: Functions mainly as attributive; can also serve as predicate.

Near Synonyms: [一望无垠] (yí wàng wú yín 一望無垠) 'boundless, vast,' [无边无际] (wú biān wú jì 無邊無際) 'without sides without borders – limitless.'

Antonyms: [咫尺之间] (zhǐ chǐ zhī jiān 咫尺之間) 'very close,' [一衣带水] (yī yī dài shuǐ 一衣帶水) 'narrow strip of water in between.'

296. 【一成不变】(一成不變) yì chéng bú biàn

成 means 'form, shape.' A literal translation of this idiom is 'once something takes shape, it doesn't change,' with a freer translation being 'fixed and unalterable, invariable.'

Example 1: 人不是一**成不变**的，而是受环境很大影响的。

Rén bú shì yìchéng-búbiàn de, ér shì shòu huánjìng hěn dà yǐngxiǎng de.

'Humans are not fixed and unalterable, but rather are strongly influenced by their environment.'

Example 2: 他已经吃腻了几十年来一**成不变**的早餐，不是煎鸡蛋就是煮鸡蛋。

Tā yǐjīng chīnìle jǐ shí nián lái yìchéng-búbiàn de zǎocān, bú shì jiān jīdàn jiùshì zhǔ jīdàn.

'He has gotten sick and tired of eating a breakfast that hasn't varied for decades; either it's fried eggs or it's boiled eggs.'

Usage: Functions mainly as attributive and predicate.

Note: Derogatory in meaning.

Near Synonyms: [墨守成规] (mò shǒu chéng guī 墨守成規) 'stick to conventions or outmoded practices,' [萧规曹随] (Xiāo guī Cáo suí 蕭規曹隨) 'Xiao's rules Cao (the famous general) follows – abide by the rules laid down by one's predecessor.'

Antonyms: [千变万化] (qiān biàn wàn huà 千變萬化) 'a great number of changes, ever changing,' [朝令夕改] (zhāo lìng xī gǎi 朝令夕改) 'morning order evening change – make frequent and unpredictable changes in policy.'

297. 【脱口而出】(脱口而出) tuō kǒu ér chū

脱 means 'break free from, escape from.' A literal translation of this idiom is 'escaping from the mouth to come out,' with freer translations including 'come out spontaneously, say without thinking, blurt out, let slip.'

Example 1: 她是古代文学教授，不论你提到哪首诗词，她都能**脱口而出**，全部背下来。

Tā shì gǔdài wénxué jiàoshòu, búlùn nǐ tídào nǎ shǒu shīcí, tā dōu néng tuōkǒu-érchū, quánbù bèixiàlái.

'She is a professor of ancient literature; no matter which poem you mention, she can recite it spontaneously without thinking.'

Example 2: 听见有人打喷嚏，旁边的人**脱口而出**，"Bless you!"

Tīngjiàn yǒu rén dǎ pēntì, pángbiān de rén tuōkǒu-érchū, "Bless you!"

'When they heard a person sneeze, the people next to the person said spontaneously, "Bless you!"'

Usage: Functions as predicate.

Near Synonym: [信口开河] (xìn kǒu kāi hé 信口開河) 'say whatever comes to mind.'

Antonym: [守口如瓶] (shǒu kǒu rú píng 守口如瓶) 'guard one's mouth like a jar lid – keep one's mouth shut.'

298. 【生气勃勃】 (生氣勃勃) shēng qì bó bó

生气 means 'vitality' and 勃勃 means 'vigorous, exuberant.' The meaning of the whole idiom is 'full of vitality.'

Example 1: 纽约总是给人一种**生气勃勃**的印象，而在美国南方则显得安静了许多。

Niǔyuē zǒngshì gěi rén yì zhǒng shēngqì-bóbó de yìnxiàng, ér zài Měiguó nánfāng zé xiǎnde ānjìngle xǔduō.

'New York always gives one an impression of great vitality, but in the south of the U.S. it appears a lot quieter.'

Example 2: 新领导掌管公司后，公司出现了巨大的变化，**生气勃勃**。

Xīn lǐngdǎo zhǎngguǎn gōngsī hòu, gōngsī chūxiànle jùdà de biànhuà, shēngqì-bóbó.

'After the new boss took charge of the company, the company experienced great changes, becoming full of energy.'

Usage: Functions mainly as attributive and predicate; can also serve as adverbial.

Note: Complimentary in meaning.

Near Synonyms: [生龙活虎] (shēng lóng huó hǔ 生龍活虎) 'bursting with energy' (when referring to people), [生机勃勃] (shēng jī bó bó 生機勃勃) 'full of vitality' (when referring to things).

Antonym: [死气沉沉] (sǐ qì chén chén 死氣沉沉) 'lifeless.'

299. 【天经地义】 (天經地義) tiān jīng dì yì

The literal meaning of this idiom is 'in accordance with the rules of heaven and the principles of earth – absolutely correct, entirely justified, unalterable.'

Example 1: 杀人偿命、欠债还钱，这是**天经地义**的事。

Shā rén cháng mìng, qiàn zhài huán qián, zhè shì tiānjīng-dìyì de shì.

'Paying for a murder with one's own life, and paying back money if one has a debt – these are absolutely correct and justified things.'

Example 2: 你在别的国家的领土上，就得遵守该国的法律，**天经地义**，没有什么好商量的。

Nǐ zài biéde guójiā de lǐngtǔ shàng, jiù děi zūnshǒu gāi guó de fǎlǜ, tiānjīng-dìyì, méiyǒu shénme hǎo shāngliáng de.

'When you are in the territory of another country, you must observe the laws of that country; this is absolutely correct and there is nothing further to talk about.'

Usage: Functions mainly as attributive, predicate, and object.

Near Synonym: [理所当然] (lǐ suǒ dāng rán 理所當然) 'of course, naturally.'

Antonym: [岂有此理] (qǐ yǒu cǐ lǐ 豈有此理) 'absurd, outrageous.'

300. 【狐假虎威】 (狐假虎威) hú jiǎ hǔ wēi

狐 means 'fox,' 假 means 'borrow,' 虎 means 'tiger,' and 威 means 'strength.' A literal translation of the whole idiom is 'a fox borrows the might of a tiger.' The extended meaning is 'rely on powerful connections with one person to bully another person.'

Example 1: 市长的秘书**狐假虎威**，在当地很狂妄。

Shìzhǎng de mìshū hújiǎ-hǔwēi, zài dāngdì hěn kuángwàng.

'The mayor's secretary relies on his connections with the mayor to bully others, acting extremely arrogantly in the local area.'

Example 2: 有的人崇洋媚外，认识了几个外国人，就**狐假虎威**起来，觉得自己好像高人一等了。

Yǒu de rén chóngyáng-mèiwài, rènshile jǐ ge wàiguórén, jiù hújiǎ-hǔwēi qǐlai, juéde zìjǐ hǎoxiàng gāo rén yì děng le.

'Some people worship and fawn over all things foreign; if they have gotten to know a few foreigners, they start relying on their connections to bully others, feeling that they are a cut above others.'

Usage: Functions as predicate, attributive, and adverbial.

Allusion: The king of Chu said to his ministers of state: "I have heard that the smaller countries in the north all very much fear our prime minister; is this really true?" Most of the ministers didn't answer; there was only one who spoke: "When a tiger catches any animal, it devours it. One day, a tiger caught a fox. The fox said: 'You dare not eat me! The heavenly emperor sent me to serve as the leader of all the animals. If you eat me, then you will be going against the command of heaven. If you don't believe me, let me walk in front, with you following behind me, and let's see if the other animals don't run away.' The tiger thought that what the fox had said made sense, so he followed behind the fox. When the other animals saw the tiger, they were terrified. But the tiger didn't realize that the other animals were afraid of it, mistakenly believing that they feared the fox. Great King, the area of your country is vast and you have great numbers of troops. The smaller countries in the north are not afraid of our prime minister, but rather they fear your army, just like the animals who were afraid of that tiger." (from "Stratagems of Chu" in *Stratagems of the Warring States*)

Note: Derogatory in meaning.

Near Synonyms: [狗仗人势] (gǒu zhàng rén shì 狗仗人勢) 'dog relies on master's influence – rely on the power of one's benefactor to bully others' (derogatory), [仗势欺人] (zhàng shì qī rén 仗勢欺人) 'rely on one's own or another's influence to bully others.'

301. 【了如指掌】(瞭如指掌) liǎo rú zhǐ zhǎng

了 means 'understand,' 如 means 'like,' and 指掌 means 'fingers and palms.' The literal meaning is 'understand as well as one's own fingers and palms,' with a freer translation being 'completely clear about, know someone or something from A to Z.'

Example 1: 警察对犯罪分子的情况**了如指掌**，只等机会来临就动手了。

Jǐngchá duì fànzuìfènzǐ de qíngkuàng liǎorú-zhǐzhǎng, zhǐ děng jīhuì láilín jiù dòngshǒu le.

'The police are completely clear about the criminals' situation, they're merely waiting for an opportunity to come for them to strike.'

Example 2: 她在联邦政府里工作了四十年，对政府里的一些内幕**了如指掌**。

Tā zài liánbāng zhèngfǔ lǐ gōngzuòle sìshí nián, duì zhèngfǔ lǐ de yìxiē nèimù liǎorú zhǐzhǎng.

'She worked in the federal government for forty years, so she knows the inner workings of the government from A to Z.'

Usage: Functions as predicate, usually preceded by coverbial construction with 对 (duì 對) 'about.'

Near Synonym: [一清二楚] (yì qīng èr chǔ 一清二楚) 'completely clear.'

Antonym: [一无所知] (yì wú suǒ zhī 一無所知) 'know absolutely nothing about something.'

302. 【别有用心】(別有用心) bié yǒu yòng xīn

别 means 'other, separate,' 有 means 'have,' and 用心 means 'intention, motive.' The whole idiom means 'harbor ulterior motives' or 'have something up one's sleeve.'

Example 1: 一些**别有用心**的人企图利用老百姓来制造混乱。

Yìxiē biéyǒuyòngxīn de rén qǐtú lìyòng lǎobǎixìng lái zhìzào hùnluàn.

'Some people with ulterior motives attempt to use the populace to create chaos.'

Example 2: 他这样做表面上是帮助你，其实**别有用心**。

Tā zhèyàng zuò biǎomiàn shàng shì bāngzhù nǐ, qíshí biéyǒuyòngxīn.

'His doing this on the surface is helping you, but actually he has ulterior motives.'

Usage: Functions mainly as attributive; can also serve as predicate.

Note: Derogatory in meaning.

Near Synonym: [居心叵测] (jū xīn pǒ cè 居心叵测) 'have evil intentions that are unpredictable' (derogatory).

Antonyms: [光明磊落] (guāng míng lěi luò 光明磊落) and [光明正大] (guāng míng zhèng dà 光明正大), both of which mean 'frank and forthright' and both of which are complimentary in meaning.

303. 【五光十色】(五光十色) wǔ guāng shí sè

光 means 'light' and 色 means 'color.' A literal translation is 'five lights and ten colors,' with a freer translation being 'all kinds of colors, multicolored.'

Example 1: 她喜欢欣赏香港街头**五光十色**的广告牌。

Tā xǐhuan xīnshǎng Xiānggǎng jiētóu wǔguāng-shísè de guǎnggàopái.

'She likes to enjoy the multicolored advertising signs on the streets of Hong Kong.'

Example 2: 他习惯了大都市的那种**五光十色**的夜生活。

Tā xíguànle dàdūshì de nà zhǒng wǔguāng-shísè de yè shēnghuó.

'He is used to the colorful nightlife of big cities.'

Usage: Functions mainly as attributive and predicate.

Note: Slightly complimentary in meaning.

Near Synonym: [五彩缤纷] (wǔ cǎi bīn fēn 五彩繽紛) 'multicolored.'

304. 【不合时宜】 (不合時宜) bù hé shí yí

合 means 'conform to,' 时 means 'at the time,' and 宜 means 'that which is appropriate.' The whole idiom means 'out of keeping with the times.'

Example 1: 社会在发展，而他的思想没有进步，因此早就**不合时宜**了。

Shèhuì zài fāzhǎn, ér tā de sīxiǎng méiyǒu jìnbù, yīncǐ zǎo jiù bùhé-shíyí le.

'Society is developing but his thought has not progressed, therefore he has for a long time now not been in tune with the times.'

Example 2: 她的情绪不太好，说了一些**不合时宜**的话。

Tā de qíngxù bú tài hǎo, shuōle yìxiē bùhé-shíyí de huà.

'She's not in a very good mood, so she said some inopportune things.'

Usage: Functions mainly as predicate and attributive.

Antonym: [因地制宜] (yīn dì zhì yí 因地制宜) 'adapt to local conditions.'

305. 【富丽堂皇】 (富麗堂皇) fù lì táng huáng

富丽 means 'magnificent' and 堂皇 means 'grand.' The meaning of the whole idiom is 'magnificent and grand.'

Example 1: 巴黎罗浮宫**富丽堂皇**，里面有很多珍贵的艺术品。

Bālí Luófúgōng fùlì-tánghuáng, lǐmiàn yǒu hěn duō zhēnguì de yìshùpǐn.

'The Louvre in Paris is magnificent and grand, inside there are many precious works of art.'

Example 2: 这所大学在一个小镇，虽然没有**富丽堂皇**的建筑，但是吸引了世界一流的学者。

Zhè suǒ dàxué zài yí ge xiǎozhèn, suīrán méiyǒu fùlì-tánghuáng de jiànzhù, dànshì xīyǐnle shìjiè yīliú de xuézhě.

'This college is in a small town; though there aren't any grand and magnificent buildings, it has attracted some of the world's top scholars.'

Usage: Functions mainly as predicate and attributive, usually used to describe buildings.

Near Synonyms: [金碧辉煌] (jīn bì huī huáng 金碧輝煌) 'resplendent in bright colors,' [美轮美奂] (měi lún měi huàn 美輪美奐) 'tall and pleasing to the eye.'

Antonyms: [家徒四壁] (jiā tú sì bì 家徒四壁) 'home only has four walls – completely destitute,' [一贫如洗] (yì pín rú xǐ 一貧如洗) 'as poor as if everything had been washed away by a flood.'

306. 【马不停蹄】(馬不停蹄) mǎ bù tíng tí

蹄 means 'hoof.' The literal meaning is 'horse doesn't stop its hooves,' with a freer translation being 'nonstop, without stopping.'

Example 1: 总统候选人**马不停蹄**地访问了一个州又一个州，到处宣传他的政策。

Zǒngtǒng hòuxuǎnrén mǎbùtíngtí de fǎngwènle yí ge zhōu yòu yí ge zhōu, dàochù xuānchuán tā de zhèngcè.

'The presidential candidate visited one state after another nonstop, publicizing his policies everywhere.'

Example 2: 一下飞机，她就**马不停蹄**地赶到了地震灾害最严重的地区。

Yí xià fēijī, tā jiù mǎbùtíngtí de gǎndàole dìzhèn zāihài zuì yánzhòng de dìqū.

'As soon as she got off the plane, she rushed without stopping to the area where the earthquake disaster had been the most serious.'

Usage: Functions mainly as adverbial; can also serve as predicate.

Near Synonyms: [夜以继日] (yè yǐ jì rì 夜以繼日) 'day and night,' [快马加鞭] (kuài mǎ jiā biān 快馬加鞭) 'fast horse add whip – at high speed.'

Antonym: [三天打鱼，两天晒网] (sān tiān dǎ yú, liǎng tiān shài wǎng 三天打魚，兩天曬網) 'go fishing for three days, dry the nets for two days – lack of perseverance; work by fits and starts.'

307. 【开门见山】(開門見山) kāi mén jiàn shān

The literal meaning of this idiom is 'open the door and see the mountain,' with a freer translation being 'come straight to the point.'

Example 1: 记者**开门见山**地问："你知道不知道这是法律不允许的？"

Jìzhě kāimén-jiànshān de wèn: "Nǐ zhīdao bù zhīdao zhè shì fǎlǜ bù yǔnxǔ de?"

'The reporter came straight to the point and asked, "Do you know this is not permitted by law?"'

Example 2: 客人**开门见山**，把他的想法直接告诉了主人。

Kèrén kāimén-jiànshān, bǎ tā de xiǎngfǎ zhíjiē gàosule zhǔrén.

'The guest came straight to the point and told his opinion directly to the host.'

Usage: Functions mainly as adverbial modifier or predicate. As an adverbial modifier, usually occurs before the verbs 问 (wèn 問) 'ask' or 说 (shuō 說) 'say.'

Near Synonyms: [直截了当] (zhí jié liǎo dàng 直截了當) 'direct, straightforward,' [单刀直入] (dān dāo zhí rù 單刀直入) 'single sword enters straight – come straight to the point,' [直言不讳] (zhí yán bú huì 直言不諱) 'speak frankly without reservation.'

Antonyms: [拐弯抹角] (guǎi wān mò jiǎo 拐彎抹角) 'take a circuitous route, beat around the bush,' [转弯抹角] (zhuǎn wān mò jiǎo 轉彎抹角) 'a tortuous route, beat around the bush.'

308. 【别具一格】(别具一格) bié jù yì gé

别 means 'other/another,' 具 means 'have,' and 格 here means 'style.'

The literal translation of this idiom is 'have another type of style,' with a freer translation being 'have a unique or distinctive style.'

Example 1: 她每年送给别人的圣诞礼物都**别具一格**。

Tā měi nián sòng gěi biérén de shèngdàn lǐwù dōu biéjù-yìgé.

'The Christmas gifts she gives others every year are always unique.'

Example 2: 我很欣赏她油画上的**别具一格**的色彩。

Wǒ hěn xīnshǎng tā yóuhuà shàng de biéjù-yìgé de sècǎi.

'I very much admire the distinctive colors of her oil paintings.'

Usage: Functions mainly as attributive or predicate.

Note: Complimentary in meaning.

Near Synonyms: [独树一帜] (dú shù yí zhì 獨樹一幟) 'fly one's own colors, have a style of one's own,' [别开生面] (bié kāi shēng miàn 別開生面) 'start something new.'

Antonyms: [千篇一律] (qiān piān yí lǜ 千篇一律) 'a thousand essays uniform – follow the same pattern, stereotyped,' [如出一辙] (rú chū yì zhé 如出一轍) 'as if emerging from the same track – one and the same, cut from the same cloth.'

309. 【一针见血】(一針見血) yì zhēn jiàn xiě

针 means 'needle' and 血 means 'blood.' A literal translation of this idiom is 'one (prick of a) needle and one sees blood.' Freer translations include 'exactly right, to the point, hit the nail on the head, go right to the heart of a matter.'

Example 1: 毛泽东**一针见血**地指出，知识分子具有两面性。

Máo Zédōng yìzhēn-jiànxiě de zhǐchū, zhīshi fènzǐ jùyǒu liǎngmiànxìng.

'Mao Zedong, getting right to the heart of the matter, pointed out that the intelligentsia possess a dual character.'

Example 2: 她说话虽然不多，但是往往**一针见血**，正中要害。

Tā shuōhuà suīrán bù duō, dànshì wǎngwǎng yìzhēn-jiànxiě, zhèngzhòng yàohài.

'Although she doesn't say much, she always hits the nail on the head with the central, crucial point.'

Usage: Functions mainly as adverbial, often followed by 地指出 (~ de zhǐchū) 'point out in a . . . manner.' Can also serve as predicate.

Note: Complimentary in meaning.

Near Synonyms: [一语中的] (yì yǔ zhòng dì 一語中的) 'with one word to hit the target – come right to the point,' [入木三分] (rù mù sān fēn 入木三分) 'enter wood 3/10 of an inch (in calligraphy) – forceful, bold, sharp.'

Antonyms: [隔靴搔痒] (gé xuē sāo yǎng 隔靴搔癢) 'scratch an itch from outside the boot – make a fruitless attempt,' [不痛不痒] (bú tòng bù yǎng 不痛不癢) 'not hurt not itch – scratching the surface, superficial.'

310. 【草木皆兵】 (草木皆兵) cǎo mù jiē bīng

草 means 'grass,' 木 means 'tree,' 皆 means 'all,' and 兵 means 'soldier.' A literal translation of the whole idiom is 'the grass and the trees all (look like enemy) soldiers,' with a freer translation being 'frightened, panic-stricken.'

Example 1: 政府军在明处，游击队躲在树林里向政府军射击，搞得政府军**草木皆兵**。

Zhèngfǔ jūn zài míngchù, yóujīduì duǒ zài shùlín lǐ xiàng zhèngfǔ jūn shèjī, gǎode zhèngfǔ jūn cǎomù-jiēbīng.

'The government troops were in the open; the guerrilla forces hid in the woods and fired at the government troops, making the government troops panic-stricken.'

Example 2: 在严打的大形势下，违过法的人感到风声鹤唳、**草木皆兵**。

Zài yándǎ de dà xíngshì xià, wéiguò fǎ de rén gǎndào fēngshēng-hèlì, cǎomù-jiēbīng.

'In the overall situation of the anti-crime crackdown, people who had disobeyed the law felt very frightened and panic-stricken.'

Usage: Functions mainly as predicate and attributive, often preceded by 风声鹤唳 (fēng shēng hè lì 風聲鶴唳) 'sound of wind and cry of cranes – frightened by the slightest sound.'

Allusion: In 383 C.E., the Former Qin emperor Fu Jian led 900,000 troops to attack Eastern Jin, and Eastern Jin sent out 80,000 of its troops to wage war. Because the Former Qin army underestimated their enemy, they suffered a great defeat. When Fu Jian saw that the grass and trees on the mountain on which the Eastern Jin army was encamped were shaped like men, he mistook them for troops and was terrified. (from "An Account of Fu Jian" in *History of the Jin Dynasty*)

Note: Derogatory in meaning.

Near Synonyms: [杯弓蛇影] (bēi gōng shé yǐng 杯弓蛇影) 'take the shadow of a bow in a cup as the shadow of a snake – very suspicious, paranoid,' [风声鹤唳] (fēng shēng hè lì 風聲鶴唳) 'sound of wind and cry of cranes – frightened by the slightest sound.'

Antonyms: [镇定自若] (zhèn dìng zì ruò 鎮定自若) 'perfectly calm and collected, in possession of oneself,' [谈笑风生] (tán xiào fēng shēng 談笑風生) 'talk and laugh merrily,' [若无其事] (ruò wú qí shì 若無其事) 'as if nothing had happened,' [稳如泰山] (wěn rú Tài shān 穩如泰山) 'as stable as Mount Tai – standing firmly in place.'

311. 【专心致志】(專心致志) zhuān xīn zhì zhì

专心 means 'concentrate one's attention,' 致 means 'utmost,' and 志 means 'intention.' The meaning of the whole idiom is 'very attentive, with single-minded devotion.'

Example 1: 她每天到图书馆里**专心致志**地看两个小时的书。

Tā měi tiān dào túshūguǎn lǐ zhuānxīn-zhìzhì de kàn liǎng ge xiǎoshí de shū.

'Every day she goes to the library and reads very attentively for two hours.'

Example 2: 她从来不拍电视剧，总是**专心致志**地拍电影。

Tā cónglái bù pāi diànshìjù, zǒngshì zhuānxīn-zhìzhì de pāi diànyǐng.

'She has never made soap operas; she always, with single-minded devotion, makes movies.'

Usage: Functions mainly as adverbial.

Note: Complimentary in meaning.

Near Synonyms: [心无旁骛] (xīn wú páng wù 心無旁騖) 'single-minded,' [聚精会神] (jù jīng huì shén 聚精會神) 'with total concentration.'

Antonyms: [心不在焉] (xīn bú zài yān 心不在焉) 'heart is not there – absent-minded, distracted,' [三心二意] (sān xīn èr yì 三心二意) 'of two minds, half-hearted,' [心猿意马] (xīn yuán yì mǎ 心猿意馬) 'heart (agile as an) ape and thoughts (swift as a) horse – fanciful and fickle, capricious.'

312. 【堂堂正正】(堂堂正正) táng táng zhèng zhèng

堂堂 means 'powerful manner' and 正正 means 'orderly manner.' The original meaning of this idiom was 'powerful and orderly' but the meaning has now become 'open and aboveboard, fair and square.'

Example 1: 他不但长得**堂堂正正**，做事也**堂堂正正**。

Tā búdàn zhǎngde tángtáng-zhèngzhèng, zuòshì yě táng táng zhèng zhèng.

'He not only looks open and aboveboard, in his work he is also open and aboveboard.'

Example 2: 我是个**堂堂正正**的人，不怕别人在背后说坏话。

Wǒ shì ge tángtáng-zhèngzhèng de rén, bú pà biérén zài bèihòu shuō huài huà.

'I'm an open and aboveboard sort of person; I'm not afraid of others saying nasty things behind my back.'

Usage: Functions mainly as attributive, adverbial, and complement.

Note: Complimentary in meaning.

Near Synonyms: [正大光明] (zhèng dà guāng míng 正大光明) 'upright and frank,' [光明磊落] (guāng míng lěi luò 光明磊落) 'frank and forthright.'

Antonym: [歪门邪道] (wāi mén xié dào 歪門邪道) 'crooked doors evil paths – dishonest ways.'

313. 【泣不成声】(泣不成聲) qì bù chéng shēng

泣 means 'cry in a low voice, sob' and 不成声 means 'it doesn't form a sound.' The meaning of the whole idiom is 'choke with sobs.'

Example 1: 那个故事还没有听完，她早已**泣不成声**了。

Nàge gùshi hái méiyǒu tīngwán, tā zǎo yǐ qìbùchéngshēng le.

'Before she finished listening to that story, she was already choking with sobs.'

Example 2: 他太感动了，**泣不成声**地说："真的太感谢您了，您真是好人！"

Tā tài gǎndòngle, qìbùchéngshēng de shuō: "Zhēn de tài gǎnxiè nín le, nín zhēn shì hǎo rén!"

'He was too moved; choking with sobs, he said: "I really thank you so much, you really are a good person!"'

Usage: Functions mainly as predicate; can also serve as adverbial.

Antonym: [开怀大笑] (kāi huái dà xiào 開懷大笑) 'laugh loudly to one's heart's content.'

314. 【无与伦比】(無與倫比) wú yǔ lún bǐ

伦 means 'peer, match.' The meaning of the whole idiom is 'unequaled, peerless, incomparable.'

Example 1: 莫扎特在音乐上的天分简直是**无与伦比**的。

Mòzhātè zài yīnyuè shàng de tiānfèn jiǎnzhí shì wúyǔlúnbǐ de.

'Mozart's genius in music was simply unparalleled.'

Example 2: 比尔•盖茨为个人计算机的普及和发展做出了**无与伦比**的贡献。

Bǐ'ěr Gàicí wèi gèrén jìsuànjī de pǔjí hé fāzhǎn zuòchūle wúyǔlúnbǐ de gòngxiàn.

'Bill Gates made unparalleled contributions for the popularization and development of the personal computer.'

Usage: Functions mainly as predicate and attributive.

Note: Complimentary in meaning.

Near Synonyms: [不可比拟] (bù kě bǐ nǐ 不可比擬) 'incomparable,' [独一无二] (dú yī wú èr 獨一無二) 'unique,' [举世无双] (jǔ shì wú shuāng 舉世無雙) 'matchless, unrivaled.'

Antonyms: [比比皆是] (bǐ bǐ jiē shì 比比皆是) 'can be found everywhere,' [不相上下] (bù xiāng shàng xià 不相上下) 'equally matched, without much difference.'

315. 【素不相识】 (素不相識) sù bù xiāng shí

素 means 'always,' 相 means 'mutually,' and 识 means 'know, be acquainted with.' The whole idiom means 'never have met someone before, not know someone.'

Example 1: 那个孩子因为家庭贫穷而失学了，许多**素不相识**的人纷纷献出爱心，资助那个孩子上学。

Nàge háizi yīnwèi jiātíng pínqióng ér shīxuéle, xǔduō sùbùxiāngshí de rén fēnfēn xiànchū àixīn, zīzhù nàge háizi shàngxué.

'When that child was unable to continue her education because her family was poor, many people who had never met her before offered their love one after another, helping her financially so she could attend school.'

Example 2: 朋友，你我**素不相识**，你为什么总是跟着我？

Péngyou, nǐ wǒ sùbùxiāngshí, nǐ wèishénme zǒngshì gēnzhe wǒ?

'Friend, you and I have never met before, why are you always following me?'

Usage: Functions mainly as attributive; can also serve as predicate.

Antonym: [一见如故] (yí jiàn rú gù 一見如故) 'the first time you see someone be like old friends.'

316. 【堂而皇之】 (堂而皇之) táng ér huáng zhī

堂皇 means 'imposing manner.' The meaning of the whole idiom is 'imposingly, ostentatiously, openly.'

Example 1: 那对影视明星不像其他人那样害怕狗仔队，**堂而皇之**地在大街上牵手走路。

Nà duì yǐngshì míngxīng bú xiàng qítā rén nàyàng hàipà gǒuzǎiduì, táng'érhuángzhī de zài dàjiē shàng qiānshǒu zǒulù.

'That pair of movie and T.V. stars is not like the others in being afraid of the paparazzi; they openly walk on the street holding hands.'

Example 2: 以前被禁止的刊物现在**堂而皇之**地摆在书店的书架上。

Yǐqián bèi jìnzhǐ de kānwù xiànzài táng'érhuángzhī de bǎi zài shūdiàn de shūjià shàng.

'Publications that formerly were prohibited now openly are placed on the bookshelves of bookstores.'

Usage: Functions mainly as adverbial followed by the adverbial marker 地 (de).

Note: Used to be pejorative in meaning but that sense is gradually disappearing.

Antonym: [偷偷摸摸] (tōu tōu mō mō 偷偷摸摸) 'surreptitiously, covertly.'

317. 【训练有素】(訓練有素) xùn liàn yǒu sù

训练 means 'train' and 素 means 'usually, always.' The meaning of the whole idiom is 'always in training, well trained.'

Example 1: 不是每个会说英语的人都能教英文，只有**训练有素**的人才能够胜任这项工作。

Bú shì měi ge huì shuō Yīngyǔ de rén dōu néng jiāo Yīngwén, zhǐyǒu xùnliàn-yǒusù de rén cái nénggòu shèngrèn zhè xiàng gōngzuò.

'Not every person who can speak English can teach English; only well-trained people are qualified for this work.'

Example 2: 看她做事的方式就知道她**训练有素**。

Kàn tā zuòshì de fāngshì jiù zhīdao tā xùnliàn-yǒusù.

'Looking at the way she works, one knows that she is well trained.'

Usage: Functions mainly as attributive; can also serve as predicate.

Note: Complimentary in meaning.

Near Synonym: [行家里手] (háng jiā lǐ shǒu 行家里手) 'expert.'

Antonym: [半路出家] (bàn lù chū jiā 半路出家) 'become a monk late in life – change careers to something for which one is not trained.'

318. 【刻骨铭心】(刻骨銘心) kè gǔ míng xīn

刻骨 means 'carved on one's bones' and 铭心 means 'engraved on one's mind.' The meaning of the whole idiom is 'engraved on one's memory, unforgettable.'

Example 1: "文革"十年，给他留下了**刻骨铭心**的记忆。

"Wén'gé" shí nián, gěi tā liúxiàle kègǔ-míngxīn de jìyì.

'The ten years of the "Cultural Revolution" left him with deeply ingrained memories.'

Example 2: 他们的初恋**刻骨铭心**，两个人永远不会忘记。

Tāmen de chūliàn kègǔ-míngxīn, liǎng ge rén yǒngyuǎn bú huì wàngjì.

'Their first love was deeply ingrained in their memory; the two of them would never forget it.'

Usage: Functions mainly as attributive and predicate.

Near Synonym: [念念不忘] (niàn niàn bú wàng 念念不忘) 'never forget.'

Antonyms: [过眼烟云] (guò yǎn yān yún 過眼煙雲) 'like smoke and clouds passing before the eyes – transient, ephemeral,' 浮光掠影 (fú guāng lüè yǐng 浮光掠影) 'floating light passing shadows – skimming over the surface, cursory.'

319. 【不屑一顾】(不屑一顧) bú xiè yí gù

屑 means 'deign to' and 顾 means 'look.' The whole idiom means 'not deign to look, be too conceited to even take a look.'

Example 1: 她喜欢看科学著作，对文学作品**不屑一顾**。

Tā xǐhuan kàn kēxué zhùzuò, duì wénxué zuòpǐn búxiè-yígù.

'She likes to read scientific works, not deigning to look at literary works.'

Example 2: "这有什么了不起？" 他的话音里带着**不屑一顾**的语气。

Zhè yǒu shénme liǎobùqǐ? Tā de huàyīn lǐ dàizhe búxiè-yígù de yǔqì.

'"What's so special about this?" His voice carried a disdainful tone of voice.'

Usage: Functions mainly as predicate, used at the end of a sentence; can also serve as attributive and adverbial.

Near Synonyms: [不足挂齿] (bù zú guà chǐ 不足掛齒) 'not worth hanging on the teeth – not worth mentioning,' [嗤之以鼻] (chī zhī yǐ bí 嗤之以鼻) 'snort at contemptuously with one's nose.'

Antonyms: [刮目相看] (guā mù xiāng kàn 刮目相看) 'hold someone in high esteem,' [举足轻重] (jǔ zú qīng zhòng 舉足輕重) 'play a decisive role.'

320. 【对牛弹琴】(對牛彈琴) duì niú tán qín

弹 means 'pluck, play' and 琴 means 'stringed instrument.' A literal translation is 'play the lute for cattle,' in other words, to discuss something complex with stupid people. English translations include 'talk over somebody's head, cast pearls to swine, preach to deaf ears, waste someone's time.'

Example 1: 跟大字不识的人讲芭蕾舞，简直是**对牛弹琴**！

Gēn dà zì bù shí de rén jiǎng bālěiwǔ, jiǎnzhí shì duìniú-tánqín!

'To discuss ballet with illiterate people is simply a waste of time!'

Example 2: 演讲的人在台上很兴奋地说个不停，台下的听众都打哈欠了，这样的演讲好像**对牛弹琴**。

Yǎnjiǎng de rén zài táishàng hěn xīngfèn de shuō ge bù tíng, táixià de tīngzhòng dōu dǎ hāqian le, zhèyàng de yǎnjiǎng hǎoxiàng duìniú-tánqín.

'On stage, the lecturer kept talking on and on excitedly, while off stage, the audience was yawning; this kind of lecture is like casting pearls to swine.'

Usage: Functions mainly as predicate, often preceded by 简直是 (jiǎnzhí shì 簡直是) 'simply is,' 好像 (hǎoxiàng) 'seems like,' 如同 (rútóng) 'is like,' or 等于 (děngyú 等於) 'equals.'

Allusion: Gong Mingyi was a famous musician of the Spring and Autumn Period who was very good at playing the lute. Once, when he played refined, ancient lute melodies for a cow, it ate grass with its head down, as if it hadn't heard. But it wasn't that the cow hadn't heard, rather it was that this kind of melody wasn't appropriate for it. Later, Gong Mingyi used his lute to imitate the sounds of mosquitoes and horseflies buzzing and the cry of a calf seeking its mother; immediately, the cow wagged its tail and straightened its ears and began walking back and forth to listen carefully. (from *Li Huo Lun* by Mou Rong, Han Dynasty)

Note: Derogatory in meaning.

Near Synonym: [无的放矢] (wú dì fàng shǐ 無的放矢) 'without a target to release arrows – make unfounded accusations.'

Antonyms: [有的放矢] (yǒu dì fàng shǐ 有的放矢) 'have an object in view,' [对症下药] (duì zhèng xià yào 對癥下藥) 'suit the medicine to the illness.'

321. 【助人为乐】(助人為樂) zhù rén wéi lè

助 means 'help,' 人 means 'other people,' 为 means 'be,' and 乐 means 'happiness.' A literal translation of the whole idiom is 'help other people is happiness,' with a freer translation being 'enjoy helping others.'

Example 1: 宗教告诫我们要多做善事，**助人为乐**，这样死后就能进入天堂。

Zōngjiào gàojiè wǒmen yào duō zuò shànshì, zhùrén-wéilè, zhèyàng sǐ hòu jiù néng jìnrù tiāntáng.

'Religion admonishes us that we should do more good works and enjoy helping others; this way, after we die, we can enter heaven.'

Example 2: 从小就要培养起**助人为乐**的好品质。

Cóng xiǎo jiù yào péiyǎng qǐ zhùrén-wéilè de hǎo pǐnzhì.

'From childhood on, one should start cultivating the good quality of enjoying helping other people.'

Usage: Functions mainly as predicate and object.

Note: Complimentary in meaning.

Near Synonym: [乐善好施] (lè shàn hào shī 樂善好施) 'charitable, benevolent.'

Antonym: [乘人之危] (chéng rén zhī wēi 乘人之危) 'take advantage of someone's precarious position.'

322. 【衣食住行】(衣食住行) yī shí zhù xíng

衣 means 'clothing,' 食 means 'food,' 住 here means 'housing,' and 行 here means 'transportation.' The literal meaning is 'clothing, food, housing, and transportation.' The connotation is 'the basic necessities of life.'

Example 1: 改革开放以后，农民在**衣食住行**各个方面都有改善。

Gǎigé kāifàng yǐhòu, nóngmín zài yīshí-zhùxíng gègè fāngmiàn dōu yǒu gǎishàn.

'After the policy of reform and opening, peasants saw improvements in every aspect of life's basic necessities.'

Example 2: 在美国，一般说来，公司对于职员的**衣食住行**都不管，那是职员自己的事情。

Zài Měiguó, yìbān shuōlái, gōngsī duìyú zhíyuán de yīshí-zhùxíng dōu bù guǎn, nà shì zhíyuán zìjǐ de shìqing.

'In the U.S., generally speaking, companies do not take care of employees' basic necessities of life; that is the employees' own business.'

Usage: Functions mainly as attributive, object, or subject. Common collocations include ～等方面 (～děng fàngmiàn), ～各方面 (～gè fàngmiàn), and ～的问题 (～de wèntí ～的問題).

Near Synonym: [生老病死] (shēng lǎo bìng sǐ 生老病死) '(such matters as) birth, senility, illness, and death.'

Antonym: [四大皆空] (sì dà jiē kōng 四大皆空) '(in Buddhism) the four major elements (earth, water, fire, air) are all void – everything is an illusion.'

323. 【不胜枚举】(不勝枚舉) bú shèng méi jǔ

不胜 means 'unable to do completely,' 枚 means 'one at a time,' and 举 means 'enumerate, list.' A literal translation of the whole idiom is 'cannot enumerate one at a time,' with a freer translation being 'too numerous to cite individually.'

Example 1: 中国的乒乓球世界冠军**不胜枚举**。

Zhōngguó de pīngpāngqiú shìjiè guànjūn búshèng-méijǔ.

'Chinese table tennis world championships are too numerous to cite individually.'

Example 2: 小公司发展壮大后吃掉大公司的例子**不胜枚举**。

Xiǎo gōngsī fāzhǎn zhuàngdà hòu chīdiào dà gōngsī de lìzi búshèng-méijǔ.

'Examples of small companies that, after growing strong, ate up big companies are too numerous to mention individually.'

Usage: Functions mainly as predicate.

Near Synonyms: [数不胜数] (shǔ bú shèng shǔ 數不勝數) 'too many to be counted, innumerable,' [不计其数] (bú jì qí shù 不計其數) 'not calculate its number – too numerous to count.'

Antonyms: [屈指可数] (qū zhǐ kě shǔ 屈指可數) 'can be counted on the fingers, very few,' [寥寥无几] (liáo liáo wú jǐ 寥寥無幾) 'very few.'

324. 【赞不绝口】(讚不絕口) zàn bù jué kǒu

赞 means 'praise,' 绝 means 'stop,' and 口 means 'mouth, talk.' A literal translation of this idiom is 'praise and not stop talking.' Freer translations include 'praise profusely, be full of praise.'

Example 1: 外国游客对中国的杂技**赞不绝口**。

Wàiguó yóukè duì Zhōngguó de zájì zànbùjuékǒu.

'Foreign tourists are full of praise for China's acrobatics.'

Example 2: 那位大音乐家对这个小女孩儿的演奏**赞不绝口**，说他二十年来没有见过这么有潜力的孩子。

Nà wèi dà yīnyuèjiā duì zhège xiǎo nǚháir de yǎnzòu zànbùjuékǒu, shuō tā èrshí nián lái méiyǒu jiànguo zhème yǒu qiánlì de háizi.

'That great musician was full of praise for this young girl's performance; he said he hadn't seen a child with such potential in twenty years.'

Usage: Functions as predicate.

Note: Complimentary in meaning.

Near Synonyms: [交口称赞] (jiāo kǒu chēng zàn 交口稱讚) 'joining mouths giving praise – overflowing with praise,' [拍案叫绝] (pāi àn jiào jué 拍案叫絕) 'hit the table and call out excellent – express admiration.'

Antonym: [破口大骂] (pò kǒu dà mà 破口大罵) 'break-open mouth great abuse – shout abuse at someone.'

325. 【大名鼎鼎】(大名鼎鼎) dà míng dǐng dǐng

鼎鼎 means 'grand, magnificent.' The meaning of the whole idiom is 'famous, well known.'

Example 1: 他就是**大名鼎鼎**的小说家金庸先生。

Tā jiù shì dàmíng-dǐngdǐng de xiǎoshuōjiā Jīnyōng xiānshēng.

'He is none other than the well-known novelist Mr. Jin Yong.'

Example 2: 这场足球比赛吸引了很多观众，因为里面有三位**大名鼎鼎**的球星。

Zhè chǎng zúqiú bǐsài xīyǐnle hěn duō guānzhòng, yīnwèi lǐmiàn yǒu sān wèi dàmíng-dǐngdǐng de qiúxīng.

'This soccer competition has attracted a lot of spectators, because in it there are three very famous soccer stars.'

Usage: Functions mainly as attributive.

Note: Complimentary in meaning. Sometimes also occurs as 鼎鼎大名 (dǐng dǐng dà míng).

Near Synonyms: [赫赫有名] (hè hè yǒu míng 赫赫有名) 'celebrated and famous, illustrious,' [如雷贯耳] (rú léi guan ěr 如雷貫耳) 'like thunder passing through one's ear,' [举世闻名] (jǔ shì wén míng 舉世聞名) 'world famous.'

Antonym: [默默无闻] (mò mò wú wén 默默無聞) 'unknown to the public.'

326. 【如数家珍】(如數家珍) rú shǔ jiā zhēn

如 means 'like,' 数 means 'count,' 家 means 'family,' and 珍 means 'treasure.' A literal translation of the whole idiom is 'like counting family treasures,' with a freer translation being 'very familiar with one's subject.'

Example 1: 一说起电影演员，她就会**如数家珍**般地给你讲出一大串。

Yì shuō qǐ diànyǐng yǎnyuán, tā jiù huì rúshǔ-jiāzhēn bān de gěi nǐ jiǎng chū yí dà chuàn.

'Once on the topic of film actors and actresses, she is so familiar with this subject that she will talk up a storm for you, going on and on.'

Example 2: 谈到本地的特产，老人**如数家珍**。

Tán dào běndì de tèchǎn, lǎorén rúshǔ-jiāzhēn.

'When talking about local specialties, the old people are as familiar with this topic as if they were counting their family treasures.'

Usage: Functions mainly as adverbial and predicate.

Note: Complimentary in meaning.

Near Synonym: [了如指掌] (liǎo rú zhǐ zhǎng 瞭如指掌) 'understand as well as one's own fingers and palms – completely clear.'

Antonym: [一无所知] (yì wú suǒ zhī 一無所知) 'know absolutely nothing about something.'

327. 【跃跃欲试】(躍躍欲試) yuè yuè yù shì

跃 usually means 'jump'; here, 跃跃 means 'impatient, anxious, in a hurry.' 欲 means 'want' and 试 means 'try.' Therefore, a literal translation of this idiom is 'impatiently want to try,' with a freer translation being 'eager to try.'

Example 1: 听说那个城市要花巨资建设会展中心，许多建筑商**跃跃欲试**。

Tīngshuō nàge chéngshì yào huā jùzī jiànshè huìzhǎn zhōngxīn, xǔduō jiànzhùshāng yuèyuè-yùshì.

'When they heard that that city was going to spend a huge amount of money to construct a conference and exhibition center, a lot of contractors were eager to give it a shot.'

Example 2: 一名外国乒乓球选手说要打败中国所有选手并夺得金牌，这引起了巨大的反响，许多选手**跃跃欲试**。

Yì míng wàiguó pīngpāngqiú xuǎnshǒu shuō yào dǎbài Zhōngguó suǒyǒu xuǎnshǒu bìng duódé jīnpái, zhè yǐnqǐle jùdà de fǎnxiǎng, xǔduō xuǎnshǒu yuèyuè-yùshì.

'When a foreign ping pong player said that he was going to defeat all the Chinese players and capture the gold medal, this touched off an enormous response, many players being eager to try.'

Usage: Functions mainly as predicate.

Near Synonyms: [摩拳擦掌] (mó quán cā zhǎng 摩拳擦掌) 'rub fists wipe palms – itching for a fight,' [蠢蠢欲动] (chǔn chǔn yù dòng 蠢蠢欲動) 'restless and about to make a move,' [咄咄逼人] (duō duō bī rén 咄咄逼人) 'threatening, agressive.'

Antonyms: [无动于衷] (wú dòng yú zhōng 無動於衷) 'unmoved, unconcerned,' [推三阻四] (tuī sān zǔ sì 推三阻四) 'decline with all sorts of excuses.'

328. 【古色古香】(古色古香) gǔ sè gǔ xiāng

A literal translation of this idiom is 'ancient color ancient flavor.' The meaning is 'antique, old-fashioned.'

Example 1: 房间里面的家具都是暗红色，显得**古色古香**的。

Fángjiān lǐmiàn de jiājù dōu shì ànhóngsè, xiǎnde gǔsè-gǔxiāng de.

'The furniture in the room was all dark red, looking antique in appearance.'

Example 2: 他的办公室里挂着一张**古色古香**的字画。

Tā de bàngōngshì lǐ guàzhe yì zhāng gǔsè-gǔxiāng de zìhuà.

'In his office hung a piece of antique calligraphy.'

Usage: Functions mainly as predicate; can also serve as attributive. Usually modifies words having to do with furniture, buildings, etc.

Note: There is an alternate form as 古香古色 (gǔ xiāng gǔ sè).

Antonym: [花里胡哨] (huā lǐ hú shào 花裏胡哨) '(of color) mixed and disorderly' (derogatory in meaning).

329. 【推波助澜】(推波助瀾) tuī bō zhù lán

推 means 'push,' 波 means 'wave,' 助 means 'help,' and 澜 means 'billow, big wave.'

A literal translation of this idiom is 'push waves and help billows.' Freer translations include 'make a situation even worse, add fuel to the fire, exacerbate.'

Example 1: 本来这是两国间的一个小摩擦，但是经过某个大国**推波助澜**后，演变成了两国大规模的军事冲突。

Běnlái zhè shì liǎng guó jiān de yí ge xiǎo mócā, dànshì jīngguò mǒu ge dàguó tuībō-zhùlán hòu, yǎnbiàn chéngle liǎng guó dà guīmó de jūnshì chōngtū.

'This used to be just a matter involving minor friction between the two countries, but after a certain major power added fuel to the fire, it developed into a large-scale military conflict between the two countries.'

Example 2: 大石油公司在这次国际油价大涨中起了**推波助澜**的作用。

Dà shíyóu gōngsī zài zhè cì guójì yóujià dà zhǎng zhōng qǐle tuībō-zhùlán de zuòyòng.

'In the sharp rise in international oil prices this time, the major oil companies had the effect of exacerbating the situation.'

Usage: Functions mainly as attributive or predicate. As attributive, often preceded by the verb construction 起了 (qǐle) 'had' and often followed by the noun 作用 (zuòyòng) 'effect.'

Note: Derogatory in meaning.

Near Synonyms: [添油加醋] (tiān yóu jiā cù 添油加醋) 'add oil add vinegar – add inflammatory details, embellish,' [火上浇油] (huǒ shàng jiāo yóu 火上浇油) 'add fuel to the flames, pour oil on the fire.'

Antonyms: [息事宁人] (xī shì níng rén 息事宁人) 'patch up a quarrel and reconcile the parties concerned,' [大事化小] (dà shì huà xiǎo 大事化小) 'disguise something major as something minor,' [小事化了] (xiǎo shì huà liǎo 小事化了) 'disregard a minor incident.'

330. 【班门弄斧】(班門弄斧) Bān mén nòng fǔ

班 refers to Lu Ban, the founder of carpentry in China, 门 means 'front door,' 弄 means 'play with,' and 斧 means 'axe.' A literal translation is 'at the front door of Lu Ban's house to play with an axe.' This means 'show off one's meager skills before an expert and not know one's own limitations.'

Example 1: "就你那点水平，还想在牛津大学演讲，别**班门弄斧**了。"

"Jiù nǐ nà diǎn shuǐpíng, hái xiǎng zài Niújīn Dàxué yǎnjiǎng, bié Bānmén-nòngfǔ le."

'"You have only very limited proficiency, and you actually want to give a lecture at Oxford; don't show off your meager skills before the experts."'

Example 2: 他非常谦虚地说，"各位专家，我就**班门弄斧**了，不对的地方请您指正。"

Tā fēicháng qiānxū de shuō, "Gèwèi zhuānjiā, wǒ jiù Bānmén-nòngfǔ le, bú duì de dìfang qǐng nín zhǐzhèng."

'He said very modestly, "All of you experts, I shall show off my meager skills before you; please do correct my mistakes."'

Usage: Functions mainly as predicate.

Allusion: The origin of this idiom is actually very ancient. But the most commonly cited source is a poem that Mei Zhihuan (1575–1641 C.E.) of the Ming Dynasty wrote when he was touring the grave of Li Bai. Li Bai (701–762 C.E.) was the most famous poet in Chinese history. After he died, he was buried on the banks of the Yangtze and, when people toured his grave, they would leave a poem, which is the reason that Mei Zhihuan also left a poem. Mei's poem read: 采石江边一堆土，李白之名高千古。来来往往一首诗，鲁班门前弄大斧。(Cǎi shí jiāng biān yì duī tǔ, Lǐ Bái zhī míng gāo qiān gǔ. Lái lái wǎng wǎng yì shǒu shī, lǔ bān mén qián nòng dà fū 採石江邊一堆土，李白之名高千古。來來往往一首詩，魯班門前弄大斧。) The general meaning of this poem is that Mei is ridiculing those who do not know their own limitations; they actually went so far as to leave poems at the poet Li Bai's tomb! It is said that Lu Ban (ca. 507–444 B.C.E.), influenced by the fact that leaves of cogon grass are shaped like the teeth of a saw, invented the saw; and that he constructed out of bamboo strips a bird that could fly in the air for three days and three nights without falling. Lu Ban had a number of different inventions, which is the reason why he is worshipped by the Chinese people as the founder of the trade of carpentry. To 'play with an axe at the doorway to Lu Ban's house' is, of course, indicative of not knowing one's own limitations.

Note: Derogatory in meaning.

Near Synonyms: [自不量力] (zì bú liàng lì 自不量力) 'not know one's own limitations,' [贻笑大方] (yí xiào dà fāng 貽笑大方) 'be laughed at by knowledgeable people.'

Antonyms: [自知之明] (zì zhī zhī míng 自知之明) 'self-knowledge,' [韬光养晦] (tāo guāng yǎng huì 韜光養晦) 'conceal one's abilities and bide one's time.'

331. 【光明磊落】(光明磊落) guāng míng lěi luò

光明 here means 'open' and 磊落 means 'candid, straightforward.' The meaning of the whole idiom is 'open and candid, frank and forthright.'

Example 1: 她一生正直，坚持原则，**光明磊落**。

Tā yìshēng zhèngzhí, jiānchí yuánzé, guāngmíng-lěiluò.

'Her whole life long she was upright, sticking to her principles and being open and candid.'

Example 2: 她为人**光明磊落**，从来不滥用自己手中的权利。

Tā wéirén guāngmíng-lěiluò, cónglái bú lànyòng zìjǐ shǒuzhōng de quánlì.

'She is an open and straightforward person who never abuses the authority in her hands.'

Usage: Functions mainly as predicate.

Note: Complimentary in meaning.

Near Synonym: [襟怀坦荡] (jīn huái tǎn dàng 襟懷坦蕩) 'magnanimous, broad-minded, open-hearted.'

Antonyms: [卑鄙小人] (bēi bǐ xiǎo rén 卑鄙小人) 'mean and vile,' [居心叵测] (jū xīn pǒ cè 居心叵測) 'have evil intentions that are unpredictable.'

332. 【川流不息】 (川流不息) chuān liú bù xī

川 means 'river,' 流 means 'flow,' and 息 means 'stop.' The meaning of the whole idiom is 'continuous flow.'

Example 1: 北京王府井大街上行人和车辆**川流不息**。

Běijīng Wángfǔjǐng Dàjiē shàng xíngrén hé chēliàng chuānliú-bùxī.

'On the streets of Wangfujing in Beijing, there is a continuous flow of pedestrians and vehicles.'

Example 2: 他去找工作，但是看到**川流不息**的求职的人，他的心很紧张。

Tā qù zhǎo gōngzuò, dànshì kàndào chuānliú-bùxī de qiúzhí de rén, tā de xīn hěn jǐnzhāng.

'He went looking for a job, but seeing the unending stream of people seeking employment, he was very anxious.'

Usage: Functions mainly as predicate, attributive, and adverbial.

Note: Typically refers to people or traffic.

Near Synonym: [络绎不绝] (luò yì bù jué 絡繹不絕) 'continuous flow.'

333. 【迎刃而解】 (迎刃而解) yíng rèn ér jiě

迎 means 'meet,' 刃 means 'knife blade,' and 解 means 'split.' The whole idiom literally means 'meet blade and split.' This originally referred to the splitting of bamboo, since when the knife-edge cuts into the bamboo, it splits all the way down. A freer translation is 'easily solved.'

Example 1: 对别人来说非常棘手的问题，他到了就**迎刃而解**。

Duì biérén lái shuō fēicháng jíshǒu de wèntí, tā dàole jiù yíngrèn-érjiě.

'Problems that are extremely difficult for others to deal with, once he arrives he can solve them with ease.'

Example 2: 只要有完备的法律，任何纠纷都会**迎刃而解**。

Zhǐyào yǒu wánbèi de fǎlǜ, rènhé jiūfēn dōu huì yíngrèn-érjiě.

'As long as there are perfect laws, any dispute will be easily solved.'

Usage: Functions as predicate, usually preceded by nouns such as 问题 (wèntí 問題) 'problem,' 难题 (nántí 難題) 'baffling problem,' and 矛盾 (máodùn) 'conflict.'

Near Synonyms: [势如破竹] (shì rú pò zhú 勢如破竹) 'situation like splitting bamboo – meet with no resistance,' [水到渠成] (shuǐ dào qú chéng 水到渠成) 'water arrives and channel is formed – when conditions are ripe success is achieved; achieved naturally and without effort,' [易如反掌] (yì rú fǎn zhǎng 易如反掌) 'as easy as turning one's palms over – very easy.'

Antonyms: [百思不解] (bǎi sī bù jiě 百思不解) 'hundreds of thoughts not understand – remain perplexed despite much thought,' [逆水行舟] (nì shuǐ xíng zhōu 逆水行舟) 'row a boat against the water – sail against the current.'

334. 【对症下药】(對癥下藥) duì zhèng xià yào

对 means 'facing, be directed at,' 症 means 'illness,' 下 here means 'prescribe,' and 药 means 'medicine.' A literal translation of the whole idiom is 'prescribe medicine that is directed at the illness,' with freer translations being 'suit the medicine to the illness' and 'act appropriately to the situation.'

Example 1: 你得先看清问题的本质，然后才能**对症下药**。

Nǐ děi xiān kàn qīng wèntí de běnzhì, ránhòu cáinéng duìzhèng-xiàyào.

'You must first see clearly the essence of the problem; only then can you act appropriately to the situation.'

Example 2: 通货膨胀的原因是生产不足，只要**对症下药**，就能从根本上解决这个问题。

Tōnghuòpéngzhàng de yuányīn shì shēngchǎn bù zú, zhǐyào duìzhèng-xiàyào, jiù néng cóng gēnběn shàng jiějué zhège wèntí.

'The reason for inflation is insufficient production; provided that we suit the medicine to the illness, we can thoroughly solve this problem.'

Usage: Functions as predicate.

Near Synonym: [有的放矢] (yǒu dì fàng shǐ 有的放矢) 'have an object in view.'

Antonym: [无的放矢] (wú dì fàng shǐ 無的放矢) 'without a target to release arrows – make unfounded accusations.'

335. 【热火朝天】(熱火朝天) rè huǒ cháo tiān

This idiom describes an atmosphere that is enthusiastic, active, and energetic. Translations include 'bustling with activity, going ahead at full steam.'

Example 1: 建筑工地上，工人们干得**热火朝天**。

Jiànzhù gōngdì shàng, gōngrénmen gàn dé rèhuǒ-cháotiān.

'At the construction site, the workers were working at full steam.'

Example 2: 澳大利亚网球公开赛正在**热火朝天**地进行，可是那名种子选手却因伤早早退出了。

Àodàlìyà Wǎngqiú Gōngkāisài zhèngzài rèhuǒ-cháotiān de jìnxíng, kěshì nà míng zhǒngzǐ xuǎnshǒu què yīn shāng zǎozǎo tuìchū le.

'Australia's tennis open is currently taking place with great enthusiasm, but that seeded player because of an injury withdrew from the tournament long ago.'

Usage: Functions mainly as predicate, adverbial or complement.

Note: Complimentary in meaning.

Near Synonym: [如火如荼] (rú huǒ rú tú 如火如荼) 'like a raging fire, flourishing.'

Antonym: [死气沉沉] (sǐ qì chén chén 死氣沉沉) 'lifeless.'

336. 【不足为奇】(不足爲奇) bù zú wéi qí

足 means 'enough' or 'worth,' 为 means 'be,' and 奇 means 'unusual.' The literal meaning of the whole idiom is 'not be enough to be considered strange' and a freer translation is 'not at all surprising, expected.'

Example 1: 三十磅的西瓜**不足为奇**，我吃过五十磅的西瓜。

Sānshí bàng de xīguā bùzú-wéiqí, wǒ chīguo wǔshí bàng de xīguā.

'A thirty-pound watermelon is nothing unusual; I've eaten fifty-pound watermelons.'

Example 2: 因为美国的中小学不教英语的语法，所以美国学生不懂得汉语的词性也就**不足为奇**了。

Yīnwei Měiguó de zhōng-xiǎoxué bù jiāo Yīngyǔ de yǔfǎ, suǒyǐ Měiguó xuésheng bù dǒngde Hànyǔ de cíxìng yě jiù bùzú-wéiqí le.

'Because U.S. elementary and middle schools don't teach English grammar, it's not surprising that U.S. students don't understand Chinese parts of speech.'

Usage: Functions as predicate.

Near Synonyms: [比比皆是] (bǐ bǐ jiē shì 比比皆是) 'can be found everywhere,' [司空见惯] (sī kōng jiàn guan 司空見慣) 'get used to seeing something and no longer find it strange.'

Antonyms: [大惊小怪] (dà jīng xiǎo guài 大驚小怪) 'make a big fuss about nothing,' [千奇百怪] (qiān qí bǎi guài 千奇百怪) 'many kinds of curious and strange things.'

337. 【脱胎换骨】(脱胎换骨) tuō tāi huàn gǔ

脱 means 'break free from, escape from,' 胎 means 'placenta,' 换 means 'change,' and 骨 means 'bones.' A literal translation of this idiom is 'break free from one's placenta and change one's bones.' This was originally a Buddhist term referring to a monk or nun obtaining enlightenment. In current usage, the meaning of the whole idiom is 'reborn, remold oneself, turn over a new leaf.'

Example 1: 英国的经济增长方式太依赖金融业，工业没有后劲，在面对世界经济危机时，必须**脱胎换骨**，才能摆脱经济危机的影响。

Yīngguó de jīngjì zēngzhǎng fāngshì tài yīlài jīnróngyè, gōngyè méiyǒu hòujìn, zài miànduì shìjiè jīngjì wēijī shí, bìxū tuōtāi-huàngǔ, cái néng bǎ ituō jīngjì wēijī de yǐngxiǎng.

'The British economic growth model relies too much on the financial sector, industry having no stamina; in facing the world economic crisis, we must remold ourselves; only then can we shake off the influence of the economic crisis.'

Example 2: 结婚以后，在妻子的帮助下，他发生了**脱胎换骨**的变化，好像变成了另外一个人。

Jiéhūn yǐhòu, zài qīzi de bāngzhù xià, tā fāshēngle tuōtāi-huàngǔ de biànhuà, hǎoxiàng biànchéngle lìngwài yí ge rén.

'After getting married, with the help of his wife, he underwent change as though he had been reborn, it appearing as if he had become another person.'

Usage: Functions mainly as attributive and predicate.

Note: Complimentary in meaning.

Near Synonyms: [洗心革面] (xǐ xīn gé miàn 洗心革面) 'reform oneself thoroughly, turn over a new leaf,' [鸟枪换炮] (niǎo qiāng huàn pào 鳥槍換炮) 'a bird rifle exchanged for a cannon – a big change for the better' (used mostly in spoken Chinese).

Antonym: [一仍其旧] (yì réng qí jiù 一仍其舊) 'everything is still the same as in the old days.'

338. 【扬眉吐气】(揚眉吐氣) yáng méi tǔ qì

扬 means 'raise,' 眉 means 'brow,' 吐 here means 'pour out,' and 气 here means 'resentment.' A literal translation of the whole idiom is 'lift one's brow and pour out one's resentment,' with freer translations being 'stand up with one's head held high' and 'feel proud and elated.'

Example 1: 时代变了，农民不再是穷困的代名词，他们终于**扬眉吐气**了。

Shídài biàn le, nóngmín bú zài shì qióngkùn de dàimíngcí, tāmen zhōngyú yángméi-tǔqì le.

'Times have changed; peasants are no longer a synonym for poverty, they have finally stood up with their heads held high.'

Example 2: 每个人都有**扬眉吐气**的时候。

Měi ge rén dōu yǒu yángméi-tǔqì de shíhou.

'Everyone has a time when he or she feels proud and elated.'

Usage: Functions mainly as predicate and attributive.

Note: Complimentary in meaning.

Near Synonym: [眉飞色舞] (méi fēi sè wǔ 眉飛色舞) 'eyebrows fly face dances – delighted, elated.'

Antonyms: [垂头丧气] (chuí tóu sàng qì 垂頭喪氣) 'hang one's head in dejection,' [忍气吞声] (rěn qì tūn shēng 忍氣吞聲) 'restrain one's anger and keep silent.'

339. 【荡然无存】(蕩然無存) dàng rán wú cún

荡 means 'cleanse, wash,' 荡然 means 'clean,' and 无存 means 'with nothing remaining.' The meaning of the whole idiom is 'vanish without a trace.'

Example 1: 我记忆中的那条小街如今已经**荡然无存**了，在那个地方盖起了高楼。

Wǒ jìyì zhōng de nà tiáo xiǎo jiē rújīn yǐjīng dàngrán-wúcún le, zài nàge dìfang gàiqǐle gāolóu.

'The little road that I remember has now vanished without a trace, in that space they have built tall buildings.'

Example 2: 那个国家的政府官员高度腐败，所以民主和法制实际上**荡然无存**。

Nàge guójiā de zhèngfǔ guānyuán gāodù fǔbài, suǒyǐ mínzhǔ hé fǎzhì shíjìshàng dàngrán-wúcún.

'Government officials from that country are highly corrupt, so democracy and the legal system in fact have vanished without a trace.'

Usage: Functions mainly as predicate at the end of a sentence.

Near Synonyms: [无影无踪] (wú yǐng wú zōng 無影無蹤) 'without a shadow without tracks – without a trace,' [烟消云散] (yān xiāo yún sàn 煙消雲散) 'smoke disappears clouds disperse – without a trace.'

Antonym: [依然故我] (yī rán gù wǒ 依然故我) 'I am still my same old self.'

340. 【叶公好龙】(葉公好龍) Yè gōng hào lóng

叶 is a Chinese surname, 公 was a term of respect for males in ancient China somewhat like 'Duke,' and 好 means 'like.' A literal translation of the whole idiom is 'Duke Ye likes dragons.' This is a metaphor for 'on the surface to like something but actually not to like it at all' or 'pretend to like what one really dislikes or fears.'

Example 1: 他口头上说欢迎大家提出不同意见，可是一旦别人真的提出了不同意见，他又很不高兴，这就有点儿**叶公好龙**了。

Tā kǒutóu shàng shuō huānyíng dàjiā tíchū bùtóng yìjiàn, kěshì yídàn biérén zhēnde tíchūle bùtóng yìjiàn, tā yòu hěn bù gāoxìng, zhè jiù yǒudiǎnr Yègōng-hàolóng le.

'He said orally that he welcomed everyone to put forward different opinions, but once someone else really put forward a different opinion, he was very unhappy; so this was a little like Duke Ye claiming that he liked dragons but actually being terrified of them.'

Example 2: 我们招收人才不是**叶公好龙**，而是让他们真正发挥才能。

Wǒmen zhāoshōu réncái búshì Yègōng-hàolóng, érshì ràng tāmen zhēnzhèng fāhuī cáinéng.

'When we recruit persons of talent, we don't say one thing and mean another; instead, we let them really bring their talents into full play.'

Usage: Functions mainly as predicate.

Allusion: In ancient China there was a rich gentleman by the name of Ye who was very fond of dragons. Dragons were embroidered on his clothes, dragons were engraved on his wine pitcher, and dragons were carved on his house; in a word, in his home dragons were everywhere. Now, when the real dragons in the heavens above heard about this, they came down from the heavens to see him. Dragon heads extended into his windows and dragon tails stretched into his living room. When he saw the real dragons, he ran in the opposite direction as if he was about to die, with an ashen expression on his face, totally unable to control himself.

Note: Derogatory in meaning.

Near Synonyms: [表里不一] (biǎo lǐ bù yī 表裡不一) 'behavior on the outside and thought on the inside are not consistent,' [言不由衷] (yán bù yóu zhōng 言不由衷) 'words are not sincere.'

Antonym: [名副其实] (míng fù qí shí 名副其實) 'worthy of the name or reputation.'

341. 【一脉相承】(一脈相承) yí mài xiāng chéng

脉 means 'blood vessel,' 相 means 'mutually,' and 承 means 'succeed.' A literal translation of the whole idiom is '(with) one blood vessel to succeed one another.' Freer translations include 'come down in a continuous line, traced to the same origin, of the same lineage.'

Example 1: 世界各地的天主教的不同派别的思想是**一脉相承**的。

Shìjiè gè dì de Tiānzhǔjiào de bùtóng pàibié de sīxiǎng shì yímài-xiāngchéng de.

'The ideology of the different factions of Catholicism everywhere in the world can be traced to the same origin.'

Example 2: 他的作品的风格跟他的老师的**一脉相承**。

Tā de zuòpǐn de fēnggé gēn tā de lǎoshī de yímài-xiāngchéng.

'The style of his works comes down in a straight line from that of his teacher.'

Usage: Functions mainly as predicate and attributive.

Near Synonym: [萧规曹随] (Xiāo guī Cáo suí 蕭規曹隨) 'Xiao's rules Cao (the famous general) follows – abide by the rules laid down by one's predecessor.'

342. 【置之不理】(置之不理) zhì zhī bù lǐ

置 means 'put,' 之 means 'it,' and 理 means 'pay attention to.' A literal translation of the whole idiom is 'put it aside and not pay attention to it,' with a freer translation being 'pay no attention to, ignore.'

Example 1: 她已经几个月没有交电话费了，电话公司几次发信，她都**置之不理**。

Tā yǐjīng jǐ ge yuè méiyǒu jiāo diànhuàfèi le, diànhuà gōngsī jǐ cì fāxìn, tā dōu zhìzhī-bùlǐ.

'She hasn't paid her telephone bill for several months; the telephone company has sent letters several times, but she pays no attention to them.'

Example 2: 他对医生的警告**置之不理**，依然抽烟喝酒，结果身体越来越差。

Tā duì yīshēng de jǐnggào zhìzhī-bùlǐ, yīrán chōuyān hējiǔ, jiéguǒ shēntǐ yuè lái yuè chà.

'He ignores the warnings of his doctors, still smoking and drinking as before; as a result, his health is getting worse and worse.'

Usage: Functions as predicate at the end of a sentence.

Note: Derogatory in meaning.

Near Synonyms: [置若罔闻] (zhì ruò wǎng wén 置若罔聞) 'turn a deaf ear to, ignore,' [束之高阁] (shù zhī gāo gé 束之高閣) 'bind and put aside in a high place – put something aside, shelve a matter.'

Antonym: [另眼看待] (lìng yǎn kàn dài 另眼看待) 'look at from a new point of view.'

343. 【身先士卒】(身先士卒) shēn xiān shì zú

身 means 'oneself,' 先 means 'in front of,' and 士卒 means 'rank-and-file soldiers.' The literal meaning of the idiom is 'oneself be in front of the rank-and-file soldiers,' with a freer translation being 'lead one's troops in a charge, provide leadership and set an example.'

Example 1: 在经济不景气的时期，公司的老板**身先士卒**，加班加点，最终率领公司
走出困境。

Zài jīngjì bù jǐngqì de shíqī, gōngsī de lǎobǎn shēnxiān-shìzú, jiābān jiādiǎn,
zuìzhōng shuàilǐng gōngsī zǒuchū kùnjìng.

'During the period when the economy was in a slump, the company boss provided
leadership to his employees; he worked extra hours and in the end led the company
out of its predicament.'

Example 2: 巴顿将军作战勇敢，**身先士卒**，有时候到战斗前线亲自观察情况。

Bādùn jiāngjūn zuòzhàn yǒnggǎn, shēnxiān-shìzú, yǒu shíhou dào zhàndòu
qiánxiàn qīnzì guānchá qíngkuàng.

'General Patton was brave in combat, himself leading his troops into battle;
sometimes he would go to the frontline of battle to personally observe the
situation.'

Usage: Functions mainly as predicate.

Note: Complimentary in meaning.

Near Synonym: [以身作则] (yǐ shēn zuò zé 以身作则) 'set an example for others.'

344. 【精神抖擞】(精神抖擻) jīng shén dǒu sǒu

抖擞 means 'stir up, rouse.' The meaning of the whole idiom is 'full of energy.'

Example 1: 休息了两天以后，他开始**精神抖擞**地上班。

Xiūxile liǎng tiān yǐhòu, tā kāishǐ jīngshén-dǒusǒu de shàngbān.

'After having rested for two days, he began to go to work full of energy.'

Example 2: 看到士兵们个个**精神抖擞**，将军非常满意。

Kàndào shìbīngmen gègè jīngshén-dǒusǒu, jiāngjūn fēicháng mǎnyì.

'On seeing that each and every one of the rank-and-file soldiers was full of energy,
the general was very satisfied.'

Usage: Functions mainly as predicate and adverbial; can also serve as attributive.

Near Synonyms: [意气风发] (yì qì fēng fā 意氣風發) 'with boundless enthusiasm,'
[容光焕发] (róng guāng huàn fā 容光煥發) 'one's face glowing with health.'

Antonym: [萎靡不振] (wěi mí bú zhèn 萎靡不振) 'dispirited.'

345. 【侃侃而谈】(侃侃而談) kǎn kǎn ér tán

侃侃 means 'confident and unhurried.' The meaning of the whole idiom is 'speak
with confidence and conviction.'

Example 1: 面对记者，他**侃侃而谈**，表达了自己的美好愿望。

Miànduì jìzhě, tā kǎnkǎn'értán, biǎodále zìjǐ de měihǎo yuànwàng.

'In front of the reporters, he spoke with confidence and conviction, expressing his own wonderful aspirations.'

Example 2: 售楼小姐与顾客**侃侃而谈**，介绍他们的楼盘的情况。

Shòulóu xiǎojiě yǔ gùkè kǎnkǎn'értán, jièshào tāmen de lóupán de qíngkuàng.

'The female real estate agent spoke with her customers with confidence and conviction, introducing the situation in their apartment building.'

Usage: Functions as predicate.

Near Synonyms: [滔滔不绝] (tāo tāo bù jué 滔滔不絕) 'talking on and on,' [娓娓道来] (wěi wěi dào lái 娓娓道來) 'talking tirelessly' (complimentary), [夸夸其谈] (kuā kuā qí tán 誇誇其談) 'full of boasts and exaggerations' (derogatory).

Antonyms: [张口结舌] (zhāng kǒu jié shé 張口結舌) 'open mouth tie tongue – at a loss for words,' [哑口无言] (yǎ kǒu wú yán 啞口無言) 'dumb and without words – speechless,' [吞吞吐吐] (tūn tūn tǔ tǔ 吞吞吐吐) 'hem and haw,' [期期艾艾] (qī qī ài ài 期期艾艾) 'stammer.'

346. 【诚心诚意】(誠心誠意) chéng xīn chéng yì

诚心 means 'sincere heart' and 诚意 means 'sincere intention.' The meaning of the whole idiom is 'earnestly and sincerely.'

Example 1: 他**诚心诚意**地向你道歉，你为什么不理他？

Tā chéngxīn-chéngyì de xiàng nǐ dàoqiàn, nǐ wèishénme bù lǐ tā?

'He apologized to you earnestly and sincerely; why do you ignore him?'

Example 2: 这个慈善家**诚心诚意**地帮助穷困地区的人民。

Zhège císhànjiā chéngxīn-chéngyì de bāngzhù qióngkùn dìqū de rénmín.

'This philanthropist earnestly and sincerely helps people from poverty-stricken areas.'

Usage: Functions mainly as adverbial and predicate.

Note: Complimentary in meaning.

Near Synonym: [真心实意] (zhēn xīn shí yì 真心實意) 'wholehearted, sincere.'

Antonym: [虚情假意] (xū qíng jiǎ yì 虚情假意) 'hypocritical, insincere.'

347. 【千军万马】(千軍萬馬) qiān jūn wàn mǎ

军 means 'soldiers, troops.' The literal meaning is 'a thousand troops and ten thousand horses,' with a freer translation being 'a vast array of infantry and cavalry, a powerful army.'

Example   1: 中国改革开放初期的高考，可以称得上是 "**千军万马**过独木桥"，能够考上大学的都是优秀的人才。

Zhōngguó gǎigé kāifàng chūqī de gāokǎo, kěyǐ chēngdeshàng shì "qiānjūn-wànmǎ guò dúmùqiáo," nénggòu kǎoshàng dàxué de dōu shì yōuxiù de réncái.

'The university entrance examination during the early period of the reforms and opening up to the outside world could be called "a thousand troops and ten thousand horses crossing a single-plank bridge," with those able to get into universities being outstanding persons of talent.'

Example 2: 公司的领导就像军队中的将军，将军要指挥**千军万马**，领导要带动全体员工。

Gōngsī de lǐngdǎo jiù xiàng jūnduì zhōng de jiāngjūn, jiāngjūn yào zhǐhuī qiānjūn-wànmǎ, lǐngdǎo yào dàidòng quántǐ yuángōng.

'The leader of a company is like a general in the armed forces; a general is supposed to command a vast array of infantry and cavalry, while a leader is supposed to spur on all of his or her staff members.'

Usage: Nominal element, functions as object or subject.

Antonym: [孤家寡人] (gū jiā guǎ rén 孤家寡人) (originally meant 'I' as spoken by the emperor, nowadays means 'an isolated man, a loner'; used mostly in speech).

348. 【绞尽脑汁】(絞盡腦汁) jiǎo jìn nǎo zhī

绞 means 'entangle,' 尽 means 'completely,' 脑 means 'brain,' and 汁 means 'juice.' The meaning of the whole idiom is 'rack one's brains.'

Example 1: 为了解决这个难题，他**绞尽脑汁**，最后终于想出了一个完美的办法。

Wèile jiějué zhège nántí, tā jiǎojìn-nǎozhī, zuìhòu zhōngyú xiǎngchūle yí ge wánměi de bànfǎ.

'In order to solve this difficult problem, he racked his brains, in the end finally thinking of the perfect way to deal with it.'

Example 2: 黑社会分子**绞尽脑汁**躲避警察的搜查。

Hēishèhuì fènzǐ jiǎojìn-nǎozhī duǒbì jǐngchá de sōuchá.

'The members of the criminal gang racked their brains to dodge the police during their search.'

Usage: Functions mainly as attributive and predicate.

Near Synonyms: [挖空心思] (wā kōng xīn sī 挖空心思) 'rack one's brains,' [千方百计] (qiān fāng bǎi jì 千方百計) 'by every possible means.'

Antonym: [灵机一动] (líng jī yí dòng 靈機一動) 'have a sudden inspiration, have a bright idea.'

349. 【垂头丧气】(垂頭喪氣) chuí tóu sàng qì

垂 means 'hang down,' 丧 means 'lose,' and 气 means 'spirit.' A literal translation of the whole idiom is 'hang head lose spirit,' with freer translations including 'hang one's head in dejection, dejected, discouraged.'

Example 1: 为了这场比赛，他们准备了一年，结果却被打得大败，队员们比赛后一个个**垂头丧气**地回了旅馆。

Wèile zhè chǎng bǐsài, tāmen zhǔnbèile yì nián, jiéguǒ què bèi dǎde dàbài, duìyuánmen bǐsài hòu yí ge ge chuítóu-sàngqì de huíle lǚguǎn.

'For this competition, they prepared for one year, and in the end, they suffered a great defeat; after the competition, each and every one of the team members returned to the hotel hanging his head in dejection.'

Example 2: 她严厉地说：看你那副**垂头丧气**的样子，哪像一个男人！

Tā yánlì de shuō: "Kàn nǐ nà fù chuítóu-sàngqì de yàngzi, nǎ xiàng yí ge nánren!"

'She said sternly: "Look at that dejected manner of yours; that isn't like a man!"'

Usage: Functions mainly as adverbial.

Note: Derogatory in meaning.

Near Synonym: [无精打采] (wú jīng dǎ cǎi 無精打采) 'listless, in low spirits.'

Antonyms: [斗志昂扬] (dòu zhì áng yáng 鬥志昂揚) 'full of fighting spirit,' [得意洋洋] (dé yì yáng yáng 得意洋洋) 'complacent, self-satisfied.'

350. 【掩耳盗铃】(掩耳盜鈴) yǎn ěr dào líng

掩 means 'cover,' 耳 means 'ear,' 盗 means 'steal,' and 铃 means 'bell.' A literal translation of this idiom is 'cover ears steal bell,' with a freer translation being 'cover one's own ears while one is stealing a bell so as to prevent others from hearing the sound of the bell.' This is a metaphor for 'deceive oneself and others.'

Example 1: 他一方面声称自己维护祖国统一，但是另一方面又秘密会晤分裂分子，这种**掩耳盗铃**的做法让人恶心。

Tā yì fāngmiàn shēngchēng zìjǐ wéihù zǔguó tǒngyī, dànshì lìng yì fāngmiàn yòu mìmì huìwù fēnliè fènzǐ, zhè zhǒng yǎn'ěr-dàolíng de zuòfǎ ràng rén ěxīn.

'On the one hand he declared that he was upholding the unification of the motherland, but on the other hand he was secretly meeting with the separatists; this way of doing things where you are deceiving yourself and others is disgusting.'

Example 2: 我们必须勇敢地面对目前的困境，不能**掩耳盗铃**。

Wǒmen bìxū yǒnggǎn de miànduì mùqián de kùnjìng, bù néng yǎn'ěr-dàolíng.

'We must bravely face our current difficulties; we should not try to deceive ourselves or others.'

Usage: Functions mainly as predicate and attributive.

Allusion: Once upon a time, when a noble family had perished, a commoner wanted to take advantage of the opportunity to steal a large bell and carry it home on his back. But the bell was too large for him to carry, so he decided to break it up with a hammer and carry it home in several pieces. While he was breaking up the bell with his hammer, the bell emitted a large "gong." Afraid that someone else would hear the sound of the bell and grab the bell away from him, the commoner immediately covered up his own ears. (from "Zi Zhi" in *Mr. Lü's Spring and Autumn Annals*)

Note: Derogatory in meaning.

Near Synonyms: [自欺欺人] (zì qī qī rén 自欺欺人) 'deceive oneself and other people,' [弄巧成拙] (nòng qiǎo chéng zhuō 弄巧成拙) 'too clever for one's own good.'

Antonyms: [光明正大] (guāng míng zhèng dà 光明正大) 'frank and upright,' [开诚布公] (kāi chéng bù gōng 開誠布公) 'have a frank and sincere talk.'

351. 【日复一日】 (日復一日) rì fù yí rì

日 means 'day' and 复 means 'again.' The literal meaning is 'a day and again one day,' with a freer translation being 'day after day, day in day out.'

Example 1: 生活就这样**日复一日**、年复一年地过下去，没有任何改变。

Shēnghuó jiù zhèyàng rìfùyírì, nián fù yì nián de guòxiàqù, méiyǒu rènhé gǎibiàn.

'Life passed in this way day after day, year after year, without any change at all.'

Example 2: 他住在费城，但是在纽约工作，因此**日复一日**地坐火车往返。

Tā zhù zài Fèichéng, dànshì zài Niǔyuē gōngzuò, yīncǐ rìfùyírì de zuò huǒchē wǎngfǎn.

'He lives in Philadelphia but works in New York; therefore, day after day he takes the train back and forth.'

Usage: Functions mainly as adverbial; can also serve as predicate and attributive. Often used in conjunction with 年复一年 (nián fù yì nián) 'year after year.'

Note: Slightly derogatory in meaning.

Antonym: [千载难逢] (qiān zǎi nán féng 千載難逢) 'once in a thousand years, the chance of a lifetime.'

352. 【奄奄一息】 (奄奄一息) yǎn yǎn yì xī

奄奄 means 'feeble breathing' and 息 means 'breath.' The meaning of the whole idiom is 'breathe feebly, one's last gasp before dying.'

Example 1: 那位病人病得很重，尽管用了最好的药，但是还是救不过来，已经**奄奄一息**了。

Nà wèi bìngrén bìngde hěn zhòng, jǐnguǎn yòngle zuì hǎo de yào, dànshì háishì jiù bú guòlái, yǐjīng yǎnyǎn-yìxī le.

'That patient is seriously ill; even though they used the best medicine, they're unable to save him; he is already on his last breath.'

Example 2: 由于经济受到国际资本的控制，这个国家的民族工业**奄奄一息**了。

Yóuyú jīngjì shòudào guójì zīběn de kòngzhì, zhège guójiā de mínzú gōngyè yǎnyǎn-yìxī le.

'Due to its economy being controlled by international capital, this country's national industry is on its last legs.'

Usage: Functions mainly as predicate and attributive.

Near Synonyms: [岌岌可危] (jí jí kě wēi 岌岌可危) 'in imminent danger,' [死到临头] (sǐ dào lín tóu 死到臨頭) 'death approaches,' [行将就木] (xíng jiāng jiù mù 行將就木) 'about to enter a coffin – on the verge of death.'

Antonyms: [朝气蓬勃] (zhāo qì péng bó 朝氣蓬勃) 'full of vigor and vitality,' [生龙活虎] (shēng lóng huó hǔ 生龍活虎) 'bursting with energy.'

353. 【千载难逢】（千載難逢） qiān zǎi nán féng

载 here means 'year' and 逢 means 'meet, encounter.' A literal translation of the entire idiom is 'in a thousand years hard to encounter.' This describes a rare opportunity. Freer translations include 'once in a thousand years, the chance of a lifetime.'

Example 1: 这是一个**千载难逢**的机会，一定要抓住。

Zhè shì yí ge qiānzǎi-nánféng de jīhuì, yídìng yào zhuāzhù.

'This is the opportunity of a lifetime; you definitely need to seize it.'

Example 2: 深圳抓住了**千载难逢**的历史机遇，于是从一个村子一跃成为国际化大都市。

Shēnzhèn zhuāzhù le qiānzǎi-nánféng de lìshǐ jīyù, yúshì cóng yí ge cūnzi yíyuè chéngwéi guójìhuà dàdūshì.

'Shenzhen seized an extremely rare historical opportunity, subsequently changing from a village to an international metropolis.'

Usage: Functions mainly as attributive; often followed by the nouns 机遇 (jīyù 機遇) 'lucky opportunity' or 机会 (jīhuì 機會) 'opportunity.'

Note: Complimentary in meaning.

Near Synonym: [百年不遇] (bǎi nián bú yù 百年不遇) 'hundred years not meet – one won't see this in a hundred years, rare.'

Antonym: [司空见惯] (sī kōng jiàn guàn 司空見慣) 'get used to seeing something and no longer find it strange.'

354. 【未雨绸缪】(未雨綢繆) wèi yǔ chóu móu

未 means 'not yet,' 雨 here means 'rain,' and 绸缪 is said to once have meant 'silk umbrella.' The idea is 'prepare one's umbrella in advance even before it rains.' Nowadays, this idiom usually means 'worry about something that hasn't happened yet, take preventive measures.'

Example 1: 她做任何事情都**未雨绸缪**，因此没有出现过重大的损失。

Tā zuò rènhé shìqing dōu wèiyǔ-chóumóu, yīncǐ méiyǒu chūxiànguo zhòngdà de sǔnshī.

'Whatever she does, she takes preventive measures; therefore, large losses have never occurred.'

Example 2: 领导者得具备**未雨绸缪**的意识，这样才能防患于未然。

Lǐngdǎozhě děi jùbèi wèiyǔ-chóumóu de yìshi, zhèyàng cái néng fánghuàn yú wèirán.

'Leaders must possess an awareness of preventive measures; only in this way can they guard against undesirable things happening in the future.'

Usage: Functions mainly as predicate and attributive; sometimes followed by 防患于未然 (fánghuàn yú wèirán 防患於未然) 'guard against something bad happening in the future.'

Note: Complimentary in meaning.

Near Synonym: [有备无患] (yǒu bèi wú huàn 有備無患) 'have preparation not have disaster – preparedness averts peril.'

Antonym: [临渴掘井] (lín kě jué jǐng 臨渴掘井) 'just before becoming thirsty dig a well – do things at the last moment.'

355. 【居高临下】(居高臨下) jū gāo lín xià

The literal meaning is 'reside in a high place and look downward,' with a freer translation being 'a commanding position or view.'

Example 1: 他的别墅在城市里的小山顶上，**居高临下**，可以看见全城。

Tā de biéshù zài chéngshì lǐ de xiǎo shāndǐng shàng, jūgāo-línxià, kěyǐ kànjiàn quánchéng.

'His villa is at the top of a little hill in the city; it's located way up there and looks down, so that you can see the whole city.'

Example 2: 有的领导总是板着脸，说话带着**居高临下**的语气。

Yǒude lǐngdǎo zǒngshì bǎnzhe liǎn, shuōhuà dàizhe jūgāo-línxià de yǔqì.

'Some leaders always keep a straight face, speaking with a tone of voice as though they were in a high position looking down.'

Usage: Functions mainly as attributive, adverbial, and predicate.

Near Synonyms: [高高在上] (gāo gāo zài shàng 高高在上) 'up very high, isolated from the masses,' [盛气凌人] (shèng qì líng rén 盛氣凌人) 'arrogant, overbearing,' [高屋建瓴] (gāo wū jiàn líng 高屋建瓴) 'operate from a strategically advantageous position.'

Antonyms: [平易近人] (píng yì jìn rén 平易近人) 'amiable and approachable.'

356. 【心安理得】(心安理得) xīn ān lǐ dé

安 means 'peaceful,' 理 means 'reason,' and 得 means 'obtain.' A literal translation is 'mind is peaceful and reason has been obtained,' with a freer translation being 'have peace of mind, have a clear conscience.'

Example 1: 这个人真是无耻，居然**心安理得**地接受别人的贿赂。

Zhège rén zhēn shì wúchǐ, jūrán xīn'ān-lǐdé de jiēshòu biérén de huìlù.

'This person is truly shameless, actually accepting bribes from others with a clear conscience.'

Example 2: 我这个年纪的人做事不求别的了，只求**心安理得**。

Wǒ zhège niánjì de rén zuòshì bù qiú biéde le, zhǐ qiú xīn'ān-lǐdé.

'Someone of my age in doing things does not seek anything else; I only seek peace of mind.'

Usage: Functions mainly as adverbial and predicate.

Note: Complimentary in meaning.

Near Synonym: [问心无愧] (wèn xīn wú kuì 問心無愧) 'have a clear conscience.'

Antonyms: [忐忑不安] (tǎn tè bù ān 忐忑不安) 'feel uneasy,' [问心有愧] (wèn xīn yǒu kuì 問心有愧) and [做贼心虚] (zuò zéi xīn xū 做賊心虛), both of which mean 'have a guilty conscience.'

357. 【一意孤行】(一意孤行) yí yì gū xíng

孤 means 'alone, isolated.' A literal translation is 'with full intention to walk in isolation.' Freer translations are 'cling obstinately to a reckless course' and 'hell-bent on having one's own way.'

Example 1: 她说如果美国**一意孤行**，对中国出口进行制裁，中国也会相应地进行报复。

Tā shuō rúguǒ Měiguó yíyì-gūxíng, duì Zhōngguó chūkǒu jìnxíng zhìcái, Zhōngguó yě huì xiāngyìng de jìnxíng bàofù.

'She said that if the U.S. obstinately clings to its own reckless course and imposes sanctions on Chinese imports, China will retaliate accordingly.'

Example 2: 董事长不顾董事会其他成员的反对，**一意孤行**，结果给公司带来了巨大的经济损失。

Dǒngshìzhǎng bú gù dǒngshìhuì qítā chéngyuán de fǎnduì, yíyì-gūxíng, jiéguǒ gěi gōngsī dàiláile jùdà de jīngjì sǔnshī.

'The chairman of the board paid no heed to the objections of the other board members, being hell-bent on having his own way, and as a result he brought the company huge economic losses.'

Usage: Functions as predicate.

Note: Derogatory in meaning.

Near Synonym: [执迷不悟] (zhí mí bú wù 執迷不悟) 'persist in one's errors and refuse to come to one's senses.'

Antonyms: [从善如流] (cóng shàn rú liú 從善如流) 'follow the good as naturally as water runs downhill – accept good advice readily,' [虚怀若谷] (xū huái ruò gǔ 虛懷若谷) 'a mind as open as a valley – very open-minded.'

358. 【三令五申】(三令五申) sān lìng wǔ shēn

令 means 'order' and 申 means 'explain.' A literal translation of the whole idiom is 'three orders five explanations,' with freer translations being 'repeated orders and commands' or 'issue orders repeatedly.'

Example 1: 虽然中央三**令五申**，地方政府还是瞒报伤亡事故。

Suīrán zhōngyāng sānlìng-wǔshēn, dìfāng zhèngfǔ háishì mánbào shāngwáng shìgù.

'Though the central authorities issued repeated orders, the local government nonetheless withheld facts in reporting about the accident that resulted in injuries and deaths.'

Example 2: 教育部三**令五申**要保证中小学教师的工资发放，可是还是有部门挪用教师工资。

Jiàoyùbù sānlìng-wǔshēn yào bǎozhèng zhōngxiǎoxué jiàoshī de gōngzī fāfàng, kěshì háishì yǒu bùmén nuóyòng jiàoshī gōngzī.

'The Ministry of Education issued orders repeatedly to guarantee the issuing of wages to secondary and elementary school teachers, but there were nevertheless departments that diverted the teachers' wages.'

Usage: Functions as predicate, with terms such as 中央政府 (zhōngyāng zhèngfǔ) 'central government' frequently serving as subject. The result in the main clause is often negative.

Near Synonym: [发号施令] (fā hào shī lìng 發號施令) 'give orders.'

Antonyms: [置若罔闻] (zhì ruò wǎng wén 置若罔聞) 'turn a deaf ear to, ignore,' [屡禁不止] (lǚ jìn bù zhǐ 屢禁不止) 'repeatedly forbidden but not stopping,' [敷衍了事] (fū yǎn liǎo shì 敷衍了事) 'do a perfunctory job.'

359. 【依依不舍】(依依不捨) yī yī bù shě

依依 means 'reluctant to part with' and 舍 means 'abandon, part.' The meaning of the whole idiom is 'feel a sense of regret when leaving, cannot bear to leave, reluctant to part from.'

Example 1: 留学生们**依依不舍**地离开北京，盼望着尽快回来。

Liúxuéshengmen yīyī-bùshě de líkāi Běijīng, pànwàngzhe jìnkuài huílái.

'The foreign students left Beijing with a great sense of regret, hoping to return as soon as possible.'

Example 2: 大熊猫被送回山里，她用**依依不舍**的眼神看着饲养了她三年的饲养员，那场面真令人感动。

Dàxióngmāo bèi sònghuí shān lǐ, tā yòng yīyī-bùshě de yǎnshén kànzhe sìyǎngle tā sān nián de sìyǎngyuán, nà chǎngmiàn zhēn lìng rén gǎndòng.

'When the panda was sent back into the mountains, she looked at the keeper who had fed her for three years with a look in her eyes indicating her reluctance to part; that scene was really touching.'

Usage: Functions mainly as adverbial and predicate; can also serve as attributive.

Note: Complimentary in meaning.

Near Synonyms: [恋恋不舍] (liàn liàn bù shě 戀戀不捨), [依依惜别] (yī yī xī bié 依依惜别), and [难舍难分] (nán shě nán fēn 難捨難分), all of which mean 'reluctant to part from.'

Antonym: [一刀两断] (yì dāo liǎng duàn 一刀兩斷) 'one (blow of a) knife two severed portions – make a clean break with.'

360. 【乐不思蜀】(樂不思蜀) lè bù sī Shǔ

乐 means 'happy,' 思 means 'think about, miss,' and 蜀 means 'the Kingdom of Shu Han (221–263 C.E.).' A literal translation of the whole idiom is 'so happy that one doesn't miss one's home country of Shu Han,' with freer translations being 'indulge in pleasure and forget home and duty, too merry to be homesick.'

Example 1: 他从费城到巴黎出差，办完公事以后仍然在那里待了一天又一天，简直**乐不思蜀**了。

Tā cóng Fèichéng dào Bālí chūchāi, bànwán gōngshì yǐhòu réngrán zài nàlǐ dāile yì tiān yòu yì tiān, jiǎnzhí lèbùsīshǔ le.

'He went from Philadelphia to Paris on a business trip; after finishing his business, he still stayed there day after day; he was simply so happy that he almost forgot he should return.'

Example 2: 她们在那里玩儿了一个月了，可是还不想回家，一副**乐不思蜀**的样子。

Tāmen zài nàlǐ wánrle yí ge yuè le, kěshì hái bù xiǎng huíjiā, yí fù lèbùsīshǔ de yàngzi.

'They've been amusing themselves there for one month now, but still don't want to return home; it appears they're having so much fun that they have forgotten their home.'

Usage: Functions mainly as predicate; can also serve as attributive.

Allusion: In 263 C.E., the king of Shu Han, Liu Chan, surrendered to another kingdom, Xi Jin, and was forced to leave the capital of his home kingdom and live in the capital of Xi Jin. One day the king of Xi Jin asked Liu Chan if he missed his native country, and Liu Chan replied: "This place is great fun; I don't miss Shu Han at all." The king of Xi Jin laughed, saying: "If a man is as shameless as him, even the smartest person in the world cannot help him."

Note: Derogatory in meaning.

Antonym: [落叶归根] (luò yè guī gēn 落葉歸根) 'falling leaves return to their roots – end one's days on one's native soil, after having resided elsewhere return to one's ancestral home.' Note that there is an alternate form of this idiom written 叶落归根 (yè luò guī gēn 葉落歸根) .

361. 【叹为观止】(嘆為觀止) tàn wéi guān zhǐ

叹 means 'sigh with emotion,' 观 means 'look,' and 止 means 'stop.' A literal translation of the whole idiom is 'sigh with emotion because once you have seen a certain place you don't need to see anything else.' Freer translations include 'in awe, sigh in wonder, acclaim something as perfect.'

Example 1: 故宫建筑群规模宏大，令人**叹为观止**。

Gùgōng jiànzhùqún guīmó hóngdà, lìng rén tànwéiguānzhǐ.

'The cluster of buildings that is the Forbidden City is on an enormous scale; it makes people sigh in awe.'

Example 2: 阿根廷球员马拉多纳的脚法令观众**叹为观止**。

Āgēntíng qiúyuán Mǎlāduōnà de jiǎofǎ lìng guānzhòng tànwéiguānzhǐ.

'The footwork of the Argentinean soccer player Maradona makes the audience sigh in wonder.'

Usage: Functions mainly as causative predicate; the usual structure is '令人～ (lìng rén) / 让人～ (ràng rén 讓) 'make someone....'

Note: Complimentary in meaning.

Near Synonym: [拍案叫绝] (pāi àn jiào jué 拍案叫絕) 'hit the table and call out excellent – express admiration.'

Antonyms: [不足挂齿] (bù zú guà chǐ 不足掛齒) 'not worth hanging on the teeth – not worth mentioning,' [不值一提] (bù zhí yì tí 不值一提) 'not worth mentioning.'

362. 【大有人在】(大有人在) dà yǒu rén zài

大 here means 'many.' The meaning of the whole idiom is 'there are many people like this.'

Example 1: 虽然支持她的人很多，但是反对的也**大有人在**。

Suīrán zhīchí tā de rén hěn duō, dànshì fǎnduì de yě dàyǒurénzài.

'Though there were many people who supported her, there were also lots of people who opposed her.'

Example 2: 你对我的评价太高了，其实比我水平高的**大有人在**。

Nǐ duì wǒ de píngjià tài gāole, qíshí bǐ wǒ shuǐpíng gāo de dàyǒurénzài.

'Your appraisal of me is too high; actually there are plenty of people with a higher level than me.'

Usage: Functions mainly as predicate at the end of a sentence.

Near Synonyms: [不乏其人] (bù fá qí rén 不乏其人) 'no lack of such people,' [比比皆是] (bǐ bǐ jiē shì 比比皆是) 'can be found everywhere.'

Antonym: [寥寥无几] (liáo liáo wú jǐ 寥寥無幾) 'very few.'

363. 【雪中送炭】(雪中送炭) xuě zhōng sòng tàn

炭 means 'charcoal.' A literal translation of the whole idiom is 'in the midst of snowy weather send charcoal.' This is a metaphor for 'provide timely and critical assistance' or 'offer opportune help.'

Example 1: 世界各地的人们给受灾者送去了大批的帐篷和棉被，真是**雪中送炭**啊！

Shìjiè gè dì de rénmen gěi shòuzāizhě sòngqùle dà pī de zhàngpéng hé miánbèi, zhēn shì xuězhōng-sòngtàn a!

'People from all over the world sent the natural disaster victims large quantities of tents and quilts, which really did provide timely and crucial assistance!'

Example 2: 整个股市处在危机之中，政府**雪中送炭**，大幅降低了银行存款利率。

Zhěnggè gǔshì chǔzài wēijī zhīzhōng, zhèngfǔ xuězhōng-sòngtàn, dàfú jiàngdīle yínháng cúnkuǎn lìlǜ.

'The entire stock market is in the midst of a crisis; the government has provided opportune assistance by greatly lowering banks' interest rates for savings.'

Usage: Functions mainly as object and predicate.

Note: Complimentary in meaning.

Near Synonym: [拔刀相助] (bá dāo xiāng zhù 拔刀相助) 'draw one's sword and help another – come to someone's rescue.'

Antonym: [落井下石] (luò jǐng xià shí 落井下石) 'someone falls in a well and someone else throws stones down at them – hit a person when he or she is down.'

364. 【一筹莫展】(一籌莫展) yì chóu mò zhǎn

筹 means 'plan,' 莫 means 'not,' and 展 here means 'implement.' A literal translation is 'even one plan not implement,' with freer translations being 'can't think of any way to solve a problem, at one's wit's end.'

Example 1: 由于这起案件中唯一的证人不幸去世了，警察因此一**筹莫展**。

Yóuyú zhè qǐ ànjiàn zhōng wéiyī de zhèngrén búxìng qùshì le, jǐngchá yīncǐ yìchóu-mòzhǎn.

'Because the only witness in this case unfortunately has died, the police therefore are at their wit's end.'

Example 2: 就在大家一**筹莫展**的时候，突然传来一个好消息。

Jiù zài dàjiā yìchóu-mòzhǎn de shíhou, tūrán chuánlái yí ge hǎo xiāoxi.

'Just when everybody was at their wit's end, suddenly a piece of good news was sent in.'

Usage: Functions mainly as predicate; can also serve as attributive. Often followed by 时 (shí 時), 的时候 (de shíhou 的時候), or 之际 (zhī jì 之際), all of which mean 'when.'

Near Synonyms: [无计可施] (wú jì kě shī 無計可施) 'at one's wit's end,' [束手无策] (shù shǒu wú cè 束手無策) 'tied hands without plan – at a complete loss about what to do.'

Antonym: [足智多谋] (zú zhì duō móu 足智多謀) 'enough wisdom and enough plans – wise and resourceful.'

365. 【水泄不通】(水泄不通) shuǐ xiè bù tōng

泄 means 'let out (water)' and 通 means 'come through.' The meaning is 'not even a drop of water could come through' – so crowded is a place, so heavy is traffic, or so tightly surrounded is some person or place.

Example 1: 示威的人群把总统府围得**水泄不通**。

Shìwēi de rénqún bǎ zǒngtǒngfǔ wéide shuǐxiè-bùtōng.

'The crowds of people who were demonstrating surrounded the Presidential Palace very tightly.'

Example 2: 购物中心新开业，商品打五折，成千上万顾客涌了过来，购物中心挤得**水泄不通**。

Gòuwù zhōngxīn xīn kāiyè, shāngpǐn dǎ wǔzhé, chéngqiān-shàngwàn gùkè yǒngle guòlai, gòuwù zhōngxīn jǐde shuǐxiè-bùtōng.

'When the shopping mall started doing business, merchandise was on sale at fifty percent off; tens of thousands of customers poured in, the shopping mall being so crowded that not even a drop of water could have gotten through.'

Usage: Functions mainly as complement for verbs such as 围 (wéi 圍) 'surround,' 挤 (jǐ 擠) 'squeeze,' and 堵 (dǔ) 'stop up.' The pattern is verb + 得 (de) + 水泄不通.

Near Synonym: [人山人海] (rén shān rén hǎi 人山人海) 'people mountain people sea – huge crowds.'

Antonyms: [四通八达] (sì tōng bā dá 四通八達) 'extend or radiate in all directions,' [畅通无阻] (chàng tōng wú zǔ 暢通無阻) 'unimpeded and unobstructed.'

366. 【相依为命】 (相依為命) xiāng yī wéi mìng

相 means 'one another,' 依 means 'depend on,' 为 means 'be,' and 命 means 'life.' A literal translation is 'several people depend on one another for their lives,' with a freer translation being 'depend on each other for survival, bound by a common destiny.'

Example 1: 因为父亲死得早，孩子跟母亲**相依为命**。

Yīnwèi fùqīn sǐde zǎo, háizi gēn mǔqin xiāngyī-wéimìng.

'Because the father died early, the children and their mother depended on one another for survival.'

Example 2: 由于生活穷困，全家五口人挤在一间屋子里**相依为命**。

Yóuyú shēnghuó qióngkùn, quán jiā wǔ kǒu rén jǐ zài yì jiān wūzi lǐ xiāngyī-wéimìng.

'Because their lives were destitute, all of the five people in the family crammed into one room, depending on each other for survival.'

Usage: Functions as predicate.

Near Synonyms: [相濡以沫] (xiāng rú yǐ mò 相濡以沫) 'moisten one another with saliva – help one another in difficult times,' [患难与共] (huàn nàn yǔ gòng 患難與共) 'go through difficulties together.'

Antonym: [各奔前程] (gè bèn qián chéng 各奔前程) 'each going her or his own way without regard for others.'

367. 【街头巷尾】(街頭巷尾) jiē tóu xiàng wěi

街头 means 'street corner' and 巷尾 means 'the end of a lane.' The meaning of the whole idiom is 'streets and lanes.'

Example 1: 在巴西**街头巷尾**踢球的少年中出现了许多后来的足球巨星。

Zài Bāxī jiētóu-xiàngwěi tīqiú de shàonián zhōng chūxiànle xǔduō hòulái de zúqiú jùxīng.

'Among the youth who kick balls in the streets and lanes of Brazil, there have emerged many a future megastar of soccer.'

Example 2: 夏天来了，**街头巷尾**出现了很多水果摊儿。

Xiàtiān láile, jiētóu-xiàngwěi chūxiànle hěn duō shuǐguǒtānr.

'Summer has come and, in the streets and lanes, there have appeared many fruit vendor stands.'

Usage: Nominal element, can function as object of coverb phrase with 在 (zài); can also serve as subject, object, and attributive.

Near Synonym: [大街小巷] (dà jiē xiǎo xiàng 大街小巷) 'all the streets and lanes.'

368. 【无微不至】(無微不至) wú wēi bú zhì

微 means 'small' and 至 means 'arrive.' A literal translation is 'there is no small (area where attention or care) did not arrive.' This idiom can be translated as 'meticulous, leaving nothing undone.'

Example 1: 在父母**无微不至**的照顾下，孩子健康地成长。

Zài fùmǔ wúwēi-búzhì de zhàogù xià, háizi jiànkāng de chéngzhǎng.

'Under the meticulous care of its parents, the child grew up in good health.'

Example 2: 医生**无微不至**地关怀所有的病人。

Yīshēng wúwēi-búzhì de guānhuái suǒyǒu de bìngrén.

'Doctors show concern for all their patients, leaving not the slightest thing undone.'

Usage: Functions mainly as adverbial and attributive.

Note: Complimentary in meaning.

Near Synonym: [关怀备至] (guān huái bèi zhì 關懷備至) 'show the utmost solicitude.'

Antonyms: [粗心大意] (cū xīn dà yì 粗心大意) 'careless, negligent,' [漠不关心] (mò bù guān xīn 漠不關心) 'indifferent,' [马马虎虎] (mǎ mǎ hū hū 馬馬虎虎) 'casual, careless' (used mostly in spoken Chinese).

369. 【不假思索】(不假思索) bù jiǎ sī suǒ

假 means 'make use of' and 思索 means 'think, ponder.' The whole idiom means 'without stopping to think, without hesitation.'

Example 1: 她**不假思索**地回答："您放心吧，没问题。"

Tā bùjiǎ-sīsuǒ de huídá: 'Nín fàngxīn ba, méiwèntí.'

'She answered without hesitating: "Relax, there's no problem."'

Example 2: 听了对方的话以后，他**不假思索**地说："不行！"

Tīngle duìfāng de huà yǐhòu, tā bùjiǎ-sīsuǒ de shuō: 'Bùxíng.'

'After he had heard the remarks from the other side, he said without hesitation: "No!"'

Usage: Functions as adverbial; usually followed by a verb meaning 'say.'

Near Synonym: [脱口而出] (tuō kǒu ér chū 脱口而出) 'blurt out.'

Antonym: [深思熟虑] (shēn sī shú lǜ 深思熟慮) 'careful deliberation or consideration.'

370. 【江郎才尽】(江郎才盡) Jiāng láng cái jìn

江 is a Chinese surname, 郎 means 'man,' 才 means 'talent,' and 尽 means 'exhausted, used up.' A literal translation is 'the talents of the man by the name of Jiang were exhausted,' with a freer translation being 'one's talents have been used up' or 'one's creative energies have become exhausted.'

Example 1: 牛顿晚年在科学上没有什么突出的贡献，这不是因为他**江郎才尽**了，而是走错了方向。

Niúdùn wǎnnián zài kēxué shàng méiyǒu shénme tūchū de gòngxiàn, zhè bú shì yīnwèi tā Jiāngláng-cáijìn le, ér shì zǒucuòle fāngxiàng.

'In his later years, Newton had no prominent contributions; this was not because his creative energies were exhausted, but because he proceeded in the wrong direction.'

Example 2: 他年轻的时候曾经凭借一个人的力量挽救过一个公司，但是晚年也有**江郎才尽**的时候。

Tā niánqīng de shíhou céngjīng píngjiè yí ge rén de lìliàng wǎnjiùguo yí ge gōngsī, dànshì wǎnnián yě yǒu Jiāngláng-cáijìn de shíhou.

'When he was young, he once – relying on his own strength – rescued a company; but in his later years, there were also times when his creative energies were exhausted.'

Usage: Functions mainly as predicate and attributive.

Allusion: Jiang Yan (444–505 C.E.) was a famous literary figure during the Southern Dynasties Period who, in his youth, wrote excellent essays. It is said that one evening during his later years, he dreamed of a handsome man by the name of Guo Pu, a famous author (276–324 C.E.). In the dream, Guo Pu said to Jiang Yan: "I have a pen that has been in your possession for many years; now you can give it back to me." When Jiang Yan felt around in his robe, he really did find a five-color pen, which he returned to Guo Pu. From this time on, the quality of Jiang Yan's poetry deteriorated dramatically. Everyone said that Jiang Yan's talent was really Guo Pu's and that now it was gone. (from *Shi Pin* by Zhong Rong)

Note: Derogatory in meaning.

Near Synonym: [黔驴技穷] (Qián lǘ jì qióng 黔驢技窮) 'the Guizhou donkey's skills have been exhausted – exhaust one's bag of clumsy tricks' (derogatory).

Antonym: [初露锋芒] (chū lù fēng máng 初露鋒芒) 'first reveal spear edge – show one's talent for the first time.'

371. 【不相上下】(不相上下) bù xiāng shàng xià

相 means 'mutually' and 上下 means 'high and low, superior and inferior.' The whole idiom means 'equally matched, without much difference, about the same.'

Example 1: 两个人的乒乓球水平**不相上下**，都很难赢对方。

Liǎng ge rén de pīngpāngqiú shuǐpíng bùxiāng-shàngxià, dōu hěn nán yíng duìfāng.

'Their level in ping pong is approximately the same, so it will be hard for either to win over the other.'

Example 2: 这两件商品的质量**不相上下**，但是价格差得就多了。

Zhè liǎng jiàn shāngpǐn de zhìliàng bùxiāng-shàngxià, dànshì jiàgé chà de jiù duō le.

'The quality of these two items of merchandise is without much difference, but the price is very different.'

Usage: Functions as predicate.

Near Synonym: [不分伯仲] (bù fēn bó zhòng 不分伯仲) 'irrespective of order of seniority among brothers – not much different.'

Antonym: [天壤之别] (tiān rǎng zhī bié 天壤之别) 'as different as heaven and earth.'

372. 【居安思危】(居安思危) jū ān sī wēi

居 means 'live in,' 安 means 'peace,' 思 means 'think about,' and 危 means 'danger.' A literal translation of the whole idiom is 'live in peace (but) think about danger.' A freer translation of the whole idiom is 'vigilant even in peacetime.'

Example 1: 现在我们的形势一片大好，但是我们不能盲目乐观，要小心谨慎，**居安思危**。

Xiànzài wǒmen de xíngshì yípiàn dàhǎo, dànshì wǒmen bùnéng mángmù lèguān, yào xiǎoxīn jǐnshèn, jū'ān-sīwēi.

'Right now our situation is that everything is excellent, but we cannot be blindly optimistic; we must be very cautious and prudent, and prepare for danger even in peacetime.'

Example 2: 上司告诫下属要加强**居安思危**的忧患意识。

Shàngsī gàojiè xiàshǔ yào jiāqiáng jū'ān-sīwēi de yōuhuàn yìshi.

'The superiors admonished the subordinates to strengthen their awareness of danger even at a time of security.'

Usage: Functions as predicate or attributive. If used as attributive, often followed by 意识 (yìshi 意識) 'awareness' or 思想 (sīxiǎng) 'mind.'

Note: Complimentary in meaning.

Near Synonyms: [防患未然] (fáng huàn wèi rán 防患未然) 'defend against possible disaster, prevent trouble before it happens,' [未雨绸缪] (wèi yǔ chóu móu 未雨綢繆) 'worry about something that hasn't happened yet.'

Antonyms: [麻痹大意] (má bì dà yì 麻痹大意) 'careless and inattentive,' [高枕无忧] (gāo zhěn wú yōu 高枕無憂) 'high pillow no worries – rest easy.'

373. 【近在咫尺】 (近在咫尺) jìn zài zhǐ chǐ

A 咫 was a unit of measurement in ancient China consisting of eight 寸 or 'Chinese inches.' A 尺 or 'Chinese foot' was another ancient measurement. Together, 咫尺 means 'short distance.' The meaning of the whole idiom is 'extremely close, close at hand.'

Example 1: 这家旅馆就在大使馆的对面，**近在咫尺**，所以住宿的人总是满着。

Zhè jiā lǚguǎn jiù zài dàshǐguǎn de duìmiàn, jìnzài-zhǐchǐ, suǒyǐ zhùsù de rén zǒngshì mǎnzhe.

'This hotel is right across from the embassy, very close at hand, so it's always fully occupied by guests.'

Example 2: 他们两个人**近在咫尺**，可是情感上却远在天涯。

Tāmen liǎng ge rén jìnzài-zhǐchǐ, kěshì qínggǎn shàng què yuǎnzài-tiānyá.

'The two of them are very close to each other in physical distance, but emotionally they're as distant from each other as the ends of the earth.'

Usage: Functions mainly as predicate and attributive.

Near Synonyms: [咫尺之遥] (zhǐ chǐ zhī yáo 咫尺之遥) 'very close,' [一衣带水] (yī yī dài shuǐ 一衣帶水) 'narrow strip of water in between.'

Antonyms: [远在天涯] (yuǎn zài tiān yá 遠在天涯) 'as distant as the ends of the earth,' [咫尺天涯] (zhǐ chǐ tiān yá 咫尺天涯) 'so near and yet so far away.'

374. 【卷土重来】(捲土重來) juǎn tǔ chóng lái

卷土 means 'sweep up dust.' This describes people and horses who are running. 重来 means 'come again.' The meaning of the whole idiom is 'stage a comeback.'

Example 1: 上次世界杯巴西失利了，这次他们**卷土重来**，非要夺取冠军不可。

Shàngcì Shìjièbēi Bāxī shīlìle, zhè cì tāmen juǎntǔ-chónglái, fēi yào duóqǔ guànjūn bùkě.

'In the last World Cup, Brazil suffered a setback; this time they are staging a comeback and are dead set on winning the championship.'

Example 2: 对于贪污腐败现象一定要持续不断地打击，因为稍微一放松，它们就会**卷土重来**。

Duìyú tānwū fǔbài xiànxiàng yídìng yào chíxù búduàn de dǎjī, yīnwèi shāowēi yí fàngsōng, tāmen jiù huì juǎntǔ-chónglái.

'We definitely should persist in cracking down on graft and corruption without interruption, because the minute you relax just a little, they will stage a comeback.'

Usage: Functions mainly as predicate.

Note: Slightly derogatory in meaning.

Near Synonyms: [东山再起] (dōng shān zài qǐ 東山再起) '(from) East Mountain rise up again – stage a comeback,' [死灰复燃] (sǐ huī fù rán 死灰復燃) 'dying embers again burn – come back to life,' [另起炉灶] (lìng qǐ lú zào 另起爐灶) 'start a new kitchen – start all over again.'

Antonyms: [一蹶不振] (yì jué bú zhèn 一蹶不振) 'unable to recover from a setback,' [万劫不复] (wàn jié bú fù 萬劫不復) 'doomed for ten thousand generations,' [偃旗息鼓] (yǎn qí xī gǔ 偃旗息鼓) 'roll up the flags and silence the drums – call everything off.'

375. 【冰天雪地】(冰天雪地) bīng tiān xuě dì

冰天 means 'icy sky' and 雪地 means 'snow-covered ground.' The whole idiom means 'all covered with ice and snow, bitterly cold.'

Example 1: 中国的东北跟美国的五大湖区差不多，冬天的时候总是**冰天雪地**。

Zhōngguó de Dōngběi gēn Měiguó de Wǔdàhú qū chàbùduō, dōngtiān de shíhou zǒngshì bīngtiān-xuědì.

'The Northeast of China is much like the Great Lakes region of the U.S., being all covered with ice and snow in the winter.'

Example 2: 旅行者迷了路，但是靠不多的一点汽油和食物，在**冰天雪地**的山林里坚持了五天，最后被人救了。

Lǚxíngzhě míle lù, dànshì kào bù duō de yìdiǎn qìyóu hé shíwù, zài bīngtiān-xuě de shānlín lǐ jiānchíle wǔ tiān, zuìhòu bèi rén jiù le.

'The travelers lost their way, but relying on their small supply of gasoline and provisions, they held on for five days in the mountainous forests that were all covered with ice and snow, until finally they were rescued.'

Usage: Functions mainly as attributive and predicate.

Near Synonym: [天寒地冻] (tiān hán dì dòng 天寒地凍) 'sky is cold and ground is frozen.'

Antonym: [春暖花开] (chūn nuǎn huā kāi 春暖花開) 'spring is warm and flowers bloom.'

376. 【有的放矢】 (有的放矢) yǒu dì fàng shǐ

的 here means 'target, goal,' 放 means 'release,' and 矢 means 'arrow.' A literal translation of the whole idiom is 'have a target and release arrows,' with freer translations being 'have an object in mind, goal-oriented.'

Example 1: 做任何事都要提前调查，这样才能**有的放矢**，取得最好的效果。

Zuò rènhé shì dōu yào tíqián diàochá, zhèyàng cáinéng yǒudì-fàngshǐ, qǔdé zuì hǎo de xiàoguǒ.

'In doing anything you should investigate beforehand; only in this way can you be goal-oriented and obtain the best results.'

Example 2: 对于罪犯，要充分了解他们成长的历史，然后**有的放矢**地进行教育。

Duìyú zuìfàn, yào chōngfèn liǎojiě tāmen chéngzhǎng de lìshǐ, ránhòu yǒudì-fàngshǐ de jìnxíng jiàoyù.

'Regarding offenders, one must sufficiently understand the history of how they grew up, and after that, in a goal-oriented manner, carry out education.'

Usage: Functions as predicate and adverbial.

Note: Complimentary in meaning.

Near Synonym: [对症下药] (duì zhèng xià yào 對癥下藥) 'suit the medicine to the illness.'

Antonym: [无的放矢] (wú dì fàng shǐ 無的放矢) 'without a target to release arrows – make unfounded accusations.'

377. 【一尘不染】 (一塵不染) yì chén bù rǎn

尘 means 'dust' and 染 means 'dye, contaminate.' A literal translation of this idiom is 'not contaminated by even a single particle of dust,' with a freer translation being 'spotless, clean, pure' (of the environment or of a person). This idiom derives from Buddhism, in which sight, sound, smell, taste, touch, and thought were called the 'six dusts,' by which a Buddhist was not supposed to be contaminated.

Example 1: 她在名利场里几十年却一**尘不染**，太难做到了。

Tā zài mínglìchǎng lǐ jǐ shí nián què yìchén-bùrǎn, tài nán zuòdàole.

'She spent decades in the circles of those seeking fame and fortune and yet remained pure; that is very hard to do.'

Example 2: 这是一家五星级的酒店，不但有一**尘不染**的环境，还有超一流的服务。

Zhè shì yì jiā wǔxīngjí de jiǔdiàn, búdàn yǒu yìchén-bùrǎn de huánjìng, hái yǒu chāo yīliú de fúwù.

'This is a five-star hotel; it not only has a spotless environment, it also has more than first-class service.'

Usage: Functions mainly as predicate and attributive.

Note: Complimentary in meaning.

Near Synonyms: [守身如玉] (shǒu shēn rú yù 守身如玉) 'keep oneself as pure as jade – maintain one's moral integrity,' [冰清玉洁] (bīng qīng yù jié 冰清玉潔) 'ice clear and jade pure – incorruptible,' [两袖清风] (liǎng xiù qīng fēng 兩袖清風) '(in one's) two sleeves (there is only) pure wind – honest and not corrupt, not a penny to one's name.'

Antonym: [欲壑难填] (yù hè nán tián 欲壑難填) 'greed is like a valley that is hard to fill – the greedy will never be satisfied.'

378. 【事半功倍】(事半功倍) shì bàn gōng bèi

功 here means 'efficacy, effect' and 倍 means 'double.' A literal translation of the whole idiom is 'work half effect double,' with a freer translation being 'twice the results with half the effort.'

Example 1: 读书要动脑筋，才能收到**事半功倍**的效果。

Dúshū yào dòng nǎojīn, cáinéng shōudào shìbàn-gōngbèi de xiàoguǒ.

'In studying you have to use your head, only then can you achieve twice the results with half the effort.'

Example 2: 高科技能起到**事半功倍**的作用。

Gāokējì néng qǐdào shìbàn-gōngbèi de zuòyòng.

'High-tech can bring about the effect of twice the results with half the effort.'

Usage: Functions mainly as attributive. Frequently preceded by verbs such as 取得 (qǔdé) 'obtain,' 收到 (shōudào) 'achieve,' 达到 (dádào 達到) 'attain,' and 获得 (huòdé 獲得) 'obtain.' Often followed by nouns such as 效果 (xiàoguǒ) 'result,' 结果 (jiéguǒ 結果) 'result,' and 作用 (zuòyòng) 'effect.'

Note: Complimentary in meaning.

Near Synonyms: [一举两得] (yì jǔ liǎng dé 一舉兩得) 'kill two birds with one stone,' [一箭双雕] (yí jiàn shuāng diāo 一箭雙鵰) 'one arrow pair (of) hawks – kill two birds with one stone.'

Antonyms: [事倍功半] (shì bèi gōng bàn 事倍功半) 'twice the work with half the result,' [得不偿失] (dé bù cháng shī 得不償失) 'the gain does not make up for the loss.'

379. 【不同凡响】(不同凡響) bù tóng fán xiǎng

不同 means 'different from,' 凡 means 'ordinary,' and 凡响 means 'common music.' The whole idiom means 'out of the ordinary, head and shoulders above the rest, outstanding.'

Example 1: 哈佛大学的教授水平就是高，观点很独特，**不同凡响**。

Hāfó Dàxué de jiàoshòu shuǐpíng jiùshì gāo, guāndiǎn hěn dútè, bùtóng-fánxiǎng.

'The level of the professors at Harvard University is just high and their points of view are unique; they stand head and shoulders above everyone else.'

Example 2: 他是一个**不同凡响**的人物，以后一定还会有大发展。

Tā shì yí ge bùtóng-fánxiǎng de rénwù, yǐhòu yīdìng hái huì yǒu dà fāzhǎn.

'He is an uncommon man; in the future he is bound to experience rapid development.'

Usage: Functions mainly as predicate and attributive.

Note: Complimentary in meaning.

Near Synonyms: [与众不同] (yǔ zhòng bù tóng 與眾不同) 'different from everyone else, out of the ordinary,' [出类拔萃] (chū lèi bá cuì 出類拔萃) 'stand out and be preeminent.'

Antonym: [平淡无奇] (píng dàn wú qí 平淡無奇) 'flat and uninteresting.'

380. 【井底之蛙】(井底之蛙) jǐng dǐ zhī wā

井 means 'well' and 蛙 means 'frog.' A literal translation of the whole idiom is 'a frog at the bottom of a well.' This is a metaphor for 'a narrow-minded or shortsighted or inexperienced person.'

Example 1: 在没有收音机、电话、电视和互联网的时代，偏远农村的人就像**井底之蛙**，对外面几乎一点都不了解。

Zài méiyǒu shōuyīnjī, diànhuà, diànshì hé hùliánwǎng de shídài, piānyuǎn nóngcūn de rén jiù xiàng jǐngdǐ-zhīwā, duì wàimiàn jīhū yìdiǎn dōu bù liǎojiě.

'During the period when there were no radios, telephones, televisions or Internet, people in the remote countryside were like frogs in the bottom of a well, understanding almost nothing about the outside.'

Example 2: 她第一次到法国，走在香榭丽舍大街上，感觉自己像一只**井底之蛙**。

Tā dìyī cì dào Fǎguó, zǒu zài Xiāng Xièlìshè dàjiē shàng, gǎnjué zìjǐ xiàng yì zhī jǐngdǐ-zhīwā.

'When she went to France for the first time, she walked along the Champs Élysées, feeling naive and inexperienced like a frog in the bottom of a well.'

Usage: Functions mainly as object.

Allusion: There was a little frog in a shallow well that said to a giant sea turtle that had come from the East Sea: "See how happy I am! When I want to go out to play, I jump around the railing at the mouth of the well; and when I wish to rest, I take a nice nap in one of the holes in the wall of the well. When I jump into the water, the water surface just reaches my waist; and when I step into the mud, the mud merely submerges my feet. How can other little critters like crabs and tadpoles compare with me? I occupy my own space, playing any way I feel like. I'm so happy! Why don't you come here more often to visit?" Before the giant sea turtle's left foot had even entered the well, its right knee had already gotten stuck in the well wall. It moved back and forth a number of times, but there was no way it could get in. So it began solemnly to tell the little frog the story of the ocean: "The ocean is thousands of miles distant and thousands of feet deep; even if in ten years there were nine years of floods, there still wouldn't appear to be more water in the ocean; and even if in eight years there were seven years of great drought, there still wouldn't appear to be less water in the ocean. The ocean is impervious to the changes of time or the amount of rainfall. These are the reasons why it is such a pleasure to live in the ocean!" When the little frog had heard this, it was very much taken aback, deeply sensing its own insignificance. (from "Qiushui" in *Zhuangzi*)

Note: Derogatory in meaning.

Near Synonyms: [夜郎自大] (Yè Láng zì dà 夜郎自大) 'parochialism and self-importance,' [一孔之见] (yì kǒng zhī jiàn 一孔之見) 'a view through a small hole – one-sided view, limited view' (modest expression).

Antonym: [见多识广] (jiàn duō shí guǎng 見多識廣) 'experienced and well informed.'

381. 【大同小异】(大同小異) dà tóng xiǎo yì

同 means 'same' and 异 means 'different.' The meaning of the whole idiom is 'mostly the same with only minor differences.'

Example 1: 这两本书看起来很不一样，其实内容**大同小异**。

Zhè liǎng běn shū kànqǐlai hěn bù yíyàng, qíshí nèiróng dàtóng-xiǎoyì.

'These two books look quite different, but actually their content is much the same.'

Example 2: 近些年，欧美国家遇到的问题**大同小异**，都差不多。

Jìn xiē nián, Ōuměi guójiā yùdào de wèntí dàtóng-xiǎoyì, dōu chàbùduō.

'In recent years, the problems that Europe and the U.S. have encountered are much the same; they're not much different.'

Usage: Functions mainly as predicate, occurring at the end of a sentence.

Antonyms: [大相径庭] (dà xiāng jìng tíng 大相徑庭) 'as different as path and yard – poles apart,' [天壤之别] (tiān rǎng zhī bié 天壤之别) 'as different as heaven and earth.'

382. 【谈笑风生】(談笑風生) tán xiào fēng shēng

风生 means 'interest, enthusiasm.' The literal meaning of the whole idiom is 'talk and laugh with interest and enthusiasm.' A freer translation is 'chat merrily, engage in witty conversation.'

Example 1: 会谈的气氛非常轻松，大家**谈笑风生**。

Huìtán de qìfēn fēicháng qīngsōng, dàjiā tánxiào-fēngshēng.

'The atmosphere at the negotiations was very relaxed, everyone chatting merrily.'

Example 2: 两个人**谈笑风生**，一起走进教室。

Liǎng ge rén tánxiào-fēngshēng, yìqǐ zǒujìn jiàoshì.

'The two of them were engaged in witty conversation as together they walked into the classroom.'

Usage: Functions as predicate.

Antonym: [默默无语] (mò mò wú yǔ 默默無語) 'completely silent and without words.'

383. 【不亦乐乎】(不亦樂乎) bú yì lè hū

亦 means 'also,' 乐 means 'happy,' and 乎 is the Classical Chinese equivalent of the Modern Chinese question particle 吗. The literal meaning of the whole idiom is 'Is it not also a happy thing?' A freer translation is 'what a pleasure' or 'what a delight.' However, in modern usage, this idiom is most commonly used to express a high degree and may be translated as 'very, extremely.'

Example 1: 圣诞节到了，孩子们都来了，这对老夫妇忙得**不亦乐乎**。

Shèngdànjié dào le, háizimen dōu lái le, zhè duì lǎo fūfù máng de búyìlèhū.

'When Christmas arrived, the children all came, and the old couple was extremely busy.'

Example 2: 两个人都很会说话，这次一吵架，吵得**不亦乐乎**。

Liǎng ge rén dōu hěn huì shuōhuà, zhè cì yì chǎojià, chǎo de búyìlèhū.

'Both of them are very articulate, so this time when they quarreled, they had quite the argument.'

Usage: Functions as complement. The predicate that comes before often expresses 'being busy.'

Note: The source of this idiom is the collection of Confucius' sayings known as *The Analects*, in which there is a line 有朋自远方来，不亦乐乎？(yǒu péng zì yuǎn fāng lái, bú yì lè hū 有朋自遠方來，不亦樂乎？) 'Is it not a delight to have friends come from afar?'

Antonym: [不可开交] (bù kě kāi jiāo 不可開交) 'a hopeless state of affairs.'

384. 【承前启后】(承前啟後) chéng qián qǐ hòu

承 means 'continue, carry on' and 启 means 'open up, begin.' A literal translation of the whole idiom is 'continue what has come before and open up what is to come after,' with freer translations being 'succeed the past and develop the future' or 'carry on the great traditions of something.'

Example 1: 莫奈在美术史上是一位**承前启后**式的画家。

Mònài zài měishùshǐ shàng shì yí wèi chéngqián-qǐhòu shì de huàjiā.

'In art history, Monet was the type of artist who built on the great traditions of the past to develop those of the future.'

Example 2: 这是一次**承前启后**、继往开来的大会。

Zhè shì yí cì chéngqián-qǐhòu, jìwǎng-kāilái de dàhuì.

'This is a conference that continues past traditions while opening up new ones, that carries on the glorious heritage of the past while developing new directions for the future.'

Usage: Functions mainly as attributive.

Near Synonyms: [承上启下] (chéng shàng qǐ xià 承上啟下) 'link the preceding with the following,' [继往开来] (jì wǎng kāi lái 繼往開來) 'carry on the glorious traditions of the past and open up the way to the future.'

Antonym: [空前绝后] (kōng qián jué hòu 空前絕后) 'never before or since.'

385. 【同甘共苦】(同甘共苦) tóng gān gòng kǔ

同 means 'together,' 甘 means 'sweet,' 共 means 'collectively,' and 苦 means 'bitter.' A literal translation of the whole idiom is 'together sweet collectively bitter,' with freer translations being 'share joys and sorrows' or 'share comforts and hardships.'

Example 1: 不少中国夫妻在艰难的时候能**同甘共苦**，但是成功后有不少问题。

Bùshǎo Zhōngguó fūqī zài jiānnán de shíhou néng tónggān-gòngkǔ, dànshì chénggōng hòu yǒu bùshǎo wèntí.

'Many Chinese couples during difficult times can share their joys and sorrows, but after they succeed, they have many problems.'

Example 2: 群众特别拥护那些能与他们**同甘共苦**的官员。

Qúnzhòng tèbié yōnghù nà xiē néng yǔ tāmen tónggān-gòngkǔ de guānyuán.

'The masses particularly support those officials who can share their joys and their sorrows.'

Usage: Functions mainly as predicate; can also serve as attributive.

Note: Complimentary in meaning.

Near Synonyms: [同舟共济] (tóng zhōu gòng jì 同舟共濟) 'same boat together cross (river) – overcome difficulties together,' [有福同享] (yǒu fú tóng xiǎng 有福同享) 'when there is good fortune together enjoy it,' [有难同当] (yǒu nàn tóng dāng 有難同當) 'when there are hardships together confront them.'

Antonym: [同床异梦] (tóng chuáng yì mèng 同床異夢) 'same bed different dreams – work together but for different ends.'

386. 【明目张胆】(明目張膽) míng mù zhāng dǎn

明目 means 'open the eyes' and 张胆 means 'gather up one's courage.' The meaning of the whole idiom is 'open, flagrant, brazen.' This refers to doing bad things openly and brazenly.

Example 1: 这座城市的治安太差了，小偷竟然**明目张胆**地在大街上偷东西。

Zhè zuò chéngshì de zhì'ān tài chà le, xiǎotōu jìngrán míngmù-zhāngdǎn de zài dàjiē shàng tōu dōngxi.

'Law and order in this city are very much lacking, thieves actually stealing things brazenly on the open street.'

Example 2: 那个大国根本不顾联合国公约，**明目张胆**地侵略别的小国。

Nàge dà guó gēnběn bú gù Liánhéguó gōngyuē, míngmù-zhāngdǎn de qīnlüè biéde xiǎo guó.

'That great power doesn't give any consideration at all to United Nations covenants, brazenly invading other smaller countries.'

Usage: Functions as adverbial.

Note: Derogatory in meaning.

Near Synonyms: [明火执仗] (míng huǒ zhí zhàng 明火執仗) 'do evil openly,' [光天化日] (guāng tiān huà rì 光天化日) 'in broad daylight.'

Antonyms: [师出有名] (shī chū yǒu míng 師出有名) 'take action with just reasons,' [名正言顺] (míng zhèng yán shùn 名正言順) 'perfectly justifiable,' [鬼鬼祟祟] (guǐ guǐ suì suì 鬼鬼祟祟) 'furtive, stealthy.'

387. 【耳闻目睹】(耳聞目睹) ěr wén mù dǔ

耳 means 'ears,' 闻 means 'hear,' 目 means 'eyes,' and 睹 means 'see.' A literal translation of the whole idiom is 'ears hear and eyes see.' This refers to hearing something with one's own ears and seeing something with one's own eyes. A freer translation would be 'what one hears and sees, observe in person.'

Example 1: 这些年，他**耳闻目睹**了一些让人气愤的事。

Zhè xiē nián, tā ěrwén-mùdǔ le yìxiē ràng rén qìfèn de shì.

'These last few years, he has personally observed some things that would make people furious.'

Example 2: **耳闻目睹**这一切后，他感动了，发誓做一个好人。

Ěrwén-mùdǔ zhè yíqiè hòu, tā gǎndòng le, fāshì zuò yí ge hǎorén.

'After he had personally observed all this, he was moved, and swore to be a good person.'

Usage: Functions mainly as predicate.

Near Synonym: [耳濡目染] (ěr rú mù rǎn 耳濡目染) 'ears immersed and eyes contaminated – influenced by what one hears and sees.'

Antonym: [闭目塞听] (bì mù sè tīng 閉目塞聽) 'close eyes and block listening – oblivious to the world.'

388. 【啼笑皆非】(啼笑皆非) tí xiào jiē fēi

啼 means 'cry,' 皆 means 'both,' and 非 means 'is not.' The literal meaning is 'cry laugh both is not.' A freer translation of this idiom is 'not know whether it is better to laugh or cry, in an awkward situation.'

Example 1: 他很严肃地讲了一个老掉牙的笑话，让人**啼笑皆非**。

Tā hěn yánsù de jiǎngle yí ge lǎo diàoyá de xiàohua, ràng rén tíxiào-jiēfēi.

'He very seriously told an old joke, making people not know whether they should laugh or cry.'

Example 2: 他提出了一种让人**啼笑皆非**的理论。

Tā tíchūle yì zhǒng ràng rén tíxiào-jiēfēi de lǐlùn.

'He proposed a theory that put people in an awkward position.'

Usage: Functions mainly as predicate after 让人 (ràng rén 讓人) / 令人 (lìng rén) / 使人 (shǐ rén) 'make someone....'

Note: Derogatory in meaning.

Near Synonym: [哭笑不得] (kū xiào bù dé 哭笑不得) 'not know whether to laugh or cry.'

389. 【死灰复燃】(死灰復燃) sǐ huī fù rán

死灰 means 'dead ashes,' 复 means 'again,' and 燃 means 'burn.' A literal translation of the whole idiom is 'dead ashes burn again,' with freer translations being 'come back to life' and 'resurgence.'

Example 1: 冬天的时候，一些在夏天高温条件下已经"死亡"的病毒常常会**死灰复燃**。

Dōngtiān de shíhou, yìxiē zài xiàtiān gāowēn tiáojiàn xià yǐjīng sǐwáng de bìngdú chángcháng huì sǐhuī-fùrán.

'In winter time, some viruses that already "died" under the conditions of high temperatures in the summer will often return to life.'

Example 2: 毒品交易在这座城市有**死灰复燃**的迹象。

Dúpǐn jiāoyì zài zhè zuò chéngshì yǒu sǐhuī-fùrán de jìxiàng.

'Narcotics trafficking in this city has indications of a resurgence.'

Usage: Functions mainly as predicate; can also serve as attributive followed by nouns such as 现象 (xiànxiàng 現象) 'appearance,' 迹象 (jìxiàng 跡象) 'indication,' and 趋势 (qūshì 趨勢) 'tendency.'

Note: Derogatory in meaning.

Near Synonyms: [东山再起] (dōng shān zài qǐ 東山再起) '(from) East Mountain rise up again – stage a comeback,' [卷土重来] (juǎn tǔ chóng lái 捲土重來) 'bounce back, stage a comeback.'

390. 【塞翁失马】(塞翁失馬) sài wēng shī mǎ

塞 means 'frontier,' 翁 means 'old man,' and 失 means 'lose.' A literal translation of the whole idiom is 'an old man living at the frontier of his country lost his horse,' with freer translations being 'a loss may turn out to be a gain, a blessing in disguise.'

Example 1: 我虽然在赌场里输了不少钱，但是**塞翁失马**，焉知非福，或许我买的股票明天就大涨了。

Wǒ suīrán zài dǔchǎng lǐ shūle bùshǎo qián, dànshì sàiwēng-shīmǎ, yānzhī-fēifú, huòxǔ wǒ mǎi de gǔpiào míngtiān jiù dà zhǎng le.

'Although I lost much money at the casino, who knows if it's not a blessing in disguise; maybe the stocks I bought will rise greatly tomorrow.'

Example 2: 她失去了那份稳定的工作后被迫做起了小贩，谁知道竟然发了大财，真是**塞翁失马**，焉知非福！

Tā shīqùle nà fèn wěndìng de gōngzuò hòu bèipò zuòqǐle xiǎofàn, shuí zhīdao jìngrán fāle dàcái, zhēn shì sàiwēng-shīmǎ, yānzhī-fēifú!

'After she lost that stable job, she was forced to become a vendor; who would have thought that she would actually make a fortune? It really is true that misfortune can be a blessing in disguise!'

Usage: Functions mainly as predicate; can also serve as object. Often followed by 焉知非福 (yān zhī fēi fú) 'How do you know it is not a blessing?'

Allusion: A man who lived on the northern frontier of China was good at riding horses. One day, for no obvious reason, his horse ran away to the nomads across the border. Everyone tried to console him, but his father said: "What makes you so sure this isn't a blessing in disguise?" Some months later, his horse returned, bringing a splendid nomad horse with it. Everyone congratulated him, but his father said, "How do you know this will not end up in disaster?" Now, the son loved to ride. One day he fell and broke his hip. Everyone tried to console him, but his father said, "What makes you so sure this isn't a blessing in disguise?" A year later, the nomads came in great force across the border, every young man taking his bow and going into battle. The Chinese frontiersmen lost nine out of every ten men. It was only because the son was lame that the father and son survived to take care of one another. Truly, a blessing can become a disaster, and a disaster can become a blessing; changes have no end, nor can the mystery be fathomed.

Near Synonym: [因祸得福] (yīn huò dé fú 因祸得福) 'because of misfortune get luck – luck grows out of adversity.'

Antonyms: [祸不单行] (huò bù dān xíng 禍不單行) 'misfortune never comes alone, misery loves company,' [乐极生悲] (lè jí shēng bēi 樂極生悲) 'joy to highest degree generates sorrow – extreme joy begets sorrow.'

391. 【口口声声】(口口聲聲) kǒu kǒu shēng shēng

口 means 'mouth' and 声 means 'voice.' The meaning of the whole idiom is 'say over and over again.'

Example 1: 上台以前，他**口口声声**地说要大胆改革，可是上台以后却没有什么行动。

Shàngtái yǐqián, tā kǒukǒu-shēngshēng de shuō yào dàdǎn gǎigé, kěshì shàngtái yǐhòu què méiyǒu shénme xíngdòng.

'Before assuming power, he said over and over again that he wanted to boldly undertake reforms, but after assuming power, he didn't take any action.'

Example 2: 她对我很客气，虽然只跟我学过几天，但是以后见面的时候**口口声声**地叫我老师。

Tā duì wǒ hěn kèqi, suīrán zhǐ gēn wǒ xuéguo jǐ tiān, dànshì yǐhòu jiànmiàn de shíhou kǒukǒu-shēngshēng de jiào wǒ lǎoshī.

'She is very polite toward me; though she had only studied with me for a few days, later when she saw me she would again and again call me "Teacher."'

Usage: Functions as adverbial.

Note: Sometimes derogatory in meaning.

Near Synonym: [信誓旦旦] (xìn shì dàn dàn 信誓旦旦) 'make a solemn pledge.'

Antonym: [绝口不提] (jué kǒu bù tí 絕口不提) 'stop talking about and never mention again.'

392. 【水落石出】(水落石出) shuǐ luò shí chū

落 means 'fall, recede.' The literal meaning is 'when the water recedes, the rocks (that are hidden under the water) will appear.' The extended meaning is 'come to light, get to the bottom of, the truth is revealed.'

Example 1: 我一定要把这个事情查个**水落石出**。

Wǒ yídìng yào bǎ zhège shìqing chá ge shuǐluò-shíchū.

'I'm definitely going to get to the bottom of this matter.'

Example 2: 经过数百检察人员几个月的调查，这起案件终于**水落石出**了。

Jīngguò shù bǎi jiǎnchá rényuán jǐ ge yuè de diàochá, zhè qǐ ànjiàn zhōngyú shuǐluò-shíchū le.

'After several months of investigations by several hundred investigators, the truth about this case is finally coming to light.'

Usage: Functions mainly as complement for the verb phrases 查个 . . . (chá ge 查個) 'investigate' and 弄个 . . . (nòng ge 弄個) 'handle.'

Near Synonyms: [真相大白] (zhēn xiàng dà bái 真相大白) 'everything is now clear, the whole truth is out,' [原形毕露] (yuán xíng bì lù 原形畢露) 'reveal one's true colors' (derogatory).

Antonym: [不明不白] (bù míng bù bái 不明不白) 'ambiguous, murky.'

393. 【我行我素】(我行我素) wǒ xíng wǒ sù

行 means 'walk' and 素 means 'always.' The idea is that however you always did things in the past, you will still do things that way now without changing them. A freer translation is 'stick to one's own way of doing things.'

Example 1: 在中央发布文件以后，下边有些地方政府依然**我行我素**，不把中央的文件放在眼里。

Zài zhōngyāng fābù wénjiàn yǐhòu, xiàbiān yǒu xiē dìfāng zhèngfǔ yīrán wǒxíng-wǒsù, bù bǎ zhōngyāng de wénjiàn fàng zài yǎn lǐ.

'After the central authorities promulgated the document, at the lower levels in some places the government still stuck to its own way of doing things, not paying attention to the central authorities' document.'

Example 2: 她在学校里**我行我素**，开始的时候大家不接受她，后来都觉得她很酷。

Tā zài xuéxiào lǐ wǒxíng-wǒsù, kāishǐ de shíhou dàjiā bù jiēshòu tā, hòulái dōu juéde tā hěn kù.

'In school she did things her own way; at the beginning, everybody didn't accept her; later they all felt she was cool.'

Usage: Functions mainly as predicate and attributive.

Note: In the past was usually derogatory in meaning but that sense has become weaker. When describing an individual, can now sometimes even be complimentary.

Near Synonym: [特立独行] (tè lì dú xíng 特立獨行) 'individualistic.'

Antonym: [言听计从] (yán tīng jì cóng 言聽計從) 'listen to someone's words and follow someone's plan – follow someone's advice.'

394. 【望而却步】(望而卻步) wàng ér què bù

望 means 'see,' 却 means 'stop,' and 步 means 'step.' A literal translation of the whole idiom is 'see something and stop one's steps,' with freer translations being 'shrink back at the sight of, flinch, frightened.'

Example 1: 那家高档饭店的菜价高得离谱，使人**望而却步**。

Nà jiā gāodàng fàndiàn de càijià gāo de lípǔ, shǐ rén wàng'érquèbù.

'The price of meals at that upmarket restaurant is unreasonably high; it makes people flinch when they see it.'

Example 2: 虽然那块地皮非常好，但是土地的拥有者开口就要两亿美元，令原本许多感兴趣的人**望而却步**。

Suīrán nà kuài dìpí fēicháng hǎo, dànshì tǔdì de yōngyǒuzhě kāikǒu jiù yào liǎng yì Měiyuán, lìng yuánběn xǔduō gǎnxìngqù de rén wàng'érquèbù.

'Although that piece of land is well located, the land owner has asked a starting price of 200 million U.S. dollars; it makes many people who were originally interested flinch upon hearing it.'

Usage: Functions mainly as predicate in structures such as 使人～ (shǐ rén ...) / 令人～ (lìng rén ...) / 让人～ (ràng rén ... 讓人～) / 叫人～ (jiào rén ...) 'make someone'; can also serve by itself as predicate.

Near Synonyms: [畏缩不前] (wèi suō bù qián 畏縮不前) 'afraid to advance,' [停滞不前] (tíng zhì bù qián 停滯不前) 'stop and stagnate and not advance – come to a standstill, get bogged down.'

Antonym: [勇往直前] (yǒng wǎng zhí qián 勇往直前) 'courageously go straight ahead – advance bravely.'

395. 【有血有肉】 (有血有肉) yǒu xuè yǒu ròu

血 means 'blood' and 肉 means 'flesh.' A literal translation of the whole idiom is 'have blood have flesh,' with a freer translation being 'vivid, lifelike.'

Example 1: 那本长篇小说成功地塑造了几十个**有血有肉**的人物形象。

Nà běn chángpiān xiǎoshuō chénggōng de sùzàole jǐ shí ge yǒuxuè-yǒuròu de rénwù xíngxiàng.

'That novel successfully depicts several dozen vivid and lifelike character images.'

Example 2: 文革时期人们把毛泽东神化了，其实他也是一个**有血有肉**的人，而不是神。

Wén'gé shíqī rénmen bǎ Máo Zédōng shénhuàle, qíshí tā yě shì yí ge yǒuxuè-yǒuròu de rén, ér bú shì shén.

'During the period of the Cultural Revolution, people deified Mao Zedong; actually, he also was a person of blood and flesh, not a god.'

Usage: Functions mainly as attributive.

Note: Complimentary in meaning.

Near Synonyms: [活灵活现] (huó líng huó xiàn 活靈活現) 'vivid, lifelike,' [呼之欲出] (hū zhī yù chū 呼之欲出) 'call it and it wants to pop out – vivid,' [栩栩如生] (xǔ xǔ rú shēng 栩栩如生) 'lifelike.'

Antonyms: [半死不活] (bàn sǐ bù huó 半死不活) 'half-dead,' [死气沉沉] (sǐ qì chén chén 死氣沉沉) 'lifeless.'

396. 【天涯海角】 (天涯海角) tiān yá hǎi jiǎo

涯 means 'edge' and 角 means 'corner.' The literal meaning of this idiom is 'heaven's edges and sea's corners,' with a freer translation being 'the ends of the earth, a very distant place, far away.'

Example 1: 无论你走到**天涯海角**，你的亲人永远关心你。

Wúlùn nǐ zǒu dào tiānyá-hǎijiǎo, nǐ de qīnrén yǒngyuǎn guānxīn nǐ.

'No matter if you go to the ends of the earth, your family will forever be concerned about you.'

Example 2: 同班同学毕业以后奔向**天涯海角**，各自找到自己的落脚点。

Tóngbān tóngxué bìyè yǐhòu bēnxiàng tiānyá-hǎijiǎo, gèzì zhǎodào zìjǐ de luòjiǎodiǎn.

'After graduation the classmates rushed off to far away places, each finding his or her own foothold.'

Usage: Functions mainly as object.

Note: Also occurs as 海角天涯 (hǎi jiǎo tiān yá). Note that in Hainan Province there is a scenic spot named 天涯海角 (tiān yá hǎi jiǎo).

Near Synonyms: [天南地北] (tiān nán dì běi 天南地北) 'far apart,' [天南海北] (tiān nán hǎi běi 天南海北) 'all over the place.'

Antonyms: [近在咫尺] (jìn zài zhǐ chǐ 近在咫尺) 'close at hand,' [咫尺之遥] (zhǐ chǐ zhī yáo 咫尺之遥) 'very close,' [一衣带水] (yī yī dài shuǐ 一衣带水) 'narrow strip of water in between.'

397. 【轻描淡写】(輕描淡寫) qīng miáo dàn xiě

轻 means 'lightly,' 描 means 'trace,' 淡 means 'light (as in color),' and 写 here means 'paint.' The literal meaning of this idiom is 'paint in light colors.' The extended meaning is 'treat a matter lightly and superficially, mention casually.'

Example 1: 别人很关心地问她，她却**轻描淡写**地说，"没事儿，一切都过去了。"

Biérén hěn guānxīn de wèn tā, tā què qīngmiáo-dànxiě de shuō, "Méi shìr, yíqiè dōu guòqùle."

'When others asked her with great concern, she just said casually, "It's nothing, it has all passed now."'

Example 2: 因为他平时的表现很好，所以虽然这次犯了错误，但是领导只是**轻描淡写**地批评了几句。

Yīnwèi tā píngshí de biǎoxiàn hěn hǎo, suǒyǐ suīrán zhè cì fànle cuòwù, dànshì lǐngdǎo zhǐ shì qīngmiáo-dànxiě de pīpíngle jǐ jù.

'Because his normal performance was very good, even though he made a mistake this time, his boss only superficially criticized him in a few sentences.'

Usage: Functions mainly as adverbial; can also serve as predicate.

Antonym: [小题大做] (xiǎo tí dà zuò 小题大做) 'make much ado about nothing.'

398. 【哭笑不得】(哭笑不得) kū xiào bù dé

得 means 'appropriate.' The meaning of the whole idiom is 'not know whether to cry or laugh.'

Example 1: 他的话弄得大家**哭笑不得**。

Tā de huà nòng de dàjiā kūxiào-bùdé.

'What he said made everyone not know whether it was appropriate to laugh or to cry.'

Example 2: 孙子的话把爷爷气得**哭笑不得**。

Sūnzi de huà bǎ yéye qì de kūxiào-bùdé.

'What the grandson said made the grandfather so angry that he didn't know whether he should laugh or cry.'

Usage: Functions mainly as complement. Often appears in the structure 让 (ràng 讓) | 使 (shǐ) | 弄 (nòng) | 令 (lìng) + 得 (de) + person + 哭笑不得.

Note: Tends to be used in spoken language.

Near Synonym: [啼笑皆非] (tí xiào jiē fēi 啼笑皆非) 'not know whether to cry or laugh.'

Antonym: [一脸正经] (yì liǎn zhèng jīng 一臉正經) 'with a serious face.'

399. 【自告奋勇】(自告奮勇) zì gào fèn yǒng

告 means 'tell, indicate' and 奋勇 means 'marshal all one's energy and courage.' A literal translation is 'oneself to indicate one's energy and courage.' Freer translations include 'offer to undertake a difficult or dangerous task, volunteer.'

Example 1: 他**自告奋勇**免费给外国人当导游。

Tā zìgào-fènyǒng miǎnfèi gěi wàiguórén dāng dǎoyóu.

'He voluntarily and free of charge serves as a tour guide for foreigners.'

Example 2: 他**自告奋勇**地说，"你就放心吧，这件事交给我了。"

Tā zìgào-fènyǒng de shuō, "Nǐ jiù fàngxīn ba, zhè jiàn shì jiāo gěi wǒ le."

'Offering to undertake a difficult task, he said, "Don't you worry, hand this matter over to me."'

Usage: Functions mainly as predicate and adverbial.

Note: Complimentary in meaning.

Near Synonym: [毛遂自荐] (Máo Suí zì jiàn 毛遂自薦) 'volunteer.'

Antonym: [畏首畏尾] (wèi shǒu wèi wěi 畏首畏尾) 'fear head fear tail – fraught with uncertainty, overcautious.'

400. 【指鹿为马】(指鹿為馬) zhǐ lù wéi mǎ

指 means 'point at' and 鹿 means 'deer.' A literal translation of the whole idiom is 'point at a deer and say it's a horse.' This is a metaphor for 'purposely confuse right and wrong,' 'misrepresent something,' or 'distort the facts.'

Example 1: 他用**指鹿为马**的伎俩打击了一大批反对他的人。

Tā yòng zhǐlù-wéimǎ de jìliǎng dǎjīle yí dà pī fǎnduì tā de rén.

'He used the trick of distorting the facts and attacked a large number of people who were opposing him.'

Example 2: 那个国家的某个时代曾经没有一点公正，到了**指鹿为马**的地步。

Nàge guójiā de mǒu ge shídài céngjīng méiyǒu yìdiǎn gōngzhèng, dàole zhǐlù-wéimǎ de dìbù.

'During a certain period in that country there was a time when there was no justice at all, when it had reached the stage of confusing right and wrong.'

Usage: Functions mainly as attributive and predicate.

Allusion: In the year 207 B.C.E., Zhao Gao, the prime minister of the state of Qin, wanted to plot a rebellion; but he was worried that the ministers of state would not obey him, so he thought of a way to test them in advance. He offered a deer to the emperor, saying "This is a horse." The emperor laughed and said: "You're wrong, saying that a deer is a horse." So Zhao Gao then asked the ministers of state. Some ministers said it was a deer, others didn't say anything, and still others said it was a horse so as to curry favor with Zhao Gao. When this all was over, Zhao Gao found pretexts to frame those ministers who had said it was a deer. Later there wasn't a single minister who did not fear Zhao Gao. (from "Qinshihuang Ben Ji" in *Records of the Grand Historian*)

Note: Derogatory in meaning.

Near Synonyms: [颠倒黑白] (diān dǎo hēi bái 顛倒黑白) 'turn black and white upside down – distort the facts,' [颠倒是非] (diān dǎo shì fēi 顛倒是非) or [混淆是非] (hùn xiáo shì fēi 混淆是非) 'confuse right and wrong,' [混淆视听] (hùn xiáo shì tīng 混淆視聽) 'mislead the public.'

Antonym: [实事求是] (shí shì qiú shì 實事求是) 'seek truth from facts.'

401. 【设身处地】(設身處地) shè shēn chǔ dì

设 here means 'assume, imagine,' 身 means 'oneself,' 处 means 'in (a certain situation),' and 地 means 'position, circumstances.' The literal meaning is 'assume that oneself is in someone else's position,' with a freer translation being 'put oneself in someone else's shoes, think from someone else's standpoint, take someone else's interests into consideration.'

Example 1: 制造商应该为消费者**设身处地**地想想，怎么样才能给他们带来更大的方便。

Zhìzàoshāng yīnggāi wèi xiāofèizhě shèshēn-chǔdì de xiǎngxiǎng, zěnmeyàng cái néng gěi tāmen dàilái gèng dà de fāngbiàn.

'Manufacturers should put themselves in the other person's shoes and think of the consumers; how they can bring them even greater convenience.'

Example 2: 你**设身处地**地想想，就不难理解对方为什么那样做了。

Nǐ shèshēn-chǔdì de xiǎngxiǎng, jiù bù nán lǐjiě duìfāng wèishénme nàyàng zuòle.

'If you put yourself in the other side's shoes, then it is not hard to understand why the other side did that.'

Usage: Functions mainly as adverbial. Often preceded by 为 (某人) (wèi [mǒu rén] 為[某人]) 'for (someone)' and followed by verbs meaning 'think,' such as 想想 (xiǎngxiǎng) and 思考 (sīkǎo).

Near Synonym: [将心比心] (jiāng xīn bǐ xīn 將心比心) 'have sympathy for others.'

Antonyms: [无所顾忌] (wú suǒ gù jì 無所顧忌) 'have no scruples or misgivings,' [不管不顾] (bù guǎn bú gù 不管不顧) 'disregard everything, without scruples.'

402. 【天方夜谭】(天方夜譚) Tiānfāng yè tán

天方 means 'Arabian' and 夜谭 means 'night talk.' The literal meaning of this idiom is 'Arabian Night Talks,' the Chinese title of the book known in English as *Arabian Nights* or *One Thousand and One Nights*. This expression has, by metaphor, gained the extended meaning of 'strange and incredible story or comment.'

Example 1: 一个三岁的孩子能够写长篇小说？这简直是**天方夜谭**。

Yí ge sān suì de háizi nénggòu xiě chángpiān xiǎoshuō? Zhè jiǎnzhí shì Tiānfāng-yètán.

'A three-year-old child can write novels? This is simply a strange and incredible story.'

Example 2: 倒退五十年，奥巴马成为总统是**天方夜谭**般的事。

Dàotuì wǔshí nián, Àobāmǎ chéngwéi zǒngtǒng shì Tiānfāng-yètán bān de shì.

'If you go back fifty years, for Obama to become President would be as incredible as a story from the *Arabian Nights*.'

Usage: Functions mainly as predicate after 是 (shì) 'be.'

Near Synonyms: [无稽之谈] (wú jī zhī tán 無稽之談) 'nonsensical talk,' [子虚乌有] (zǐ xū wū yǒu 子虛烏有) 'sheer fiction,' [胡说八道] (hú shuō bā dào 胡說八道) 'talk nonsense' (in speech).

Antonym: [引经据典] (yǐn jīng jù diǎn 引經據典) 'quote the classics.'

403. 【雅俗共赏】(雅俗共賞) yǎ sú gòng shǎng

雅 here means 'cultured or refined people,' 俗 means 'ordinary people,' and 赏 means 'appreciate, enjoy.' A literal translation of this idiom is 'cultured people and ordinary people can all enjoy it,' with a freer translation being 'appeal to both cultured and popular tastes.'

Example 1:《007》可以说是一系列**雅俗共赏**的电影。

007 kěyǐ shuō shì yí xìliè yǎsú-gòngshǎng de diànyǐng.

'007 can be said to be a series of films enjoyed by both cultured and ordinary people.'

Example 2: 乡村音乐称得上是**雅俗共赏**。

Xiāngcūn yīnyuè chēngdeshàng shì yǎsú-gòngshǎng.

'Country music can be said to be something enjoyed by both cultured and ordinary people alike.'

Usage: Functions mainly as attributive and predicate.

Note: Complimentary in meaning.

Near Synonym: [老少咸宜] (lǎo shào xián yí 老少咸宜) 'suitable for both old and young.'

Antonym: [曲高和寡] (qǔ gāo hè guǎ 曲高和寡) 'the higher the melody the fewer the singers.'

404. 【无所适从】(無所適從) wú suǒ shì cóng

适 here means 'go' and 从 means 'follow.' A literal translation of the whole idiom is 'have nowhere to go and nothing to follow,' with freer translations being 'at a loss how to proceed, not know what to do.'

Example 1: 孩子以前总有父母照顾，现在独立生活，往往会感到**无所适从**。

Háizi yǐqián zǒng yǒu fùmǔ zhàogù, xiànzài dúlì shēnghuó, wǎngwǎng huì gǎndào wúsuǒshìcóng.

'Before the child always had her parents to look after her, now she lives independently; she often feels at a loss about what to do.'

Example 2: 前任领导定下了一套规矩，新任领导又定下了另一套规矩，搞得员工们**无所适从**。

Qiánrèn lǐngdǎo dìngxiàle yí tào guīju, xīnrèn lǐngdǎo yòu dìngxiàle lìng yí tào guīju, gǎode yuángōngmen wúsuǒshìcóng.

'The former leader made up one set of rules, and the new leader made up another set of rules, making it so that the employees were at a loss about how to proceed.'

Usage: Functions mainly as predicate.

Near Synonym: [不知所措] (bù zhī suǒ cuò 不知所措) 'not know what to do.'

Antonyms: [萧规曹随] (Xiāo guī Cáo suí 蕭規曹隨) 'Xiao's rules Cao (the famous general) follows – abide by the rules laid down by one's predecessor,' [上行下效] (shàng xíng xià xiào 上行下效) 'the actions of superiors are imitated by subordinates,' [照猫画虎] (zhào māo huà hǔ 照貓畫虎) 'draw a tiger with a cat as a model – follow a model' (spoken style).

405. 【不容置疑】(不容置疑) bù róng zhì yí

容 means 'allow' and 置疑 means 'raise doubts.' The whole idiom means 'allow no doubts, undeniable.'

Example 1: 她的文章材料丰富，论证合理，结论**不容置疑**。

Tā de wénzhāng cáiliào fēngfù, lùnzhèng hélǐ, jiélùn bùróng-zhìyí.

'She has abundant data for her article and her proof is convincing; the conclusion is undeniable.'

Example 2: 不少人认为毛泽东的话句句是真理，是**不容置疑**的。

Bùshǎo rén rènwéi Máo Zédōng de huà jù jù shì zhēnlǐ, shì bùróng-zhìyí de.

'Many people believed that every one of Mao Zedong's words was the truth; this is undeniable.'

Usage: Functions mainly as predicate and attributive.

Note: [毋庸置疑] (wù yōng zhì yí 毋庸置疑) and [无庸置疑] (wú yōng zhì yí 無庸置疑) are more formal, written equivalents.

Near Synonym: [千真万确] (qiān zhēn wàn què 千真萬確) 'absolutely true.'

Antonym: [荒诞不经] (huāng dàn bù jīng 荒誕不經) 'fantastic, incredible.'

406. 【流连忘返】(流連忘返) liú lián wàng fǎn

流连 means 'cannot bear to leave, linger,' 忘 means 'forget,' and 返 means 'return.' A literal translation of the whole idiom is 'unwilling to leave and forget to return.' Freer translations of the idiom include 'enjoy oneself so much as to forget to return home, hate to leave.'

Example 1: 阿尔卑斯山的风景美得跟画一样，真让人**流连忘返**。

Ā'ěrbēisī Shān de fēngjǐng měi de gēn huà yíyàng, zhēn ràng rén liúlián-wàngfǎn.

'The scenery in the Alps is as beautiful as a painting; it really makes people unwilling to leave and return home.'

Example 2: 迪斯尼乐园好玩极了，令孩子们**流连忘返**。

Dísīní lèyuán hǎowán jí le, lìng háizǐmen liúlián-wàngfǎn.

'Disney World is so much fun; it makes children feel that they don't want to leave.'

Usage: Functions as predicate.

Near Synonyms: [恋恋不舍] (liàn liàn bù shě 戀戀不捨) 'reluctant to part from,' [依依不舍] (yī yī bù shě 依依不捨) 'feel a sense of regret when leaving,' [乐不思蜀]

(lè bù sī Shǔ 樂不思蜀) 'so happy one doesn't think of the ancient state of Shu – so happy as to forget home and duty.'

407. 【翻来覆去】(翻來覆去) fān lái fù qù

翻 means 'turn over' and 覆 means 'turn back around.' The whole idiom can have two different meanings: 'turn over back and forth, toss and turn' (as when sleeping) or 'repeat something again and again.'

Example 1: 晚上，她**翻来覆去**睡不好觉，想不出一个好法子。

Wǎnshàng, tā fānlái-fùqù shuìbùhǎo jiào, xiǎngbùchū yí ge hǎo fǎzi.

'At night, she tossed and turned, not being able to sleep well; she couldn't think of any good way (to deal with her problem).'

Example 2: 他的那个笑话**翻来覆去**地用了好几年了，一点儿都不可笑了。

Tā de nàge xiàohuà fānlái-fùqù de yòngle hǎo jǐ nián le, yìdiǎr dōu bù kěxiào le.

'He has been using that joke of his over and over again for a number of years now; it's not at all funny any more.'

Usage: Functions mainly as adverbial.

Near Synonym: [辗转反侧] (zhǎn zhuǎn fǎn cè 輾轉反側) 'toss and turn (because one is unable to sleep).'

Antonym: [一锤定音] (yì chuí dìng yīn 一錘定音) 'with one beat of the gong to set the tune – have the final word.'

408. 【无中生有】(無中生有) wú zhōng shēng yǒu

A literal translation of this idiom is 'in the midst of nothing there is engendered something.' It is frequently translated as 'fabricated, groundless.'

Example 1: 狗仔队常常**无中生有**，编造娱乐明星的各种小道消息。

Gǒuzǎiduì chángcháng wúzhōng-shēngyǒu, biānzào yúlè míngxīng de gè zhǒng xiǎodào xiāoxi.

'Paparazzi often create rumors out of nothing, fabricating all kinds of hearsay about stars from the entertainment world.'

Example 2: 面对**无中生有**的谣言，他根本不在乎。

Miànduì wúzhōng-shēngyǒu de yáoyán, tā gēnběn bú zàihu.

'Facing groundless rumors, he didn't pay any attention at all.'

Usage: Functions mainly as predicate, attributive, and adverbial.

Note: Derogatory in meaning.

Near Synonyms: [无事生非] (wú shì shēng fēi 無事生非) 'when there are no problematic matters give birth to trouble – create problems when none exist,' [颠倒黑白] (diān dǎo hēi bái 顛倒黑白) 'turn black and white upside down – distort the facts,' [信口雌黄] (xìn kǒu cí huáng 信口雌黄) 'talk irresponsibly.'

Antonyms: [铁证如山] (tiě zhèng rú shān 鐵證如山) 'iron evidence like a mountain – ironclad evidence,' [板上钉钉] (bǎn shàng dìng dīng 板上釘釘) 'nail nails into a plank – definite, fixed.'

409. 【庞然大物】(龐然大物) páng rán dà wù

庞然 means 'gigantic' and 大物 means 'big thing.' The meaning of the whole idiom is 'a monster, a giant, a colossus.'

Example 1: 波音747飞机是个**庞然大物**，里面可以载四百多名乘客。

Bōyīn 747 fēijī shì ge **pángrán-dàwù**, lǐmiàn kěyǐ zài sì bǎi duō míng chéngkè.

'A Boeing 747 is a colossus, which on the inside can carry over 400 passengers.'

Example 2: 沃尔玛在零售市场业中是个**庞然大物**，没有公司能动摇她的地位。

Wò'ěrmǎ zài língshòu shìchǎngyè zhōng shì ge **pángrán-dàwù**, méiyǒu gōngsī néng dòngyáo tā de dìwèi.

'Walmart is a giant in the retail industry whose position no company can shake.'

Usage: Nominal element, functions mainly as object.

Note: Slightly derogatory in meaning.

Near Synonym: [硕大无朋] (shuò dà wú péng 碩大無朋) 'unequalled in size.'

Antonym: [微乎其微] (wēi hū qí wēi 微乎其微) 'very little, next to nothing.'

410. 【黔驴技穷】(黔驢技窮) Qián lǘ jì qióng

黔 is an ancient name for Guizhou Province, 驴 means 'donkey,' 技 means 'skill,' and 穷 means 'exhaust.' A literal translation is 'the Guizhou donkey's skills have been exhausted,' with a freer translation being 'exhaust one's (limited) bag of tricks' or 'have used up all the (limited) skills that one possesses.'

Example 1: 他已经**黔驴技穷**了，不过，要小心他狗急了跳墙，做出一些违法的事。

Tā yǐjīng **Qiánlǘ-jìqióng** le, búguò, yào xiǎoxīn tā gǒu jíle tiàoqiáng, zuòchū yìxiē wéifǎ de shì.

'He has already used up his bag of tricks; however, we have to be careful lest he gets desperate and does something illegal.'

Example 2: **黔驴技穷**的她只好承认自己失败了。

Qiánlǘ-jìqióng de tā zhǐhǎo chéngrèn zìjǐ shībàile.

'She, having used up her bag of tricks, had no choice but to admit defeat.'

Usage: Functions mainly as predicate and attributive.

Allusion: It is said that in Guizhou and vicinity there are no donkeys. A troublemaker once used a boat to bring in a donkey from the outside, but when it arrived, it proved to be of no use, so the troublemaker set the donkey free in the mountains. A tiger saw it and considered the donkey to be a very large animal; thinking that it must be a god, the tiger only dared to hide in the forest and watch the donkey secretly. Later, the tiger slowly approached the donkey but was very careful, since it didn't know what the donkey really was. One day the donkey brayed loudly, frightening the tiger, which thought the donkey wanted to eat it, so the tiger fled far away. But the tiger, observing everything closely from afar, felt that the donkey did not possess any outstanding talent. Moreover, the tiger slowly became accustomed to the donkey's braying and once again began approaching the donkey, though it still didn't dare to fight with it. Finally, the tiger slowly approached the donkey, its attitude no longer so solemn, and purposely collided with the donkey so as to provoke it. The donkey was furious and with its hoofs kicked the tiger. Now the tiger was glad, thinking: "This is all the talent it's got?" And so the tiger jumped high, roared loudly, and bit and broke the donkey's neck, eating up all its flesh, after which it left. (from "The Donkey of Qin" in *Three Things to Abstain From* by Liu Zongyuan, Tang Dynasty)

Note: Derogatory in meaning.

Near Synonyms: [无计可施] (wú jì kě shī 無計可施) 'at one's wit's end' (neutral in meaning), [束手无策] (shù shǒu wú cè 束手無策) 'at a complete loss about what to do' (neutral in meaning).

Antonym: [神通广大] (shén tōng guǎng dà 神通廣大) 'all-powerful, omnipotent.'

411. 【三三两两】(三三兩兩) sān sān liǎng liǎng

The literal meaning is 'three three two two,' with a freer translation being 'in twos and threes, not many people.'

Example 1: 因为太早，集市上冷冷清清，只能看到三三**两两**的人群。

Yīnwèi tài zǎo, jíshì shàng lěnglěng qīngqīng, zhǐ néng kàndào sānsān-liǎngliǎng de rénqún.

'Because it was too early, the market was deserted, one only being able to see small groups of people in twos and threes.'

Example 2: 晚会开始前的半个小时，大家三三**两两**地来到了现场。

Wǎnhuì kāishǐ qián de bàn ge xiǎoshí, dàjiā sānsān-liǎngliǎng de láidàole xiànchǎng.

'During the half hour before the party started, everyone arrived on the scene in groups of two and three.'

Usage: Functions mainly as attributive and adverbial.

Near Synonym: [稀稀拉拉] (xī xī lā lā 稀稀拉拉) 'sparse, scattered.'

Antonym: [川流不息] (chuān liú bù xī 川流不息) 'continuous flow without stopping (of people or traffic).'

412. 【发号施令】(發號施令) fā hào shī lìng

Both 号 and 令 mean 'a command, an order' while 施 means 'carry out, execute.' The meaning of the whole idiom is 'give orders, boss people around.'

Example 1: 每个国家的主权都平等，我们不接受任何国家对我们**发号施令**。

Měi ge guójiā de zhǔquán dōu píngděng, wǒmen bù jiēshòu rènhé guójiā duì wǒmen fāhào-shīlìng.

'Every country's sovereignty is equal, so we don't accept any country's giving us orders.'

Example 2: 当领导的**发号施令**后，手下的人就开始忙了。

Dāng lǐngdǎo de fāhào-shīlìng hòu, shǒuxià de rén jiù kāishǐ máng le.

'After the leader had given her orders, the subordinates began their work.'

Usage: Functions mainly as predicate and attributive.

Near Synonyms: [调兵遣将] (diào bīng qiǎn jiàng 調兵遣將) 'transfer troops and dispatch generals – make good use of personnel,' [颐指气使] (yí zhǐ qì shǐ 頤指氣使) 'arrogant and bossy.'

Antonym: [唯唯诺诺] (wéi wéi nuò nuò 唯唯諾諾) 'a yes-man.'

413. 【心旷神怡】(心曠神怡) xīn kuàng shén yí

旷 means 'open,' 神 means 'spirits,' and 怡 means 'happy.' A literal translation of this idiom is 'heart open spirits happy,' with a freer translation being 'relaxed and joyful, cheerful and happy.'

Example 1: 黄石公园风景优美，使人**心旷神怡**。

Huángshí Gōngyuán fēngjǐng yōuměi, shǐ rén xīnkuàng-shényí.

'The scenery in Yellowstone National Park is exquisite, making one feel open and relaxed in one's heart and joyful in one's spirits.'

Example 2: 行走在巴黎的街道上，一边听着缓缓的古典音乐，一边慢慢地欣赏着美丽的街景，真的令人**心旷神怡**。

Xíngzǒu zài Bālí de jiēdào shàng, yìbiān tīngzhe huǎnhuǎn de gǔdiǎn yīnyuè, yìbiān mànmàn de xīnshǎngzhe měilì de jiējǐng, zhēn de lìng rén xīnkuàng-shényí.

'Walking on the streets of Paris, on the one hand listening to the leisurely classical music and on the other hand unhurriedly appreciating the beautiful sights on the streets, really does make one relaxed and joyful.'

Usage: Used mostly after the causative verbs 使 (shǐ), 让 (ràng 讓), and 令 (lìng), all of which mean 'cause or make (someone something).'

Note: Complimentary in meaning.

Near Synonyms: [赏心悦目] (shǎng xīn yuè mù 賞心悅目) 'pleasing to the mind and eye,' [悠然自得] (yōu rán zì dé 悠然自得) 'content and leisurely.'

Antonym: [心烦意乱] (xīn fán yì luàn 心煩意亂) 'worried and upset.'

414. 【雷厉风行】(雷厲風行) léi lì fēng xíng

雷 means 'thunder,' 厉 means 'violence,' and 行 here means 'swift.' A literal translation of the whole idiom is 'as violent as thunder and as swift as wind,' with a freer translation being 'vigorous and resolute, in a sweeping manner.'

Example 1: 他在军队里养成了**雷厉风行**的作风。

Tā zài jūnduì lǐ yǎngchéngle léilì-fēngxíng de zuòfeng.

'He cultivated a vigorous and resolute manner in the military.'

Example 2: 他做事**雷厉风行**，说干就干。

Tā zuòshì léilì-fēngxíng, shuō gàn jiù gàn.

'He has a vigorous and resolute manner in his work, and does what he promises.'

Usage: Functions mainly as predicate and attributive.

Note: Complimentary in meaning.

Near Synonyms: [大张旗鼓] (dà zhāng qí gǔ 大張旗鼓) 'openly show flags and bang drums – with a lot of fanfare,' [干净利落] (gān jìng lì luò 干淨利落) 'neat and tidy – very efficient.'

Antonyms: [拖泥带水] (tuō ní dài shuǐ 拖泥帶水) 'drag through mud and water – do things sloppily,' [优柔寡断] (yōu róu guǎ duàn 優柔寡斷) 'irresolute and hesitant, indecisive.'

415. 【朝夕相处】(朝夕相處) zhāo xī xiāng chǔ

朝 means 'morning,' 夕 means 'evening,' and 相处 means 'live together.' The meaning of the whole idiom is 'constantly together.'

Example 1: 他们在同一所学校里，**朝夕相处**，后来产生了爱情。

Tāmen zài tóng yì suǒ xuéxiào lǐ zhāoxī-xiāngchǔ, hòulái chǎnshēngle àiqíng.

'They were in the same school, constantly together, and later they fell in love.'

Example 2: 就要告别**朝夕相处**的教练，运动员们禁不住哭了。

Jiù yào gàobié **zhāoxī-xiāngchǔ** de jiàoliàn, yùndòngyuánmen jīnbúzhù kū le.

'When they were about to take leave of their coach, with whom they had been together night and day for such a long time, the athletes couldn't help but cry.'

Usage: Functions mainly as predicate and attributive; can also serve as adverbial.

Near Synonym: [形影不离] (xíng yǐng bù lí 形影不離) 'as inseparable as body and shadow.'

Antonym: [聚少离多] (jù shǎo lí duō 聚少離多) 'apart most of the time.'

416. 【踌躇满志】(躊躇滿志) chóu chú mǎn zhì

踌躇 means 'pleased with oneself,' 满 means 'content,' and 志 means 'ideals.' The meaning of the whole idiom is 'self-satisfied, puffed up with pride.'

Example 1: 她在数万人的大会上兴奋地演讲，一副**踌躇满志**的样子。

Tā zài shù wàn rén de dàhuì shàng xīngfèn de yǎnjiǎng, yí fù **chóuchú-mǎnzhì** de yàngzi.

'At a mass meeting of tens of thousands of people, she lectured excitedly, with a smug expression on her face.'

Example 2: 总统在就职典礼上大谈他会如何如何改革，对未来**踌躇满志**。

Zǒngtǒng zài jiùzhí diǎnlǐ shàng dà tán tā huì rúhé rúhé gǎigé, duì wèilái **chóuchú-mǎnzhì**.

'At the inauguration, the president spoke on and on about how he would reform things, puffed up with pride about the future.'

Usage: Functions as predicate, adverbial, and attributive.

Note: Complimentary in meaning.

Near Synonym: [心满意足] (xīn mǎn yì zú 心滿意足) 'completely satisfied.'

Antonym: [垂头丧气] (chuí tóu sàng qì 垂頭喪氣) 'hang one's head in dejection.'

417. 【金碧辉煌】(金碧輝煌) jīn bì huī huáng

金碧 means 'gold and green pigments' and 辉煌 means 'glorious, magnificent.' The meaning of the whole idiom is 'resplendent in bright colors.'

Example 1: 故宫**金碧辉煌**，是中国古代宫廷建筑的代表。

Gùgōng **jīnbì-huīhuáng**, shì Zhōngguó gǔdài gōngtíng jiànzhù de dàibiǎo.

'The Forbidden Palace is resplendent in bright colors; it's the representative of ancient Chinese palace architecture.'

Example 2: 他们参观了西藏**金碧辉煌**的寺庙。

Tāmen cānguānle Xīzàng jīnbì-huīhuáng de sìmiào.

'They visited the brightly colored temples of Tibet.'

Usage: Functions mainly as attributive and predicate; used to describe buildings.

Near Synonym: [富丽堂皇] (fù lì táng huáng 富麗堂皇) 'magnificent and grand.'

Antonym: [黯然无光] (àn rán wú guāng 黯然無光) 'dim and without light.'

418. 【同舟共济】(同舟共濟) tóng zhōu gòng jì

同 means 'same,' 舟 means 'boat,' 济 means 'cross a river,' and 共 means 'together.' A literal translation of the whole idiom is 'cross the river together in the same boat.' Freer translations include 'overcome difficulties together, pull together to resolve problems, stand together in time of need.'

Example 1: 在这个危难的关头，大家要**同舟共济**，否则全部遭殃。

Zài zhège wēinàn de guāntóu, dàjiā yào tóngzhōu-gòngjì, fǒuzé quánbù zāoyāng.

'At this dangerous juncture, everybody must pull together to overcome this difficulty; otherwise, all will suffer disaster.'

Example 2: 公司高层领导与普通员工**同舟共济**，终于度过了这段最艰难的经济危机时期。

Gōngsī gāocéng lǐngdǎo yǔ pǔtōng yuángōng tóngzhōu-gòngjì, zhōngyú dùguòle zhè duàn zuì jiānnán de jīngjì wēijī shíqī.

'The senior leaders of the company and the ordinary workers pulled together, finally passing through this period of a most difficult economic crisis.'

Usage: Functions mainly as predicate, can also serve as attributive.

Note: Complimentary in meaning.

Near Synonyms: [风雨同舟] (fēng yǔ tóng zhōu 風雨同舟) 'wind and rain same boat – bear hardships together,' [患难与共] (huàn nàn yǔ gòng 患難與共) 'go through difficulties together,' [生死与共] (shēng sǐ yǔ gòng 生死與共) 'live and die together,' [同甘共苦] (tóng gān gòng kǔ 同甘共苦) 'together sweet collectively bitter – share joys and sorrows.'

Antonyms: [反目为仇] (fǎn mù wéi chóu 反目為仇) 'have a falling out and be enemies,' [反目成仇] (fǎn mù chéng chóu 反目成仇) 'have a falling out and become enemies,' [同床异梦] (tóng chuáng yì mèng 同床異夢) 'same bed different dreams – work together but for different ends.'

419. 【志同道合】(志同道合) zhì tóng dào hé

志 means 'aspiration' and 道 means 'road.' A literal translation of this idiom is 'aspiration the same and road conforming,' with a freer translation being 'have the same aspirations, have common goals.'

Example 1: 他有一位美丽善良、**志同道合**的妻子。

Tā yǒu yí wèi měilì shànliáng, zhìtóng-dàohé de qīzi.

'He has a beautiful, kindhearted wife who has the same aspirations he has.'

Example 2: 他们寻找**志同道合**的朋友，然后一起建立一家新公司。

Tāmen xúnzhǎo zhìtóng-dàohé de péngyou, ránhòu yìqǐ jiànlì yì jiā xīn gōngsī.

'They are looking for friends with the same aspirations; then together they will set up a new company.'

Usage: Functions mainly as attributive; can also serve as predicate.

Note: Complimentary in meaning.

Near Synonyms: [情投意合] (qíng tóu yì hé 情投意合) 'perfectly suited to each other,' [党同伐异] (dǎng tóng fá yì 黨同伐異) 'help one's own faction and hamper outsiders.'

Antonyms: [貌合神离] (mào hé shén lí 貌合神離) 'appearance united spirits apart – seemingly agreed but actually at variance, in name or appearance only,' [不共戴天] (bú gòng dài tiān 不共戴天) 'cannot live under the same sky – irreconcilable hatred.'

420. 【唇亡齿寒】(唇亡齒寒) chún wáng chǐ hán

唇 means 'lip,' 亡 means 'lose,' 齿 means 'tooth,' and 寒 means 'cold.' A literal translation of this idiom is 'when the lips are gone the teeth are cold.' The extended meaning is 'closely related and share common concerns.'

Example 1: 朝鲜跟中国东北是**唇亡齿寒**的关系，这也就是为什么中国在朝鲜战争中出兵援助朝鲜的原因。

Cháoxiǎn gēn Zhōngguó dōngběi shì chúnwáng-chǐhán de guānxi, zhè yě jiùshì wèishénme Zhōngguó zài Cháoxiǎn zhànzhēng zhōng chūbīng yuánzhù Cháoxiǎn de yuányīn.

'North Korea and northeast China are very closely related, this being the reason why China, during the Korean War, dispatched troops to assist North Korea.'

Example 2: 总统和副总统关系密切，如果副总统出了事，**唇亡齿寒**，总统也会受到牵连。

Zǒngtǒng hé fùzǒngtǒng guānxi mìqiè, rúguǒ fùzǒngtǒng chūle shì, chúnwáng-chǐhán, zǒngtǒng yě huì shòudào qiānlián.

'The relationship between the president and the vice president is very close; if anything happened to the vice president, given that the two of them are as close as the lips and the teeth, the president would also become involved.'

Usage: Functions mainly as predicate and attributive, sometimes preceded by 唇齿相依 (chún chǐ xiāng yī 唇齒相依) 'lips and teeth mutually dependent – closely related and interdependent' or 辅车相依 (fǔ chē xiāng yī 輔車相依) 'interdependent.'

Allusion: During the Spring and Autumn Period, the country of Jin was a major power, while the country of Yu, which was to the south of Jin, was a minor power, as was the country of Guo, to the south of Yu. In 655 B.C.E., the king of Jin bribed the king of Yu with a piece of jade, saying that he wanted to have temporary access to one of the roads in Yu so as to go to the south to fight Guo. A minister of Yu requested that the king not provide access to the road, saying that Yu and Guo depended on each other and that the relationship between the two countries was one of interdependence and shared goals, as the lips are to the teeth. However, the king of Yu did not accept the recommendation from his minister. Sure enough, after Jin had destroyed Guo, its troops took advantage of the opportunity to also destroy Yu on their way back home. (from "The Fifth Year of Duke Xi" in *The Chronicle of Zuo*)

Near Synonyms: [息息相关] (xī xī xiāng guān 息息相關) 'interrelated, closely linked,' [辅车相依] (fǔ chē xiāng yī 輔車相依) 'interdependent,' [休戚相关] (xiū qī xiāng guān 休戚相關) 'share joys and sorrows.'

Antonyms: [隔岸观火] (gé àn guān huǒ 隔岸觀火) 'from the opposite side of the river to watch the fire – indifferent to another's plight,' [坐山观虎斗] (zuò shān guān hǔ dòu 坐山觀虎鬥) 'sit on a mountain and watch the tigers fight – watch a fight from a safe distance (and then reap the spoils when both sides are exhausted).'

421. 【柳暗花明】(柳暗花明) liǔ àn huā míng

The literal meaning of this idiom is 'willows shady flowers bright.' It describes a beautiful scene where willow trees create shade and where flowers are blooming, dazzling the eyes with their bright colors. Later this idiom was also used as a metaphor for hope in the midst of difficulty, or for a bright future after a period of difficulty. This idiom can sometimes be translated as 'joy after sorrow' or 'good fortune after hardship.'

Example 1: 集邮市场曾经有过一段时间不景气，但是现在**柳暗花明**了，因为社会上对集邮的兴趣又高涨了。

Jíyóu shìchǎng céngjīng yǒuguo yí duàn shíjiān bù jǐngqì, dànshì xiànzài liǔ'ànhuāmíng le, yīnwèi shèhuì shàng duì jíyóu de xìngqù yòu gāozhǎng le.

'The stamp collecting market in the past had a period that was depressed, but now there is a bright future after a period of difficulty, because interest in stamp collecting in society has risen again.'

Example 2: 他的事业三起三落，曾经陷入过低谷，也曾经**柳暗花明**过。

Tā de shìyè sānqǐ-sānluò, céngjīng xiànrùguo dīgǔ, yě céngjīng liǔ'àn-huāmíng guò.

'His career has had its ups and downs; in the past there have been times when it sank into the pits, and there have also been times when it blossomed forth brightly after periods of difficulty.'

Usage: Functions mainly as predicate.

Note: This idiom derives from a poem by the Song Dynasty poet Lu You. The whole verse, which is often quoted in its entirety, is: 山重水复疑无路，柳暗花明又一村 (shān chóng shuǐ fù yí wú lù, liǔ àn huā míng yòu yì cūn 山重水復疑無路，柳暗花明又一村) 'The mountains multiply and the streams double so that I suspect there is no road, the willows are shady and the flowers are bright and then there is another village.'

Near Synonyms: [时来运转] (shí lái yùn zhuǎn 時來運轉) 'a change in one's fortune for the better,' [苦尽甘来] (kǔ jìn gān lái 苦盡甘來) 'when the bitter is exhausted sweetness comes.'

Antonyms: [穷途末路] (qióng tú mò lù 窮途末路) 'dead end, impasse,' [走投无路] (zǒu tóu wú lù 走投無路) 'have no way out, have nowhere to turn.'

422. 【袖手旁观】（袖手旁觀）xiù shǒu páng guān

袖 means 'put in one's sleeves,' 旁 means 'from the sides,' and 观 means 'look on.' A literal translation of this idiom is 'put one's hands in one's sleeves and look on from the sidelines.' A freer translation is 'stand by with one's arms folded, stand idly by.'

Example 1: 该国的外交政策是，如果东亚发生了战争，他们不会**袖手旁观**，而是要积极参与。

Gāi guó de wàijiāo zhèngcè shì, rúguǒ dōngyà fāshēngle zhànzhēng, tāmen bú huì xiùshǒu-pángguān, ér shì yào jījí cānyù.

'The foreign policy of that country is that, if in East Asia war erupts, they will not stand idly by but will participate actively.'

Example 2: 你们是好朋友，现在他遇到了那么大的麻烦，你怎么能**袖手旁观**呢？

Nǐmen shì hǎo péngyou, xiànzài tā yùdàole nàme dà de máfan, nǐ zěnme néng xiùshǒu-pángguān ne?

'You're good friends; now that he has encountered such big trouble, how can you just look on from the sidelines?'

Usage: Functions mainly as predicate.

Note: Derogatory in meaning.

Near Synonyms: [作壁上观] (zuò bì shàng guān 作壁上觀) 'stand by and watch,' [坐山观虎斗] (zuò shān guān hǔ dòu 坐山觀虎鬥) 'sit on a mountain and watch the tigers fight – watch a fight from a safe distance (and then reap the spoils when both sides are exhausted).'

Antonyms: [拔刀相助] (bá dāo xiāng zhù 拔刀相助) 'draw one's sword and help another – come to someone's rescue,' [挺身而出] (tǐng shēn ér chū 挺身而出) 'step forward courageously.'

423. 【豁然开朗】(豁然開朗) huò rán kāi lǎng

豁然 means 'open' and 开朗 means 'open and bright.' The literal meaning is 'open and bright,' with a freer translation being 'suddenly see the light.'

Example 1: 他们钻出山洞，眼前**豁然开朗**。

Tāmen zuānchū shāndòng, yǎnqián huòrán-kāilǎng.

'When they had made their way out of the cave, before their eyes it suddenly became open and bright.'

Example 2: 听老师解释以后，他**豁然开朗**，一下子明白了。

Tīng lǎoshī jiěshì yǐhòu, tā huòrán-kāilǎng, yíxiàzi míngbai le.

'After hearing the teacher's explanation, he suddenly saw the light.'

Usage: Functions mainly as predicate.

Near Synonyms: [恍然大悟] (huǎng rán dà wù 恍然大悟) 'suddenly understand,' [茅塞顿开] (máo sè dùn kāi 茅塞顿開) 'suddenly see the light.'

Antonyms: [大惑不解] (dà huò bù jiě 大惑不解) 'puzzled, baffled,' [一窍不通] (yí qiào bù tōng 一竅不通) 'one gate not opened – know nothing about something.'

424. 【诗情画意】(詩情畫意) shī qíng huà yì

诗 means 'poem,' 情 means 'feeling,' and 意 means 'meaning, idea.' The literal meaning is 'poem-feeling painting-idea,' with a freer translation being 'rich in poetic and artistic flavor.'

Example 1: 大学生活不纯粹是**诗情画意**，也充满了就业前的准备。

Dàxué shēnghuó bù chúncuì shì shīqíng-huàyì, yě chōngmǎnle jiùyè qián de zhǔnbèi.

'University life is not purely poetry and art; it's also filled with preparation prior to employment.'

Example 2: 浪漫主义作品给人以**诗情画意**般的享受。

Làngmàn zhǔyì zuòpǐn gěi rén yǐ shīqíng-huàyì bān de xiǎngshòu.

'Works of Romanticism give one a poetic and artistic kind of enjoyment.'

Usage: Functions mainly as object of the verbs 富有 (fùyǒu) 'rich in' and 充满 (chōngmǎn 充滿) 'full of.'

Note: Complimentary in meaning.

Near Synonym: [如诗如画] (rú shī rú huà 如詩如畫) 'like poems and paintings.'

Antonym: [平淡无奇] (píng dàn wú qí 平淡無奇) 'flat and uninteresting.'

425. 【同日而语】 (同日而語) tóng rì ér yǔ

同 means 'same,' 日 means 'day,' and 语 means 'speak.' The literal meaning of this idiom is 'speak about on the same day,' with a freer translation being 'talk about at the same time, mention in the same breath, compare with.'

Example 1: 迈克尔•乔丹第二次复出后，水平跟以前不可**同日而语**。

Màikè'ěr Qiáodān dì'èr cì fùchū hòu, shuǐpíng gēn yǐqián bù kě tóngrì-éryǔ.

'After Michael Jordan resurfaced the second time, his level couldn't compare with before.'

Example 2: 他大学毕业后在很多国家工作过，到过很多不同的地方，因此现在的见识岂能跟大学时期的**同日而语**？

Tā dàxué bìyè hòu zài hěn duō guójiā gōngzuòguo, dàoguò hěn duō bùtóng de dìfang, yīncǐ xiànzài de jiànshi qǐ néng gēn dàxué shíqī de tóngrì-éryǔ?

'After graduating from college, he worked in many countries and visited many different places; so how could his current knowledge be mentioned in the same breath as that of the period when he was in college?'

Usage: Functions as predicate, usually in negative sentences and rhetorical questions.

Near Synonym: [相提并论] (xiāng tí bìng lùn 相提並論) 'mention in the same breath.'

Antonym: [今非昔比] (jīn fēi xī bǐ 今非昔比) 'the present does not compare with the past.'

426. 【曾几何时】 (曾幾何時) céng jǐ hé shí

曾 is Classical Chinese for the modern 曾经 and means 'before, once,' 几何 means 'how much,' and 时 means 'time.' A literal translation of the whole idiom is 'not very much time (has passed).' A freer translation is 'it was not so long ago that . . . , it was not long before. . . .' However, this idiom is not infrequently misused to mean 'at some point in the past' or 'long ago,' which is gradually becoming accepted usage.

Example 1: **曾几何时**，水果是过节的象征，是去亲戚朋友家的礼品。

Céngjǐhéshí, shuǐguǒ shì guòjié de xiàngzhēng, shì qù qīnqi péngyou jiā de lǐpǐn.

'It was not so long ago that fruit was the symbol for celebrating holidays, or a gift when going to the homes of relatives and friends.'

Example 2: **曾几何时**，《周易》热了一段时间。

Céngjǐhéshí, *Zhōu Yì* rèle yí duàn shíjiān.

'It was not so long ago that *The Book of Changes* was "hot" for a period of time.'

Usage: Functions independently as adverbial.

Note: Very literary in style. Because of the strong tendency of Chinese idioms to be analyzed in groups of two characters, this idiom is usually pronounced with a brief pause in the middle as 曾几 ‖ 何时(céng jǐ ‖ hé shí).

Near Synonyms: [弹指之间] (dàn zhǐ zhī jiān 彈指之間) 'in the time it takes to flick a finger – in a moment,' [稍纵即逝] (shāo zòng jí shì 稍縱即逝) 'fleeting.'

Antonyms: [久而久之] (jiǔ ér jiǔ zhī 久而久之) 'in the course of time,' [遥遥无期] (yáo yáo wú qī 遙遙無期) 'not in the foreseeable future.'

427. 【高高在上】(高高在上) gāo gāo zài shàng

This idiom means 'up very high, isolated from the masses.'

Example 1: 当领导的不能给别人一种**高高在上**的感觉，否则没人愿意跟你接近。

Dāng lǐngdǎo de bùnéng gěi biérén yì zhǒng gāogāo-zàishàng de gǎnjúe, fǒuzé méi rén yuànyì gēn nǐ jiējìn.

'Those who serve as leaders must not give others the feeling that they are very high in position, otherwise there won't be anyone who wants to approach you.'

Example 2: 这个话剧是讽刺那些**高高在上**的法官的。

Zhège huàjù shì fěngcì nàxiē gāogāo-zàishàng de fǎguān de.

'This play satirizes those judges who have such high positions.'

Usage: Functions mainly as predicate, attributive, and adverbial.

Note: Slightly derogatory in meaning.

Near Synonym: [至高无上] (zhì gāo wú shàng 至高無上) 'highest, supreme.'

Antonym: [平易近人] (píng yì jìn rén 平易近人) 'amiable and approachable.'

428. 【一往情深】(一往情深) yì wǎng qíng shēn

The meaning of this idiom is 'fall passionately in love with, head over heels in love with.'

Example 1: 虽然丈夫出了车祸，双腿残疾，但是妻子对丈夫一**往情深**地说："我永远不会离开你。"

Suīrán zhàngfu chūle chēhuò, shuāng tuǐ cánjí, dànshì qīzi duì zhàngfu yìwǎng-qíngshēn de shuō: "Wǒ yǒngyuǎn bú huì líkāi nǐ."

'Though the husband had an automobile accident and lost the use of both of his legs, the wife said to the husband, deeply in love with him: "I shall never leave you."'

Example 2: 她对舞蹈事业一**往情深**，六十多岁了还亲自登台演出。

Tā duì wǔdǎo shìyè yìwǎng-qíngshēn, liùshí duō suì le hái qīnzì dēngtái yǎnchū.

'She is passionately in love with dance; at the age of over sixty, she still personally gets on stage to perform.'

Usage: Functions mainly as predicate and adverbial, usually preceded by 对 (duì 對).

Note: Complimentary in meaning.

Near Synonyms: [情深意厚] (qíng shēn yì hòu 情深意厚) 'feelings are deep and intentions are thick,' [情意绵绵] (qíng yì mián mián 情意綿綿) 'continuous love and affection.'

Antonyms: [朝三暮四] (zhāo sān mù sì 朝三暮四) 'three in the morning and four at night – fickle and inconstant,' [朝秦暮楚] (zhāo Qín mù Chǔ 朝秦暮楚) 'serve Qin in the morning and Chu in the evening – fickle and inconstant.'

429. 【痛心疾首】(痛心疾首) tòng xīn jí shǒu

痛 means 'hurt,' 疾 means 'pain,' and 首 means 'head.' A literal translation of the idiom is 'hurt the heart and pain the head,' with a freer translation being 'very distressing or distressed, full of resentment.'

Example 1: 长江受到这么严重的污染，真让人**痛心疾首**。

Chángjiāng shòudào zhème yánzhòng de wūrǎn, zhēn ràng rén tòngxīn-jíshǒu.

'That the Yangtze River was so seriously polluted has really distressed people.'

Example 2: 在中国的成长的历史上，发生过**痛心疾首**的事。

Zài Zhōngguó de chéngzhǎng de lìshǐ shàng, fāshēngguo tòngxīn-jíshǒu de shì.

'In the history of China's growth, there have occurred very distressing things.'

Usage: Functions mainly as predicate after causative verbs; can also serve as attributive or adverbial.

Near Synonym: [肝肠寸断] (gān cháng cùn duàn 肝腸寸斷) 'great pain and grief.'

Antonym: [眉飞色舞] (méi fēi sè wǔ 眉飛色舞) 'eyebrows fly face dances – delighted, elated.'

430. 【鹬蚌相争，渔翁得利】(鷸蚌相爭，漁翁得利)
yù bàng xiāng zhēng, yú wēng dé lì

鹬 means 'snipe (a type of water bird),' 蚌 means 'clam,' 相 means 'mutually,' 争 means 'fight,' 渔翁 means 'fisherman,' and 利 means 'benefit.' A literal translation of the whole idiom is 'when the snipe and the clam fought with each other, the fisherman obtained the benefit' (since he could grab them both while they were distracted). This is a metaphor for a third party's benefiting when two parties are engaged in a quarrel and neither is willing to yield.

Example 1: 二十世纪八十年代，美国和前苏联**鹬蚌相争**的时候，中国得到了很多好处。

Èrshí shìjì bāshí niándài, Měiguó hé qián Sūlián yùbàng-xiāngzhēng de shíhou, Zhōngguó dédàole hěn duō hǎochù.

'During the 1980s in the 20th century, when the U.S. and the former Soviet Union were involved in disputes much like the proverbial "snipe and clam," China reaped many benefits.'

Example 2: 总统大选初选的时候，候选人都盼望着其他候选人**鹬蚌相争**，他们好**渔翁得利**。

Zǒngtǒng dàxuǎn chūxuǎn de shíhou, hòuxuǎnrén dōu pànwàngzhe qítā hòuxuǎnrén yùbàng-xiāngzhēng, tāmen hǎo yú wēng dé lì.

'In the primaries of the presidential election, the candidates all hoped that the other candidates would fight with each other like the proverbial "snipe and clam," so that they could "reap the benefit of the fisherman."'

Usage: Functions mainly as predicate and attributive.

Allusion: During the Warring States Period, the state of Zhao wanted to attack the state of Yan. Under the command of the king of Zhao, there was a minister of state by the name of Su Dai who said to the king: "On my way to see you this morning, I passed a river where I saw a clam that had opened its shell to sun itself. Just then, a water bird stretched over and put its long beak into the clam's shell, wanting to eat the clam. The clam quickly clamped down on the bird's beak with the two halves of its shell. The bird said, 'If it doesn't rain today and it doesn't rain tomorrow, you'll die.' But the clam said, 'If your beak can't break free today, and if it can't break free tomorrow, you'll die.' Neither the clam nor the bird were willing to give up, so both were easily caught by a fisherman." Understanding what Su Dai meant, the king of Zhao gave up his plan to attack the country of Yan. (from "Stratagems of Yan" in *Stratagems of the Warring States*)

Note: Derogatory in meaning.

Near Synonyms: [乘人之危] (chéng rén zhī wēi 乘人之危) 'take advantage of someone's precarious position,' [坐山观虎斗] (zuò shān guān hǔ dòu 坐山觀虎鬥) 'sit on a mountain and watch the tigers fight – watch a fight from a safe distance (and reap the spoils when both sides are exhausted).'

Antonym: [拔刀相助] (bá dāo xiāng zhù 拔刀相助) 'draw one's sword and help another – come to someone's rescue.'

431. 【无时无刻】 (無時無刻) wú shí wú kè

A literal translation of this idiom is 'there isn't an hour and there isn't a quarter hour.' The meaning is 'constantly, incessantly, all the time.'

Example 1: 她**无时无刻**不在思念远方的丈夫。

Tā wúshí-wúkè bú zài sīniàn yuǎnfāng de zhàngfu.

'There wasn't a moment when she wasn't longing for her faraway husband.'

Example 2: 贫困**无时无刻**都在阻止发展中国家的进步。

Pínkùn wúshí-wúkè dōu zài zǔzhǐ fāzhǎnzhōng guójiā de jìnbù.

'Poverty is constantly preventing the progress of developing countries.'

Usage: Often used before 不在 (bú zài) as adverbial.

Near Synonyms: [分分秒秒] (fēn fēn miǎo miǎo 分分秒秒) 'every minute and every second,' [长年累月] (cháng nián lěi yuè 長年累月) 'year after year and month after month.'

432. 【欢天喜地】 (歡天喜地) huān tiān xǐ dì

A literal translation of this idiom is 'happy heaven happy earth.' The meaning is 'completely overjoyed.'

Example 1: 他们**欢天喜地**地搬进了新房子。

Tāmen huāntiān-xǐdì de bānjìnle xīn fángzi.

'They moved into their new home completely overjoyed.'

Example 2: 这个大家庭新添了一个孙子，全家人都**欢天喜地**的。

Zhège dàjiātíng xīntiānle yí ge sūnzi, quán jiā rén dōu huāntiān-xǐdì de.

'This large family newly added a grandson, so everyone in the family was overjoyed.'

Usage: Functions mainly as adverbial and predicate.

Near Synonym: [喜气洋洋] (xǐ qì yáng yáng 喜氣洋洋) 'jubilant.'

Antonyms: [愁眉苦脸] (chóu méi kǔ liǎn 愁眉苦臉) 'worried eyebrows bitter face – distressed,' [悲痛欲绝] (bēi tòng yù jué 悲痛欲絕) 'sorrowful and desperate.'

433. 【殚精竭虑】 (殫精竭慮) dān jīng jié lǜ

殚 means 'use up,' 精 means 'energy,' 竭 also means 'use up,' and 虑 means 'thought.' The literal meaning of the whole idiom is 'use up all one's energy and thought,' with a freer translation being 'rack one's brains.'

Example 1: 文化大革命期间，周恩来总理**殚精竭虑**，努力保护了一批老同志。

Wénhuà Dàgémìng qījiān, Zhōu Ēnlái zǒnglǐ dānjīng-jiélǜ, nǔlì bǎohùle yì pī lǎotóngzhì.

'During the Cultural Revolution, Premier Zhou Enlai racked his brains trying to protect a group of old comrades.'

Example 2: 为了儿子的婚事，父母**殚精竭虑**，明显瘦了许多。

Wéile érzi de hūnshì, fùmǔ dānjīng-jiélǜ, míngxiǎn shòule xǔduō.

'For the sake of their son's marriage, his parents racked their brains, obviously losing a lot of weight.'

Usage: Functions mainly as predicate.

Note: Somewhat complimentary in meaning.

Near Synonyms: [处心积虑] (chǔ xīn jī lǜ 處心積慮) 'deliberately plan something,' [煞费苦心] (shà fèi kǔ xīn 煞費苦心) 'take great pains.'

434. 【通情达理】(通情達理) tōng qíng dá lǐ

通 means 'understand,' 情 means 'situation,' 达 means 'attain,' and 理 means 'reason.' The meaning of the whole idiom is 'very reasonable or sensible.'

Example 1: 她很**通情达理**，因此交了很多朋友。

Tā hěn tōngqíng-dálǐ, yīncǐ jiāole hěn duō péngyou.

'She is very sensible, therefore she has made many friends.'

Example 2: 温网的观众是最**通情达理**的观众，也给失败者很多掌声。

Wēnwǎng de guānzhòng shì zuì tōngqíng-dálǐ de guānzhòng, yě gěi shībàizhě hěn duō zhǎngshēng.

'The spectators at the Wimbledon Open are extremely reasonable spectators, also giving the losers a lot of applause.'

Usage: Functions mainly as predicate and attributive.

Note: Complimentary in meaning.

Near Synonym: [善解人意] (shàn jiě rén yì 善解人意) 'good at understanding others' intentions.'

Antonyms: [蛮不讲理] (mán bù jiǎng lǐ 蠻不講理) 'quite unreasonable,' [强词夺理] (qiǎng cí duó lǐ 強詞奪理) 'use far-fetched arguments.'

435. 【从天而降】(從天而降) cóng tiān ér jiàng

降 means 'fall.' The literal meaning of the whole idiom is 'fall from the sky.' A freer English equivalent is 'come out of a clear blue sky.'

Example 1: 这条坏消息简直**从天而降**，让人一点准备也没有。

Zhè tiáo huài xiāoxi jiǎnzhí cóngtiān-érjiàng, ràng rén yìdiǎn zhǔnbèi yě méiyǒu.

'This piece of bad news simply came out of a clear blue sky, there being no way that one could have been prepared.'

Example 2: 她买彩票中了特等奖，财富**从天而降**，一下子发了大财。

Tā mǎi cǎipiào zhòngle tèděngjiǎng, cáifù cóngtiān-érjiàng, yíxiàzi fāle dà cái.

'She bought a lottery ticket and won the special prize, with riches falling from the sky; all of a sudden, she struck it rich.'

Usage: Functions mainly as predicate.

Note: Can be used literally or figuratively.

Near Synonym: [突如其来] (tū rú qí lái 突如其來) 'appear suddenly.'

Antonym: [意料之中] (yì liào zhī zhōng 意料之中) 'as might be expected.'

436. 【井井有条】 (井井有條) jǐng jǐng yǒu tiáo

井井 means 'orderly, well arranged.' 有条 means 有条理, which also means 'orderly, well arranged.' The meaning of the whole idiom is 'orderly, in good order, methodical.'

Example 1: 他太太把家里收拾得**井井有条**，干净利落。

Tā tàitai bǎ jiā lǐ shōushí de jǐngjǐng-yǒutiáo, gānjìng-lìluò.

'His wife arranged everything in their home in good order, clean and tidy.'

Example 2: 秘书把事情安排得**井井有条**，领导非常满意。

Mìshū bǎ shìqing ānpái de jǐngjǐng-yǒutiáo, lǐngdǎo fēicháng mǎnyì.

'The secretary arranged matters in an orderly manner, the boss being extremely satisfied.'

Usage: Functions mainly as complement and predicate.

Near Synonym: [秩序井然] (zhì xù jǐng rán 秩序井然) 'in methodical order.'

Antonyms: [杂乱无章] (zá luàn wú zhāng 雜亂無章) 'disorganized,' [乱七八糟] (luàn qī bā zāo 亂七八糟) 'in great disorder, a mess' (limited mostly to spoken Chinese).

437. 【苦口婆心】 (苦口婆心) kǔ kǒu pó xīn

苦口 means 'urge with great patience,' 婆 means 'old woman,' and 婆心 means 'kindheartedness.' The meaning of the whole idiom is 'admonish over and over with good intentions.'

Example 1: 父母**苦口婆心**地跟孩子讲为什么要上大学的道理。

Fùmǔ **kǔkǒu-póxīn** de gēn háizi jiǎng wèishénme yào shàng dàxué de dàolǐ.

'Admonishing them over and over again with good intentions, the parents explained to their children the reasons why they should attend college.'

Example 2: 传教士**苦口婆心**地劝说人们信仰上帝。

Chuánjiàoshì **kǔkǒu-póxīn** de quànshuō rénmen xìnyǎng Shàngdì.

'Admonishing them over and over with good intentions, the missionary urged the people to believe in God.'

Usage: Functions mainly as attributive.

Near Synonyms: [不厌其烦] (bú yàn qí fán 不厭其煩) 'not mind the trouble,' [语重心长] (yǔ zhòng xīn cháng 語重心長) 'sincere, heartfelt.'

Antonym: [油腔滑调] (yóu qiāng huá diào 油腔滑調) 'slick tunes smooth melodies – glib.'

438. 【人山人海】(人山人海) rén shān rén hǎi

The literal translation of this idiom is 'people-mountain and people-sea.' The meaning is 'many people, huge crowds.'

Example 1: 国庆节的时候，天安门广场游客非常多，**人山人海**。

Guóqìngjié de shíhou, Tiānānmén guǎngchǎng yóukè fēicháng duō, rénshān-rénhǎi.

'On National Day, there were extremely many sightseers on Tiananmen Square – crowds and crowds.'

Example 2: 她是现在最有名的歌星，在她的演唱会现场，**人山人海**。

Tā shì xiànzài zuì yǒumíng de gēxīng, zài tā de yǎnchànghuì xiànchǎng, rénshān-rénhǎi.

'She is currently the most famous singer; at the site of her performances, there are always huge crowds of people.'

Usage: Functions mainly as predicate.

Near Synonyms: [川流不息] (chuān liú bù xī 川流不息) 'continuous flow without stopping' (of people or traffic) (unlike 人山人海, which can only refer to people, 川流不息 can also refer to traffic).

Antonym: [三三两两] (sān sān liǎng liǎng 三三兩兩) 'in twos and threes, not many people.'

439. 【运筹帷幄】(運籌帷幄) yùn chóu wéi wò

运筹 means 'map out tactics, plan' and 帷幄 means 'army tent.' A literal translation is 'map out strategic plans in an army tent.' Nowadays, this idiom is usually employed with the extended meaning 'good at strategies and planning.'

Example 1: 国共战争期间，毛泽东**运筹帷幄**，只用了四年时间就打败了蒋介石的八百万军队，真是军事史上的奇迹。

Guó-Gòng zhànzhēng qījiān, Máo Zédōng yùnchóu-wéiwò, zhǐ yòngle sì nián shíjiān jiù dǎbàile Jiǎng Jièshí de bābǎi wàn jūnduì, zhēn shì jūnshìshǐ shàng de qíjì.

'At the time of the war between the Kuomintang and the Communists, Mao Zedong excelled at strategic planning, it taking him only four years to defeat Chiang Kai-shek's eight million troops; it really was a miracle in military history.'

Example 2: 巴菲特**运筹帷幄**，即使在股市大跌的时期依然能赚到不少钱。

Bāfēitè yùnchóu-wéiwò, jíshǐ zài gǔshì dàdiē de shíqī yīrán néng zhuàndào bù shǎo qián.

'U.S. investor Warren Buffett is good at strategies and planning; even at the time of the sharp drop in the stock market, he still was able to earn quite a bit of money.'

Usage: Functions mainly as predicate.

Note: Complimentary in meaning.

Near Synonyms: [决胜千里] (jué shèng qiān lǐ 決勝千里) 'determine the final outcome,' [神机妙算] (shén jī miào suàn 神機妙算) 'divine stratagem, marvelous scheme.'

Antonym: [屡战屡败] (lǚ zhàn lǚ bài 屢戰屢敗) 'repeatedly wage war and repeatedly be defeated.'

440. 【才高八斗】(才高八斗) cái gāo bā dǒu

才 means 'talent' (especially literary talent) and 斗 was a unit of measurement in ancient China, with ten *dou* making up a *dan*. A literal translation of this idiom is 'talent high to the extent of eight *dou*,' with a freer translation being 'lots of talent, extremely talented.'

Example 1: 王教授古典文学基础深厚，**才高八斗**，学富五车，写副对联不费什么功夫。

Wáng jiàoshòu gǔdiǎn wénxué jīchǔ shēnhòu, cáigāo-bādǒu, xuéfù-wǔchē, xiě fù duìlián bú fèi shénme gōngfu.

'Professor Wang's foundation in classical literature is very deep, and he is extremely talented and well-read; composing a couplet expends no effort on his part.'

Example 2: 那些自以为**才高八斗**的评论家，人家的作品他根本没有看完就乱发评论。

Nà xiē zìyǐwéi cáigāo-bādǒu de pínglùnjiā, rénjiā de zuòpǐn tā gēnběn méiyǒu kànwán jiù luàn fā pínglùn.

'Those critics who consider themselves extremely talented, they haven't even finished reading someone's works and already they indiscriminately issue their criticisms.'

Usage: Functions mainly as predicate and attributive, often followed by 学富五车 (xué fù wǔ chē 學富五車) 'well-read, learned.'

Allusion: The famous Southern Dynasties poet Xie Lingyun once said: "In the whole world, there is in all only one *dan*'s (equals ten *dou*) worth of literature. The poet Cao Zhi alone accounts for eight *dou*, and I account for one *dou*; everyone else in the world must together share the remaining *dou*." (from "Explaining the Common Saying *Badouzhicai*," anonymous)

Note: Complimentary in meaning.

Near Synonyms: [学富五车] (xué fù wǔ chē 學富五車) 'well-read, learned,' [才华横溢] (cái huá héng yì 才華橫溢) 'overflowing with talent.'

Antonyms: [才疏学浅] (cái shū xué qiǎn 才疏學淺) 'little talent and shallow learning' (self-deprecatory term), [志大才疏] (zhì dà cái shū 志大才疏) 'great ambition but little talent.'

441. 【沾沾自喜】(沾沾自喜) zhān zhān zì xǐ

沾沾 means 'frivolous, flighty,' 自 means 'oneself,' and 喜 means 'like, happy with.' A literal translation of this idiom is 'frivolous and happy with oneself,' with freer translations including 'pleased with oneself, self-satisfied, complacent.'

Example 1: 他取得了不小的成就，但是没有**沾沾自喜**，而是继续奋斗。

Tā qǔdéle bù xiǎo de chéngjiù, dànshì méiyǒu zhānzhān-zìxǐ, ér shì jìxù fèndòu.

'He obtained great achievements, but was not complacent, continuing to struggle.'

Example 2: 第二次世界大战前，法国人以为德国不会进攻法国及其盟国，因而**沾沾自喜**的时候，德国的坦克已经悄悄地出发了。

Dì'èr Cì Shìjiè Dàzhàn qián, Fǎguórén yǐwéi Déguó bú huì jìngōng Fǎguó jí qí méngguó, yīn'ér zhānzhān-zìxǐ de shíhou, Déguó de tǎnkè yǐjīng qiāoqiāo de chūfāle.

'Before World War II, the French thought that Germany would not attack France and its allies; therefore, while it was feeling self-satisfied, the German tanks were already secretly setting out.'

Usage: Functions mainly as predicate; can also serve as adverbial and attributive.

Note: Derogatory in meaning.

Near Synonyms: [洋洋自得] (yáng yáng zì dé 洋洋自得) 'complacent, self-satisfied,' [自鸣得意] (zì míng dé yì 自鳴得意) 'pleased with oneself.'

Antonyms: [戒骄戒躁] (jiè jiāo jiè zào 戒驕戒躁) 'guard against arrogance and impetuosity,' [谦虚谨慎] (qiān xū jǐn shèn 謙虛謹慎) 'modest and prudent.'

442. 【皆大欢喜】(皆大歡喜) jiē dà huān xǐ

皆 means 'all,' 大 means 'greatly,' and 欢喜 means 'joyful, happy, delighted.' The meaning of the whole idiom is 'everyone is happy, to the satisfaction of all.'

Example 1: 事情的结果是双方**皆大欢喜**。

Shìqing de jiéguǒ shì shuāngfāng jiēdàhuānxǐ.

'The result of the matter was that both sides were very pleased.'

Example 2: 市长改善了城市的交通，市民们**皆大欢喜**。

Shìzhǎng gǎishànle chéngshì de jiāotōng, shìmínmen jiēdàhuānxǐ.

'The mayor improved city traffic, so the city residents were all very happy.'

Usage: Functions mainly as predicate.

Near Synonym: [尽如人意] (jìn rú rén yì 盡如人意) 'completely as one wishes.'

Antonym: [怨声载道] (yuàn shēng zǎi dào 怨聲載道) 'complaints are heard everywhere.'

443. 【大千世界】(大千世界) dà qiān shì jiè

大千 means 'the infinite universe.' The meaning of the whole idiom is 'the vast world, the infinite universe.'

Example 1: **大千世界**，无奇不有。

Dàqiān-shìjiè, wúqí-bùyǒu.

'Anything under the sun.' (lit. 'In the vast world, there is no strange thing that does not exist.')

Example 2: 人生活在**大千世界**里，总会遇到自己喜欢的人。

Rén shēnghuó zài dàqiān-shìjiè lǐ, zǒng huì yùdào zìjǐ xǐhuan de rén.

'People live in such a vast world, eventually they will come across someone they like.'

Usage: Nominal element, occurs mainly as object.

Note: This idiom, which is a common cliché, was originally a Buddhist term.

Near Synonym: [花花世界] (huā huā shì jiè 花花世界) 'the mortal world of tempting pleasures.'

444. 【举一反三】 (舉一反三) jǔ yī fǎn sān

举 means 'mention, give an example' and 反 means 'infer.' A literal translation of the whole idiom is 'when one (corner of a room) is mentioned, you infer the other three (corners of the room),' with a freer translation being 'infer other things from one fact that is already known, extrapolate.'

Example 1: 她聪明绝顶，**举一反三**，什么事情一点就透。

Tā cōngmíng juédǐng, jǔyī-fǎnsān, shénme shìqing yì diǎn jiù tòu.

'She is utterly brilliant, and can infer other things from one fact; she can understand anything right away with just a little bit of information.'

Example 2: 我们要善于抓住事情的本质，然后**举一反三**，这样才能有大收获。

Wǒmen yào shànyú zhuāzhù shìqing de běnzhì, ránhòu jǔyī-fǎnsān, zhèyàng cáinéng yǒu dà shōuhuò.

'We must be good at capturing the essence of things, and then infer other things from one fact; only in this way can we have great achievements.'

Usage: Functions mainly as predicate.

Note: Complimentary in meaning. This idiom originated from Confucius's saying 举一隅不以三隅反，则不复也 (Jǔ yī yú bù yǐ sān yú fǎn, zé bú fù yě 舉一隅不以三隅反，則不復也). The whole saying means: 'If you saw one corner of a room but could not infer the other three, then I would not try to enlighten you again.'

Near Synonyms: [触类旁通] (chù lèi páng tōng 觸類旁通) 'touch one kind others known – know the rest of a kind by analogy,' [融会贯通] (róng huì guàn tōng 融會貫通) 'gain a thorough understanding after comprehensive study.'

Antonyms: [一窍不通] (yí qiào bù tōng 一竅不通) 'one gate not opened – know nothing about something,' [囫囵吞枣] (hú lún tūn zǎo 囫圇吞棗) 'swallow a date whole – accept something uncritically without careful consideration.'

445. 【不了了之】 (不了了之) bù liǎo liǎo zhī

了 means 'end, finish.' The whole idiom means 'settle a matter by leaving it unsettled, let an issue disappear.'

Example 1: 那件事情因为没有人继续追究了，最后也就**不了了之**了。

Nà jiàn shìqing yīnwèi méiyǒu rén jìxù zhuījiūle, zuìhòu yě jiù bùliǎo-liǎozhī le.

'Because nobody continued looking into it, that matter in the end disappeared on its own.'

Example 2: 他们的恋爱关系没有发展下去，时间久了，就**不了了之**了。

Tāmen de liàn'ài guānxi méiyǒu fāzhǎn xiàqù, shíjiān jiǔ le, jiù bùliǎo-liǎozhī le.

'Their romance did not continue developing; with time, it ended on its own.'

Usage: Functions as predicate.

Near Synonym: [置之不理] (zhì zhī bù lǐ 置之不理) 'pay no attention to, ignore.'

Antonym: [一了百了] (yī liǎo bǎi liǎo 一了百了) 'when you die everything comes to an end.'

446. 【得不偿失】(得不償失) dé bù cháng shī

得 means 'get, gain,' and 偿 means 'compensate.' The meaning of the whole idiom is 'the gain does not make up for the loss.'

Example 1: 这样做有很大的风险，如果失败，就**得不偿失**了。

Zhèyàng zuò yǒu hěn dà de fēngxiǎn, rúguǒ shībài, jiù débùchángshī le.

'Doing this is very risky; if you fail, any gain won't make up for the loss.'

Example 2: 那家大公司在这件新产品上光打广告就花了五百万美元，结果卖得并不好，**得不偿失**了。

Nà jiā dà gōngsī zài zhè jiàn xīn chǎnpǐn shàng guāng dǎ guǎnggào jiù huāle wǔbǎi wàn Měiyuán, jiéguǒ mài de bìng bù hǎo, débùchángshī le.

'That large firm spent five million dollars just on advertising for this new product, and the result was that it didn't sell well at all, so the gain didn't equal the loss.'

Usage: Functions mainly as predicate at the end of a sentence.

Note: Has a negative implication.

Near Synonym: [因小失大] (yīn xiǎo shī dà 因小失大) 'for a small gain lose a lot.'

Antonyms: [钵满盆溢] (bō mǎn pén yì 钵满盆溢) (also written as [钵满盆盈] (bō mǎn pén yíng 钵满盆盈) or [钵满盆满] (bō mǎn pén mǎn 钵满盆满)) 'bowl is full and basin overflows.'

447. 【偷工减料】(偷工减料) tōu gōng jiǎn liào

偷 means 'steal,' 工 means 'work,' 减 means 'reduce,' and 料 means 'materials.' The meaning of the whole idiom is 'do shoddy work by skimping on materials.' This recently has gained the extended meaning of 'not be responsible in one's work, careless, deceive others.'

Example 1: 建筑商**偷工减料**，都是"豆腐渣"工程，结果地震的时候许多建筑都倒塌了。

Jiànzhùshāng tōugōng-jiǎnliào, dōu shì "dòufūzhā" gōngchéng, jiéguǒ dìzhèn de shíhou xǔduō jiànzhù dōu dǎotāle.

'The builders did shoddy work and skimped on materials, it all being construction of the quality of the "bean waste" that is left over after making soy milk; as a result, when the earthquake occurred, many buildings collapsed.'

Example 2: 做功课的时候要认真，不能**偷工减料**。

Zuò gōngkè de shíhou yào rènzhēn, bù néng tōugōng-jiǎnliào.

'When you do your homework you should be diligent; you can't take shortcuts.'

Usage: Functions mainly as predicate.

Note: Derogatory in meaning.

Near Synonym: [敷衍了事] (fū yǎn liǎo shì 敷衍了事) 'do a perfunctory job.'

Antonym: [一丝不苟] (yì sī bù gǒu 一絲不苟) 'not the least bit negligent.'

448. 【高屋建瓴】(高屋建瓴) gāo wū jiàn líng

屋 means 'roof,' 建 here means 'to pour water,' and 瓴 here means 'water vase.' A literal translation would be 'on a high rooftop pour water down.' A freer translation is 'operate from a strategically advantageous position.'

Example 1: 首长的讲话**高屋建瓴**，对我们以后的工作具有十分重要的意义。

Shǒuzhǎng de jiǎnghuà gāowū-jiànlíng, duì wǒmen yǐhòu de gōngzuò jùyǒu shífēn zhòngyào de yìyì.

'A leading cadre's speech is from a strategically advantageous position; it will have very important significance for our jobs in the future.'

Example 2: 她**高屋建瓴**地对以前的研究进行了一个简要的总结。

Tā gāowū-jiànlíng de duì yǐqián de yánjiū jìnxíngle yí ge jiǎnyào de zǒngjié.

'From a strategically advantageous position, she made a brief summary of previous research.'

Usage: Functions mainly as predicate, adverbial and attributive, often used to describe a person's speech.

Note: Complimentary in meaning.

Near Synonyms: [高瞻远瞩] (gāo zhān yuǎn zhǔ 高瞻遠矚) 'look out from on high and see far – far sighted,' [居高临下] (jū gāo lín xià 居高臨下) 'reside in a high place and look downward – a commanding position or view.'

Antonym: [坐井观天] (zuò jǐng guān tiān 坐井觀天) 'sit in a well and look at the sky – have a limited outlook.'

449. 【恋恋不舍】 (戀戀不捨) liàn liàn bù shě

恋恋 means 'lovingly, with great affection' and 舍 means 'abandon, leave.' A literal translation of the whole idiom is 'lovingly not willing to leave,' with freer translations being 'very reluctant to leave, hate to part from.'

Example 1: 他让司机开得慢一点儿，不停地回头看，**恋恋不舍**地离开了生活过十年的总统府。

Tā ràng sījī kāide màn yìdiǎr, bù tíng de huítóu kàn, liànliàn-bùshě de líkāile shēnghuóguo shí nián de zǒngtǒngfǔ.

'He had the driver drive slower, incessantly looking back; very reluctant to depart, he left the presidential palace where he had lived for ten years.'

Example 2: 她**恋恋不舍**地跟男朋友告别。

Tā liànliàn-bùshě de gēn nánpéngyou gàobié.

'Very reluctant to part, she took leave of her boyfriend.'

Usage: Functions mainly as adverbial, used in situations involving leave-taking.

Near Synonyms: [依依不舍] (yī yī bù shě 依依不舍) 'feel a sense of regret when leaving,' [难舍难分] (nán shě nán fēn 難舍難分) 'reluctant to part from.'

Antonyms: [一刀两断] (yì dāo liǎng duàn 一刀兩斷) 'one (blow of a) knife two severed portions – make a clean break with,' [扬长而去] (yáng cháng ér qù 揚長而去) 'swagger off haughtily.'

450. 【围魏救赵】 (圍魏救趙) wéi Wèi jiù Zhào

围 means 'encircle, surround,' 魏 was the name of a state in ancient China, 救 means 'rescue,' and 赵 was the name of another state in ancient China. A literal translation of this idiom is 'encircle the state of Wei and rescue the state of Zhao.' This is a metaphor for 'attack an enemy's rear in order to force it to give up its own attack.'

Example 1: 二战中，1940年8月26日，英国空军用**围魏救赵**的方法袭击了德国的首都柏林，从而减小了英国方面的压力。

Èrzhàn zhōng, yī-jiǔ-sì-líng nián bá yuè èrshiliù rì, Yīngguó kōngjūn yòng wéi Wèi jiù Zhào de fāngfǎ xíjīle Déguó de shǒudū Bólín, cóng'ér jiǎnxiǎole Yīngguó fāngmiàn de yālì.

'During World War II, on August 26, 1940, the British air force used the method of "encircling the state of Wei to rescue the state of Zhao" and attacked the German capital of Berlin, thereby lessening the pressure on England.'

Example 2: 甲公司想整个吞并乙公司，乙公司找到甲公司支柱产品的漏洞，通过起诉甲公司的做法起到了**围魏救赵**的效果。

Jiǎ gōngsī xiǎng zhěnggè tūnbìng yǐ gōngsī, yǐ gōngsī zhǎodào jiǎ gōngsī zhīzhù chǎnpǐn de lòudòng, tōngguò qǐsù jiǎ gōngsī de zuòfǎ qǐdàole wéi Wèi jiù Zhào de xiàoguǒ.

'When Company A wanted to completely swallow up Company B, Company B found a flaw in one of Company A's signature products and, by suing Company A, brought about the result of "encircling Wei to save Zhao," so that Company A was forced to give up its attack.'

Usage: Functions mainly as attributive.

Allusion: In 354 B.C.E., the state of Wei sent its army to besiege Handan, the capital of the state of Zhao. When Zhao sought assistance from the state of Qi, Qi sent Tian Ji and Sun Bin to bring troops to help Zhao. Tian Ji believed that the troops should be brought to Handan, the Zhao capital, but Sun Bin thought that most of the Wei troops were besieging the Zhao capital and that the Wei capital was therefore empty, so it would be better to take advantage of the opportunity to attack the capital of Wei. In that case, the Wei troops would definitely turn around to save Wei, so the Qi troops could lie in wait halfway along the way and make a surprise attack on the Wei troops. And in exactly this manner, the Qi troops really did defeat the Wei troops and save Zhao. (From "Sunzi Wuqi Lie Zhuan" in *Records of the Grand Historian*)

Near Synonym: [声东击西] (shēng dōng jī xī 聲東擊西) 'announce east attack west – use diversionary tactics.'

451. 【花团锦簇】(花團錦簇) huā tuán jǐn cù

This idiom means 'masses of flowers and piles of brocade.' This can also refer to well-dressed people or beautiful decorations.

Example 1: 国庆节的时候，北京城的大街小巷，**花团锦簇**。

Guóqìngjié de shíhou, Běijīngchéng de dàjiē-xiǎoxiàng, huātuán-jǐncù.

'At the time of National Day, all the streets and lanes of the city of Beijing are filled with masses of flowers and piles of brocade.'

Example 2: 广州的春天**花团锦簇**，非常漂亮。

Guǎngzhōu de chūntiān huātuán-jǐncù, fēicháng piàoliang.

'At spring time in Guangzhou, you see masses of flowers and piles of brocade; it's very pretty.'

Usage: Functions mainly as predicate; can also serve as attributive.

Near Synonyms: [姹紫嫣红] (chà zǐ yān hóng 姹紫嫣紅) 'beautiful flowers of all colors,' [万紫千红] (wàn zǐ qiān hóng 萬紫千紅) 'colors of every hue, multicolored.'

452. 【悲欢离合】(悲歡離合) bēi huān lí hé

The four characters literally mean 'sad, happy, separate, reunite.' The whole idiom means 'sorrows, joys, partings, and reunions' or 'the vicissitudes of human life.' Though 欢 and 合 have a positive sense, the overall meaning of this idiom emphasizes 悲 and 离, with their negative sense.

Example 1: 罗密欧与朱丽叶**悲欢离合**的爱情故事感动了一代又一代人。

Luómì'ōu yǔ Zhūlìyè bēihuān-líhé de àiqíng gùshi gǎndòngle yí dài yòu yí dài rén.

'The love story of Romeo and Juliet with its sorrows, joys, partings, and reunions has moved one generation after another.'

Example 2: 每次战争中都有很多**悲欢离合**。

Měicì zhànzhēng zhōng dōu yǒu hěn duō bēihuān-líhé.

'In every war there are many sorrows, joys, partings, and reunions.'

Usage: Functions mainly as attributive or predicate.

Note: This idiom has become popularized through a *ci* or lyric poem by the famous Song Dynasty poet Su Dongpo, in which he writes 人有悲欢离合，月有阴晴圆缺，此事古难全 (rén yǒu bēihuān-líhé, yuè yǒu yīnqíng-yuánquē, cǐ shì gǔ nán quán 人有悲歡離合，月有陰晴圓缺，此事古難全) 'People have their sorrows and joys, their partings and reunions; the moon has its dark and cloudy times, its waxing and its waning; these things have not been ideal since ancient times.'

Near Synonyms: [酸甜苦辣] (suān tián kǔ là 酸甜苦辣) 'sour, sweet, bitter, pungent,' [喜怒哀乐] (xǐ nù āi lè 喜怒哀樂) 'delight, anger, sorrow, happiness.'

453. 【今非昔比】(今非昔比) jīn fēi xī bǐ

昔 means 'former times.' The meaning of the whole idiom is 'the present does not compare with the past, times have changed.'

Example 1: 中国经过三十多年稳定的高速的发展，实力已经**今非昔比**了。

Zhōngguó jīngguò sānshí duō nián wěndìng de gāosù de fāzhǎn, shílì yǐjīng jīnfēixībǐ le.

'After over thirty years of stable and rapid development, China's real power has become unprecedented in her history.'

Example 2: 那个电影明星老了以后，影响力也下降了，**今非昔比**了。

Nàge diànyǐng míngxīng lǎole yǐhòu, yǐngxiǎnglì yě xiàjiàng le, jīnfēixībǐ le.

'After that movie star aged, his influence declined; his situation today can't compare with that in the past.'

Usage: Functions as predicate, often in the pattern 已 (经) ～了 (yǐ (jīng) . . . le 已 (經) ～了).

Near Synonyms: [日新月异] (rì xīn yuè yì 日新月異) 'change rapidly with each new day,' [鸟枪换炮] (niǎo qiāng huàn pào 鳥槍換炮) 'a bird gun exchanged for a cannon – a big change for the better' (limited mostly to spoken Chinese).

Antonyms: [今不如昔] (jīn bù rú xī 今不如昔) 'the present is worse than the past,' [每况愈下] (měi kuàng yù xià 每況愈下) 'go from bad to worse.'

454. 【一事无成】(一事無成) yí shì wú chéng

成 here means 'accomplishment.' The meaning of the whole idiom is 'accomplish or achieve nothing, get nowhere.'

Example 1: 他自以为聪明，但是做事不认真，结果一辈子**一事无成**。

Tā zìyǐwéi cōngmíng, dànshì zuòshì bú rènzhēn, jiéguǒ yíbèizi yíshì-wúchéng.

'He considered himself smart, but he wasn't diligent in his work, with the result that his whole life long he accomplished nothing.'

Example 2: 如果一个人过于保守，什么都不敢尝试，很可能会**一事无成**。

Rúguǒ yí ge rén guòyú bǎoshǒu, shénme dōu bù gǎn chángshì, hěn kěnéng huì yíshì-wúchéng.

'If someone is excessively conservative, not daring to try anything, it is quite possible that they will achieve nothing.'

Usage: Functions as predicate.

Note: Derogatory in meaning.

Near Synonym: [无所作为] (wú suǒ zuò wéi 無所作為) 'do or accomplish nothing.'

Antonyms: [功成名就] (gōng chéng míng jiù 功成名就) 'make a name for oneself,' [无往不利] (wú wǎng bú lì 無往不利) 'there is no place one goes where it is not advantageous – go smoothly everywhere.'

455. 【不伦不类】(不倫不類) bù lún bú lèi

Both 伦 and 类 mean 'class, category.' The meaning of the whole idiom is 'not one thing not another, neither fish nor fowl, nondescript.'

Example 1: 这座建筑下面四四方方的，像是中国传统的建筑，可是上面有个很高的尖顶，看起来**不伦不类**的。

Zhè zuò jiànzhù xiàmiàn sìsìfāngfāng de, xiàng shì Zhōngguó chuántǒng de jiànzhù, kěshì shàngmiàn yǒu ge hěn gāo de jiāndǐng, kànqǐlai bùlún-búlèi de.

'This building is square-shaped below, like traditional Chinese buildings, but on top there is a very tall apex that looks neither here nor there.'

Example 2: 有人把豆汁翻译成北京可乐，听起来**不伦不类**的。

Yǒu rén bǎ dòuzhī fānyì chéng Běijing kělè, tīngqǐlai bùlún-búlèi de.

'There is someone who has translated *douzhi* (fermented mung bean juice) as "Beijing cola," which sounds rather nondescript.'

Usage: Functions mainly as predicate and attributive.

Note: Derogatory in meaning.

Near Synonyms: [不三不四] (bù sān bú sì 不三不四) 'not three not four, neither fish nor fowl,' [非驴非马] (fēi lú fēi mǎ 非驢非馬) 'not donkey not horse, neither fish nor fowl.'

Antonym: [正经八百] (zhèng jīng bā bǎi 正經八百) 'seriously.'

456. 【家常便饭】(家常便飯) jiā cháng biàn fàn

家常 means 'home-style' and 便饭 means 'simple meal,' so the literal meaning of this idiom is 'simple home-style food.' This idiom is often used with the literal meaning, but it is just as often employed as a metaphor for anything that is very common or ordinary.

Example 1: 这是**家常便饭**，请随便用，不要客气。

Zhè shì jiācháng-biànfàn, qǐng suíbiàn yòng, búyào kèqi.

'This is simple home-style cooking, please help yourself, don't be polite.'

Example 2: 他是个工作狂，加班到晚上十一、二点是**家常便饭**。

Tā shì ge gōngzuòkuáng, jiābān dào wǎnshang shíyī-èr diǎn shì jiācháng-biànfàn.

'He's a workaholic; for him to work overtime until 11 or 12 p.m. is a common occurrence.'

Usage: Functions mainly as predicate.

Near Synonyms: [粗茶淡饭] (cū chá dàn fàn 粗茶淡飯) 'plain food,' [司空见惯] (sī kōng jiàn guàn 司空見慣) 'get used to seeing something and no longer find it strange.'

Antonym: [别开生面] (bié kāi shēng miàn 別開生面) 'start something new.'

457. 【平心而论】(平心而論) píng xīn ér lùn

平心 means 'with an impartial heart' and 论 means 'discuss.' The meaning of the whole idiom is 'objectively speaking, in all fairness, to be honest.'

Example 1: **平心而论**，这位总统虽然很有成就，但是也有不完美的地方。

Píngxīn-érlùn, zhè wèi zǒngtǒng suīrán hěn yǒu chéngjiù, dànshì yě yǒu bù wánměi de dìfang.

'In all fairness, though this president has lots of achievements, there are also areas that are not perfect.'

Example 2: **平心而论**，这篇文章写得不算太好。

Píngxīn-érlùn, zhè piān wénzhāng xiěde bú suàn tài hǎo.

'To be honest, this essay was not written particularly well.'

Usage: Functions as independent adverbial.

458. 【变本加厉】(變本加厲) biàn běn jiā lì

变 means 'change,' 本 means 'basic nature,' 加 means 'add,' and 厉 means 'severity.' The whole idiom means 'intensify, become worse.'

Example 1: 外资企业对当地工人的剥削**变本加厉**了，不但没有涨工资，反而降了一些。

Wàizī qǐyè duì dāngdì gōngrén de bōxuē biànběn-jiālì le, búdàn méiyǒu zhǎng gōngzī, fǎn'ér jiàngle yìxiē.

'The exploitation of local workers by foreign enterprises has intensified; not only have wages not risen but, on the contrary, they have fallen a little.'

Example 2: 东南沿海一带的走私活动**变本加厉**了，从开始的香烟、摩托车，到现在的汽车、石油。

Dōngnán yánhǎi yídài de zǒusī huódòng biànběn-jiālì le, cóng kāishǐ de xiāngyān, mótuóchē, dào xiànzài de qìchē, shíyóu.

'Smuggling in the southeastern coastal area has intensified, from the initial cigarettes and motorcycles to the present automobiles and petroleum.'

Usage: Functions mainly as predicate.

Note: Derogatory in meaning.

Near Synonyms: [肆无忌惮] (sì wú jì dàn 肆無忌憚) 'unscrupulous, unbridled,' [小题大做] (xiǎo tí dà zuò 小題大做) 'make much ado about nothing.'

459. 【名正言顺】(名正言順) míng zhèng yán shùn

The literal meaning is 'with right titles and proper words – fitting and proper, perfectly justifiable.'

Example 1: 双方父母终于同意了这对年轻人的婚事，于是他们**名正言顺**地结婚了。

Shuāngfāng fùmǔ zhōngyú tóngyìle zhè duì niánqīngrén de hūnshì, yúshì tāmen míngzhèng-yánshùn de jiéhūn le.

'Both parents finally agreed on the young couple's marriage; as a result, they got married in a fitting and proper way.'

Example 2: 你这样做**名正言顺**，什么都不用担心！

Nǐ zhèyàng zuò míngzhèng-yánshùn, shénme dōu búyòng dānxīn!

'If you do things in a fitting and proper way, you don't have to worry about anything!'

Usage: Functions mainly as adverbial modifier, predicate, or attribute.

Note: The negative form is 名不正则言不顺 from *The Analects* of Confucius.

Near Synonym: [理直气壮] (lǐ zhí qì zhuàng 理直氣壯) 'bold through being in the right, with righteous self-assurance.'

Antonyms: [理屈词穷] (lǐ qū cí qióng 理屈詞窮) 'in the wrong and out of arguments,' [师出无名] (shī chū wú míng 師出無名) 'send the army out without a righteous cause – act without any justifiable reason.'

460. 【望梅止渴】(望梅止渴) wàng méi zhǐ kě

望 means 'gaze or look at,' 梅 means 'plum,' 止 means 'stop,' and 渴 means 'thirsty.' A literal translation of this idiom is 'gaze at plums to quench one's thirst.' This is a metaphor for merely consoling oneself with fantasies and being unable to realize one's goals. One possible English translation is 'feed on illusions.'

Example 1: 奢侈品店里的东西一般人是买不起的，有的人只好看看橱窗里的样品**望梅止渴**了。

Shēchǐpǐndiàn lǐ de dōngxi yìbān rén shì mǎibuqǐ de, yǒu de rén zhǐhǎo kànkan chúchuāng lǐ de yàngpǐn wàngméi-zhǐkě le.

'Ordinary people are unable to afford the things in the luxury goods store; some people have no choice but to look at the samples in the display windows as if they were "gazing at plums to quench their thirst."'

Example 2: 指望他帮忙就像**望梅止渴**，其实根本是帮不上的。

Zhǐwàng tā bāngmáng jiù xiàng wàngméi-zhǐkě, qíshí gēnběn shì bāngbushàng de.

'Expecting his help is feeding on illusions; in truth, he is completely unable to help.'

Usage: Functions mainly as predicate.

Allusion: During the Three Kingdoms Period, the famous general Cao Cao was hurrying along the troops that he commanded. It was an unusually hot day, but there were no water sources along the road, so the soldiers were extremely thirsty. Cao Cao said to his soldiers: "Up in front there is a big expanse of plum groves with an abundance of plums that are both sweet and sour. They'll quench your thirst." When the soldiers heard this, the saliva flowed in their mouths, so that they had the energy to keep hurrying along. And in the end they finally did reach a water source. (from "Jia Jue," No. 27, in *New Account of Tales of the World*)

Note: Derogatory in meaning.

Near Synonym: [画饼充饥] (huà bǐng chōng jī 畫餅充饑) 'draw cakes to still one's hunger – feed on illusions.'

461. 【意气风发】(意氣風發) yì qì fēng fā

意气 means 'enthusiasm' and 风发 means 'energetic.' The meaning of the whole idiom is 'enthusiastic and energetic, with boundless enthusiasm.'

Example 1: 年轻人总是**意气风发**，充满活力。

Niánqīng rén zǒngshì yìqì-fēngfā, chōngmǎn huólì.

'Young people are always enthusiastic and energetic, full of vigor.'

Example 2: 新市长**意气风发**地对记者说，"我希望本市的经济三年大变样，五年翻一番。"

Xīn shìzhǎng yìqì-fēngfā de duì jìzhě shuō, "Wǒ xīwàng běnshì de jīngjì sān nián dà biànyàng, wǔ nián fān yì fān."

'The new mayor, with boundless enthusiasm, told the reporter, "I hope that the economy of this city will in three years look very different and in five years double."'

Usage: Functions mainly as predicate, adverbial, and attributive.

Note: Complimentary in meaning.

Near Synonym: [英姿勃发] (yīng zī bó fā 英姿勃發) 'heroic.'

Antonyms: [萎靡不振] (wěi mí bú zhèn 萎靡不振) 'dispirited,' [垂头丧气] (chuí tóu sàng qì 垂頭喪氣) 'hang one's head in dejection,' [心灰意冷] (xīn huī yì lěng 心灰意冷) 'downhearted.'

462. 【双管齐下】(雙管齊下) shuāng guǎn qí xià

双 means 'two, a pair' and 管 means 'pen, brush.' A literal translation is 'paint with two brushes at the same time.' Later this was used as a metaphor for 'doing two things simultaneously' or 'simultaneously using two ways to achieve one goal.'

Example 1: 只有**双管齐下**才能解决目前的难题，一方面要提高销量，另一方面要节省开支。

Zhǐ yǒu shuāngguǎn-qíxià cái néng jiějué mùqián de nántí, yì fāngmiàn yào tígāo xiāoliàng, lìng yì fāngmiàn yào jiéshěng kāizhī.

'Only by doing two things simultaneously can we solve the current difficulty; on the one hand, we must raise sales volume and on the other, we must save on expenditures.'

Example 2: 为了有利地解决这次国际争端，该国政府采取了**双管齐下**的办法，一边呼吁国际社会进行介入调解，一边加强了军事准备。

Wèile yǒulì de jiějué zhè cì guójì zhēngduān, gāi guó zhèngfǔ cǎiqǔle shuāngguǎn-qíxià de bànfǎ, yìbiān hūyù guójì shèhuì jìnxíng jièrù tiáojiě, yìbiān jiāqiángle jūnshì zhǔnbèi.

'To resolve this international dispute in a beneficial manner, the government of the country in question adopted an approach of simultaneously using two ways to achieve one goal; on the one hand, it appealed to the international community to undertake and get involved in mediation and, on the other hand, it strengthened its military preparations.'

Usage: Functions mainly as predicate.

Near Synonym: [齐头并进] (qí tóu bìng jìn 齊頭並進) 'do many things at once.'

463. 【含辛茹苦】(含辛茹苦) hán xīn rú kǔ

含 means 'hold in the mouth,' 辛 means 'hot spicy,' 茹 means 'eat,' and 苦 means 'bitter,' so that the literal meaning of this idiom is 'mouth something spicy and eat something bitter.' A freer translation is 'suffer great hardships and difficulties.'

Example 1: 你父母**含辛茹苦**，把你们两个养大，很不容易。

Nǐ fùmǔ hánxīn-rúkǔ, bǎ nǐmen liǎng ge yǎngdà, hěn bù róngyì.

'Your parents suffered tremendous hardships in raising the two of you; it was really difficult.'

Example 2: 为了得到第一手的资料，他到偏远落后的地区**含辛茹苦**地调查了几个月。

Wèile dédào dìyīshǒu de zīliào, tā dào piānyuǎn luòhòu de dìqū hánxīn-rúkǔ de diàochále jǐ ge yuè.

'To obtain first-hand data, he went to remote, backward regions and, suffering great hardships, conducted research for several months.'

Usage: Functions mainly as predicate and adverbial.

Near Synonyms: [相濡以沫] (xiāng rú yǐ mò 相濡以沫) 'moisten one another with saliva – help one another in difficult times,' [千辛万苦] (qiān xīn wàn kǔ 千辛萬苦) 'many sufferings and hardships.'

Antonym: [养尊处优] (yǎng zūn chǔ yōu 養尊處優) 'have a respected position and live in affluence.'

464. 【立竿见影】(立竿見影) lì gān jiàn yǐng

立 means 'raise up,' 竿 means 'pole,' and 影 means 'shadow.' The literal meaning of this idiom is 'put up a pole and see its shadow.' A freer translation is 'get quick results.'

Example 1: 这服药非常神奇，产生了**立竿见影**的效果。

Zhè fù yào fēicháng shénqí, chǎnshēngle lìgān-jiànyǐng de xiàoguǒ.

'This dose of medicine was extremely miraculous; it brought about immediate results.'

Example 2: 他的经济政策**立竿见影**，取得了良好的经济效益。

Tā de jīngjì zhèngcè lìgān-jiànyǐng, qǔdéle liánghǎo de jīngjì xiàoyì.

'His economic policy got off to a quick start, obtaining excellent economic results.'

Usage: Functions mainly as attributive; can also serve as predicate.

Note: Somewhat complimentary in meaning.

Near Synonym: [马到成功] (mǎ dào chéng gōng 馬到成功) 'horse arrives achieve success – imminent success.'

Antonym: [旷日持久] (kuàng rì chí jiǔ 曠日持久) 'long and drawn out, time-consuming.'

---

465. **【冲锋陷阵】(衝鋒陷陣)** chōng fēng xiàn zhèn

冲锋 means 'charge forward and attack,' 陷 means 'break through or breach,' and 阵 means 'battle formation.' The meaning of the whole idiom is 'charge forward and submerge the enemy lines' or 'dash to the front of battle.'

Example 1: 这位将军从普通的士兵当起，一辈子**冲锋陷阵**，为国家立了大功。

Zhè wèi jiāngjūn cóng pǔtōng de shìbīng dāngqǐ, yíbèizi chōngfēng-xiànzhèn, wèi guójiā lìle dàgōng.

'This general has been serving since he was an ordinary rank-and-file soldier; his whole life long he has been charging forward. He has made very meritorious contributions for his country.'

Example 2: 他又勇敢又有智谋，这件事可以叫他去**冲锋陷阵**。

Tā yòu yǒnggǎn yòu yǒu zhìmóu, zhè jiàn shì kěyǐ jiào tā qù chōngfēng-xiànzhèn.

'He is both courageous and resourceful, so in this matter we can have him charge forward.'

Usage: Functions mainly as predicate and attributive.

Note: Complimentary in meaning.

Near Synonyms: [赴汤蹈火] (fù tāng dǎo huǒ 赴湯蹈火) 'go through fire or water,' [出生入死] (chū shēng rù sǐ 出生入死) 'risk one's life.'

Antonym: [临阵脱逃] (lín zhèn tuō táo 臨陣脫逃) 'flee just before battle.'

466. 【水到渠成】(水到渠成) shuǐ dào qú chéng

渠 means 'a channel (for water)' and 成 means 'is formed.' The literal meaning is 'water arrives and channel is formed,' with a freer translation being 'when conditions are ripe success is achieved; achieved naturally and without effort.'

Example 1: 他为竞选做了大量的准备，所以成功是**水到渠成**的事。

Tā wèi jìngxuǎn zuòle dàliàng de zhǔnbèi, suǒyǐ chénggōng shì shuǐdào-qúchéng de shì.

'He made a great deal of preparations for the campaign, so it was natural and only to be expected that he would be successful.'

Example 2: 等欧洲各国经济上完全融合以后，政治上的统一自然**水到渠成**。

Děng Ōuzhōu gè guó jīngjì shàng wánquán rónghé yǐhòu, zhèngzhì shàng de tǒngyī zìrán shuǐdào-qúchéng.

'Once the economies of the various European countries have completely merged, political union will naturally achieve success.'

Usage: Functions mainly as predicate and attributive. Often preceded by the near synonym 瓜熟蒂落 (guā shú dì luò) 'when the melon is ripe it falls off the vine,' with which it co-occurs.

Near Synonyms: [瓜熟蒂落] (guā shú dì luò 瓜熟蒂落) 'when the melon is ripe it falls off the vine,' [顺理成章] (shùn lǐ chéng zhāng 順理成章) 'do something in a reasonable and orderly manner.'

Antonym: [无疾而终] (wú jí ér zhōng 無疾而終) 'without illness to die, pass away peacefully.'

467. 【危言耸听】(危言聳聽) wēi yán sǒng tīng

危言 means 'words said to frighten people' and 耸听 means 'frightening things one hears.' The meaning of the whole idiom is 'purposely say startling things in order to frighten people and create a sensation.'

Example 1: 这绝不是**危言耸听**，历史上出现过类似的情况。

Zhè jué bú shì wēiyán-sǒngtīng, lìshǐ shàng chūxiànguo lèisì de qíngkuàng.

'This is absolutely not a case of startling things being said to frighten people and create a sensation; in history there have occurred similar situations.'

Example 2: 他喜欢吓唬人，总讲一些**危言耸听**的话。

Tā xǐhuan xiàhu rén, zǒng jiǎng yìxiē wēiyán-sǒngtīng de huà.

'He likes to frighten people, always saying some startling things so as to create a sensation.'

Usage: Functions mainly as predicate in negative sentences; can also serve as attributive.

Note: Derogatory in meaning.

Near Synonyms: [骇人听闻] (hài rén tīng wén 駭人聽聞) 'shocking, terrifying,' [耸人听闻] (sǒng rén tīng wén 聳人聽聞) 'shake people up, sensationalize.'

468. 【何去何从】(何去何從) hé qù hé cóng

The first 何 means 'where?' so that 何去 means 'go where?' The second 何 means 'what?' The verb 从 here means 'do' so that 何从 means 'do what?' The meaning of the whole idiom is 'what path to take and what to do.'

Example 1: 大学毕业以后，他有些茫然，不知道自己该**何去何从**。

Dàxué bìyè yǐhòu, tā yǒuxiē mángrán, bù zhīdao zìjǐ gāi héqù-hécóng.

'After graduating from college, he was a little lost, not knowing what path he should take or what he should do.'

Example 2: 英国地处欧洲，但是一向跟美国友好，现在美国跟欧盟有了重大矛盾，英国将**何去何从**？

Yīngguó dìchǔ Ōuzhōu, dànshì yíxiàng gēn Měiguó yǒuhǎo, xiànzài Měiguó gēn Ōuméng yǒule zhòngdà máodùn, Yīngguó jiāng héqù-hécóng?

'England is located in Europe, but has always been friendly toward the U.S.; now that the U.S. and the European Union have had a major clash, what path will England take and what will it do?'

Usage: Functions mainly as predicate.

Antonyms: [听天由命] (tīng tiān yóu mìng 聽天由命) 'abide by the will of heaven, accept one's fate,' [听之任之] (tīng zhī rèn zhī 聽之任之) 'allow things to go any old way, let matters drift.'

469. 【有求必应】(有求必應) yǒu qiú bì yìng

求 means 'request,' 必 means 'certainly,' and 应 means 'respond.' A literal translation of this idiom is 'if there is a request certainly respond,' with a freer translation being 'respond to every plea, grant every request.'

Example 1: 他很富有，又很大方，所以他的朋友有困难的时候都去找他帮助，而他每次**有求必应**。

Tā hěn fùyǒu, yòu hěn dàfāng, suǒyǐ tā de péngyou yǒu kùnnán de shíhou dōu qù zhǎo tā bāngzhù, ér tā měi cì yǒuqiú-bìyìng.

'He is very wealthy and also very generous, so when his friends have difficulties, they all go looking for him to help, and each time he responds to every request.'

Example 2: 那位大牌网球球星没有一点明星的架子，观众请他签名的时候几乎**有求必应**。

Nà wèi dàpái wǎngqiú qiúxīng méiyǒu yìdiǎn míngxīng de jiàzi, guānzhòng qǐng tā qiānmíng de shíhou jīhū yǒuqiú-bìyìng.

'That big-name tennis star doesn't have even a little of the haughtiness of a star; when spectators ask him for an autograph, he grants almost every request.'

Usage: Functions as predicate.

Note: Complimentary in meaning.

Near Synonyms: [来者不拒] (lái zhě bú jù 來者不拒) 'one who comes is not refused – no one is rejected,' [乐善好施] (lè shàn hào shī 樂善好施) 'charitable, benevolent.'

Antonym: [拒之门外] (jù zhī mén wài 拒之門外) 'refuse her or him outside the entrance – refuse someone entrance.'

470. 【杯弓蛇影】 (杯弓蛇影) bēi gōng shé yǐng

杯 means 'cup,' 弓 means 'bow (as in archery),' 蛇 means 'snake,' and 影 here means 'reflection.' A literal translation of the whole idiom is '(mistakenly to take the reflection of a) bow in one's cup as a snake's reflection,' with freer translations being 'entertain imaginary fears, very suspicious, paranoid.'

Example 1: 逃犯听见尖锐的声音就以为是警车，简直**杯弓蛇影**。

Táofàn tīngjiàn jiānruì de shēngyīn jiù yǐwéi shì jǐngchē, jiǎnzhí bēigōng-shéyǐng.

'When the escaped convict heard the piercing sound, he thought it was a police car; he was simply paranoid.'

Example 2: 投资者要大胆自信，不能**杯弓蛇影**。

Tóuzīzhě yào dàdǎn zìxìn, bùnéng bēigōng-shéyǐng.

'Investors must be bold and self-confident; they cannot entertain imaginary fears.'

Usage: Functions mainly as predicate.

Allusion: In ancient times there was a man whose superior once invited him to go drinking with him. Hanging on the wall there was a bow which, in the sunlight, was reflected on the wine cup so that it looked just like a snake. The man felt quite uncomfortable, but the other person was his superior, so he couldn't very well not drink, and so he drank. When he went home, he felt such severe pain in his chest and abdomen that he couldn't eat; he tried laxatives but they didn't help. Later, because of some business, his superior went to his home and, seeing him like that, asked him what was wrong. The subordinate said he feared nothing more than that kind of snake, and now the snake had already entered his belly. His superior went home and thought for a long time; suddenly he saw the bow on the wall and understood immediately. He then sent someone to take his subordinate to the place where they had originally gone drinking; in the cup there again was the reflection of a snake. The superior asked the subordinate if it had been this kind of snake, and the subordinate said that, yes, it had been this kind of snake. Then the superior told the subordinate that the 'snake' was the reflection of the bow on the wall. The subordinate understood immediately, and so he recovered right away from his serious illness.

Note: Derogatory in meaning.

Near Synonyms: [惊弓之鸟] (jīng gōng zhī niǎo 驚弓之鳥) 'a bird afraid of a bow – once bitten twice shy,' [草木皆兵] (cǎo mù jiē bīng 草木皆兵) 'grass and trees all look like the enemy – panic-stricken,' [疑神疑鬼] (yí shén yí guǐ 疑神疑鬼) 'suspect gods suspect devils – very suspicious and fearful.'

Antonyms: [泰然处之] (tài rán chǔ zhī 泰然處之) 'calmly handle it – handle something with composure,' [谈笑自若] (tán xiào zì ruò 談笑自若) 'go on as if nothing had happened.'

471. 【风平浪静】(風平浪靜) fēng píng làng jìng

A literal translation of this idiom is 'wind calm waves still.' The meaning is 'calm and tranquil, uneventful.'

Example 1: 暴雨过后，海面上**风平浪静**。

Bàoyǔ guòhòu, hǎimiàn shàng fēngpíng-làngjìng.

'After the rainstorm, the surface of the sea was calm and tranquil.'

Example 2: 这几天，股票市场看起来好像**风平浪静**，但是大家都清楚，过几天就会不平静了。

Zhè jǐ tiān, gǔpiào shìchǎng kànqǐlai hǎoxiàng fēngpíng-làngjìng, dànshì dàjiā dōu qīngchu, guò jǐ tiān jiù huì bù píngjìng le.

'The last few days the stock market has looked calm and tranquil, but everyone is clear, in a few days it won't be calm anymore.'

Usage: Functions mainly as predicate.

Near Synonyms: [波澜不惊] (bō lán bù jīng 波瀾不驚) 'mighty waves not risen – uneventful,' [平安无事] (píng ān wú shì 平安無事) 'peaceful and without troubling matters, all is well.'

Antonyms: [轩然大波] (xuān rán dà bō 軒然大波) 'major disturbance,' [波涛汹涌] (bō tāo xiōng yǒng 波濤洶涌) 'roaring waves.'

472. 【逍遥法外】(逍遙法外) xiāo yáo fǎ wài

逍遥 means 'carefree and unencumbered' and 法外 means 'outside or beyond the law.' This idiom refers to those who have broken the law but remain unpunished and free. A freer translation is 'at large.'

Example 1: 这起案件已经发生一年多了，可是凶手依然**逍遥法外**，真让人愤怒。

Zhè qǐ ànjiàn yǐjīng fāshēng yì nián duō le, kěshì xiōngshǒu yīrán xiāoyáo-fǎwài, zhēn ràng rén fènnù.

'This case occurred over a year ago, yet the murderer is still at large; it really makes one angry.'

Example 2: 有的高干子弟以为父母有权有钱，他们犯了罪以后仍可以**逍遥法外**。

Yǒu de gāogàn zǐdì yǐwéi fùmǔ yǒu quán yǒu qián, tāmen fànle zuì yǐhòu réng kěyǐ xiāoyáo-fǎwài.

'The sons and daughters of some high-level cadres believe that because their parents have power and money, after they have committed crimes they can still remain free and beyond the reach of the law.'

Usage: Functions as predicate.

Note: Derogatory in meaning.

Near Synonym: [无法无天] (wú fǎ wú tiān 無法無天) 'without morality, lawless.'

Antonyms: [法网难逃] (fǎ wǎng nán táo 法網難逃) 'law net hard to escape – the arm of the law reaches far,' [天网恢恢] (tiān wǎng huī huī 天網恢恢) 'heavenly net very vast – justice is inescapable.'

473. 【灯红酒绿】 (燈紅酒綠) dēng hóng jiǔ lǜ

A literal translation is 'lantern is red and wine is green.' The meaning is 'debauchery.'

Example 1: 他进了大城市，受不了**灯红酒绿**的诱惑，慢慢地没有追求了。

Tā jìnle dàchéngshì, shòubùliǎo dēnghóng-jiǔlǜ de yòuhuò, mànmàn de méiyǒu zhuīqiú le.

'On entering the big city, he was unable to endure the temptations of debauchery, gradually not having anything that he pursued anymore.'

Example 2: 这条街**灯红酒绿**，不由得让人想起纽约、东京和香港。

Zhè tiáo jiē dēnghóng-jiǔlǜ, bùyóude ràng rén xiǎngqǐ Niǔyuē, Dōngjīng hé Xiānggǎng.

'This street is full of bars and brothels; one can't help but think of New York, Tokyo, and Hong Kong.'

Usage: Nominal element, functions mainly as attributive and predicate.

Note: Pejorative in meaning.

Near Synonyms: [花天酒地] (huā tiān jiǔ dì 花天酒地) 'flowers in the sky and wine on the ground – lead a frivolous life,' [纸醉金迷] (zhǐ zuì jīn mí 紙醉金迷) 'intoxicated by paper and mesmerized by gold – indulge in wanton and luxurious living.'

Antonym: [克勤克俭] (kè qín kè jiǎn 克勤克儉) 'hardworking and thrifty.'

474. 【顶天立地】 (頂天立地) dǐng tiān lì dì

The literal meaning is 'with one's head reaching the sky and one's feet on the ground.' A freer translation is 'having a heroic or indomitable spirit.'

Example 1: 他是一个好丈夫，既能在外面奋斗，又很照顾妻子和孩子，是个**顶天立地**的男子汉。

Tā shì yí ge hǎo zhàngfu, jì néng zài wàimiàn fèndòu, yòu hěn zhàogù qīzi hé háizi, shì ge dǐngtiān-lìdì de nánzǐhàn.

'He is a good husband, both able to struggle on the outside and taking good care of his wife and children – a "real man" of indomitable spirit.'

Example 2: 这么大的国家当然需要**顶天立地**的人来领导。

Zhème dà de guójiā dāngrán xūyào dǐngtiān-lìdì de rén lái lǐngdǎo.

'So large a country of course needs a person of heroic spirit to lead it.'

Usage: Functions mainly as attributive and predicate.

Note: Complimentary in meaning.

Antonym: [卑躬屈膝] (bēi gōng qū xī 卑躬屈膝) 'bow low and humiliate oneself, submissive or deferential.'

475. 【有鉴于此】 (有鑒於此) yǒu jiàn yú cǐ

鉴 here means 'experience,' 于 means 'from,' and 此 means 'this.' A literal translation of the whole idiom is 'having the experience obtained from this.' Freer translations are 'taking this into consideration, in view of this.'

Example 1: 人们的寿命明显增长了，**有鉴于此**，政府应该加快完善社会养老保障体系。

Rénmen de shòumìng míngxiǎn zēngzhǎngle, yǒujiàn-yúcǐ, zhèngfǔ yīnggāi jiākuài wánshàn shèhuì yǎnglǎo bǎozhàng tǐxì.

'People's life spans have clearly increased; in view of this, the government should accelerate the perfection of a system for social retirement safeguards.'

Example 2: 英语热兴起了，全民都在学英语，**有鉴于此**，电视台、出版社纷纷推出跟英语有关的节目和书籍。

Yīngyǔ rè xīngqǐle, quánmín dōu zài xué Yīngyǔ, yǒujiàn-yúcǐ, diànshìtái, chūbǎnshè fēnfēn tuīchū gēn Yīngyǔ yǒuguān de jiémù hé shūjí.

'An "English fad" has started up, with everyone learning English; in view of this, television stations and publishers are one after another putting out programs and books related to English.'

Usage: Functions mainly as independent element.

Note: Written style.

Antonym: [另当别论] (lìng dāng bié lùn 另當別論) 'regarded as another matter entirely.'

476. 【义愤填膺】(義憤填膺) yì fèn tián yīng

义 means 'righteousness,' 愤 means 'indignation,' 填 means 'fill,' and 膺 means 'breast, chest.' A literal translation of this idiom is 'righteous indignation fills the breast,' with a freer translation being 'filled with righteous indignation.'

Example 1: 日本右翼分子歪曲第二次世界大战的历史，这令中国人民**义愤填膺**。

Rìběn yòuyì fènzǐ wāiqū Dì'èr Cì Shìjiè Dàzhàn de lìshǐ, zhè lìng Zhōngguó rénmín yìfèn-tiányīng.

'Japanese right-wingers distort the history of World War II; this fills the Chinese people with righteous indignation.'

Example 2: 他**义愤填膺**地说，"你这样做会得到报应的。"

Tā yìfèn-tiányīng de shuō, "Nǐ zhèyàng zuò huì dédào bàoyìng de."

'Filled with righteous indignation, he said, "Your doing this will receive retribution."'

Usage: Functions mainly as predicate; can also serve as adverbial.

Note: Complimentary in meaning.

Near Synonyms: [满腔义愤] (mǎn qiāng yì fèn 滿腔義憤) 'filled with righteous indignation,' [天怒人怨] (tiān nù rén yuàn 天怒人怨) 'the wrath of God and enmity of man – seething discontent.'

Antonyms: [无动于衷] (wú dòng yú zhōng 無動於衷) 'unmoved, unconcerned,' [麻木不仁] (má mù bù rén 麻木不仁) 'numb, apathetic.'

477. 【不可告人】(不可告人) bù kě gào rén

告 means 'tell, inform.' The whole idiom means 'secretive, confidential, cannot bear the light of day.'

Example 1: 他们两个总是背着别人偷偷地说话，好像有**不可告人**的目的。

Tāmen liǎng ge zǒngshì bèizhe biérén tōutōu de shuōhuà, hǎoxiàng yǒu bùkě-gàorén de mùdì.

'The two of them always talk in secret with their backs turned to others; it seems they have some secret purpose.'

Example 2: 如果你没有**不可告人**的事情，为什么不当着大家的面讲出来？

Rúguǒ nǐ méiyǒu bùkě-gàorén de shìqing, wèishénme bù dāngzhe dàjiā de miàn jiǎng chūlái?

'If you don't have anything confidential, why don't you just say it to everyone's face?'

Usage: Functions as attributive.

Note: Derogatory in meaning.

Near Synonym: [别有用心] (bié yǒu yòng xīn 别有用心) 'harbor ulterior motives.'

Antonym: [光明正大] (guāng míng zhèng dà 光明正大) 'frank and upright.'

478. 【指手画脚】(指手畫腳) zhǐ shǒu huà jiǎo

指 means 'point,' 画 means 'draw,' and 脚 means 'foot.' A literal translation is 'point with the hands and draw with the feet.' The meaning is 'gesticulate' or, by extension, 'make indiscrete remarks, interfere in the affairs of others, criticize.'

Example 1: 中国反对任何国家在人权问题上对中国**指手画脚**。

Zhōngguó fǎnduì rènhé guójiā zài rénquán wèntí shàng duì Zhōngguó zhǐshǒu-huàjiǎo.

'China is opposed to any country's criticism of China in the area of human rights issues.'

Example 2: 他**指手画脚**地说，"你们看看，我当初怎么说来着？如果你们当初听了我的忠告，现在就不会这么惨了吧？"

Tā zhǐshǒu-huàjiǎo de shuō, "Nǐmen kànkan, wǒ dāngchū zěnme shuō láizhe? Rúguǒ nǐmen dāngchū tīngle wǒ de zhōnggào, xiànzài jiù bú huì zhème cǎnle ba?"

'Gesticulating with his hands he said, "See, what did I say at the outset? If you had listened to my advice at the outset, then I suppose you wouldn't be in such a terrible situation now?"'

Usage: Functions mainly as predicate and adverbial.

Note: Derogatory in meaning.

Near Synonyms: [品头论足] (pǐn tóu lùn zú 品頭論足) 'overly critical of small details, nitpick,' [多管闲事] (duō guǎn xián shì 多管閑事) 'mind other people's business.'

479. 【简明扼要】(簡明扼要) jiǎn míng è yào

扼 means 'grasp' and 要 means 'main points.' The meaning of the whole idiom is 'brief and to the point, clear and concise.'

Example 1: 警察局长**简明扼要**地回答了记者提出的问题。

Jǐngchájúzhǎng jiǎnmíng-èyào de huídále jìzhě tíchū de wèntí.

'The police station chief briefly and concisely answered the questions raised by the reporters.'

Example 2: 这篇文章条理清晰，**简明扼要**，通俗易懂。

Zhè piān wénzhāng tiáolǐ qīngxī, jiǎnmíng-èyào, tōngsú-yìdǒng.

'This essay is well-ordered and clear, brief and to the point, and easy to understand.'

Usage: Functions mainly as adverbial and predicate.

Note: Complimentary in meaning.

Near Synonym: [短小精悍] (duǎn xiǎo jīng hàn 短小精悍) 'short of stature but energetic and brave.'

Antonym: [长篇累牍] (cháng piān lěi dú 長篇累牘) 'long essay.'

---

480. 【螳螂捕蝉，黄雀在后】(螳螂捕蟬，黄雀在後)
táng láng bǔ chán, huáng què zài hòu

螳螂 means 'mantis,' 捕 means 'catch,' 蝉 means 'cicada,' and 黄雀 is a type of finch. A literal translation of this idiom is 'mantis catches cicada, finch is behind,' with a freer translation being 'when a mantis catches a cicada, a finch is right behind.' By metaphor this refers to people who single-mindedly plot against someone else, unaware that another person is also plotting against them.

Example 1: 他一辈子算计别人，没想到**螳螂捕蝉，黄雀在后**，最后他自己被他的秘书算计了。

Tā yíbèizi suànjì biérén, méi xiǎngdào tángláng-bǔchán, huángquè-zàihòu, zuìhòu tā zìjǐ bèi tā de mìshū suànjìle.

'His whole life long he schemed against others, never thinking that "when a mantis catches a cicada, the finch is right behind"; in the end, he himself was plotted against by his secretary.'

Example 2: 他得意地说："想不到**螳螂捕蝉，黄雀在后**吧？我盯着你已经好久了。"

Tā déyì de shuō: "Xiǎngbúdào tángláng-bǔchán, huángquè-zàihòu ba? Wǒ dīngzhe nǐ yǐjīng hǎojiǔ le."

'He said with satisfaction: "I guess you didn't think that 'when a mantis catches a cicada, the finch is never far behind,' or did you? I've been keeping a close watch on you for a long time now."'

Usage: Functions mainly as predicate; also used independently.

Allusion: During the Spring and Autumn Period, the king of the state of Wu was determined to fight the state of Chu and said to his ministers of state that if anyone tried to dissuade him, they would have to die. The king of Wu had a young retainer who wanted to dissuade him, but the retainer didn't dare to dissuade the king too directly. And so, early one morning, he took his slingshot and walked in the garden, the dew making all his clothes wet. He did this for three consecutive days. The king of Wu was curious and asked him why he did this. The retainer answered:

"In the garden there was a tree, and on the tree there was a cicada. The cicada only knew to sing on the tree, not realizing that there was a mantis behind it that was getting ready to catch it. The mantis with one heart and one mind was preparing to catch the cicada, but it didn't realize that there was a finch next to it preparing to eat the mantis. The finch stretched its neck, preparing to eat the mantis, but it didn't realize that I was in back, preparing to shoot it with a slingshot. The mantis, the finch, and I all wished to obtain that which we wanted, but we all forgot that we ourselves were in danger." The king of Wu felt that the retainer's words made a lot of sense, so he gave up his plan to fight the state of Chu. (from "Zhengjian," Book 9, in *Shuoyuan*)

Note: Derogatory in meaning.

Near Synonym: [害人如害己] (hài rén rú hài jǐ 害人如害己) 'harming other people is like harming oneself.'

Antonym: [智者千虑, 必有一失] (zhì zhě qiān lǜ, bì yǒu yì shī 智者千虑, 必有一失) 'wise people have a thousand concerns, there is sure to be a mistake.'

481. 【一举两得】(一舉兩得) yì jǔ liǎng dé

举 means 'action' and 得 means 'obtain.' A literal translation of this idiom is 'one action two acquisitions,' with a freer translation being 'kill two birds with one stone.'

Example 1: 夏季到中国去学中文，还能参观旅游，可谓一**举两得**。

Xiàjì dào Zhōngguó qù xué Zhōngwén, hái néng cānguān lǚyóu, kě wèi yìjǔ-liǎngdé.

'Going to China in the summer to study Chinese, and in addition being able to see the sites and tour, this can be called "killing two birds with one stone."'

Example 2: 把工厂建到农村，既降低了成本，又解决了当地的就业，真是一**举两得**的好办法。

Bǎ gōngchǎng jiàndào nóngcūn, jì jiàngdīle chéngběn, yòu jiějuéle dāngdì de jiùyè, zhēn shì yìjǔ-liǎngdé de hǎo bànfǎ.

'Constructing the factory in the countryside has both reduced costs and solved local employment; it's really a good approach that "kills two birds with one stone."'

Usage: Functions mainly as predicate; can also serve as attributive.

Note: Complimentary in meaning.

Near Synonyms: [一石二鸟] (yì shí èr niǎo 一石二鳥) 'one stone two birds,' [一箭双雕] (yí jiàn shuāng diāo 一箭雙雕) 'one arrow pair hawks – kill two birds with one stone,' [事半功倍] (shì bàn gōng bèi 事半功倍) 'twice the results with half the effort,' [两全其美] (liǎng quán qí měi 兩全其美) 'satisfy both sides.'

Antonyms: [事倍功半] (shì bèi gōng bàn 事倍功半) 'twice the work with half the result,' [得不偿失] (dé bù cháng shī 得不償失) 'the gain does not make up for the loss.'

482. 【置之度外】(置之度外) zhì zhī dù wài

置 means 'put,' 之 means 'it,' and 度 means 'consider.' A literal translation of the whole idiom is 'put it outside of one's consideration,' with a freer translation being 'disregard, give no thought to.'

Example 1: 那位警察把生死**置之度外**，勇敢地跟歹徒搏斗。

Nà wèi jǐngchá bǎ shēngsǐ **zhìzhī-dùwài**, yǒnggǎn de gēn dǎitú bódòu.

'That policeman disregarded life and death, bravely fighting with the evildoer.'

Example 2: 这场球赛，她把胜负**置之度外**，因此打得十分放松。

Zhè chǎng qiúsài, tā bǎ shèngfù **zhìzhī-dùwài**, yīncǐ dǎde shífēn fàngsōng.

'In this match, she gave no thought to victory or defeat; therefore, she played in a very relaxed manner.'

Usage: Functions as predicate, often preceded by constructions involving 把 (bǎ) or 将 (jiāng 將), and frequently with the objects 生死 (shēngsǐ) 'life and death,' 安危 (ānwēi) 'safety and danger,' 得失 (déshī) 'gain and loss,' 荣辱 (róngrǔ 榮辱) 'honor and dishonor,' 胜负 (shèngfù 勝負) 'victory or defeat,' 利益 (lìyì) 'benefit,' and 生命 (shēngmìng) 'life.'

Note: Complimentary in meaning.

Near Synonyms: [念念不忘] (niàn niàn bú wàng 念念不忘) 'never forget,' [耿耿于怀] (gěng gěng yú huái 耿耿於懷) 'take to heart, brood over.'

483. 【永垂不朽】(永垂不朽) yǒng chuí bù xiǔ

永 means 'forever,' 垂 here means 'hand down,' and 朽 means 'decay.' A literal translation of the whole idiom is 'forever hand down and not decay.' Freer translations include 'immortal, live in one's heart forever.'

Example 1: 雷锋精神**永垂不朽**!

Léi Fēng jīngshen **yǒngchuí-bùxiǔ**!

'The spirit of Lei Feng will live forever!' (*Note:* Lei Feng, 1940–1962, was a model soldier in the Chinese People's Liberation Army.)

Example 2: 他的英明和事业将**永垂不朽**。

Tā de yīngmíng hé shìyè jiāng **yǒngchuí-bùxiǔ**.

'His brilliance and his causes will be immortal.'

Usage: Functions mainly as predicate; used on solemn occasions, especially in texts and speeches about the deceased.

Note: Complimentary in meaning.

Near Synonyms: [名垂青史] (míng chuí qīng shǐ 名垂青史) 'go down in history,' [流芳千古] (liú fāng qiān gǔ 流芳千古) 'leave a good name through the ages.'

Antonym: [遗臭万年] (yí chòu wàn nián 遗臭萬年) 'leave behind a stink for ten thousand years – have one's name live in everlasting infamy.'

484. 【美中不足】(美中不足) měi zhōng bù zú

美 means 'good,' 中 means 'within,' and 不足 means 'insufficient.' A literal translation of the whole idiom is 'the insufficiency within the goodness.' In other words, something is overall quite good but there are still areas where improvement is needed. Freer English translations include 'a minor flaw in something otherwise perfect,' 'a small defect,' and 'what's missing is. . . .'

Example 1: 他们夫妻和睦，儿子也很可爱。但是**美中不足**的是只有一个孩子，如果再有一个女儿就完美了。

Tāmen fūqī hémù, érzi yě hěn kě'ài. Dànshì měizhōng-bùzú de shì zhǐ yǒu yí ge háizi, rúguǒ zài yǒu yí ge nǚ'ér jiù wánměi le.

'Husband and wife get along harmoniously, and their son is cute. But the one thing that's missing is they have only one child; if in addition they had a daughter, then it would be perfect.'

Example 2: 这部电影拍得很成功，不过**美中不足**的是结局有些悲惨，让观众心里挺沉重的。

Zhè bù diànyǐng pāide hěn chénggōng, búguò měizhōng-bùzú de shì jiéjú yǒu xiē bēicǎn, ràng guānzhòng xīn lǐ tǐng chénzhòng de.

'This movie was made very successfully; however, the one minor flaw is that the ending is a little too tragic; it makes the audience have a very serious and heavy feeling in their hearts.'

Usage: Functions mainly as subject in the structure 美中不足的是 (měi zhōng bù zú de shì) 'what's missing is. . . .' Also functions as attribute in 美中不足的地方 (měi zhōng bù zú de dìfang) and 美中不足之处 (měi zhōng bù zú zhī chù 美中不足之處), both 'a minor flaw in something otherwise perfect.'

Near Synonyms: [白璧微瑕] (bái bì wēi xiá 白璧微瑕) 'white jade tiny flaw – a flaw or defect in somebody or something otherwise perfect,' [瑕不掩瑜] (xiá bù yǎn yú 瑕不掩瑜) 'flaw does not hide luster – the weakness does not detract from the virtues.'

Antonyms: [十全十美] (shí quán shí měi 十全十美) 'perfect,' [尽善尽美] (jìn shàn jìn měi 盡善盡美) 'completely perfect.'

485. 【人声鼎沸】(人聲鼎沸) rén shēng dǐng fèi

人声 means 'human voices,' a 鼎 is a kind of ancient pot, and 沸 means 'boil.' 鼎沸 means 'water is boiling in a big pot, bubbling like in a cauldron.' The meaning of the whole idiom is 'noisy voices, a hubbub or confusion of voices.'

Example 1: 法庭里对同性恋婚姻辩论得很激烈，法庭外支持者和反对者都很多，**人声鼎沸**。

Fǎtíng lǐ duì tóngxìngliàn hūnyīn biànlùn de hěn jīliè, fǎtíng wài zhīchízhě hé fǎnduìzhě dōu hěn duō, rénshēng-dǐngfèi.

'Inside the courtroom, gay marriage was being debated intensely; outside the courtroom, there were many supporters and many opponents, their voices creating a loud hubbub.'

Example 2: 他喜欢在**人声鼎沸**的闹市区逛街。

Tā xǐhuan zài rénshēng-dǐngfèi de nàoshìqū guàngjiē.

'He likes to go strolling through the noisy downtown area.'

Usage: Functions mainly as predicate; can also serve as attributive.

Antonym: [鸦雀无声] (yā què wú shēng 鴉雀無聲) 'crow sparrow no sound – complete silence.'

486. 【天真烂漫】(天真爛漫) tiān zhēn làn màn

天真 means 'innocent, naive' and 烂漫 means 'unaffected, innocent.' The meaning of the whole idiom is 'lively and cute, naive and unaffected, pure and natural.'

Example 1: 一群**天真烂漫**的孩子在公园里玩耍，非常可爱。

Yì qún tiānzhēn-lànmàn de háizi zài gōngyuán lǐ wánshuǎ, fēicháng kě'ài.

'A group of innocent and unaffected children were playing in the park; they were very cute.'

Example 2: 她多想回到**天真烂漫**的童年啊！

Tā duō xiǎng huídào tiānzhēn-lànmàn de tóngnián a!

'How much she wishes she could go back to the naive and innocent years of childhood!'

Usage: Functions mainly as attributive and predicate.

Note: Complimentary in meaning.

Near Synonyms: [天真无邪] (tiān zhēn wú xié 天真無邪) 'innocent and free of evil intention,' [活泼可爱] (huó pō kě ài 活潑可愛) 'lively and cute.'

Antonyms: [少年老成] (shào nián lǎo chéng 少年老成) 'young but experienced,' [老成持重] (lǎo chéng chí zhòng 老成持重) 'experienced and discreet.'

487. 【就事论事】(就事論事) jiù shì lùn shì

就 means 'concerning, regarding, according to.' The meaning of the whole idiom is 'consider the matter in and of itself.'

Example 1: 我的话不是针对某个人，而是**就事论事**。

Wǒ de huà bú shì zhēnduì mǒu ge rén, érshì jiùshì-lùnshì.

'My words are not directed at any individual, but are considering the matter in and of itself.'

Example 2: 我们不应该停留在**就事论事**的阶段，而应该从大局来看待这件事情。

Wǒmen bù yīnggāi tíngliú zài jiùshì-lùnshì de jiēduàn, ér yīnggāi cóng dàjú lái kàndài zhè jiàn shìqing.

'We shouldn't stop at the stage where you consider a matter in and of itself, but should treat this matter as seen from the overall situation.'

Usage: Functions mainly as predicate; can also serve as attributive and adverbial.

Note: In order to give the person concerned face, Chinese people usually say that the comments they make are about a matter itself (就事论事), and are not directed at any individual.

Near Synonyms: [对号入座] (duì hào rù zuò 對號入座) 'according to the ticket number take one's seat,' [以偏概全] (yǐ piān gài quán 以偏概全) 'take a part for the whole.'

488. 【大手大脚】(大手大腳) dà shǒu dà jiǎo

A literal translation of this idiom is 'big hands big feet.' The meaning is 'extravagant, wasteful.'

Example 1: 他花钱**大手大脚**的，太浪费了。

Tā huāqián dàshǒu-dàjiǎo de, tài làngfèi le.

'He's extravagant in the way he spends money – just too wasteful!'

Example 2: 结婚后，她改变了**大手大脚**买东西的毛病。

Jiéhūn hòu, tā gǎibiànle dàshǒu-dàjiǎo mǎi dōngxi de máobìng.

'After she married, she changed her bad habit of making extravagant purchases.'

Usage: Functions mainly as adverbial. Modifies verbs related to spending money or consuming resources.

Note: Derogatory in meaning.

Near Synonym: [挥金如土] (huī jīn rú tǔ 揮金如土) 'throw money around like dirt.'

Antonyms: [省吃俭用] (shěng chī jiǎn yòng 省吃儉用) 'economical in everyday necessities,' [克勤克俭] (kè qín kè jiǎn 克勤克儉) 'hardworking and thrifty.'

489. 【漫山遍野】 (漫山遍野) màn shān biàn yě

漫 means 'all over, everywhere,' 遍 also means 'all over, everywhere,' and 野 means 'wilderness.' The literal meaning is 'all over the mountains and all over the wilderness,' with a freer translation being 'all over, in great numbers.'

Example 1: 新英格兰的秋天，**漫山遍野**都是红叶，非常漂亮。

Xīn Yīnggélán de qiūtiān, mànshān-biànyě dōu shì hóng yè, fēicháng piàoliàng.

'At the time of fall in New England, there are red leaves all over, it's very beautiful.'

Example 2: 听说那座山上有千年的人参，人们连夜赶到那里去挖，**漫山遍野**都是人。

Tīngshuō nà zuò shān shàng yǒu qiān nián de rénshēn, rénmen liányè gǎndào nàlǐ qù wā, mànshān-biànyě dōu shì rén.

'When they heard that on that mountain there was 1,000-year-old ginseng, people rushed there to dig straight through the night; there were people everywhere.'

Usage: Functions as subject, attributive, predicate, and adverbial.

Near Synonym: [俯拾皆是] (fǔ shí jiē shì 俯拾皆是) 'so many you can bend down and pick them up easily.'

Antonym: [寥若晨星] (liáo ruò chén xīng 寥若晨星) 'few as the morning stars – very few.'

490. 【刻舟求剑】 (刻舟求劍) kè zhōu qiú jiàn

刻 means 'carve,' 舟 means 'boat,' 求 means 'seek,' and 剑 means 'sword.' A literal translation of the whole idiom is 'carve marks on a boat (to serve as a reminder of where to) seek the sword (that fell overboard).' This is a metaphor for 'not know how to adapt to changed conditions,' 'act foolishly without regard to changed circumstances,' or 'incorrect or inappropriate method for solving a problem.'

Example 1: 你这样做就是**刻舟求剑**，十年以后情况不一定变化成啥样呢。

Nǐ zhèyàng zuò jiùshì kèzhōu-qiújiàn, shí nián yǐhòu qíngkuàng bù yídìng biànhuà chéng sháyàng ne.

'Your doing it this way is just like the man who made a notch on a boat to mark where a sword had fallen overboard – you don't know what the situation will be like in ten years.'

Example 2: 看事情的时候得用发展的眼光去看，否则就是**刻舟求剑**了。

Kàn shìqing de shíhou děi yòng fāzhǎn de yǎnguāng qù kàn, fǒuzé jiùshì kèzhōu-qiújiàn le.

'When looking at things you must look at them from a progressive perspective; otherwise, you'll be like the man who made a notch on a boat to mark where a sword had fallen overboard – that is, you won't know how to adapt to changed conditions.'

Usage: Functions mainly as predicate and adverbial.

Allusion: In ancient times there was a man who was crossing the Yangtze River. Because he didn't pay attention, the treasured sword he was carrying fell into the water. Very calmly, he made a mark on the boat, saying: "This is the place where my sword fell into the water." When the boat reached the river bank, he jumped into the water to look for his sword at the place where he had made the mark, but of course he couldn't find it. (from "Cha Jin" in *Mr. Lü's Spring and Autumn Annals*)

Note: Derogatory in meaning.

Near Synonyms: [守株待兔] (shǒu zhū dài tù 守株待兔) 'keep watch over a tree stump waiting for hares – hope to attain something without working for it,' [墨守成规] (mò shǒu chéng guī 墨守成規) 'stick to conventions or outmoded practices.'

Antonyms: [见机行事] (jiàn jī xíng shì 見機行事) 'look for a good opportunity to take some action, play by ear,' [八面玲珑] (bā miàn líng lóng 八面玲瓏) 'smooth and slick, get along well with everyone.'

491. 【生龙活虎】(生龍活虎) shēng lóng huó hǔ

龙 means 'dragon' and 虎 means 'tiger.' A literal translation is 'live dragon live tiger.' The extended meaning is 'lively and vigorous, bursting with energy.'

Example 1: 在球场上，小伙子们一个个**生龙活虎**，拼得很凶。

Zài qiúchǎng shàng, xiǎohuǒzimen yī ge ge shēnglóng-huóhǔ, pīnde hěn xiōng.

'On the ball field, each and every one of the kids was brimming with energy, giving it their utmost.'

Example 2: 原来**生龙活虎**的一个人，怎么病了几天之后，就这么没有精神？

Yuánlái shēnglóng-huóhǔ de yí ge rén, zěnme bìngle jǐ tiān zhīhòu, jiù zhème méiyǒu jīngshen?

'A person who formerly was bursting with energy, how come that after being sick for a couple of days, he is this lacking in energy?'

Usage: Functions mainly as attributive and predicate.

Note: Complimentary in meaning.

Near Synonyms: [生气勃勃] (shēng qì bó bó 生氣勃勃) 'full of vitality,' [龙腾虎跃] (lóng téng hǔ yuè 龍騰虎躍) 'dragon soars tiger leaps – bustle of activity.'

Antonyms: [死气沉沉] (sǐ qì chén chén 死氣沉沉) 'lifeless,' [老气横秋] (lǎo qì héng qiū 老氣橫秋) 'lacking vitality.'

492. 【不甘示弱】 (不甘示弱) bù gān shì ruò

不甘 means 'not resigned to, not reconciled to, unwilling to,' 示 means 'show,' and 弱 means 'weak.' A literal translation of the whole idiom is 'unwilling to show weakness (in comparison with others),' with a freer translation being 'unwilling to be outdone.'

Example 1: 红、白两队进行唱歌比赛，白队赢得了全场掌声，红队**不甘示弱**，唱起了她们最拿手的歌。

Hóng, bái liǎng duì jìnxíng chànggē bǐsài, bái duì yíngdéle quán chǎng zhǎngshēng, hóng duì bùgān-shìruò, chàngqǐle tāmen zuì náshǒu de gē.

'The two teams – red and white – held a singing contest, with the white team winning the applause of the entire audience; the red team, unwilling to be outdone, began singing their signature song.'

Example 2: 美国宣布对欧盟某项商品实行制裁，欧盟**不甘示弱**，马上宣布对美国某重要出口产品进行反倾销调查。

Měiguó xuānbù duì Ōuméng mǒu xiàng shāngpǐn shíxíng zhìcái, Ōuméng bùgān-shìruò, mǎshàng xuānbù duì Měiguó mǒu zhòngyào chūkǒu chǎnpǐn jìnxíng fǎn qīngxiāo diàochá.

'When the U.S. announced that it was implementing sanctions against a certain European Union commodity, the European Union, unwilling to be outdone, immediately announced that it was implementing an anti-dumping investigation of a certain important U.S. export product.'

Usage: Functions mainly as predicate.

Near Synonyms: [不甘人后] (bù gān rén hòu 不甘人後) 'not reconciled to being behind someone else,' [力争上游] (lì zhēng shàng yóu 力爭上游) 'strive to go upstream – strive to be best.'

Antonyms: [甘拜下风] (gān bài xià fēng 甘拜下風) 'candidly admit defeat,' [心服口服] (xīn fú kǒu fú 心服口服) 'sincerely convinced in one's mind about something and say so sincerely.'

493. 【循循善诱】 (循循善誘) xún xún shàn yòu

循循 means 'in proper order,' 善 means 'well,' and 诱 means 'guide.' A literal translation is 'in proper order good at guiding others.' This idiom is often translated as 'good at guiding others, teach in a systematic and patient manner.'

Example 1: 王教授讲课的时候不是枯燥地讲解，而是给出很多例子，**循循善诱**。

Wáng jiàoshòu jiǎngkè de shíhou bú shì kūzào de jiǎngjiě, ér shì gěi chū hěn duō lìzi, xúnxún-shànyòu.

'When Professor Wang teaches, she doesn't dryly lecture, but gives lots of examples; she is good at guiding others.'

Example 2: 他是一位**循循善诱**的电视访谈节目主持人。

Tā shì yí wèi xúnxún-shànyòu de diànshì fǎngtán jiémù zhǔchírén.

'He is a television talk show host who is good at guiding others.'

Usage: Functions mainly as predicate; can also serve as attributive and adverbial.

Note: Complimentary in meaning.

Near Synonym: [谆谆教导] (zhūn zhūn jiào dǎo 諄諄教導) 'instruct earnestly.'

494. 【万家灯火】 (萬家燈火) wàn jiā dēng huǒ

万家 means 'ten thousand families' or 'very many families,' while 灯火 means 'lights.' A literal translation is 'ten thousand families' lamps.' This often refers to a city that is ablaze with lights.

Example 1: 虽然已经深夜里，上海依然**万家灯火**，这是一个不眠的城市。

Suīrán yǐjīng shēn yèlǐ, Shànghǎi yīrán wànjiā-dēnghuǒ, zhè shì yí ge bù mián de chéngshì.

'Though it was already late at night, Shanghai was still ablaze with lights; this was a city that did not sleep.'

Example 2: 她站在楼顶，欣赏着**万家灯火**的美景。

Tā zhàn zài lóudǐng, xīnshǎngzhe wànjiā-dēnghuǒ de měijǐng.

'She stood on the roof, enjoying the beautiful sights of a city ablaze with lights.'

Usage: Functions mainly as object and attributive.

Near Synonym: [灯火通明] (dēng huǒ tōng míng 燈火通明) 'brightly lit.'

Antonym: [灯火阑珊] (dēng huǒ lán shān 燈火闌珊) 'with lights dimming.'

495. 【执迷不悟】 (執迷不悟) zhí mí bú wù

执 means 'persist,' 迷 means 'confused,' and 悟 means 'realize, understand.' A literal translation is 'persist in being confused and not realize it.' A freer translation is 'persist in one's errors and refuse to come to one's senses.'

Example 1: 你要看清形势，不要**执迷不悟**。

Nǐ yào kànqīng xíngshì, bú yào zhímí-búwù.

'You should see the situation clearly; don't persist in your errors and refuse to come to your senses.'

Example 2: 科学和历史早已证明世上没有什么长生不老的药，可是还有些**执迷不悟**的人努力寻找。

Kēxué hé lìshǐ zǎoyǐ zhèngmíng shìshàng méiyǒu shénme cháng shēng bù lǎo de yào, kěshì hái yǒu xiē zhímí-búwù de rén nǔlì xúnzhǎo.

'Science and history have long ago proven that there is no medicine in the world that can let you live forever, but there are still some people who refuse to come to their senses who try hard to find it.'

Usage: Functions mainly as predicate; can also serve as attributive.

Note: Derogatory in meaning.

Near Synonyms: [冥顽不化] (míng wán bú huà 冥頑不化) 'stubbornly not change,' [一意孤行] (yí yì gū xíng 一意孤行) 'cling obstinately to a reckless course.'

Antonyms: [迷途知返] (mí tú zhī fǎn 迷途知返) 'lose one's way but know how to get back – realize and rectify one's errors,' [知错就改] (zhī cuò jiù gǎi 知錯就改) 'as soon as you realize a mistake, correct it.'

496. 【千疮百孔】 (千瘡百孔) qiān chuāng bǎi kǒng

疮 means 'wound' and 孔 means 'hole.' The literal meaning is 'a thousand wounds and a hundred holes,' with a freer translation being 'riddled with gaping wounds, afflicted with any disorder imaginable.' This idiom is also used metaphorically to mean 'full of flaws or shortcomings.'

Example 1: 战后的城市**千疮百孔**，看起来非常悲惨。

Zhànhòu de chéngshì qiānchuāng-bǎikǒng, kànqǐlai fēicháng bēicǎn.

'The post-war city was riddled with gaping wounds, looking extremely tragic.'

Example 2: 如何挽救一家**千疮百孔**的亏损的企业，让新来的领导非常发愁。

Rúhé wǎnjiù yìjiā qiānchuāng-bǎikǒng de kuīsǔn de qǐyè, ràng xīn lái de lǐngdǎo fēicháng fāchóu.

'How to rescue a business that was riddled with flaws and that was losing money made the recently arrived leader very worried.'

Usage: Functions as predicate and attributive.

Note: Somewhat derogatory in meaning.

Antonym: [焕然一新] (huàn rán yì xīn 焕然一新) 'look brand-new, change beyond recognition.'

497. 【悬崖勒马】 (懸崖勒馬) xuán yá lè mǎ

悬 means 'hang,' 崖 means 'precipice,' 悬崖 means 'sheer cliff,' and 勒 means 'rein in.' A literal translation is 'rein in a horse at the edge of a precipice,' with the extended meaning being 'realize and escape from danger just in the nick of time.'

Example 1: 现在你的情况非常危险，如果再不**悬崖勒马**，肯定会出大事的。

Xiànzài nǐ de qíngkuàng fēicháng wēixiǎn, rúguǒ zài bù xuányá-lèmǎ, kěndìng huì chū dà shì de.

'Now your situation is very dangerous; if you still don't escape from danger just in the nick of time, you will definitely have a big accident.'

Example 2: 中国警告对方**悬崖勒马**，否则后果自负。

Zhōngguó jǐnggào duìfāng xuányá-lèmǎ, fǒuzé hòuguǒ zìfù.

'China warned the other side to escape from danger in the nick of time, otherwise they themselves must take responsibility for the consequences.'

Usage: Functions mainly as predicate.

Antonym: [执迷不悟] (zhí mí bú wù 執迷不悟) 'persist in one's errors and refuse to come to one's senses.'

498. 【半斤八两】 (半斤八兩) bàn jīn bā liǎng

半 means 'half,' 斤 is a unit of weight often translated as 'catty,' and 两 is another unit of weight often translated as 'ounce.' The literal translation of this idiom is 'half a catty (is the equivalent of) eight ounces,' with freer translations being 'six of one and half a dozen of the other, tweedledum and tweedledee, the same.'

Example 1: 一个人骂对方，另一个人打对方，两个人**半斤八两**，都有错儿。

Yí ge rén mà duìfāng, lìng yí ge rén dǎ duìfāng, liǎng ge rén bànjīn-bāliǎng, dōu yǒu cuòr.

'One person scolded the other party, and the other party hit the first person; it's six of one and half a dozen of the other – they were both wrong.'

Example 2: 这种做法跟那种做法**半斤八两**，都不省力。

Zhè zhǒng zuòfǎ gēn nà zhǒng zuòfǎ bànjīn-bāliǎng, dōu bù shěnglì.

'This method is about the same as that method; neither saves labor.'

Explanation: In the traditional Chinese weight system, one *jin* (斤) equals sixteen *liang* (两), so half a *jin* equals eight *liang*. Currently in the P.R.C., one *jin* equals ten *liang*, but in Hong Kong and Taiwan, the traditional system is often still used.

Usage: Functions mainly as predicate at the end of a sentence.

Note: This is colloquial-style usage. It has a somewhat negative connotation.

Near Synonyms: [不相上下] (bù xiāng shàng xià 不相上下) 'equally matched, without much difference,' [旗鼓相当] (qí gǔ xiāng dāng 旗鼓相當) '(two armies) of the same number of banners and drums – well-matched (in strength).'

Antonyms: [大相径庭] (dà xiāng jìng tíng 大相徑庭) 'as different as path and yard – poles apart,' [天差地远] (tiān chā dì yuǎn 天差地遠) 'poles apart.'

499. 【共襄盛举】(共襄盛舉) gòng xiāng shèng jǔ

共 means 'together,' 襄 means 'help,' 盛 means 'great,' and 举 means 'undertaking.' A literal translation is 'together help each other in great undertakings,' with a freer translation being 'join together to accomplish a great task.'

Example 1: 我们中国代表团团长说："我们衷心地希望海内外中华儿女**共襄盛举**，完成祖国统一大业。"

Wǒmen Zhōngguó dàibiǎotuán tuánzhǎng shuō: "Wǒmen zhōngxīn de xīwàng hǎinèiwài Zhōnghuá érnǚ gòngxiāng-shèngjǔ, wánchéng zǔguó tǒngyī dàyè."

'The head of our Chinese delegation said: "We hope with all our hearts that the sons and daughters of China all over the world will join together to accomplish a great task, and complete the unification of the motherland."'

Example 2: 发生了大地震，大陆及港、澳、台三地艺人为了救灾**共襄盛举**，举办了多场演唱会。

Fāshēngle dà dìzhèn, dàlù jí Gǎng, Ào, Tái sān dì yìrén wèile jiùzāi gòngxiāng-shèngjǔ, jǔbànle duō chǎng yǎnchànghuì.

'When the major earthquake occurred, entertainers from the mainland and the three areas of Hong Kong, Macao, and Taiwan joined together to accomplish the great task of providing disaster relief, holding numerous performances.'

Usage: Functions as predicate.

Note: Complimentary in meaning.

Near Synonyms: [齐心协力] (qí xīn xié lì 齊心協力) 'work as one,' [与有荣焉] (yǔ yǒu róng yān 與有榮焉) 'take pride in someone' (written style).

Antonym: [各自为政] (gè zì wéi zhèng 各自為政) 'each does things in her or his own way.'

500. 【五十步笑百步】(五十步笑百步) wǔ shí bù xiào bǎi bù

步 means 'pace, step' and 笑 means 'laugh at.' A literal translation of the whole idiom is '(a man who retreated only) fifty paces laughed at (another man who retreated) a hundred paces.' This means 'disparage someone else for essentially the same thing you yourself have done.'

Example 1: 他以前老笑话别人有绯闻，现在自己有了，真是**五十步笑百步**。

Tā yǐqián lǎo xiàohuà biérén yǒu fēiwén, xiànzài zìjǐ yǒu le, zhēnshì wǔshíbù-xiàobǎibù.

'He used to always laugh at others for having affairs; now he himself is involved in one; it really is a situation of his having disparaged others for the same thing he himself is doing.'

Example 2: 两个人同时受审，在审判的过程中，两个人同时揭发对方贪污受贿，并指责对方人品低劣，这不过是**五十步笑百步**罢了。

Liǎng ge rén tóngshí shòushěn, zài shěnpàn de guòchéng zhōng, liǎng ge rén tóngshí jiēfā duìfāng tānwū shòuhuì, bìng zhǐzé duìfāng rénpǐn dīliè, zhè búguò shì wǔshíbù-xiàobǎibù bàle.

'The two of them stood trial simultaneously; during the course of the trial, the two of them simultaneously exposed each other as being corrupt and having taken bribes, and moreover they found fault with each other for being of bad moral character; this is merely disparaging someone else for essentially the same thing you yourself have done.'

Usage: Functions mainly as predicate.

Allusion: During the Warring States Period, King Hui of Liang was fond of waging war. Mencius went to exhort him. King Hui of Liang said, "As far as my country is concerned, I think I can be considered to have done my best. Wherever there is a natural disaster, I will send people to provide relief. Based on my observation, the kings of other countries are not as conscientious as I am. But the population of the neighboring countries has not decreased, and the population in my own country has not increased. Why is this?" Mencius replied: "King, you are fond of war. Let me offer you an example from war. The battle drums are beating and the armies from the two sides are fighting at close quarters. Unavoidably, there will be some soldiers who flee to the rear. There is one soldier who doesn't stop running until he has run a hundred paces, and there is another who stops after he has run fifty paces. The soldier who ran fifty paces makes fun of the one who ran a hundred paces. Do you think this is right?" King Hui of Liang said: "No, he merely didn't run a hundred paces; he still ran, just like the other soldier." Mencius replied: "Great King, since you understand this reasoning, do not in the future expect that the population of your country will be greater than that of your neighboring countries." (from "King Hui of Liang," Book One, in *The Mencius*)

Note: Derogatory in meaning.

Near Synonym: [天下乌鸦一般黑] (tiān xià wū yā yì bān hēi 天下烏鴉一般黑) 'in the whole world crows are the same black – bad people are bad everywhere, things are the same the world over.'

Appendix one: common structural patterns of Chinese idioms

The following twenty-one structural patterns that are frequently encountered in Chinese idioms are especially productive, well over a thousand Chinese idioms being patterned on them. Learners of Chinese who are familiar with these patterns and who pay careful attention to the context will be able to make educated guesses about the meanings of many unfamiliar idioms. Note that in the list below, an asterisk (*) represents a Chinese character.

1. *天*地：Because 天 (天 tiān) 'heaven' and 地 (地 dì) 'earth' are extreme contrasts, this pattern generally describes extreme degrees of something. Examples: 欢天喜地 (歡天喜地 huān tiān xǐ dì) 'overjoyed,' 惊天动地 (驚天動地 jīng tiān dòng dì) 'earthshaking,' 花天酒地 (花天酒地 huā tiān jiǔ dì) 'flowers in the sky and wine on the ground – lead a frivolous life,' 谢天谢地 (謝天謝地 xiè tiān xiè dì) 'very thankful.'

2. 东*西*：Since 东 (東 dōng) means 'east' and 西 (西 xī) means 'west,' the literal translation of this pattern is 'do something from east to west,' in other words, over a wide range or scope. This pattern is often derogatory in meaning. Examples: 东张西望 (東張西望 dōng zhāng xī wàng) 'look around in all directions,' 东奔西走 (東奔西走 dōng bēn xī zǒu) 'rush about all over the place,' 东拉西扯 (東拉西扯 dōng lā xī chě) 'pull a large number of different things randomly into one's speech, talk incoherently with many irrelevant details.'

3. 不*不*：This pattern means 'neither . . . nor. . . .' Examples: 不三不四 (不三不四 bù sān bú sì) 'neither fish nor fowl,' 不慌不忙 (不慌不忙 bù huāng bù máng) 'neither panicky nor in a rush,' 不屈不挠 (不屈不撓 bù qū bù náo) 'refuse to submit.'

4. 一*一*：This pattern often expresses the meanings 'each, every, all.' Examples: 一言一行 (一言一行 yì yán yì xíng) 'every word and every deed,' 一草一木 (一草一木 yì cǎo yí mù) 'every blade of grass and every tree,' 一心一意 (一心一意 yì xīn yí yì) 'with one heart and one mind, wholeheartedly.'

5. 千*万*：Since, especially in ancient China, 'thousand' and 'ten thousand' were large numbers, this pattern typically means 'large number of, many.' Examples: 千辛万苦 (千辛萬苦 qiān xīn wàn kǔ) 'many sufferings and hardships,' 千变万化 (千變萬化 qiān biàn wàn huà) 'a great number of changes, ever changing,' 千军万马 (千軍萬馬 qiān jūn wàn mǎ) 'a large number of infantry and cavalry.'

6. 无*无*：'Have no . . . at all' and 'not even a little . . .' are common translations of this idiom. Examples: 无忧无虑 (無憂無慮 wú yōu wú lǜ) 'have no worries or anxieties at all,' 无穷无尽 (無窮無盡 wú qióng wú jìn) 'have no limits whatsoever,' 无声无息 (無聲無息 wú shēng wú xī) 'no sound no breath – silent,' 无时无刻 (無時無刻 wú shí wú kè) 'constantly, incessantly, all the time.'

7. 七*八*：This pattern often denotes confusion or disorder, especially in speech. Examples: 七嘴八舌 (七嘴八舌 qī zuǐ bā shé) 'seven mouths eight tongues – everyone talking at

the same time and expressing completely different opinions,' 七手八脚 (七手八腳 qī shǒu bā jiǎo) 'seven hands eight feet – hands and feet flying every which way – very confused,' 七上八下 (七上八下 qī shàng bā xià) 'seven up and eight down – flustered, perturbed, upset.'

8. *头*脑: This pattern, which is common in spoken Chinese, describes a person's 头脑 (tóunǎo) 'head, brains.' Except for 虎头虎脑 (虎頭虎腦 hǔ tóu hǔ nǎo) 'robust and good-natured,' which is complimentary in meaning, the other idioms containing this pattern are generally derogatory. More examples: 呆头呆脑 (呆頭呆腦 dāi tóu dāi nǎo) 'dull and slow-witted,' 愣头愣脑 (愣頭愣腦 lèng tóu lèng nǎo) 'rash, reckless,' 摇头晃脑 (搖頭晃腦 yáo tóu huàng nǎo) 'absent-minded, in a daze.'

9. 天*地*: Since there is a great contrast between天 (天 tiān) 'heaven' and 地 (地 dì) 'earth,' this pattern describes a very high degree of something. Examples: 天长地久 (天長地久 tiān cháng dì jiǔ) 'as eternal as the universe,' 天经地义 (天經地義 tiān jīng dì yì) 'unalterable principle, entirely justified,' 天昏地暗 (天昏地暗 tiān hūn dì àn) 'very dark,' 天崩地裂 (天崩地裂 tiān bēng dì liè) 'earth-shattering.'

10. *三*四: This pattern generally is derogatory in meaning. Examples: 朝三暮四 (朝三暮四 zhāo sān mù sì) 'three in the morning and four at night – fickle and inconstant,' 不三不四 (不三不四 bù sān bú sì) 'neither fish nor fowl,' 丢三落四 (丟三落四 diū sān luò sì) 'lose three drop four – forgetful, absent-minded,' 挑三拣四 (挑三揀四 tiāo sān jiǎn sì) 'choosy.'

11. 龙*虎*: Since 龙 (龍 lóng) 'dragons' and 虎 (虎 hǔ) 'tigers' are both bold and fearless creatures, this pattern is complimentary or commendatory in meaning. Examples: 龙腾虎跃 (龍騰虎躍 lóng téng hǔ yuè) 'dragon soars tiger leaps – bustle of activity,' 龙争虎斗 (龍爭虎鬥 lóng zhēng hǔ dòu) 'dragon fights tiger struggles – fierce fighting between formidable foes,' 龙潭虎穴 (龍潭虎穴 lóng tán hǔ xué) 'dragon pool tiger cave – dangerous place' (the latter idiom being neutral in meaning).

12. 不可**: This pattern means 'unable to.' Examples: 不可思议 (不可思議 bù kě sī yì) 'unable to imagine – inconceivable,' 不可多得 (不可多得 bù kě duō dé) 'unable to obtain more – hard to come by,' 不可理喻 (不可理喻 bù kě lǐ yù) 'unable to reason with – will not listen to reason.'

13. 一*不*: This pattern in general means 'not even a little.' Examples: 一丝不苟 (一絲不苟 yì sī bù gǒu) 'not the least bit negligent,' 一毛不拔 (一毛不拔 yì máo bù bá) 'not willing to pull out even one hair – not lift a finger to help,' 一尘不染 (一塵不染 yì chén bù rǎn) 'not contaminated by even a single particle of dust – clean, spotless,' 一窍不通 (一竅不通 yí qiào bù tōng) 'one gate not opened – know nothing about something.'

14. 有*无*: This pattern usually means 'have . . . not have . . .' with the first half of the pattern being emphasized. Examples: 有备无患 (有備無患 yǒu bèi wú huàn) 'have preparation not have disaster – preparedness averts peril,' 有恃无恐 (有恃無恐 yǒu shì wú kǒng) 'have someone one can rely on and not have fear – feel secure because one has strong backing,' 有气无力 (有氣無力 yǒu qì wú lì) 'have spirit not have strength – listless,' 有名无实 (有名無實 yǒu míng wú shí) 'have name not have reality – in name only.'

15. 金*玉*: Because 金 (金 jīn) 'gold' and 玉 (玉 yù) 'jade' are both valuable commodities of which the Chinese people in general have always been very fond, this pattern is highly complimentary and very positive in meaning. Examples: 金童玉女 (金童玉女 jīn tóng yù nǚ) 'young boys and girls (who serve the immortals in Taoism),' 金枝玉叶 (金枝玉葉 jīn zhī yù yè) 'person of upper class or noble birth,' 金科玉律 (金科玉律 jīn kē yù lǜ) 'golden rule.'

16. 一*半*: Because 一 (一 yī) 'one' and 半 (半 bàn) 'half' are both very small numerical amounts, this pattern describes small quantities of something or a low degree of

something. Examples: 一知半解 (一知半解 yì zhī bàn jiě) 'one know half understand – have only superficial knowledge of something,' 一年半载 (一年半載 yì nián bàn zǎi) 'one year half year – six months to a year,' 一男半女 (一男半女 yì nán bàn nǚ) 'one male half female – one or two children,' 一官半职 (一官半職 yì guān bàn zhí) 'one official half post – unimportant official post.'

17. 不*而*: This pattern basically means 'not/no . . . but. . . .' Examples: 不约而同 (不約而同 bù yuē ér tóng) 'not agree (beforehand) but (end up being) the same – take the same action or have the same view without prior consultation,' 不言而喻 (不言而喻 bù yán ér yù) 'it goes without saying, obvious,' 不翼而飞 (不翼而飛 bú yì ér fēi) 'not winged but fly – vanish into thin air.'

18. 三*两*: This pattern, which is used most commonly in speech, is often somewhat negative in meaning. Examples: 三番两次 (三番兩次 sān fān liǎng cì) 'three times two times – over and over again,' 三拳两脚 (三拳兩腳 sān quán liǎng jiǎo) 'three fists two feet – with just two or three blows or kicks, without great effort,' 三言两语 (三言兩語 sān yán liǎng yǔ) 'three words two words – in a few words,' 三长两短 (三長兩短 sān cháng liǎng duǎn) 'three long two short – mishap, accident.'

19. 以*为*: The verb 以 (以 yǐ) means 'take' and the verb 为 (為 wéi) means 'be.' This pattern can often be translated as 'use . . . as. . . .' Examples: 以退为进 (以退為進 yǐ tuì wéi jìn) 'use retreating as a way to advance,' 以守为攻 (yǐ shǒu wéi gōng) 'use guarding something as a way to attack,' 以人为鉴 (yǐ rén wéi jiàn) 'use a person as a mirror – draw lessons from others.'

20. 大*大*: Since 大 (大 dà) means 'big, large, great,' this pattern ordinarily describes a high degree of something. Examples: 大风大浪 (大風大浪 dà fēng dà làng) 'big winds big waves – great storms, great social upheavals,' 大摇大摆 (大搖大擺 dà yáo dà bǎi) 'big swing big sway – swagger, stagger,' 大起大落 (大起大落 dà qǐ dà luò) 'big rise big fall – major rises and falls.'

21. 一*千*: This structure often has the general meaning that the number involved is small but that the result may be very great. Examples: 一诺千金 (一諾千金 yí nuò qiān jīn) 'one promise is worth a thousand pieces of gold,' 一字千金 (一字千金 yí zì qiān jīn) 'one character is worth a thousand pieces of gold – not one word may be changed.'

Appendix two: Pinyin index of 500 common Chinese idioms

References are to entry numbers.

A

ān jū lè yè	安居乐业	62
àn tú suǒ jì	按图索骥	180

B

bā xiān guò hǎi	八仙过海	70
bá miáo zhù zhǎng	拔苗助长	200
bǎi huā qí fàng	百花齐放	211
Bān mén nòng fǔ	班门弄斧	330
bàn jīn bā liǎng	半斤八两	498
bēi gōng shé yǐng	杯弓蛇影	470
bēi huān lí hé	悲欢离合	452
bèi dào ér chí	背道而驰	214
běn lái miàn mù	本来面目	226
bǐ bǐ jiē shì	比比皆是	143
biàn běn jiā lì	变本加厉	458
bié chū xīn cái	别出心裁	265
bié jù yì gé	别具一格	308
bié kāi shēng miàn	别开生面	176
bié yǒu yòng xīn	别有用心	302
bīn bīn yǒu lǐ	彬彬有礼	243
bīng tiān xuě dì	冰天雪地	375
bó dà jīng shēn	博大精深	201
bù dé ér zhī	不得而知	287
bú dòng shēng sè	不动声色	156
bù gān shì ruò	不甘示弱	492
bù hé shí yí	不合时宜	304
bù jiǎ sī suǒ	不假思索	369
bú jiàn jīng zhuàn	不见经传	266
bù jiě zhī yuán	不解之缘	208
bù kān shè xiǎng	不堪设想	192
bù kě duō dé	不可多得	256
bù kě gào rén	不可告人	477
bù kě huò quē	不可或缺	203
bù kě sī yì	不可思议	21

bù liǎo liǎo zhī	不了了之	445
bù lún bú lèi	不伦不类	455
bù qū bù náo	不屈不挠	136
bù róng zhì yí	不容置疑	405
bú shèng méi jǔ	不胜枚举	323
bù tóng fán xiǎng	不同凡响	379
bù xiāng shàng xià	不相上下	371
bú xiè yí gù	不屑一顾	319
bù yán ér yù	不言而喻	128
bú yàn qí fán	不厌其烦	264
bù yí yú lì	不遗余力	206
bù yǐ wéi rán	不以为然	45
bú yì lè hū	不亦乐乎	383
bù yóu zì zhǔ	不由自主	52
bù yuē ér tóng	不约而同	47
bù zé shǒu duàn	不择手段	251
bù zhé bú kòu	不折不扣	103
bù zhī suǒ cuò	不知所措	66
bù zú wéi qí	不足为奇	336

C

cái gāo bā dǒu	才高八斗	440
cǎo mù jiē bīng	草木皆兵	310
céng chū bù qióng	层出不穷	73
céng jǐ hé shí	曾几何时	426
cháng zhì jiǔ ān	长治久安	61
chē shuǐ mǎ lóng	车水马龙	294
chéng qiān shàng wàn	成千上万	11
chéng qián qǐ hòu	承前启后	384
chéng xīn chéng yì	诚心诚意	346
chí zhī yǐ héng	持之以恒	233
chōng fēng xiàn zhèn	冲锋陷阵	465
chóu chú mǎn zhì	踌躇满志	416
chù mù jīng xīn	触目惊心	147
chuān liú bù xī	川流不息	332
chuí tóu sàng qì	垂头丧气	349

chún wáng chǐ hán	唇亡齿寒	420
cǐ qǐ bǐ fú	此起彼伏	189
cóng tiān ér jiàng	从天而降	435

D

dà dāo kuò fǔ	大刀阔斧	205
dà jiē xiǎo xiàng	大街小巷	51
dà jīng xiǎo guài	大惊小怪	268
dà míng dǐng dǐng	大名鼎鼎	325
dà qiān shì jiè	大千世界	443
dà shì suǒ qū	大势所趋	186
dà shǒu dà jiǎo	大手大脚	488
dà tóng xiǎo yì	大同小异	381
dà yǒu kě wéi	大有可为	152
dà yǒu rén zài	大有人在	362
dà yǒu zuò wéi	大有作为	284
dà zhāng qí gǔ	大张旗鼓	242
dān jīng jié lǜ	殚精竭虑	433
dāng wù zhī jí	当务之急	13
dāng zhī wú kuì	当之无愧	216
dàng rán wú cún	荡然无存	339
dé bù cháng shī	得不偿失	446
dé cái jiān bèi	德才兼备	83
dé gāo wàng zhòng	德高望重	262
dé tiān dú hòu	得天独厚	43
dēng hóng jiǔ lǜ	灯红酒绿	473
diào yǐ qīng xīn	掉以轻心	188
dǐng tiān lì dì	顶天立地	474
dōng chuāng shì fā	东窗事发	240
Dōng Shī xiào pín	东施效颦	270
dú lì zì zhǔ	独立自主	14
dú shù yí zhì	独树一帜	238
dú yī wú èr	独一无二	101
duì niú tán qín	对牛弹琴	320
duì zhèng xià yào	对症下药	334
duō duō bī rén	咄咄逼人	217

E

| ěr mù yì xīn | 耳目一新 | 123 |
| ěr wén mù dǔ | 耳闻目睹 | 387 |

F

fā hào shī lìng	发号施令	412
fā yáng guāng dà	发扬光大	68
fān lái fù qù	翻来覆去	407
fán róng chāng shèng	繁荣昌盛	93
fāng xīng wèi ài	方兴未艾	141
fèi fèi yáng yáng	沸沸扬扬	257

fèn bú gù shēn	奋不顾身	291
fēng chén pú pú	风尘仆仆	259
fēng fēng yǔ yǔ	风风雨雨	98
fēng gōng wěi jì	丰功伟绩	155
fēng píng làng jìng	风平浪静	471
fēng yún biàn huàn	风云变幻	131
fù lì táng huáng	富丽堂皇	305

G

gāo gāo zài shàng	高高在上	427
gāo wū jiàn líng	高屋建瓴	448
gāo zhān yuǎn zhǔ	高瞻远瞩	144
gé gé bú rù	格格不入	273
gēn shēn dì gù	根深蒂固	158
gōng bù yìng qiú	供不应求	23
gòng xiāng shèng jǔ	共襄盛举	499
gǔ sè gǔ xiāng	古色古香	328
gǔ wǎng jīn lái	古往今来	283
gù quán dà jú	顾全大局	69
guā mù xiāng kàn	刮目相看	97
guāng míng lěi luò	光明磊落	331

H

hán xīn rú kǔ	含辛茹苦	463
hào hào dàng dàng	浩浩荡荡	165
hé qù hé cóng	何去何从	468
hōng hōng liè liè	轰轰烈烈	74
hòu gù zhī yōu	后顾之忧	82
hú jiǎ hǔ wēi	狐假虎威	300
hú lún tūn zǎo	囫囵吞枣	280
huā tuán jǐn cù	花团锦簇	451
huà lóng diǎn jīng	画龙点睛	90
huà shé tiān zú	画蛇添足	230
huān tiān xǐ dì	欢天喜地	432
huàn rán yì xīn	焕然一新	194
huǎng rán dà wù	恍然大悟	173
huò rán kāi lǎng	豁然开朗	423
huò zhēn jià shí	货真价实	289

J

jī quǎn shēng tiān	鸡犬升天	290
jí gōng jìn lì	急功近利	161
jí sī guǎng yì	集思广益	285
jì wǎng kāi lái	继往开来	122
jiā cháng biàn fàn	家常便饭	456
jiā yù hù xiǎo	家喻户晓	56
jiān chí bú xiè	坚持不懈	22
jiān dìng bù yí	坚定不移	7

jiān kǔ fèn dòu	艰苦奋斗	2
jiǎn míng è yào	简明扼要	479
jiàn yì yǒng wéi	见义勇为	34
Jiāng láng cái jìn	江郎才尽	370
jiǎo jìn nǎo zhī	绞尽脑汁	348
jiǎo tà shí dì	脚踏实地	64
jiē dà huān xǐ	皆大欢喜	442
jiē èr lián sān	接二连三	248
jiē tóu xiàng wěi	街头巷尾	367
jié rán bù tóng	截然不同	79
jīn fēi xī bǐ	今非昔比	453
jīn bì huī huáng	金碧辉煌	417
jīn jīn lè dào	津津乐道	223
jīn jīn yǒu wèi	津津有味	252
jìn zài zhǐ chǐ	近在咫尺	373
jīng dǎ xì suàn	精打细算	292
jīng gōng zhī niǎo	惊弓之鸟	220
jīng jīng yè yè	兢兢业业	102
jīng shén dǒu sǒu	精神抖擞	344
jīng tiān dòng dì	惊天动地	239
jīng xīn dòng pò	惊心动魄	63
jīng yì qiú jīng	精益求精	182
jǐng dǐ zhī wā	井底之蛙	380
jǐng jǐng yǒu tiáo	井井有条	436
jiǔ ér jiǔ zhī	久而久之	159
jiù shì lùn shì	就事论事	487
jū ān sī wēi	居安思危	372
jū gāo lín xià	居高临下	355
jǔ shì zhǔ mù	举世瞩目	35
jǔ yī fǎn sān	举一反三	444
jǔ zú qīng zhòng	举足轻重	33
jù jīng huì shén	聚精会神	142
juǎn tǔ chóng lái	卷土重来	374

K

kāi mén jiàn shān	开门见山	307
kǎn kǎn ér tán	侃侃而谈	345
kě gē kě qì	可歌可泣	219
kè bù róng huǎn	刻不容缓	78
kè gǔ míng xīn	刻骨铭心	318
kè zhōu qiú jiàn	刻舟求剑	490
kǒu kǒu shēng shēng	口口声声	391
kū xiào bù dé	哭笑不得	398
kǔ kǒu pó xīn	苦口婆心	437
kuài zhì rén kǒu	脍炙人口	227

L

lái zhī bú yì	来之不易	67
làn yú chōng shù	滥竽充数	250

lè bù sī Shǔ	乐不思蜀	360
léi lì fēng xíng	雷厉风行	414
lǐ suǒ dāng rán	理所当然	27
lǐ zhí qì zhuàng	理直气壮	87
lì bù cóng xīn	力不从心	212
lì gān jiàn yǐng	立竿见影	464
liàn liàn bù shě	恋恋不舍	449
liàng lì ér xíng	量力而行	164
liǎo rú zhǐ zhǎng	了如指掌	301
lín láng mǎn mù	琳琅满目	91
lín lí jìn zhì	淋漓尽致	132
liú lián wàng fǎn	流连忘返	406
liǔ àn huā míng	柳暗花明	421
luò yì bù jué	络绎不绝	46

M

mǎ bù tíng tí	马不停蹄	306
màn shān biàn yě	漫山遍野	489
Máo Suì zì jiàn	毛遂自荐	140
měi zhōng bù zú	美中不足	484
míng fù qí shí	名副其实	41
míng liè qián máo	名列前茅	55
míng luò Sūn Shān	名落孙山	190
míng mù zhāng dǎn	明目张胆	386
míng zhèng yán shùn	名正言顺	459
mò míng qí miào	莫名其妙	17
mò mò wú wén	默默无闻	111
mù bù zhuǎn jīng	目不转睛	293

N

nài rén xún wèi	耐人寻味	92
nán néng kě guì	难能可贵	94
nán yuán běi zhé	南辕北辙	150
niàn niàn bú wàng	念念不忘	236
nòng xū zuò jiǎ	弄虚作假	38

O

ǒu xīn lì xuè	呕心沥血	139

P

pái yōu jiě nàn	排忧解难	58
páng rán dà wù	庞然大物	409
píng xīn ér lùn	平心而论	457
pò bù jí dài	迫不及待	112
pò fǔ chén zhōu	破釜沉舟	100
pò zài méi jié	迫在眉睫	146
pū shuò mí lí	扑朔迷离	20
pū tiān gài dì	铺天盖地	241

Q

qí xīn xié lì	齐心协力	49
qí zhì xiān míng	旗帜鲜明	99
Qǐ rén yōu tiān	杞人忧天	130
qì bù chéng shēng	泣不成声	313
qì chuǎn xū xū	气喘吁吁	229
qià dào hǎo chù	恰到好处	222
qiān chuāng bǎi kǒng	千疮百孔	496
qiān fāng bǎi jì	千方百计	3
qiān jiā wàn hù	千家万户	32
qiān jūn wàn mǎ	千军万马	347
qiān lǐ tiáo tiáo	千里迢迢	272
qiān qiān wàn wàn	千千万万	48
qiān xīn wàn kǔ	千辛万苦	269
qiān zǎi nán féng	千载难逢	353
Qián lú jì qióng	黔驴技穷	410
qián suǒ wèi yǒu	前所未有	6
qián yí mò huà	潜移默化	187
qiè ér bù shě	锲而不舍	177
qīng ér yì jǔ	轻而易举	109
qīng miáo dàn xiě	轻描淡写	397
qíng bú zì jìn	情不自禁	44
qiú tóng cún yì	求同存异	105
qǔ cháng bǔ duǎn	取长补短	224
qǔ ér dài zhī	取而代之	157
quán lì yǐ fù	全力以赴	26
quán shén guàn zhù	全神贯注	178
quán xīn quán yì	全心全意	4

R

rán méi zhī jí	燃眉之急	263
rè huǒ cháo tiān	热火朝天	335
rén shān rén hǎi	人山人海	438
rén shēng dǐng fèi	人声鼎沸	485
rèn zhòng dào yuǎn	任重道远	118
rì fù yí rì	日复一日	351
rì xīn yuè yì	日新月异	42
rú huǒ rú tú	如火如荼	274
rú shǔ jiā zhēn	如数家珍	326
rù mù sān fēn	入木三分	120

S

sài wēng shī mǎ	塞翁失马	390
sān gù máo lú	三顾茅庐	170
sān lìng wǔ shēn	三令五申	358
sān sān liǎng liǎng	三三两两	411
shǎng xīn yuè mù	赏心悦目	282
shè shēn chǔ dì	设身处地	401

shēn rù qiǎn chū	深入浅出	253
shēn sī shú lǜ	深思熟虑	237
shēn tǐ lì xíng	身体力行	88
shēn xiān shì zú	身先士卒	343
shēn wù tòng jué	深恶痛绝	255
shěn shí duó shì	审时度势	184
shēng lóng huó hǔ	生龙活虎	491
shēng qì bó bó	生气勃勃	298
shī qíng huà yì	诗情画意	424
shí shì qiú shì	实事求是	1
shí zì lù kǒu	十字路口	198
shǐ wú qián lì	史无前例	153
shǐ zhōng bù yú	始终不渝	162
shì bàn gōng bèi	事半功倍	378
shì ér bú jiàn	视而不见	174
shì zài bì xíng	势在必行	215
shǒu zhū dài tù	守株待兔	210
shù shǒu wú cè	束手无策	197
shuāng guǎn qí xià	双管齐下	462
shuǐ dào qú chéng	水到渠成	466
shuǐ luò shí chū	水落石出	392
shuǐ xiè bù tōng	水泄不通	365
shùn lǐ chéng zhāng	顺理成章	204
sī kōng jiàn guàn	司空见惯	247
sǐ huī fù rán	死灰复燃	389
sì miàn bā fāng	四面八方	28
sì miàn Chǔ gē	四面楚歌	160
sì tōng bā dá	四通八达	218
sì wú jì dàn	肆无忌惮	279
sù bù xiāng shí	素不相识	315
sù rán qǐ jìng	肃然起敬	275
suí xīn suǒ yù	随心所欲	154
suǒ zuò suǒ wéi	所作所为	81

T

tán hé róng yì	谈何容易	185
tán xiào fēng shēng	谈笑风生	382
tàn wéi guān zhǐ	叹为观止	361
táng ér huáng zhī	堂而皇之	316
táng táng zhèng zhèng	堂堂正正	312
táng láng bǔ chán, huáng què zài hòu	螳螂捕蝉,黄雀在后	480
tāo tāo bù jué	滔滔不绝	126
tǎo jià huán jià	讨价还价	85
tí xiào jiē fēi	啼笑皆非	388
tí xīn diào dǎn	提心吊胆	288
tiān fān dì fù	天翻地覆	127
Tiān fāng yè tán	天方夜谭	402
tiān jīng dì yì	天经地义	299
tiān yá hǎi jiǎo	天涯海角	396

tiān zhēn làn màn	天真烂漫	486
tǐng shēn ér chū	挺身而出	125
tōng qíng dá lǐ	通情达理	434
tóng gān gòng kǔ	同甘共苦	385
tóng rì ér yǔ	同日而语	425
tóng xīn tóng dé	同心同德	86
tóng zhōu gòng jì	同舟共济	418
tòng xīn jí shǒu	痛心疾首	429
tōu gōng jiǎn liào	偷工减料	447
tū fēi měng jìn	突飞猛进	96
tū rú qí lái	突如其来	115
tuī bō zhù lán	推波助澜	329
tuō kǒu ér chū	脱口而出	297
tuō tāi huàn gǔ	脱胎换骨	337
tuō yǐng ér chū	脱颖而出	15

W

wáng yáng bǔ láo	亡羊补牢	110
wàn jiā dēng huǒ	万家灯火	494
wàn wú yì shī	万无一失	179
wàng ér què bù	望而却步	394
wàng méi zhǐ kě	望梅止渴	460
wēi bù zú dào	微不足道	77
wēi yán sǒng tīng	危言耸听	467
wéi Wèi jiù Zhào	围魏救赵	450
wèi rán chéng fēng	蔚然成风	267
wèi yǔ chóu móu	未雨绸缪	354
wǒ xíng wǒ sù	我行我素	393
wò xīn cháng dǎn	卧薪尝胆	50
wú dòng yú zhōng	无动于衷	145
wú jì yú shì	无济于事	148
wú jiā kě guī	无家可归	119
wú kě nài hé	无可奈何	16
wú lùn rú hé	无论如何	5
wú néng wéi lì	无能为力	106
wú shí wú kè	无时无刻	431
wú suǒ shì cóng	无所适从	404
wú wēi bú zhì	无微不至	368
wú yǐng wú zōng	无影无踪	245
wú yǔ lún bǐ	无与伦比	314
wú zhōng shēng yǒu	无中生有	408
wǔ cǎi bīn fēn	五彩缤纷	171
wǔ guāng shí sè	五光十色	303
wǔ huā bā mén	五花八门	104
wǔ shí bù xiào bǎi bù	五十步笑百步	500
wǔ yán liù sè	五颜六色	196

X

| xī xī rǎng rǎng | 熙熙攘攘 | 244 |

xī xī xiāng guān	息息相关	75
xǐ chū wàng wài	喜出望外	225
xǐ qì yáng yáng	喜气洋洋	202
xǐ wén lè jiàn	喜闻乐见	117
xiāng dé yì zhāng	相得益彰	235
xiāng fǔ xiāng chéng	相辅相成	84
xiāng tí bìng lùn	相提并论	254
xiāng yī wéi mìng	相依为命	366
xiǎng fāng shè fǎ	想方设法	31
xiāo yáo fǎ wài	逍遥法外	472
xiǎo xīn yì yì	小心翼翼	36
xīn ān lǐ dé	心安理得	356
xīn kuàng shén yí	心旷神怡	413
xīn píng qì hé	心平气和	261
xīn xīn xiàng róng	欣欣向荣	169
xíng xíng sè sè	形形色色	54
xíng zhī yǒu xiào	行之有效	24
xìng gāo cǎi liè	兴高采烈	57
xìng zhì bó bó	兴致勃勃	29
xiōng yǒu chéng zhú	胸有成竹	278
xiù shǒu páng guān	袖手旁观	422
xǔ xǔ rú shēng	栩栩如生	138
xuán yá lè mǎ	悬崖勒马	497
xuě shàng jiā shuāng	雪上加霜	258
xuě zhōng sòng tàn	雪中送炭	363
xún xù jiàn jìn	循序渐进	124
xún xún shàn yòu	循循善诱	493
xùn liàn yǒu sù	训练有素	317
xùn sī wǔ bì	徇私舞弊	65

Y

yǎ sú gòng shǎng	雅俗共赏	403
yǎn ěr dào líng	掩耳盗铃	350
yǎn huā liáo luàn	眼花缭乱	135
yǎn yǎn yì xī	奄奄一息	352
yáng cháng bì duǎn	扬长避短	276
yáng méi tǔ qì	扬眉吐气	338
Yè gōng hào lóng	叶公好龙	340
yè yǐ jì rì	夜以继日	232
yì běn zhèng jīng	一本正经	172
yì chén bù rǎn	一尘不染	377
yì chéng bú biàn	一成不变	296
yì chóu mò zhǎn	一筹莫展	364
yì fān fēng shùn	一帆风顺	183
yì jǔ liǎng dé	一举两得	481
yì jǔ yí dòng	一举一动	167
yí mài xiāng chéng	一脉相承	341
yì míng jīng rén	一鸣惊人	30
yì mú yí yàng	一模一样	95
yí mù liǎo rán	一目了然	163

yì rú jì wǎng	一如既往	19
yī shí zhù xíng	衣食住行	322
yí shì tóng rén	一视同仁	195
yí shì wú chéng	一事无成	454
yì sī bù gǒu	一丝不苟	76
yì wǎng qíng shēn	一往情深	428
yí wàng wú jì	一望无际	295
yì wú suǒ yǒu	一无所有	209
yì wú suǒ zhī	一无所知	107
yì xí zhī dì	一席之地	108
yì xīn yí yì	一心一意	114
yī yī bù shě	依依不舍	359
yí yì gū xíng	一意孤行	357
yì yīng jù quán	一应俱全	286
yì zhēn jiàn xiě	一针见血	309
yǐ shēn zuò zé	以身作则	72
yì bù róng cí	义不容辞	89
yì fèn tián yīng	义愤填膺	476
yì hū xún cháng	异乎寻常	281
yì jūn tū qǐ	异军突起	116
yì kǒu tóng shēng	异口同声	213
yì qì fēng fā	意气风发	461
yì wèi shēn cháng	意味深长	121
yì wú fǎn gù	义无反顾	193
yīn dì zhì yí	因地制宜	9
yīn shì lì dǎo	因势利导	271
yǐn rén rù shèng	引人入胜	191
yǐn rén zhù mù	引人注目	8
yīng yǒu jìn yǒu	应有尽有	149
yíng rèn ér jiě	迎刃而解	333
yìng yùn ér shēng	应运而生	53
yǒng chuí bù xiǔ	永垂不朽	483
yōu xīn chōng chōng	忧心忡忡	133
yǒu dì fàng shǐ	有的放矢	376
yǒu jiàn yú cǐ	有鉴于此	475
yǒu mù gòng dǔ	有目共睹	168
yǒu qiú bì yìng	有求必应	469
yǒu shēng yǒu sè	有声有色	113
yǒu tiáo bù wěn	有条不紊	175
yǒu xuè yǒu ròu	有血有肉	395
yǒu zhāo yí rì	有朝一日	151
yú gōng yí shān	愚公移山	80
yǔ rì jù zēng	与日俱增	199
yǔ hòu chūn sǔn	雨后春笋	166
yǔ zhòng xīn cháng	语重心长	137
yù bàng xiāng zhēng, yú wēng dé lì	鹬蚌相争, 渔翁得利	430
yuán yuǎn liú cháng	源远流长	37
yuè yuè yù shì	跃跃欲试	327
yùn chóu wéi wò	运筹帷幄	439

Z

zài jiē zài lì	再接再厉	129
zàn bù jué kǒu	赞不绝口	324
zhān zhān zì xǐ	沾沾自喜	441
zhǎn dīng jié tiě	斩钉截铁	249
zhāo sān mù sì	朝三暮四	260
zhāo xī xiāng chǔ	朝夕相处	415
zhēn fēng xiāng duì	针锋相对	234
zhēn xīn shí yì	真心实意	221
zhēng zhēng rì shàng	蒸蒸日上	277
zhí jié liǎo dàng	直截了当	134
zhí mí bú wù	执迷不悟	495
zhǐ lù wéi mǎ	指鹿为马	400
zhǐ shàng tán bīng	纸上谈兵	40
zhǐ shǒu huà jiǎo	指手画脚	478
zhì gāo wú shàng	至高无上	246
zhì tóng dào hé	志同道合	419
zhì zhī bù lǐ	置之不理	342
zhì zhī dù wài	置之度外	482
zhòng suǒ zhōu zhī	众所周知	25
zhū rú cǐ lèi	诸如此类	181
zhù rén wéi lè	助人为乐	321
zhuān xīn zhì zhì	专心致志	311
zhuó yǒu chéng xiào	卓有成效	12
zì gào fèn yǒng	自告奋勇	399
zì lǐ háng jiān	字里行间	207
zì lì gēng shēng	自力更生	18
zì qiáng bù xī	自强不息	59
zì rán ér rán	自然而然	71
zì xiāng máo dùn	自相矛盾	10
zì yán zì yǔ	自言自语	39
zì yóu zì zài	自由自在	228
zǒu mǎ guān huā	走马观花	60
zuò wú xū xí	座无虚席	231

Appendix three: stroke index of 500 common Chinese idioms

References are to entry numbers.

One stroke

一心一意	114
一无所有	209
一无所知	107
一丝不苟	76
一本正经	172
一目了然	163
一如既往	19
一尘不染	377
一帆风顺	183
一成不变	296
一应俱全	286
一针见血	309
一事无成	454
一往情深	428
一视同仁	195
一鸣惊人	30
一举一动	167
一举两得	481
一脉相承	341
一席之地	108
一望无际	295
一意孤行	357
一筹莫展	364
一模一样	95

Two strokes

了如指掌	301
人山人海	438
人声鼎沸	485
入木三分	120
八仙过海	70
力不从心	212
十字路口	198

Three strokes

万无一失	179
万家灯火	494
三三两两	411
三令五申	358
三顾茅庐	170
久而久之	159
义不容辞	89
义无反顾	193
义愤填膺	476
亡羊补牢	110
千千万万	48
千方百计	3
千军万马	347
千辛万苦	269
千里迢迢	272
千疮百孔	496
千家万户	32
千载难逢	353
口口声声	391
大刀阔斧	205
大千世界	443
大手大脚	488
大同小异	381
大名鼎鼎	325
大有人在	362
大有可为	152
大有作为	284
大张旗鼓	242
大势所趋	186
大惊小怪	268
大街小巷	51
小心翼翼	36
川流不息	332
才高八斗	440
马不停蹄	306

Four strokes

不了了之	445
不见经传	266
不以为然	45
不可多得	256
不可告人	477
不可或缺	203
不可思议	21
不甘示弱	492
不由自主	52
不亦乐乎	383
不伦不类	455
不动声色	156
不厌其烦	264
不合时宜	304
不同凡响	379
不约而同	47
不折不扣	103
不言而喻	128
不足为奇	336
不屈不挠	136
不择手段	251
不知所措	66
不相上下	371
不胜枚举	323
不容置疑	405
不屑一顾	319
不假思索	369
不得而知	287
不堪设想	192
不遗余力	206
不解之缘	208
与日俱增	199
专心致志	311
丰功伟绩	155
五十步笑百步	500

五光十色	303
五花八门	104
五彩缤纷	171
五颜六色	196
井井有条	436
井底之蛙	380
今非昔比	453
从天而降	435
双管齐下	462
天方夜谭	402
天经地义	299
天真烂漫	486
天涯海角	396
天翻地覆	127
开门见山	307
引人入胜	191
引人注目	8
心平气和	261
心安理得	356
心旷神怡	413
方兴未艾	141
无与伦比	314
无中生有	408
无可奈何	16
无动于衷	145
无论如何	5
无时无刻	431
无所适从	404
无济于事	148
无家可归	119
无能为力	106
无微不至	368
无影无踪	245
日复一日	351
日新月异	42
比比皆是	143
毛遂自荐	140

气喘吁吁	229
水到渠成	466
水泄不通	365
水落石出	392
见义勇为	34
车水马龙	294
长治久安	61
风云变幻	131
风风雨雨	98
风平浪静	471
风尘仆仆	259

Five strokes

东施效颦	270
东窗事发	240
乐不思蜀	360
以身作则	72
半斤八两	498
发号施令	412
发扬光大	68
古色古香	328
古往今来	283
可歌可泣	219
史无前例	153
叶公好龙	340
司空见惯	247
叹为观止	361
四面八方	28
四面楚歌	160
四通八达	218
对牛弹琴	320
对症下药	334
平心而论	457
扑朔迷离	20
未雨绸缪	354
本来面目	226
永垂不朽	483
生气勃勃	298
生龙活虎	491
目不转睛	293
立竿见影	464
讨价还价	85
训练有素	317

Six strokes

任重道远	118
众所周知	25
光明磊落	331
全力以赴	26
全心全意	4

全神贯注	178
共襄盛举	499
兴致勃勃	29
兴高采烈	57
再接再厉	129
冰天雪地	375
冲锋陷阵	465
危言耸听	467
同心同德	86
同日而语	425
同甘共苦	385
同舟共济	418
名正言顺	459
名列前茅	55
名副其实	41
名落孙山	190
后顾之忧	82
因地制宜	9
因势利导	271
如火如荼	274
如数家珍	326
字里行间	207
守株待兔	210
安居乐业	62
异口同声	213
异乎寻常	281
异军突起	116
当之无愧	216
当务之急	13
成千上万	11
执迷不悟	495
扬长避短	276
扬眉吐气	338
有目共睹	168
有血有肉	395
有声有色	113
有条不紊	175
有求必应	469
有的放矢	376
有朝一日	151
有鉴于此	475
欢天喜地	432
此起彼伏	189
死灰复燃	389
江郎才尽	370
灯红酒绿	473
百花齐放	211
耳目一新	123
耳闻目睹	387
自力更生	18
自由自在	228

自告奋勇	399
自言自语	39
自相矛盾	10
自强不息	59
自然而然	71
至高无上	246
行之有效	24
衣食住行	322
设身处地	401
齐心协力	49

Seven strokes

何去何从	468
别开生面	176
别出心裁	265
别有用心	302
别具一格	308
助人为乐	321
含辛茹苦	463
呕心沥血	139
囫囵吞枣	280
围魏救赵	450
坚定不移	7
坚持不懈	22
层出不穷	73
应有尽有	149
应运而生	53
弄虚作假	38
形形色色	54
志同道合	419
忧心忡忡	133
我行我素	393
杞人忧天	130
束手无策	197
来之不易	67
求同存异	105
纸上谈兵	40
花团锦簇	451
走马观花	60
身先士卒	343
身体力行	88
迎刃而解	333
运筹帷幄	439
近在咫尺	373
针锋相对	234
鸡犬升天	290

Eight strokes

事半功倍	378
侃侃而谈	345

供不应求	23
依依不舍	359
刮目相看	97
刻不容缓	78
刻舟求剑	490
刻骨铭心	318
势在必行	215
卓有成效	12
卧薪尝胆	50
卷土重来	374
取长补短	224
取而代之	157
咄咄逼人	217
垂头丧气	349
夜以继日	232
奄奄一息	352
奋不顾身	291
始终不渝	162
实事求是	1
审时度势	184
居安思危	372
居高临下	355
庞然大物	409
念念不忘	236
所作所为	81
承前启后	384
拔苗助长	200
斩钉截铁	249
明目张胆	386
杯弓蛇影	470
欣欣向荣	169
沸沸扬扬	257
沾沾自喜	441
泣不成声	313
狐假虎威	300
画龙点睛	90
画蛇添足	230
直截了当	134
肃然起敬	275
艰苦奋斗	2
苦口婆心	437
视而不见	174
诗情画意	424
诚心诚意	346
货真价实	289
轰轰烈烈	74
迫不及待	112
迫在眉睫	146
金碧辉煌	417
雨后春笋	166
顶天立地	474

Nine strokes

举一反三	444
举世瞩目	35
举足轻重	33
前所未有	6
南辕北辙	150
变本加厉	458
徇私舞弊	65
急功近利	161
恍然大悟	173
恰到好处	222
持之以恒	233
指手画脚	478
指鹿为马	400
按图索骥	180
挺身而出	125
柳暗花明	421
津津乐道	223
津津有味	252
独一无二	101
独立自主	14
独树一帜	238
皆大欢喜	442
相依为命	366
相得益彰	235
相辅相成	84
相提并论	254
突飞猛进	96
突如其来	115
络绎不绝	46
绞尽脑汁	348
美中不足	484
耐人寻味	92
背道而驰	214
草木皆兵	310
荡然无存	339
语重心长	137
轻而易举	109
轻描淡写	397
顺理成章	204

Ten strokes

哭笑不得	398
唇亡齿寒	420
家常便饭	456
家喻户晓	56
座无虚席	231
恋恋不舍	449
息息相关	75

栩栩如生	138
根深蒂固	158
格格不入	273
流连忘返	406
浩浩荡荡	165
热火朝天	335
班门弄斧	330
真心实意	221
破釜沉舟	100
素不相识	315
继往开来	122
胸有成竹	278
脍炙人口	227
莫名其妙	17
袖手旁观	422
诸如此类	181
谈何容易	185
谈笑风生	382
逍遥法外	472
通情达理	434
难能可贵	94
顾全大局	69
高屋建瓴	448
高高在上	427
高瞻远瞩	144

Eleven strokes

偷工减料	447
堂而皇之	316
堂堂正正	312
彬彬有礼	243
得不偿失	446
得天独厚	43
悬崖勒马	497
情不自禁	44
惊弓之鸟	220
惊天动地	239
惊心动魄	63
掉以轻心	188
排忧解难	58
接二连三	248
推波助澜	329
掩耳盗铃	350
望而却步	394
望梅止渴	460
淋漓尽致	132
深入浅出	253
深思熟虑	237
深恶痛绝	255
焕然一新	194

理所当然	27
理直气壮	87
眼花缭乱	135
脚踏实地	64
脱口而出	297
脱胎换骨	337
脱颖而出	15
跃跃欲试	327
随心所欲	154
雪上加霜	258
雪中送炭	363

Twelve strokes

博大精深	201
啼笑皆非	388
喜气洋洋	202
喜出望外	225
喜闻乐见	117
富丽堂皇	305
就事论事	487
循序渐进	124
循循善诱	493
悲欢离合	452
提心吊胆	288
曾几何时	426
朝三暮四	260
朝夕相处	415
殚精竭虑	433
琳琅满目	91
痛心疾首	429
街头巷尾	367
赏心悦目	282
量力而行	164
铺天盖地	241
雅俗共赏	403
集思广益	285

Thirteen strokes

塞翁失马	390
微不足道	77
想方设法	31
意气风发	461
意味深长	121
愚公移山	80
源远流长	37
滔滔不绝	126
滥竽充数	250
简明扼要	479

置之不理	342
置之度外	482
肆无忌惮	279
蒸蒸日上	277
触目惊心	147
雷厉风行	414

Fourteen strokes

兢兢业业	102
截然不同	79
旗帜鲜明	99
漫山遍野	489
熙熙攘攘	244
精打细算	292
精神抖擞	344
精益求精	182
聚精会神	142
蔚然成风	267
踌躇满志	416
锲而不舍	177

Fifteen strokes

德才兼备	83
德高望重	262
潜移默化	187

Sixteen strokes

燃眉之急	263
赞不绝口	324
黔驴技穷	410
默默无闻	111

Seventeen strokes

繁荣昌盛	93
螳螂捕蝉, 黄雀在后	480
豁然开朗	423
鹬蚌相争, 渔翁得利	430

Eighteen strokes

翻来覆去	407